Suharto and His Generals
Indonesian Military Politics 1975 – 1983

David Jenkins

Monograph Series
(Publication no. 64)

Cornell Modern Indonesia Project
Southeast Asia Program
Cornell University
Ithaca, New York
1984

PRICE: $12.50

For Ann

CONTENTS

TABLES

ILLUSTRATIONS

Following page 12

Inner Circle

1. Lt. Gen. Ali Murtopo
2. General Yoga Sugama
3. Admiral Sudomo
4. General Benny Murdani

Outer Circle

5. General Maraden Panggabean
6. General Widodo
7. General Mohammad Jusuf
8. General Sumitro
9. Lt. Gen. Sutopo Juwono
10. General Darjatmo

Fosko Group

11. General A. H. Nasution
12. Lt. Gen. H. R. Dharsono
13. Lt. Gen. Djatikusumo
14. Lt. Gen. Ali Sadikin
15. General Hugeng Imam Santoso
16. Lt. Gen. Mohammad Jasin
17. Lt. Gen. Mokoginta

18. President Suharto

ACKNOWLEDGMENTS

This monograph has its origins in the four years I spent in In-donesia in 1976-80 as a correspondent for the *Far Eastern Economic Review* but is based more particularly on research carried out under a fourteen-month research grant at the Institute of Southeast Asian Studies in Singapore in 1981-82.

The number of people to whom I am indebted for help and ad-vice is, of course, enormous. But I would like to express my partic-ular thanks to all those Indonesians, both civilian and military, who took time out to explain, patiently and generously, something about the workings of the Indonesian political and military systems.

By its very nature, much of the research work centered on prominent retired officers who were critical of the way in which the New Order had, they felt, failed to live up to the expectations of 1966. Here, I am particularly indebted to General A. H. Nasution, who, despite his own heavy writing commitments, provided me with many insights into the role of the armed forces in both the Old and New Order periods. I also owe a very great debt to Brig. Gen. Ab-dulkadir Besar, Lt. Gen. H. R. Dharsono, Lt. Gen. G. P. H. Djati-kusumo, General Hugeng Imam Santoso, Lt. Gen. Ibnu Sutowo, Lt. Gen. Mohammad Jasin, Col. Alex Kawilarang, the late Lt. Gen. A. J. Mokoginta, Lt. Gen. Ali Sadikin, and the late Maj. Gen. Achmad Sukendro. Other retired officers who provided invaluable insights included Lt. Gen. T. B. Simatupang and General Sumitro.

It would have been virtually impossible, however, to produce a rounded account of the internal debate over the military's role in so-ciety without the help and understanding of those officers still in power at the time this debate took place. Here, I owe a special debt of gratitude to Admiral Sudomo, General Benny Murdani, and General Mohammad Jusuf. I am also indebted to Lt. Gen. Alamsjah Ratu Per-wiranegara, General Darjatmo, Maj. Gen. August Marpaung, Brig. Gen. (Hon.) Nugroho Notosusanto, Lt. Gen. Sutopo Juwono, General Supardjo Rustam, General Widodo, and General Yoga Sugama. A number of these senior officers expressed the view that a study of this kind, if it were to have any value at all, should present the picture "warts and all." If they feel that in writing this account I have included too many--or too few--warts, then I can only ask for their further indulgence.

Many Indonesian civilians also provided invaluable insights and background information, and in particular I would like to thank Rus-lan Abdulgani, Sabam Siagian, Mohammad Natsir, Slamet Bratanata,

Harry Tjan Silalahi, and Jusuf Wanandi. I am also indebted to Toeti Adhitama, Alex Alatas, Amir Daud, Gunawan Mohomad, Fikri Jufri, the late Jusuf Ismail, Jusuf Ronodipuro, Aristides Katoppo, Lie Tek Tjeng, Mochtar Lubis, Adam Malik, Onghokham, Buyung Nasution, Subadio Sastrosatomo, Juwono Sudarsono, and Sudjatmoko.

Mention must also be made of Col. George Benson, a former United States defense attaché at the embassy in Jakarta and a man who traces his links with many of Indonesia's most senior military figures back to the days when they were captains and majors. He provided insights into the thinking of senior army officers over a quarter of a century and on one occasion arranged an interview with an officer not normally inclined to share his opinions with others. Col. Joe Uttinger, likewise defense attaché at the U.S. embassy for many years, was also very generous in sharing his knowledge about the Indonesian armed forces.

Perhaps my greatest debt is to Prof. Herbert Feith and Prof. J. A. C. Mackie, who, when I was a very junior foreign correspondent in Jakarta in 1969-70 for the Melbourne *Herald*, and later at Monash University, opened my eyes to the study of Indonesian politics and generously shared their knowledge about the country. A number of people have read or commented on one or more draft chapters of the manuscript and offered many invaluable suggestions and criticisms. Apart from Herb Feith and Jamie Mackie, the others include Brig. Gen. Abdulkadir Besar, Benedict Anderson, Slamet Bratanata, Harold Crouch, Don Emmerson, Michael Leifer, General Nasution, Brig. Gen. Nugroho Notosusanto, Sabam Siagian, Lt. Gen. Simatupang, Leo Suryadinata, and Jusuf Wanandi. I am particularly indebted to Don Emmerson for his very valuable comments on the arrangement of the material in the opening chapters. Yuli Ismartono and Fatmi Ronodipuro helped me find my way through some of the more opaque writings on Indonesian military doctrine. Any errors or omissions are, of course, my own responsibility.

Finally, I would like to thank Prof. Kernial Singh Sandhu of the Institute of Southeast Asian Studies for his kindness in arranging for me to spend fourteen months at the institute on a research grant, with provision for three one-month visits to Indonesia. I am also grateful to Derek Davies, the editor of the *Far Eastern Economic Review*, who allowed me to take more than a year's leave of absence from the magazine. Without this, the monograph could never have been written.

PREFACE

In writing this monograph I have been guided by two separate but interrelated goals. The first has been to provide an histori-cal-descriptive record of the "challenge" posed to President Suharto within the Armed Forces of the Republic of Indonesia (ABRI) during the period 1975-82 and the debate that developed over ABRI's role in society. Although this debate sprawled across the whole canvas of military involvement in society, it can be said to have focused essen-tially on two key issues. The first, which was debated with consid-erable vigor during the period 1977-80, involved ABRI's relations with other social-political groups in society, and in particular the political parties. The center of this debate was the "contradiction" between ABRI's claim to be above all groups in society and the reality of its continuing support for Golkar, the political grouping which held a majority of the seats in the DPR (Parliament). Due largely to the in-tervention of the president, this debate was resolved in favor of the status quo and by 1980 it appeared unlikely that there would be any substantial changes during the remainder of the Suharto presidency.

The second issue, which became of increasing importance after 1980, centered on the appointment of military officers to nonmilitary functions. There were in the mid-1970s more than 20,000 military men serving in a *kekaryaan* (nonmilitary, or "functional") capacity, as ministers, ambassadors, parliamentarians, senior executives in gov-ernment corporations, bankers, senior civil servants, university rec-tors, provincial governors, subdistrict heads, and even village head-men. Answerable to the chief of staff for functional affairs (Kaskar), they acted as "reinforcing rods" to ensure that the bureaucracy was responsive to the commands of those at the top--a role that was not unlike that of the Communist Party in many Communist states. In the view of the critics, ABRI's heavy involvement in kekaryaan activities, although understandable in terms of recent Indonesian history, was excessive and needed to be scaled back. On this front, some gov-ernment concessions seemed possible, if only because the armed forces were short of manpower. Even so, any cutback in the kekaryaan ABRI was likely to be both slow and from the bottom up, with the commanding heights of the system remaining firmly in the hands of the military leaders.

A related--but less central--thread that ran through the debate was the need for "purification," this being a theme which found its fullest expression in the statements of a number of prominent retired officers, men who looked askance at what they saw as the moral dis-solution of the times and who felt that widespread corruption was not only being tolerated but encouraged by the contemporary armed forces' leadership.

These challenges, although brushed aside with comparative ease by the ruling group, raised fundamental questions about the sort of society that was being created in Indonesia. What developed was, in a sense, a debate between different factions within the outgoing Generation of '45, the officers who had fought in the independence struggle against the Dutch, about the sort of values that should be passed on to a new generation of military leaders, a competition for their attention.

Criticisms of the government came from a whole pantheon of former military leaders, including Nasution, R. Sudirman, Djatikusumo, Dharsono, Sukendro, Mokoginta, Kawilarang, Jasin, Ali Sadikin, and Hugeng. But it was much more than a campaign mounted by retired officers, most of whom were depicted by the ruling group as members of a socalled "Barisan Sakit Hati" (Sick at Heart Brigade). Two of the key officers in the command structure--the 1978–83 minister of defense, General Mohammad Jusuf, and the 1978–80 army chief of staff, General Widodo--were in sympathy with its aims, as were members of the teaching staff at Seskoad, the Army Staff and Command School in Bandung, and members of Lemhannas, the National Defense Institute, including Lt. Gen. Sutopo Juwono, the 1978–83 governor of that body.

On the other hand, it should not be supposed that this issue divided the army down the middle to such an extent that it transcended everything else. Most officers at the middle and lower levels, although comprising the "audience" that each side was seeking to reach, were "apolitical" in the sense that for one reason or another they did not take sides. In the final analysis, the silent majority could be expected to follow whatever dictates came down from on high --at least for the time being. The debate took place very much at the apex of the military pyramid and the sympathies of most of the key figures there were well enough known, at least to those within the system. Even at that level, however, there were officers who managed to commit themselves to neither side.

This debate brought forth (and was in turn reflected in) a series of papers which dealt at some length with the army's role in society. The first such paper, produced by members of the teaching staff at Seskoad, appeared in mid-1977, shortly after the general elections. Reacting to the "excesses" of Golkar's 1977 election campaign, the authors of the "Seskoad paper" urged that ABRI refrain in the future from siding with one of the contestants in a general election. Instead, they said, it should return to its "pure" role as a body which was not the property of any one group in society but belonged to the nation as a whole. In the period that followed, papers produced by Fosko, a "forum" for retired senior army officers, came to broadly similar conclusions, as did papers produced by the Institute for the Promotion of Constitutional Awareness (LKB), an association of "retired generals and retired politicians," which counted amongst its founders Dr. Mohammad Hatta, the former vice president, as well as General Nasution, the former minister of defense.

The second major army paper--issued by the army chief of staff, General Widodo, in October 1978--came to almost identical conclusions. Indeed, the "Widodo paper" incorporated much of the thinking that had been present in the earlier Seskoad document, as well as material from Fosko and Lemhannas. But the Widodo paper was much more than this. Prepared after close consultations with senior army staff and command officers, it put forward an interpretation of the military's *dwifungsi* (dual function) that appeared to be starkly at odds with the thinking of the ruling Suharto group.

During the period from late 1978 until early 1980, General Jusuf was conducting a widely publicized campaign aimed at reunifying ABRI and the people and stressing, as the Seskoad and Widodo papers had done, that ABRI was not the property of any one group in society but was above all groups, an assurance that gave hope to many that the armed forces would not throw their weight behind Golkar in future elections.

It will be argued in this paper that Suharto, aware of the widening gap between the armed forces and society and knowing that something had to be done about this, lent a degree of support to the Jusuf campaign to "reunite" ABRI and the people and have it stand above all groups in society. However, it will be suggested that Suharto, who appeared to see the interests of ABRI and Golkar as indistinguishable and who had had himself elected chairman of the Golkar "politburo" in October 1978, had no deep-seated commitment to the notion of ABRI standing above all groups. Further, it will be suggested that Suharto relied on Admiral Sudomo, one of the members of his inner circle, to undermine much of the Jusuf campaign almost from the start.

By 1981, it will be shown, the ruling group had reasserted itself and dealt with the various heresies that had been taking root. Widodo, a favorite of neither Suharto nor Jusuf and a man whose performance as chief of staff had come under criticism from other members of the inner group, had been pushed into retirement and replaced by his deputy, General Poniman, a bland and malleable command officer. Jusuf had had the rug pulled out from under him when Suharto, addressing the RAPIM ABRI (Armed Forces Commanders Call) in March 1980, had made it plain that ABRI would again support Golkar and not stand above all sociopolitical groups. Fosko had been "frozen" and its members rebuked (and later penalized) for the criticisms they had continued to launch. Nasution and other members of the LKB who had signed a "Petition of Fifty" strongly critical of Suharto had likewise been dealt with.

It only remained for the ruling group to formulate their own counter to the Seskoad and Widodo papers. This they did when a "Hankam paper"--*Fighters and Soldiers: The Concept and Implementation of ABRI's Dual Function*--was issued in 1981. Prepared by a team of trusted senior officials, the Hankam paper sought to provide an ideological justification for the status quo and defend the way in which the dwifungsi was being implemented.

The second goal has been to provide an analytical-speculative conclusion that seeks to characterize the regime and estimate the future role of the armed forces within it. This looks not just at the twin themes of "elevation" (ABRI above all groups), which got nowhere, and at the limited military disengagement from ostensibly civilian positions, which did get somewhere, and which, if only for reasons of ABRI's self-interest, might well make further progress during the remainder of the 1980s. It also looks at generational change, the prospects for intramilitary conflict along generational lines and at the wider subject of the character and future of Suharto's military regime as a whole. Looked at in another way, the manuscript is about two levels of conflict. One is about the identity and role of the armed forces; the second is more basically about the exercise of power. The aim has been to merge and separate the two as judiciously as possible.

In considering these various issues, the study draws heavily on two kinds of evidence: documentary (doctrinal) and recollected (events). Basically, the latter is used to illustrate the former, and vice versa. To limit oneself to the former would be to assume that scripture and reality were synonymous, while to focus only on the latter would be to dismiss the importance, however limited, of the doctrinal debate in a welter of recollection and anecdotal material.[1]

In preparing the manuscript, I was fortunate in having been provided by key participants in the debate with copies of all the major papers that were prepared during the 1975-83 period on ABRI doctrine and ideology. Even more fortunately, I was able to interview, in most cases on tape, a broad cross-section of senior military officers, both active and retired. To these men I owe an enormous debt. Not only were they exceedingly generous with their time but they spoke with remarkable candor--and with the benefit of first-hand knowledge--about the key issues under discussion. What is more, they were willing in all but a very few instances to have their views attributed, a rare phenomenon when one is dealing with matters of policy and planning that are often quite sensitive. As a result, it has been possible to provide a sense of the personalities behind the debate and to give an idea of which officers lined up on which sides of certain key issues.

In an earlier paper,[2] I made an attempt to trace the development of Indonesia's military doctrine over the years 1945-75 and to show how the increasingly elaborate formulations of that doctrine in

---

1. I am indebted to Don Emmerson for making this point.

2. See David Jenkins, "The Evolution of Indonesian Army Doctrinal Thinking: The concept of *Dwifungsi*," *Southeast Asian Journal of Social Science*, [Singapore], 11, 2 (1983); 15-30.

the years after 1957 were related to, and helped legitimize, the army's expanding role in political and economic affairs; a brief outline of that process is set out in the Introduction, as is an outline of the estrangement which has developed since independence between the army and the forces of political Islam. Chapter One reviews some of the literature on patrimonialism and praetorianism to orient the subject matter of subsequent chapters, which is not the regime as a whole but the particular role of the army within it. The chapter then describes the "core group" of senior officers around Suharto, their ideology and outlook and the institutions over which they preside. Chapter Two looks at the way in which Suharto has restructured the political landscape in the years since 1966 and at the way in which he has come to depend on the loyalty of the government administrative structure--in particular the Departments of Defense and Home Affairs--to implement his designs. The following four chapters trace government attempts to ensure a satisfactory outcome during the 1977 general election; the initiatives for reform that were coming from various quarters, both inside ABRI and outside; the various bodies that were created to give expression to this concern; the way in which Golkar was brought still more firmly under the control of the president during its 1978 national conference, and the way in which Jusuf attempted to ensure that ABRI was at one with (*manuggal*) the people.

Chapter Seven looks at Suharto's decisive March 1980 speech at Pekanbaru, in the course of which he ruled out suggestions that the armed forces should in fact be above all groups in society and stressed that ABRI should "choose friends" who truly supported Pancasila, the five-point state ideology, and the 1945 Constitution. The remaining chapters look at the Hankam paper, in which the ruling group in effect put forth its own view of ABRI's role, at the views of General Nasution, the founder of the dual function doctrine and a prominent critic of Suharto and his system of government, and at the other retired officers who clashed with the ruling military leaders during this period. As indicated above, an attempt is made to draw these threads together in the Conclusion and to look at ABRI's likely future role in Indonesian society.

INTRODUCTION

AN IDEOLOGY TAKES SHAPE

In the first three decades after the proclamation of independence in 1945, Indonesian military doctrine passed through five fairly distinct periods. The first period, which spanned the years of the physical revolution (1945-49), produced no shared military doctrine. However, the experiences of army leaders during these critical formative years gave birth to a strongly shared ethos, as well as a range of arguments about the role that the armed forces should play in society. Of central importance was the shared perception that the Indonesian National Army (Tentara Nasional Indonesia, TNI) was created by the Indonesian people, not by civilian political leaders. The notion that the army emerged from the people, that it fought for independence alongside the populace (even when the civilian political leaders had "surrendered"), and that it had participated extensively in nominally "civilian" matters during that time was to give birth to the idea that the armed forces were justified in playing an extensive role in nonmilitary affairs.

During the second period--which coincided more or less with the years of liberal democracy (1949-57)--these notions and ambitions were, in the main, contained, as the Dutch-trained leadership sought to rationalize and modernize a large, cumbersome, and imperfectly integrated army left over from the revolution. Occasionally, however, military dissatisfaction with the civilian leadership manifested itself in bids for greater power, most notably in the "October 17 Affair" of 1952, a so-called "half coup" in which many of the Dutch-trained officers were involved.

The third period--1957-59--stands in marked contrast to its predecessor. With the outbreak of the regional rebellions and the declaration of martial law (events which coincided with and marked the death knell of liberal-style parliamentary democracy), military leaders acquired enormous powers in the nonmilitary sector, powers they were not at all loath to use in their quest both to "improve" the working of the system and further their own political and economic interests. In these two years, military leaders abandoned any willingness to accept civilian ideas of the army being an apolitical instrument of the state and took their place alongside President Sukarno as one of the two main pillars of the government, with their *bête noire*, the electorally popular Indonesian Communist Party (PKI), just outside the government. This dramatic enhancement of the army's influence in society was legitimized first by martial law

1

and then by General Nasution's doctrines of the dual function (dwi-fungsi).

On November 11, 1958, three years after he had been reap-pointed army chief of staff, Nasution delivered his most important speech on the position of the TNI in society. Speaking without notes at a graduation ceremony at the military academy at Magelang, the chief of staff said that the position of the TNI was not like that of an army in a Western country, in which the military was solely an "instrument of the government." Neither was it like that of various Latin American armies which monopolized political power. Rather, the TNI was one of the forces of the people's struggle which was at the same level and which fought shoulder to shoulder with other forces, such as parties.[1] The army itself would not be politically active, yet neither would it be simply a spectator. Indi-vidual officers must be granted an opportunity to participate in the government and to make use of their nonmilitary skills in helping develop the nation. Officers must be permitted to participate in determining economic, financial, international, and other policies at the highest levels of government. Therefore they must have a place in *all* the institutions of the state, not just in the National Council and the cabinet, as was already the case, but also in the National Planning Council, the diplomatic corps, Parliament, and elsewhere in the government. If this did not happen, Nasution warned, the army might react violently to discrimination against its officers.

Nasution's concern at this time, Lev has argued, was to en-sure that the military continued to exercise an influence in decision making, if only to keep the political parties, and in particular the increasingly powerful PKI, at bay.[2] The difficulty, however, was that martial law was temporary and under attack. To make perma-nent the army's right to participate in the direction of national af-fairs, says Lev, Nasution claimed for it a new and explicitly politi-cal status.

In the fourth period between 1959 and 1965, military leaders extended and defended their position in the nonmilitary sector, their doctrines (increasingly formulated by Brig. Gen. Suwarto, the head of Seskoad, the Army Staff and Command School in Bandung), being used to legitimize what was now known as "the army's middle way,"[3] and ensure the continuation of a military role in society; these efforts were motivated, in part at least, by the army's impla-

---

1. Because this speech was made without a text, the only record of it is in contemporary newspaper reports.

2. Daniel S. Lev, "The Political Role of the Army in Indonesia," *Pacific Affairs* 36 (Winter 1963-1964), 349-64.

3. It was Prof. Djokosutono, not Nasution, who dubbed the con-cept "the army's middle way" (*jalan tengah tentara*).

cable opposition to the PKI, which, in the years 1962-65, formed the third corner of the Sukarno-army-PKI "triangle."

In mid-1962 Sukarno was able to outmanoeuver Nasution and replace him as army chief of staff with General Achmad Yani, a Javanese officer who, though he shared the dominant army concern about the PKI, was more inclined to defer to Sukarno's leadership. Yani pledged to unite himself (*menyatukan diri*) "with the leadership of Bung Karno," and within a short time had secured the removal of a number of regional commanders who had opposed the president, particularly on Communist issues. As the influence of the palace grew, the pro-Sukarnoist views of certain key officers became increasingly apparent. Thus in 1964, the Siliwangi commander, Maj. Gen. Ibrahim Adjie, had the phrase "Bung Karno is my leader" (*Bung Karno adalah pemimpinku*) written into the "Caturlaksana" (Four Guides for Implementation) of the Siliwangi.[4]

Seen from outside, Sukarnoist influence in the army reached its zenith during the first army seminar, organized by Yani in April 1965. The new military doctrine produced by this gathering--the *Tri Ubaya Cakti*, or Three Sacred Vows--was so heavily laced with Sukarnoist imagery and ideology that it was to be subjected to a "total correction" at a second seminar held fifteen months later, following Sukarno's decline. At the same time, the seminar formally adopted the concept of the dual function, affirming that the armed forces had a dual role as both a "military force" and a "social-political force." As a social-political force, the army's activities covered "the ideological, political, social, economic, cultural, and religious fields."

In the aftermath of the pro-Communist coup attempt of September 30, 1965, in which Yani and five other senior officers were killed, leadership of the army was assumed by Maj. Gen. Suharto, the commander of Kostrad, the army strategic reserve. The ruthless purge of the PKI, which was accused of having masterminded the coup, eliminated the party as an effective political force during

---

4. Interview with General A. H. Nasution, August 9, 1983. Adjie was not so much a pro-Sukarnoist in the ideological sense but felt a strong personal loyalty to the president. Adjie had gone in the face of Nasution's strict moral code when he had divorced his first wife. He had compounded the offense by returning from Yugoslavia, where he served as military attaché, with a second, Yugoslav wife. Nasution's indignation was such that he refused to reassign Adjie for more than seven months and may even have intended to edge him out of the service. Sukarno stepped in, however, and forced Nasution to appoint Adjie chief of staff of the Siliwangi, leaving Adjie, who moved up to become panglima ten months later, with a personal debt to the president. See Ulf Sundhaussen, *The Road to Power, Indonesian Military Politics 1945-1967* (Kuala Lumpur: Oxford University Press, 1982), pp. 150-51. Adjie was also close to Hartini, Sukarno's third wife.

the closing months of 1965. In many areas army officers cooperated with anti-Communist civilian groups in a massacre that claimed the lives of anywhere between 200,000 and 300,000 party activists. Half a million more were arrested. This left Sukarno, whom some army leaders suspected of complicity in the death of the generals, in a greatly weakened position vis-à-vis the army and culminated in his ouster in March 1967. The former balance of forces irreparably shattered, the army now stood as the dominant actor on the political stage with Suharto moving quickly to consolidate his power. Within a month of the coup Suharto had succeeded in filling virtually all key positions in the army general staff with his own appointees and had begun the process of excluding Nasution from the center of decision making. During 1966 he launched a thoroughgoing purge of pro-PKI and pro-Sukarno elements in the army, particularly in East and Central Java. Thousands of officers and men were arrested, suspended, transferred, or dishonorably discharged.

In these circumstances, senior officers moved to reformulate military doctrine. This involved stripping away the "excesses" of the "Old Order" period and putting together a creed that would provide the doctrinal basis for a "New Order" government. When a second army seminar was held in Bandung in August 1966, the notion that the army had a dual role was developed still further; the army not only had a right and duty to assume responsibilities outside the military field, the seminar declared, but had been "forced" into expanding its nonmilitary activities. "All the people's hopes for well being are focused on the armed forces in general and the army in particular," the seminar declared. Therefore, the army had no choice but to live up to the expectations of the people, which entailed securing the formation of a responsible, strong, and progressive government.[5]

The holding of such a seminar was timely. As Harold Maynard has observed, military men were daily undertaking new and expanded functions, yet no consensus had been reached on their role. A military program was required which would receive the widespread support of army leaders.

The conclusions reached at the army seminar in Bandung were disseminated to the armed forces as a whole at a defense and security seminar in November, one which was attended by senior officers of all four services--the army, navy, air force, and police. This meeting produced a *Doctrine of National Defense and Security and a Doctrine for the Struggle of the Armed Forces of the Republic of Indonesia.* Subtitled *Four Missions, One Fate (Catur Dharma Eka Karma)*, the document stressed the fact that the four services

---

5. Doktrin Perjuangan TNI-AD "Tri Ubaya Cakti," quoted in Ulf Sundhaussen, "The Military: Structure, Procedures, and Effects on Indonesian Society," in *Political Power and Communications in Indonesia*, ed. Karl D. Jackson and Lucian W. Pye (Berkeley: University of California Press, 1978), p. 69.

were joined by one doctrine. Maynard argues that this 121-page document was most notable for the fact that it expanded and solidified the concept of dwifungsi.[6]

The principal statement of New Order military doctrine, the document begins by stressing the familiar theme that the armed forces were born of the people's struggle during the revolution. Those forces, it emphasizes, have always remained loyal to the precepts of the Pancasila. Depicting the armed forces in centrist terms, the document says that military units have been employed in what amounts to a continuous struggle against elements of the extreme left (the 1948 Madiun revolt and the 1965 coup attempt) and the extreme right (the Darul Islam and the PRRI-Permesta regional rebellion of 1957-61).

In this fifth period--from 1965--one can distinguish, as during Guided Democracy, between an initial phase (1966-67), in which the key doctrines were established, and a later one in which they were maintained and in some ways modified. At the second army seminar in 1966 the New Order leaders were conscious not only of the need to "perfect" the Tri Ubaya Cakti doctrine and rid it of its Sukarnoist and leftist embellishments but to develop a comprehensive doctrinal statement, justifying and rationalizing the military's dominant influence in society. (By 1983, further refinement seemed likely, there being a growing feeling in military circles that the Catur Dharma Eka Karma doctrine, though still reflecting the basic philosophy of the armed forces, needed to be amended to take into account the structural changes that had been made in 1969 and thereafter. At the same time, there was a feeling that it would be appropriate to discard certain words that were carryovers from the Old Order lexicon--"revolution" was a case in point--and no longer quite in keeping with ABRI's outlook.)

For at least two decades, the notion that ABRI has a legitimate role to play as a "social-political force" has been enshrined in every important publication dealing with military doctrine and has gained considerable acceptance in society at large. However, the acceptable parameters of armed forces' intervention in society have always been controversial.

Not even with the physical elimination of the PKI in 1965-66 and the subsequent eclipse of Sukarno were many key army leaders inclined to give much thought to the notion that military officers wielded "too much" power. The instability generated by the collapse of the old triangular relationship convinced army leaders that they were justified in playing a still more dominant role "to help fill the vacuum and restore order." This view found a good deal of initial acceptance amongst those groups in society who accepted

---

6. See Harold Ward Maynard, "A Comparison of Military Elite Role Perceptions in Indonesia and the Philippines" (Ph.D. thesis, The American University, 1976), p. 154.

membership in the army-led New Order "partnership." By the mid-1970s, however, the situation had changed. Stability had been re-stored and the groundwork undertaken to prepare the nation for "twenty-five years of accelerated modernization." Yet it appeared that the army—or, more particularly, the dominant group around President Suharto—envisaged no significant reduction in military in-fluence. The government view seemed to be that the situation had to remain much as it was to ensure that the hard-won stability was not overturned. This development—along with other alleged short-comings of New Order rule—disturbed a number of Indonesians, civilian and military alike, their concern manifesting itself in vari-ous ways. The ranks of those critical of the government included Nasution, now retired, and a number of likeminded officers who felt that Suharto and his group had overstated the role of the military, to the clear detriment of civilian institutions.

*   *   *   *   *

These attempts to forge a coherent military doctrine took place at a time of growing estrangement between the army and the forces of political Islam, an estrangement which was a more-or-less permanent backdrop to Indonesian politics during the years 1975-82. The differences between the army and political Islam have their roots in the basic cleavage that exists between the two cultural ori-entations of Java, that between the *santri*, the devoutly Muslim minority, and the *abangan*, those who, while nominally Muslim, are more attuned to a philosophy and culture that dates from Java's pre-Islamic past. These differences, which were sharpened during the revolution by a clash between regular army units and irregular guerrilla forces oriented to Muslim political groups, have invariably focused on the place of religion in the state.

During the thirties, nationalist leaders had debated this ques-tion in a series of lively polemical exchanges, their deliberations being marked by a surprising degree of intellectual tolerance and mutual respect. With the approach of independence in 1945, how-ever, the place of Islam became the subject of an intense and in-creasingly acrimonious debate, particularly in the BPKI, the Body to Investigate Measures for the Preparation of Indonesian Indepen-dence, an organization dominated by those of a secular nationalist cast of mind.

In his study of the Indonesian national revolution, Anthony Reid has noted that Muslim representatives had "always argued the need for a Muslim state in which religious law would be enforce-able."[7] Sukarno's position, which had been outlined in his famous Pancasila speech of June 1, 1945, was that the state should be based on "belief in the One, Supreme God," whether worshipped in

---

7.   Anthony J. S. Reid, *Indonesian National Revolution: 1945-1950* (Melbourne: Longman, 1974), p. 20.

Muslim or Christian terms. If the Muslims wanted more than this, Sukarno held, they were free to strive for it through the democratic process. The Muslims were offended that Sukarno had treated Islam as merely one religion among many, and they sought, in subsequent subcommittee meetings of the BPKI, to strengthen the position of Islam. In this they met with some success. The subcommittee's draft preamble to the Constitution, which came to be known as the Jakarta Charter, provided in one centrally important passage that Indonesia would be a republic founded not only on the basis of unity, a righteous and civilized humanity, democracy, and social justice, but also on belief in God "with the obligation for those who profess the Islamic faith to abide by Islamic laws," seven words (in the original Indonesian version) which gave rise to a constitutional controversy that continues to this day. In July 1945, the BPKI made the further concession that the president should be a Muslim. "Although well short of Muslim hopes," Reid notes, "this was to prove the highest point in their pursuit of an Islamic state."[8] By August, the "seven words" had been dropped from the preamble (as had the reference in the Constitution to the fact that the president should be a Muslim), largely, it appears, because Dr. Hatta accepted Christian arguments that a phrase that referred to only one religion was discriminatory.[9] In its final form, the preamble to the Constitution was a Sukarno-inspired compromise between two key groups--the nationalists, who sought to build a secular state, and the Islamic group, which wished to build an Islamic state. The compromise enshrined in that document was that there should be a state that was neither secular nor Islamic. Rather, there would be a state which was built on "belief in the One, Supreme God," a concept sufficiently general to cover all religions.

8. Ibid.

9. On August 17, 1945, after the proclamation of independence, Hatta received a Japanese naval officer who came as an envoy of the Kaigun (Japanese navy). The officer said that representatives of the Protestant and Catholic communities of Eastern Indonesia, an area under Kaigun administration, were "very disturbed" at the inclusion of the seven words in the preamble. They felt, the officer said, that "the inclusion of such a requirement in such a vital part of the Constitution implied a form of discrimination against minorities." If such "discrimination" was to be retained, they felt they would be better off outside the Republic of Indonesia. Though he argued that there was no discrimination in the Jakarta Charter, Hatta decided it would be wise to remove the sentence in order to prevent "splitting" the new nation. The next day the BPKI unanimously approved the change. See *Mohammad Hatta, Indonesian Patriot: Memoirs*, ed. C. L. M. Penders (Singapore: Gunung Agung, 1981), pp. 240-43. According to a source closely connected with these events, the Japanese approach to Hatta was almost certainly made at the behest of Dr. Sam Ratulangi, an astute Christian politician from Menado, North Sulawesi. Confidential communication.

Against this backdrop of santri-abangan relations and the debate over the most appropriate form of the soon-to-be proclaimed
state, there developed a cleavage between regular army units, most
of them made up of former officers and men of the Peta, the Japanese-sponsored self-defense force, and irregular *lasykar* units,
many of them associated with Islamic political parties. The seeds of
this conflict were sown in 1944 when the Hizbullah (Army of Allah)
was set up on Java as an Islamic paramilitary group independent of
the Peta. This established the principle of a separate Muslim military organization, and in the period thereafter "youth from the
pious Muslim (santri) community was channelled separately into the
revolution."[10] Acting in league with the Islamic parties, says
McVey, the Hizbullah "thus entered on the anti-army side into the
rivalry between the regular and the irregular forces."[11] When in
early 1948 the Siliwangi division of the regular army withdrew from
West Java in accordance with the Renville Agreement with the
Dutch, Hizbullah units remained to carry on a guerrilla war. In
March 1948 the group established itself as the Darul Islam, an
autonomous organization with its own army, the Islamic Army of Indonesia (Tentara Islam Indonesia, TII). In August, its leader,
S. M. Kartosuwirjo, proclaimed the Islamic State of Indonesia (Negara Islam Indonesia), organized on what he took to be Koranic
lines.[12] This development triggered off a religious revolt that was
to last thirteen years, exacerbating the tensions between orthodox
Muslims and army leaders. As McVey has noted,

> The long years of warfare against Muslim rebellion en-
> couraged a tradition of army distrust of militant Islam,
> and the many Javanese officers of *abangan* persuasion
> were strengthened in their objection to Muslim aggres-
> siveness. As a result of all this, the secularizing ten-
> dency common to the modern professional military was,

---

10. Ruth McVey, "The Post-Revolutionary Transformation of the Indonesian Army (Part I)," *Indonesia* 11 (April 1971): 138.

Islam had been treated with suspicion by the Dutch colonial authorities. However, the Japanese actively encouraged Islamic groups
and during their occupation of the East Indies young Indonesian
Muslims were brought into the civil service in increasing numbers.
A number of these young men later found themselves in military
service, not always in the Hizbullah. Among those who joined the
Peta were Sudirman, Muljadi Djojomartono, and Kasman Singodimedjo, all of whom were members of the Muhammadiyah, the modern-
ist Islamic social and educational organization.

11. Ibid.

12. See Herbert Feith, *The Decline of Constitutional Democracy in
Indonesia* (Ithaca: Cornell University Press, 1962), p. 54, and
Reid, *Indonesian National Revolution*, p. 158.

in the Indonesian case, particularly marked; the *santri* officer became a rare bird . . .[13]

Less than one year after the Dutch transfer of sovereignty in 1949, an important confrontation took place in Jakarta between the leaders of the army on the one hand and the leaders of the Masyumi, at that time the major Muslim political party in Indonesia, on the other. The prime minister, Mohammad Natsir, was a leading member of the Masyumi, and senior army officers, who were at the time engaged in operations against the Darul Islam, professed to be anxious to know where the Masyumi stood on the rebellion. With the support of his fellow officers, the armed forces chief of staff, Col. T. B. Simatupang, a Christian who was later to become chairman of the Indonesian Council of Churches, approached Natsir and asked if the Masyumi could issue a statement condemning the Darul Islam. Natsir sidestepped the issue by pointing out that he was no longer chairman of the party, referring Simatupang instead to Jusuf Wibisono, the acting chairman of the organization. At the end of an almost day-long session with the armed forces' representative, Wibisono and his fellow Masyumi leaders said that the maximum their party could say on the matter of the Negara Islam was that the Masyumi had its own way. According to Simatupang, the armed forces' leadership took this to mean that the Masyumi favored the idea of a Negara Islam but that they had their own way of achieving this; that is, they would seek to do so democratically and constitutionally.[14]

The notion of a "Negara Islam," says Simatupang, found its way into the language of Indonesian politics because of the Darul Islam, and became linked with political Islam as a whole because the Masyumi leaders had felt they could not be seen to be "underbidding" the Darul Islam. This had been a tragedy for Indonesia and a tragedy for Islam in Indonesia. Until then, the army and Islamic groups had been able to work essentially for the same goals. Now, the army feared that the whole question of the shape of the state was being reopened. Partly as a result of this, the army had

---

13. McVey, "Post-Revolutionary Transformation," p. 139. In this context, it may be worth noting that when the three big Java divisions--the Siliwangi, Diponegoro, and Brawijaya--were formed, the military leadership showed a distinct preference for pre-Islamic names. Siliwangi was the last great pre-Islamic king of West Java, Brawijaya the last non-Islamic emperor of East Java. And while Prince Diponegoro was a Muslim, he was honored more for his nationalist, than his Islamic credentials. In the opinion of some, the heroes of the pre-Islamic past have a special link in the minds of the military leadership with nationalist aspirations, their names more evocative, more suited to efforts to mobilize the spirit of the nation.

14. Interviews with Lt. Gen. Simatupang, July 8 and 10, 1982.

taken steps to introduce the Sapta Marga, the oath of loyalty, with
its uncompromising declaration that the army was committed to uphold the Pancasila (and, by extension, reject any attempt to set up
an Islamic state).

Islam remained the great political issue of the fifties and Muslim politicians worked tirelessly to advance their cause, their setback at the 1955 general elections (when the combined Islamic vote
accounted for only 44 percent of the total) notwithstanding. In
1959, as Indonesia moved towards the readoption of the 1945 Constitution (it had been dropped two months after its introduction), the
Islamic political groupings tried once again to have "the seven
words" written back into the preamble of that document. The attempt proved unsuccessful, meeting with the combined opposition of
President Sukarno, the Indonesian National Party (Partai Nasional
Indonesia, PNI), the PKI, the Christian parties, and, ultimately,
the army. However, the decree announcing the return to the 1945
Constitution was couched in language that was deliberately ambiva-
lent. "Considering that the Jakarta Charter influences/influenced
the Constitution," it said, that Constitution was again valid. In
Bahasa Indonesia there are no verbal roots inflected for tenses and
the sentence can be read either as a statement of historical fact or
as an acknowledgment that the Jakarta Charter has a continuing influence on the Constitution.[15]

In the opinion of the current ruling group--and in the opinion of Christian leaders like Simatupang--talk of the Pancasila *plus
the Jakarta Charter* is totally unacceptable. Such a call is not only
discriminatory, it is argued, but opens up a Pandora's box of delicate questions: Once it is said in the Constitution that Muslims must
abide by the *syariah* (Islamic law), the argument runs, the state is
given power to enforce the syariah. As a result, the state must
then make up its mind just what the syariah encompasses, with all
the problems that entails. In short, it is argued, any such move
would alter the whole nature of the state.

In these circumstances, some Indonesians contend, it is up to
wise and thoughtful Muslim leaders to take the initiative and convince the army leadership that Islamic groups have abandoned their
dreams of an Islamic state. The army, this argument runs, is
aware that many Muslims speak disparagingly about the Pancasila
and that some among them are arguing that only through acts of
force and even violence can Islam gain its rightful place in the
scheme of things. In view of this, it is said, it is understandable
that the army leadership will go on suspecting the Islamic group.

To others there are drawbacks to this line of reasoning,
drawbacks that go well beyond the fact that it is difficult, given

---

15. The view that the Jakarta Charter still applies owing to the
confusion in the 1959 wording is found, for example, in Saifuddin
Anshari, *The Jakarta Charter of June 1945* (Kuala Lumpur: Muslim
Youth Movement of Malaysia, 1979), especially pp. 104-5.

the way the army has structured the situation, for any strong and self-confident Islamic leadership to emerge. In this view, the burden of proof is being put on the Islamic community to show that it is not against the Pancasila when in fact this is no longer an issue of any importance. Since 1945 according to this argument, having Islamic aspirations has not meant that one doubts the Pancasila, a point that both Sukarno and Hatta had explained clearly on many occasions. What is needed, it is argued, is a government which is sufficiently enlightened and sufficiently self-confident to come to terms with the question of political Islam, not a government that treats it as something dark and malevolent. "There is no question Islam is in crisis," an Indonesian scholar noted in 1978.

> Islam has just begun to come to grips with the modern world and the essentially secular aspect of the political process and Islam will be a problem for a long time. But one doesn't deal with the problem by throwing all the Muslims onto one heap and dealing with them. There is a fundamental identity with Islam in Indonesia, even with the abangan. People wouldn't vote for a party which had an important element of Christians in it.[16]

There were, as we have seen, understandable reasons why the army was wary of political Islam. The Darul Islam and the PRRI-Permesta had caused enormous dislocations, and suppression of the Darul Islam in particular had cost the army dearly in terms of loss of life. The PRRI-Permesta rebellion, however, had not been entirely a Muslim affair and not all Muslims had sided with it. (Many of the most prominent PRRI military leaders were Christians, including Warouw, Simbolon, Kawilarang, and Sumual). And though the Darul Islam leaders had sought to create an Islamic state, few in the mid-1970s were still thought to nurture that dream.

The army, however, had taken this basic fear of Islam--a fear which struck a responsive chord in its own breast--and had, many believed, played upon it for its own political ends. The fear, it was suggested, had been greatly exaggerated. And that, in turn, had led the government to ignore the great changes that were taking place amongst Muslims. Many of the younger Muslim intellectuals had left the idea of an Islamic state behind them. There was still, it was true, a fundamentalist fringe in Indonesia. But it was no more than this. Even so, as one scholar notes

> it is a fact that there is enough combustible material in our society to keep alive the fear of Islam. What kept Sukarno in power so long? It was the fact that the

---

16. For my understanding of the role of Islam in Indonesia politics I am particularly indebted to a prominent Indonesian scholar who wishes to remain anonymous.

abangan, the Catholics and the Protestants were more afraid of Islam than of the Communists. The same groups support the army and I think that fear is being manipulated for power reasons. Many seriously fear it [Islam] but a leadership that would know how to handle the Muslims and had closer cooperation with them would be able to reduce the fear to more manageable proportions.[17]

What made matters worse was that there had been a backlash against the greed and materialism associated with development. This was a moral backlash which, given the transitional nature of the society, had assumed religious overtones. Muslims, disturbed by what they saw around them, had tended to become even more Muslim. There was, essentially, a yearning for moral rectitude in the face of morally reprehensible behavior, and its impact had already been felt in Iran, in Pakistan, in Bangladesh to some extent, and in Malaysia. "We are really involved in great historical processes which we very rarely see let alone understand but which are of great importance in the Third World," this scholar noted. "In a way, it might make Indonesia more difficult to govern. It is not just a matter of how is the government doing, how is the military doing. Over and above that there are processes going on which we only dimly perceive and even less understand. This only highlights the government's fear of Islam."[18]

As the Muslim world went through these convulsions, the army view of Islam remained static. The army liked to see itself as centrist in outlook, a group, neither of the right nor the left, which had been called on repeatedly to save the nation from extremism of one kind or another. Pancasila, Liddle has noted, is currently interpreted in centrist terms, "containing all the strengths and none of the weaknesses of left or right, and Dwi Fungsi is the guarantee that Indonesia will remain a Panca Sila state."[19]

---

17. Confidential communication.

18. Ibid.

19. R. W. Liddle, "The 1977 Indonesian Election and New Order Legitimacy," *Southeast Asian Affairs* (1978), p. 123.

1. Lt. Gen. Ali Murtopo (reprinted
by permission of *Tempo*)

2. General Yoga Sugama

3. Admiral Sudomo (reprinted
by permission of *Tempo*)

4. General Benny Murdani

Inner Circle

5. General Maraden Panggabean

6. General Widodo

7. General Mohammad Jusuf

Outer

8. General Sumitro

9. Lt. Gen. Sutopo Juwono (reprinted by permission of *Tempo*)

10. General Darjatmo

Circle

11. General A. H. Nasution

12. Lt. Gen. H. R. Dharsono (reprinted
by permission of *Tempo*)

13. Lt. Gen. Djatikusumo (reprinted
by permission of *Tempo*)

Fosko

14. Lt. Gen. Ali Sadikin

15. General Hugeng Imam Santoso
(reprinted by permission of *Tempo*)

16. Lt. Gen. Mohammad Jasin

17. Lt. Gen. Mokoginta

Group

18. President Suharto

CHAPTER ONE

ARMY OFFICERS AND KRATON POLITICS

> After Malari Pak Harto asked me. . . . 'Well, what do
> you think about the idea of Ali [Murtopo] becoming Chief
> of Bakin?' 'No'! I rejected it. I told Pak Harto, 'It is
> not because I don't like Ali, Pak! It is because we have
> to create a very good impression with the whole intelli-
> gence effort'. Intelligence officers should not play games
> in the political processes.
>
> -- General Sumitro, 1981[1]

For anyone studying the Indonesian political scene in the early
1980s, the most obvious phenomenon was the preeminent position of
President Suharto, a retired army officer whose political skills were
still sometimes underestimated. Suharto's bland, almost avuncular,
manner concealed astuteness and craft, and the personal graciousness
he exhibited to guests disguised strongly held--and surprisingly
rigid--views about the sort of society he was seeking to build. Suharto had spent the years since 1965 extending and defending his
power base and he was now very much more than the *primus inter
pares* in a collegial army leadership. Suharto stood at the apex of
the pyramid; his appointees sat in each of the key executive, legislative, and judicial branches of government. He dominated the cabinet
and the state bureaucracy. He dominated the armed forces (Angkatan
Bersenjata Republic Indonesia, ABRI) and had hand-picked both the
minister of defense and the commander of Kopkamtib, the powerful
Operational Command for the Restoration of Security and Order. He
dominated the People's Consultative Assembly (Majelis Permusyawaratan Rakyat, MPR)--the body that continued to reelect him for
successive five-year terms--and had selected a trusted military colleague to preside over its deliberations. He was the central figure in
Golkar, the army-backed political movement, and had crippled the effectiveness of the two "opposition" political parties. He dominated the
judicial branch, weak as it was, and had stacked its key positions
with long-time associates, all of them generals. He appointed the men
who sat in the Supreme Advisory Council (Dewan Pertimbangan
Agung, DPA). His writ extended into every department and into
every state-run corporation; it reached down, if he chose, to every
village. He wielded enormous power both because the 1945 Constitu-

---

1. Interview with General Sumitro, March 17, 1981.

tion confers enormous power on the president and because he was the dominant influence over the army, itself the dominant force in society. In short, he had established himself as the paramount figure in a society in which deference to authority is deeply rooted.

This power, however, needs to be seen in context. Though Suharto had an extraordinary capacity to influence the course of events in Indonesia, his power was by no means unlimited. In a discussion of the constitutional deliberations of 1945, John Legge has made the point that, while the outlines of the 1945 Constitution appear to provide for an almost dictatorial president, "the wide dispersion of power in Indonesia was likely to tell against any heavy-handed exercise of authority. Any president would, in practice, have to conciliate pressure groups."[2] This has, in fact, been the case, for Suharto no less than it was for Sukarno. In formal terms, Suharto's influence over society seems almost unfettered. In practice, Suharto has been obliged on most issues to be a consensus seeker, meeting endlessly with the leaders of major social and political groups, bending them, where possible, to his will. In this sense, he has been almost as "political" as his predecessor, the army's proclaimed disdain for politics notwithstanding.

A Patrimonial or a Praetorian State?

Many observers have commented on the fact that the system of government in contemporary Indonesia bears a marked resemblance to that which was found in precolonial Java, a line of argument which finds its most elegant formulation in Benedict Anderson's 1972 essay on "The Idea of Power in Javanese Culture."[3]

Perhaps the most exact image of the ordered Javanese polity, Anderson suggested in that essay, "is that of a cone of light cast downwards by a reflector lamp."[4] Traditional Javanese thought implicitly denied a hierarchical approach, "since a hierarchy presupposes a certain degree of autonomy at each of its various levels"; instead, it sought ideally a single, pervasive source of power and authority, the core of the traditional polity being the ruler, who personified the unity of society.[5] Turning to the traditional relationship between the ruler and the governmental structure through which he ruled, Anderson noted that Schrieke's picture of the administrative

---

2. See J. D. Legge, *Sukarno: A Political Biography* (New York: Praeger, 1972), pp. 189-90.

3. See Benedict R. O'G. Anderson, "The Idea of Power in Javanese Culture" in *Culture and Politics in Indonesia*, ed. Claire Holt et al. (Ithaca: Cornell University Press, 1972), pp. 1-69. Anderson, it should be said, has now largely abandoned this view.

4. Ibid., p. 22.

5. Ibid.

structure of the precolonial Javanese kingdom admirably fits Max Weber's model of the patrimonial state. According to this model, the central government is essentially an extension of the ruler's personal household and staff. Officials are granted their positions and the perquisites that go with them as personal favors of the ruler and may be dismissed or degraded at his personal whim. "The administrative structure, while formally hierarchical, is in effect composed of stratified clusters of patron-client relationships," Anderson noted. "Both in the regions and in the center, officials gather around them clusters of personal dependents, on the model of the ruler himself," the destinies of these dependents being linked with the success or failure of their patrons.

What one sees here, said Anderson, is the marked consonance of the traditional Javanese concept of Power with the political structures and behavior of the patrimonial state. Moreover, he suggested, the "indigenization" of bureaucratic structures and behavior in Indonesia that was so marked after the middle 1950s "can be usefully viewed as a reemergence of the patrimonial model."[6] And while the major cause of this reemergent patrimonialism was doubtless the fact that the rational-legal bureaucracy of Dutch times proved economically unsustainable in a period of economic decline "the holding power of patrimonialism was probably also accentuated by the persistence of traditional perspectives so consonant with it."[7] In Anderson's view, the signal unwillingness of the *pusat* (center) to accede to demands for decentralization and regional autonomy in the late parliamentary period (1956-58), while clearly stemming from fears for the national exchequer, could also be attributed in part to the continuing impact of old conceptions of center-province relationships as indicators of the "health" of the regime. A parallel line of argument was suggested for patterns of administrative behavior at the center, particularly after the restoration of the 1945 Constitution in 1959. This Constitution, it was pointed out, provides explicitly that cabinet ministers are to be the assistants of the president and responsible to him alone.

> Under the 1945 Constitution, formal norms and traditional propensities tended to coincide. Insofar as real Power is seen to flow out of the concentrated center and not from the diffuse perimeter, ministerial behavior should reflect the wishes of the former rather than the latter. The same argument helps to explain the ease with which many Javanese accepted the emergence under both the authoritarian Sukarno and Suharto regimes of informal power-groups outside the "rational-legal" structure of the bureaucracy. The so-called *golongan istana* (palace group) under Guided Democracy and the President's SPRI (private staff) under the New Order represented the

---

6. Ibid., p. 36.

7. Ibid.

kitchen cabinet of the ruler, his personal agents and confidants. The enormous power they in fact wielded depended solely on the fact that their proximity to the center was recognized by the entire politico-administrative
elite. [8]

This "reemergence" of precolonial patterns of government has
been frequently commented on--and condemned--by Indonesians, not
least by a number of prominent army officers who had hoped that the
New Order would live up to its promise of 1966 to bring about a
"total correction" after the various excesses of the past. Many of
these critics refer deprecatingly to the state over which Suharto rules
as "the new Mataram," an allusion to the dominant kingdom on Java in
the years after 1582 and to the president's success in evoking the atmosphere of a Javanese *kraton* (palace), in which politics is frequently a matter of court intrigue and in which one powerful "prince"
is played off against another for the greater good of the ruler.
Other critics have drawn attention to the fact that patrimonial practices are rampant in the economy; one does not have to look far,
these critics contend, to find a ruler who, true to traditional patterns, underpins his authority by the allocation of specified benefices
to his subordinates.

Given all this, it would be hard to deny the continuing "pull"
of patrimonialism in Indonesia. On the other hand, one should not
make too much of this. Postindependence Indonesia is not precolonial
Java, and while some of the patterns of the past may indeed be
"shadowing" contemporary Indonesia there are obvious deficiencies in
neo-patrimonial explanations of the present. The danger is that
"neo-patrimonialism" provides an all-too-convenient rationalization of
and "explanation" for almost any conceivable excess of centrism or
authoritarianism, explanations which bring with them comforting assurances that any such developments are in harmony with something
in the Javanese soul. The concept is a useful adjunct to our understanding but is simply too all-embracing to be of much value on its
own. [9]

Suharto's style of leadership during the early years of the New
Order certainly encouraged the belief that he followed an essentially
patrimonial approach, great authority being delegated to those like
Lt. Col. (later Lt. Gen.) Ali Murtopo who were acquaintances of long
standing and who tended to operate outside the "rational-legal" structures of government. However, this phenomenon needs to be seen in
the context of the times. The postcoup period was one of great uncertainty in Indonesia, in the army no less than in other institutions,
and there were compelling reasons why a new leader would seek to

---

8. Ibid., pp. 37-38.

9. This is not to suggest that Anderson has rushed to rationalize
excesses of authoritarianism; his interest was in the mind of the
Javanese rather than in any putative soul.

bring with him, and work with, associates on whom he could depend explicitly, rather than associate himself with "outsiders." While it would be a mistake to discount the continuing impact of "feudal" or "patrimonial" influences on Suharto, a case can be made for the argument that the president is, in fact, a "rationalizer" and "modernizer," a man who moved, once he was securely in office, to formalize the administration and put it on a more rational-legal basis. In 1966, for example, the most prominent of the Indonesian "technocrats"--Dr. Widjojo Nitisastro, Dr. Ali Wardhana, Dr. Emil Salim, Dr. Mohammad Sadli, and Dr. Subroto--were members of a special team attached to Suharto's personal staff. By 1971, all of them had been appointed to the cabinet. Suharto, it is true, did not "dismiss" the remaining members of his kitchen cabinet, most of whom were senior army officers, until forced to do so in 1974 by outside events. But several of his personal assistants had by then moved across into the bureaucracy proper, or had at least a nominal position within it, a trend which continued in the years thereafter.[10] In time, the distinction between those who were "inside" and those who were "outside" the rational-legal structure became less relevant. As this process continued, the New Order leaders were strengthening and extending parallel civilian-military administrative structures which, reaching down to the village level, gave the regime a base far more resilient, interlocking, and permanent than anything based on the more transitory nature of personal loyalty. Though officials not infrequently adopted a "feudal" manner in their dealings with both their subordinates and the public, the existence of the administrative framework made patrimonial explanations of contemporary Indonesian leadership less than adequate. As Donald Emmerson has correctly observed, Suharto is more than a neopatrimonial prince dispensing favors and fiats. "He has not only built a government but around it a regime, whose structures are more solid than a purely personalistic or Javanese-cultural conception of power in the New Order would allow."[11]

---

10. Much the same sort of thing occurred in the United States when Dr. Henry Kissinger moved across from the Nixon White House (where he had served as national security adviser) to become secretary of state. In practical terms, the distinctions about being "inside" or "outside" the system seem largely irrelevant. In this context, there are interesting similarities between the Indonesian and the US presidential systems. If the former bestows on the Head of State much of the power and panoply of a precolonial Javanese king, then the latter, as Thomas Jefferson averred in 1787, was created as an "elective monarchy." "The office," says Huntington, "was designed to embody much of the power of the British king; and the politics that surround it are court politics." See Samuel P. Huntington, *Political Order in Changing Societies* (New Haven: Yale University Press, 1968), p. 114.

11. Donald K. Emmerson, "Indonesian Politics in the 1980s: Pressure and Counterpressure," (Paper delivered at State Department meeting on Indonesia, April 1981), p. 6.

An alternative--and perhaps more appropriate--approach would be to describe Indonesia in "praetorian" terms, as a nation in which, in Nordlinger's words, military officers are "major or predominant political actors by virtue of their actual or threatened use of force."[12] The term praetorianism comes from the elite Praetorian Guard of the Roman Empire, first established to protect the emperor but which eventually used its military power to overthrow emperors and to control the appointment of their successors. Praetorianism (or military intervention) occurs, Nordlinger suggests, in various coup situations, and most particularly when officers themselves take control of the government. In such cases, civilian regimes are transformed into military regimes, even though certain civilian individuals and groups often enjoy a good measure of political influence.

In delimiting the subject of praetorianism, Nordlinger says, it is necessary to ask whether a military regime is still so considered ten or twenty years after the coup, even if it is "civilianized," with the leaders shedding their military uniforms and taking on the title of president or prime minister. The answer, he suggests, is yes, if the military took power by means of a coup, the highest government officials have served (or continue to serve) in the armed forces, and the governors are primarily dependent upon the support of the officer corps for the retention of power.

Praetorians invariably portray themselves as responsible and patriotic officers who have intervened in civilian affairs because of an overriding responsibility to constitution and nation, taking it upon themselves to decide if the constitution has been violated or the national interest subverted, and thus whether or not intervention is warranted. The military argue that they have a special responsibility, "a crucial mission that transcends their obligations to existing authorities." This, says Nordlinger, is praetorianism's basic public rationale.

> Particular coups are justified by charging the former civilian incumbents with a shorter or longer list of performance failures. The soldiers almost invariably claim that constitutional principles have been flouted by the corrupt, arbitrary, or illegal actions of the civilian incumbents. They are also commonly accused of having acted contrary to the national interest by allowing subversive groups to threaten the country's internal security, by fomenting class and communal conflicts and thereby encouraging political disorder and violence, by adopting policies that resulted in low economic growth rates, widespread unemployment, and inflationary spirals, or by failing to undertake programs of socioeconomic modernization and reform.

---

12. Eric A. Nordlinger, *Soldiers in Politics: Military Coups and Governments* (New Jersey: Prentice Hall, 1977), p. 2.

At the same time the praetorians confidently assert
that they will restore the country to political and econom-
ical good health. They are willing and able to do so because the officer corps is highly patriotic, detached from
the interests of particular class and communal groups,
devoid of the politicians' weaknesses, and highly skilled
in technical and managerial matters. Given these at-
tributes, along with the determination to succeed, the
military governors announce that they will eliminate corruption, root out subversive elements, curb political dis-
order, generate economic growth, and bring a halt to in-
flationary spirals. Some praetorians go on to announce
their intentions to modernize the economy and implement
progressive socioeconomic policies. But the predominant
theme is that of praetorians as saviors, promising to
remedy and rectify past civilian failures, rather than
committing themselves to the fashioning of a better or different society.

Lastly, almost all praetorians announce their intention
to hand over the reins of government to democratically
elected civilians in the near or distant future. . . .[13]

There are, Nordlinger argues, three kinds of praetorian offi-
cers--moderators, guardians, and rulers. Praetorian moderators exercise a veto power over a varied range of governmental decisions,
without however taking control of the government themselves.
Praetorian guardians are those who, having overthrown a civilian
government, retain governmental power in their own hands, usually
for a period of two to four years. Ruler-type praetorians not only
control the government but dominate the regime, and their political
and economic objectives are exceptionally ambitious. The far-reaching
nature of the intended changes and the realization that the changes
will take considerable time to become securely rooted "necessitates regime dominance and an indefinite period of military rule." Ruler-type
praetorians seek to bring about basic changes in the distribution of
power by eliminating nearly all existing power centers. Some ruler-
type praetorians "attempt to mobilize the population by creating mass
parties (or movements) over which they have exclusive control.
Polity, economy, and society are to be penetrated from above."

Contemporary Indonesia, it is suggested, displays many if not
all of the characteristics described by Nordlinger and fits without any
great difficulty into what he describes as a ruler-type praetorian category.[14] At the same time, there are certain features that make

---

13. Ibid., pp. 20-21.

14. The army did not come to power in Indonesia through a coup
launched by senior officers, one of the basic givens in Nordlinger's
concept of praetorianism. As we have seen, there had been a progressive expansion in army involvement since the late 1950s, culminat-

the Indonesian experience unique. For one thing, the military's right to participate in nonmilitary affairs, which is traced back to the revolutionary period and which has been imbued with an almost mystical significance, is said to be everlasting. As Anderson has noted, "unlike even the Pinochet regime in Chile, the New Order holds out no prospects whatever of a 'return to civilian rule' or a 'restoration of parliamentary government.'"[15] For another, the ruler-type praetorianism that is found in Indonesia is centered to an extraordinary degree on the person of Suharto and a few key members of his inner circle. The army, although enormously powerful in day-to-day administration, has surprisingly little influence on policy formation. For the most part, army officers merely implement decisions that have been taken by others in Jakarta; they generally have little, if any, say in those decisions, a situation very different from that which prevailed twenty years ago. Under Suharto, power is not only centralized but held in very few hands. The president, in the final analysis, depends on the services of perhaps a dozen key military officers, each of whom presides in turn over tightly organized and often mutually-antagonistic pyramids of authority.

The "Core Group" Around Suharto

In the mid-1970s, the members of this "core group" included General Maraden Panggabean, the minister of defense and security/commander of the armed forces; Lt. Gen. (later Gen.) Amir Machmud, the minister of home affairs; Lt. Gen. (later Gen.) Yoga Sugama, the head of Bakin, the State Intelligence Coordinating Board; Lt. Gen. Ali Murtopo, the deputy head of Bakin and former head of the president's "kitchen cabinet" for political affairs; Admiral Sudomo, the chief of staff (later commander) of Kopkamtib; Maj. Gen. (later Gen.) Benny Murdani,[16] the assistant for intelligence to the minister of defense; Lt. Gen. Sudharmono, the state secretary; Lt. Gen. (later Gen.) Darjatmo, the chief of staff for nonmilitary affairs at the Minis-

---

ing in a full take-over in the mid-1960s. Even so, Indonesia would appear to be in all other respects a near-perfect example of a ruler-type praetorian society.

15. Benedict R. Anderson, "Nationalism and the State in Modern Indonesia" (Paper contributed to the Japanese Political Science Association Round Table Conference on National Interest and Political Leadership, Tokyo, 1982), p. 41.

16. Murdani, being younger than the others, was in a category of his own. Although he had joined the revolutionary struggle, at the age of sixteen, in December 1948, he was not in any sense of the revolutionary generation. "Even Benny says his relationship with the president is like that of father and son. He makes no bones about it. He doesn't eyeball to eyeball like Sumitro or Ali." Confidential communication, November 14, 1981.

try of Defense; Lt. Gen. Ibnu Sutowo, the president director of Pertamina, the huge state-owned oil company; and perhaps one or two others.[17] (Two prominent and powerful members of the group--General Sumitro, the former commander of Kopkamtib/deputy commander of the armed forces; and Lt. Gen. Sutopo Juwono, the former head of Bakin--had been forced onto the sidelines following the so-called "Malari" riots of January 1974. Ibnu Sutowo, a man on whom Suharto had depended to a very great extent for extra-budgetary financing, was likewise forced out in early 1975 following disclosures that Pertamina was on the brink of bankruptcy.)

Each of the officers in the core group could count on the support (either personal or institutional) of his own particular "pyramid." For example, the "Amir Machmud group" centered on the powerful Ministry of Home Affairs and thus commanded the support of those serving in what was, after the Ministry of Defense and Security (Hankam), the most important government department. The "Ali Murtopo group" was built around Murtopo's position as a powerful force in the intelligence community and included, under the same umbrella, the Centre for Strategic and International Studies (CSIS), a "think tank" modeled on the Rand Corporation and largely run by Chinese Catholic intellectuals with whom Murtopo had become associated during the anti-Sukarno actions of the mid-1960s. The "Sudharmono group" was a cluster of senior officers in or close to the State Secretariat, the most important members of which were graduates of the Military Law Academy (AHM) in Jakarta. By the early eighties, when the influence of this group was at its peak, the Sudharmono group exercised almost untrammeled control of the Indonesian judicial system. Its members included the minister of justice, Lt. Gen. Ali Said; the attorney general, Maj. Gen. Ismail Saleh; and the chief justice of the Supreme Court, Lt. Gen. Mudjono. Other members were Maj. Gen. E. J. Kanter, the effective head of the Opstib anti-graft operation, and Maj. Gen. August Marpaung, the general manager of Antara, the government-run news agency. As state secretary, Sudharmono not only had constant access to the president (while controlling the access of almost all others); he also had authority, after the introduction of Presidential Decision No. 10 of 1980, to screen all government purchases for goods and services of more than Rp. 500 million (US \$770,000), a power which greatly enhanced his position and influence.

---

17. Other generals, many of whom had an economic-logistics background, were associated with Suharto in a more private capacity. Maj. Gen. (retd) Sudjono Humardhani, a financial-economic adviser to the president over many years, was widely regarded at this time as Suharto's spiritual "senior" and adviser on *kepercayaan* (Javanese mystic beliefs). Maj. Gen. Bustanil Arifin, head of Bulog, the National Logistics Board, was likewise a member of Suharto's private circle. (Bustanil's wife was related to Madame Suharto.) Maj. Gen. Surjo Wirjohadiputro, Suharto's onetime assistant for financial affairs, also retained links with the president, at least initially.

Each of these groupings was in orbit around Suharto, and the president was able to manipulate them in such a way that they were not united but remained in competition with one another. Highly skilled at playing one "prince" off against another and believing in the need for a "creative tension" between those who served him, Suharto had adopted a style of divide and rule under which the position of potential rivals was effectively weakened while his own position was effectively enhanced.

Within this constellation of forces there was an "inner core group"--known variously as the "kitchen cabinet" or the "central committee"--made up of Javanese officers who enjoyed particularly close relations with Suharto.

The "Inner Core Group"

When Suharto came to power in the mid-1960s, he relied to a very considerable extent on a small group of advisers drawn from the army.[18] In August 1966 he established a private staff (Staf Pribadi, or SPRI) which consisted of six army officers and two teams of civilian specialists on economic affairs. By 1968, the SPRI had twelve members and was widely regarded as an "invisible government" which enjoyed greater powers than the cabinet, particularly in the field of policy formation. SPRI members were responsible for such matters as finance, politics, foreign intelligence, domestic intelligence, social welfare, and general elections affairs, as well as "general affairs" and "special affairs."[19] The dominant members of this group were officers with whom Suharto had been associated for a number of years. The coordinator of the SPRI, Maj. Gen. Alamsjah Ratu Perwiranegara, had been a close friend of Suharto since the two men served together on the headquarters of the army staff in 1960. Three others--Ali Murtopo, Sudjono Humardhani, and Yoga Sugama--had served on Suharto's staff when he was commander of the Central Java Diponegoro military region in the late 1950s and had been with him again later in Kostrad, the army strategic reserve. Alamsjah and Sudjono Humardhani had a background in army finance. Ali Murtopo and Yoga Sugama were intelligence officers, Ali heading an independent intelligence unit known as Opsus (Special Operations), which had been set up within Kostrad in 1964 to seek ways of putting an end to "Confrontation" with Malaysia.

Although the SPRI was dissolved in June 1968 following student and press protests, key members of the group retained their influence. Alamsjah, who had been appointed state secretary in February that year, was now given control over the president's official staff. Yoga Sugama, the SPRI officer responsible for domestic intelligence,

---

18. Harold Crouch, *The Army and Politics in Indonesia* (Ithaca: Cornell University Press, 1978), p. 307.

19. Ibid.

became deputy head and then head of Bakin in the same year. Meanwhile, Maj. Gen. (later Lt. Gen.) Surjo Wirjohadiputro, the SPRI officer in charge of finance, Sudjono Humardhani (economy), and Ali Murtopo (foreign intelligence) were appointed personal assistants (ASPRI) to Suharto; Murtopo's Opsus continued to undertake "special operations" on behalf of the president, the opposition of some senior staff generals (and in particular General Sumitro) notwithstanding.

The composition of this inner group around Suharto was not unchanging. In 1971 Alamsjah was sent as ambassador to the Netherlands, partly because he had failed to finesse several difficult assignments, partly because of intrigues carried out by other members of the inner group, most notably Ali Murtopo. In 1974, following the Malari Affair, Suharto dissolved the ASPRI and "dismissed" Murtopo, Humardhani, and Surjo. All three, however, maintained their links with the president, even if, in the case of Humardhani and Surjo, these did tend to fade with the passing of the years. Surjo, whose name had been linked with a major fraud case in 1970-71, was appointed president director of the Hotel Indonesia and later given permission to build two large new Jakarta hotels, the Mandarin and the Hilton. Humardhani maintained his interest in forging closer economic links with Japan, while serving also as a spiritual counsellor to the president, a follower of *kebatinan* (Javanese mystic beliefs). Murtopo's star, meanwhile, was at its zenith. His key rival, Sumitro, had been forced into retirement and replaced as head of Kopkamtib by Admiral Sudomo, an officer with whom Murtopo had good working relations. A Murtopo protégé, Brig. Gen. Benny Murdani, had been brought in to replace an associate of Sumitro as assistant for intelligence to the minister of defense.[20] Murtopo had excellent relations with Lt. Gen. Ibnu Sutowo, the freewheeling president director of Pertamina, and would soon see another of his protégés, Brig. Gen. Abdul Rahman Ramly, installed as head of the state tin company. Murtopo was the deputy in charge of operations at Bakin, retained his control over Opsus, a body answerable only to Suharto, and was co-sponsor (along with Sudjono Humardhani) of the CSIS.

In the mid-1970s, the four most important members of the "inner core group" were Yoga Sugama, Ali Murtopo, Sudomo, and Benny Murdani. This was not in any sense a homogeneous body; its members enjoyed close relations with the president more on an individual than a group basis. Nevertheless, there was a certain unanimity of view on key issues and an ability to work together in times of stress. The members of the "inner core group" were men with whom Suharto had not only had close relations for many years but with whom he felt most comfortable. Officers like Mohammad Jusuf,

---

20. As in the case of earlier key appointments, Suharto fell back on officers with whom he had a long-established relationship and on whom he felt he could depend; Sudomo and Murdani, both Javanese Christians, had been associated with Suharto in the early 1960s when he was head of the Mandala Command for the liberation of West Irian.

who was appointed minister of defense in 1978, Panggabean, and (before his downfall) Sumitro, could work in close cooperation with the president, but could never be considered his closest confidants. Even Amir Machmud, a blunt but loyal instrument of the president, was outside this innermost circle. "Sudomo, Benny, and Yoga are closest to Suharto," a retired general observed in 1981. "They have personal relations, outside their official relations. If you talk about Amir Machmud and Jusuf and Sumitro they have their relations more according to their work, not personal."[21]

What was most striking about this inner group, apart from its members' loyalty to, and length of association with, the president, was the predominance of officers with an intelligence or security background. Three of the four men on whom Suharto depended most --Ali Murtopo, Benny Murdani, and Yoga Sugama--were from the intelligence field while the fourth--Sudomo--held extraordinary security powers. If in the late 1970s and early 1980s policy was decided at the top of the army pyramid in Jakarta, then that policy was shaped to a quite extraordinary degree by intelligence and security officers. This tended to antagonize many senior officers at the Ministry of Defense and Security and sharpen traditional rivalries between officers from the intelligence and operations branches of the army.[22]   Al-

---

21.   Confidential communication, March 2, 1981.

22.   These rivalries appear to have peaked at the time of the Indonesian invasion of East Timor in 1975. The invasion plans were drawn up by Maj. Gen. Benny Murdani without the knowledge or participation of key members of the operational staff. The deputy commander of the armed forces (Wapangab), General Surono Reksodimedjo, who was as much in the dark as anyone else, registered his displeasure by going off shortly thereafter on the *haj*, leaving Murdani's group to complete the takeover. Surono felt that as Wapangab he should have known what was planned. Surono was not the only officer upset over the invasion. The Kostrad commander, Lt. Gen. Leo Lopulisa, who would in the normal course of events have played a central role in any such operation, was in Paris at the time and received a cable advising him that the invasion had gone through, without ever having been asked if his troops were ready. Lopulisa confided to a retired colleague not long after the invasion, "I am only the manager of a funeral parlor. Only that! I am not involved. I am only in charge of the funerals of the men who didn't come back." (Confidential communication, March 23, 1982.) In the view of some senior officers from the operational side, Suharto was operating outside normal channels in bypassing Kostrad and relying on the Kopassandha (Komando Pasukan Sandhi Yudha, or Secret Warfare Force) and the intelligence community in such an operation. This view did not make allowance for the fact that in many ways an expanded Kopassandha had taken over some of the functions that were formerly the responsibility of Kostrad. However, there were dangers in such methods, quite apart from any considerations of operating "outside" the formal system. Al-

though seldom explicit, this rivalry was to run like a thread through the debate which took part in the late 1970s and early 1980s over ABRI's role in Indonesian society. This dominance of intelligence and security officers both reflected and reinforced Suharto's preoccupation with a "security and development" approach to nation building.

A second feature was the unusual "doubling up" of functions in the hands of the most trusted members of Suharto's inner circle. As the editors of the bi-annual Cornell University journal *Indonesia* noted in 1980, Sudomo had been effectively running Kopkamtib since January 1974 and had been deputy commander of the armed forces since April 1978.[23] Murdani had not only been assistant for intelligence in the Defense Ministry since August 1974, but had also had the functions of head of the Strategic Intelligence Center since August 1977 and deputy head of Bakin since early 1978. Yoga Sugama, who had been the head of Bakin since January 1974, had served as chief of staff of Kopkamtib from 1978 to 1980.[24] Although not a member of

---

though Kopassandha units fought well and were able to penetrate deeply into enemy territory, they were not good at holding the ground they had taken; "real" infantry, it was argued, would be able to do this. In 1978, after he had stepped down as the secretary general of ASEAN, Lt. Gen. Dharsono spoke with the newly installed minister of defense, General Jusuf, about the differences that existed between the operational and intelligence branches of the armed forces. Jusuf, according to Dharsono, was "having trouble at that time with Murtopo," and the former Siliwangi commander suggested in effect that some parts of that intelligence service be placed more firmly under the control of Hankam. Jusuf is said to have listened and implicitly conceded that there may have been a problem. However, he did not comment on the proposal. Interview with Lt. Gen. Dharsono, March 26, 1982.

23. See "Current Data on the Indonesian Military Elite," *Indonesia* 39 (April 1980), p. 156. In March 1983 Sudomo was named minister for labor in the fourth Suharto cabinet.

24. According to one senior military officer in the Suharto "inner core group," Yoga was only made chief of staff of Kopkamtib so that he could get his fourth star. According to this account, Yoga felt "upset" that other officers had been promoted to full general while he was still a three-star officer. Because Bakin is nominally a civilian agency, it was arranged that he could come back into the military command structure, where he would be able to gain this promotion. Yoga, it is said, did "nothing" at Kopkamtib during his two years as chief of staff of that body. (Confidential communication, February 28, 1981.) Yoga flatly rejects this account, arguing that he was, in fact, heavily involved in Kopkamtib affairs during this time. (Interview, July 15, 1981.) While this may be open to question, there would seem no reason for him to have taken on a "military" job in order to be promoted. There was no rule against officers being promoted while they were out on kekaryaan (nonmilitary) duties; indeed, Amir

Table I. *Overlapping Areas of Responsibility Within Suharto's
Inner Circle (1978–80)*

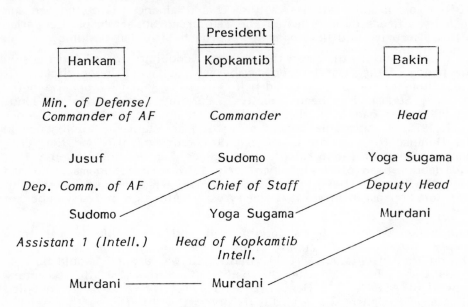

Murdani was also Kapusintelstrat (head of the Strategic Intelligence Center).   Unlike the assistant 1 slot, which had a coordinating function, this position carried executive responsibility; in an
emergency, Murdani would have had operational command of all Kopassandha forces.

The commander of the Kopassandha, Major General Yogie Suardi
Memet, was, at the same time, commander of Kodam VI/Siliwangi (West
Java).   Murdani and Yogie Memet were graduates of the postrevolu-
tionary *Pusat Pendidikan Perwiraan-Angkatan Darat* (P3-AD, or Army
Officers' Training Center) in Bandung.   As such, they were members
of a group of about 100 officers who formed a link between the
Generation of '45 and the post-1960 graduates of the Armed Forces
Academy in Magelang.   Popular with both Jusuf and Murdani, Yogi
Memet had served as a link between these two officers on occasions
when relations between them were not harmonious.

Within Bakin, there were other officers with personal links to
Suharto.   Maj. Gen. Rudjito, the head of one of the four Bakin departments, was a Diponegoro officer who had been Suharto's intelligence officer in the Mandala Command in the early 1960s.   Brig. Gen.
Raden Mas Jono Hatmodjo, fourth deputy to the chief of Bakin in the
late 1970s, was a member of the Mangkunegoro royal family and a relative of Ibu Tien Suharto.   (In April 1980, Jono Hatmodjo was installed as the director general for security and foreign relations at
the Ministry of Foreign Affairs.)

this inner group, Maj. Gen. Yogie Suardi Memet had been commander of the Kopassandha (Army Paracommandos) since May 1975 and commander of Military Region VI/Siliwangi (West Java) since October 1978.[25] This doubling of functions served Suharto well. For a start, it allowed the president to fill many of the most important government and army posts without going outside his immediate circle. At the same time, it created a system of checks and balances under which the power and influence of key aides was kept in rough equilibrium. (The appointment of Murdani to serve as deputy head of Bakin under Yoga Sugama was a case in point; neither man had much time for the other and each tended to go his own way, reporting directly to Suharto.)

A third--and closely related--feature was that the trusted members of the "inner core group" had tended to be left in key positions well beyond the normal two-year tour of duty. As noted above, three members of this group--Sudomo, Murdani, and Yoga Sugama--had remained in charge of the most important intelligence and security positions since 1974. In similar vein, General Darjatmo, a longtime associate of the president, had served as chief of staff for functional affairs, an extremely powerful position in the social-political field, for nine years (1969-78). This "immobility" in the intelligence/security and sociopolitical fields contrasted with a fairly rapid turnover in troop commands. Members of the inner core group were prepared to admit in private that this practice hampered normal personnel management; appointments, they said, were based more on trust than on capability. However, this was understandable, they argued. Intelligence was an extremely sensitive area--the situation in South Korea at the time of the 1979 assassination of President Park Chung Hee was often held up as an example--and it was very difficult, in the words of one Suharto confidant, "to find someone you can really trust."[26]

A fourth feature was the unique position and "reach" of Murdani. The three key pillars of Suharto's rule were Hankam, Kopkamtib, and Bakin, each one headed, as we have seen, by a Suharto loyalist. Under the "doubling up" of functions noted above, between 1978 and 1983 Sudomo occupied a key position in two of these institutions (Hankam and Kopkamtib), while Yoga Sugama served for a time in another two (Kopkamtib and Bakin). Murdani, however, spanned all three. Between 1978-83 he was assistant for intelligence (Asintel) at Hankam, assistant for intelligence at Kopkamtib

---

Machmud and Mohammad Jusuf had been regularly promoted while serving outside Hankam in ministerial capacities.

25. In February 1983 Yogie Memet replaced Lt. Gen. Wijogo Atmodarminto as commander of Kowilhan II, the unified Regional Defense Command for Java, Madura, and Nusatenggara. He later gave up the posts of commander of Kodam VI/Siliwangi and commander of the Kopassandha.

26. Confidential communication, February 28, 1981.

(Asintelkopkamtib), and deputy head (Wakil Ketua) of Bakin. He was also, as we have seen, head of the Strategic Intelligence Center (Kapusintelstrat) in Hankam, a position which, like that of Asintel, was technically under the chief of staff for operations. As such, his responsibilities transcended those of coordination and planning in the intelligence field. In his capacity as Asintelkopkamtib, Murdani was the head of Satgasintel (Satuan Tugas Intelijen, or Intelligence Task Unit); this empowered him, using the Kopkamtib decree, to detain people for 48 hours or more. In his capacity of Kapusintelstrat, Murdani would, in an emergency, have operational control of all Kopassandha forces, the 5,000-man "praetorian guard" of Hankam.[27] Beyond this, he was used by Suharto in a variety of other semi-clandestine roles, mainly in the foreign affairs field; he had planned and directed the Indonesian invasion of East Timor, had negotiated the purchase of reconditioned A-4 Skyhawk jet fighters from Israel, had made two secret visits (in 1980 and 1981) to Hanoi, held private talks in Switzerland with the government's key opponent in a sensitive corruption case, and jointly supervised (with Yoga Sugama) the storming of a hijacked Garuda jetliner in Bangkok. He had overall responsibility for developments in East Timor, on both the military and nonmilitary fronts, and overall responsibility for the resettlement abroad of all Vietnamese refugees in Indonesia. At the same time, he had become an indispensable member of the presidential entourage whenever Suharto made important overseas visits, serving, inter alia, as the unofficial head of the presidential bodyguard unit. Staunchly loyal to Suharto, holding down key positions in each of the three major power centers and with up to 5,000 highly-trained paratroops at his disposal in an emergency, Murdani had become one of the most powerful men in Suharto's Indonesia.[28]

---

27. Confidential communication, March 8, 1981, confirmed by two four-star generals. Formerly known as the RPKAD (Resimen Para Komando Angkatan Darat, Army Paracommando Regiment), the Kopassandha is divided into four *grup* (groups). There are two *parakom* (para-commando) groups, each of 1,800 men, and two Sandhi Yudha (Secret Warfare) groups, each of about 550-600 men. The two parakom groups are stationed in West Java; the other two were moved to Ujung Pandang under General Jusuf's plan to transfer some forces out of Java. Members of the Kopassandha undergo an extremely rugged 28-week training course. Administratively, Kopassandha is under the army chief of staff; operationally, it would be deployed through Hankam, the army being merely told to provide. The name Kopassandha was substituted for RPKAD on February 17, 1971. For additional details on the origins of the force, see "29 Tahun Usia Kopassandha Kita," in *Merdeka*, April 22, 1981.

28. Murdani's influence also extended into other government departments. For example, Satari, the able and extroverted director general for Asia and the Pacific at the Ministry of Foreign Affairs, was widely considered a Murdani man. There were others too on whom Murdani could call. For example, Maj. Gen. Nichlany Sudarjo,

A fifth feature was that two of the four members of this core group--Ali Murtopo and Yoga Sugama--were abangan (nominal Muslim) Javanese from Suharto's home province of Central Java while the two others--Sudomo and Murdani--were Javanese Christians; this, it will be argued, was a predisposing factor in the socalled "Islam-phobia" of the ruling group. (At the time of the 1977 general elections, Suharto received Ignatius Joseph Kasimo, Frans Seda, and several other leaders of the former Catholic Party. Before the group was seated the president is said to have declared: "Our common enemy is Islam!")[29]

Sixth, in common with a number of other senior military officers, the members of the inner core group shared a similar outlook on matters of business. They believed in being able to operate successfully outside the legal-rational economic system, in having mutually beneficial links with cukong (financiers, often Chinese) and with foreign capital. These links were maintained not so much to increase the net wealth of the officers in question (although that, in most cases, was a not unimportant consideration) but more to buttress the financial base of the individual core groups, each of which needed a more or less regular income in order to maintain its activities and its position relative to the other groups. These shared business interests were, in true patrimonial style, a major part of the cement holding the ruling elite together, even if there was room at times for as much conflict as cooperation between different economic groups.

What is also striking about this "core group" around Suharto was that its members were of a singularly "pragmatic"--some might say "Machiavellian"--cast of mind. And this, it will be argued, was

---

a CPM (military police) officer with considerable experience in intelligence matters, had become a close acquaintance of Murdani's in the mid-1970s when he (Nichlany) was serving as military attaché in Washington and Murdani was assistant for intelligence at Hankam. This connection was of some use to Murdani when Nichlany served as director general for immigration (1980-82). According to a member of the Ali Murtopo group, Nichlany, who was associated with the Sumitro-Sutopo Juwono group, had been sent to Washington by Yoga Sugama after Yoga returned as head of Bakin in 1974, a move fully supported by Murtopo. (Confidential communication, May 24, 1984.) According to another source, Nichlany was sent to Washington "just about 48 hours after he had an argument with Ali Murtopo. He stayed there six years." (Confidential communication, February 19, 1981.) Brig. Gen. Datuk R. Mulia SH, a member of the AHM (Military Law Academy) group, had become associated with Murdani while serving as deputy director for domestic intelligence in Murdani's office. This link was useful when Datuk Mulia was later installed as deputy attorney general, intelligence. In March 1983 Murdani was appointed commander of the armed forces (Pangab), this position having been separated from that of minister of defense.

29. Confidential communication, March 25, 1982.

not simply a function of the demands imposed by their particular calling. The Indonesian officer corps in general, and the intelligence
agencies in particular, are riven by a cleavage between those who
could be categorized as "pragmatic" and those who might best be described as "principled." Suharto, for whatever reasons, has always
appeared to be more comfortable with members of the former group
and more inclined to take their counsel. This cleavage existed, for
the most part, below the surface and was often subsumed by a host
of other issues. However, it tended to become apparent in times of
stress. Thus, in 1974, the pragmatic-principled dichotomy ran
parallel to, and reinforced the divisions that existed between, what
Harold Crouch has described as the "military professionals" at Hankam
and the "political" and "financial" generals associated with the
Palace.[30] In the intelligence field, this cleavage between "military
professionals/principled" officers on the one side and "political/
pragmatic" officers on the other was personified by Lt. Gen. Sutopo
Juwono, at that time head of Bakin, and Maj. Gen. Ali Murtopo, at
that time his deputy. By the late seventies, it will be argued, officers were once more placing themselves on one side of this divide or
the other. And though it was no longer entirely accurate to speak of
a Hankam-Palace cleavage, it was nonetheless true that the pragmatic
officers tended to be those clustered around Suharto. The more
"principled" group tended to be more closely associated with the army
proper, or at any rate with its nonintelligence sectors. There was in
all this an obvious correlation between "pragmatism" and "power holding" on the one hand and "principle/removed from power" on the
other. However, it would be wrong to see this as being no more
than an "in" group, "out" group phenomenon.

Those officers who might be described as "military pragmatists"
took the view that Indonesian society was still in transition and that
it was essential for the armed forces to play a major or dominant role
in everyday life. It was necessary, they believed, to channel political developments in carefully determined directions. And if for some
reason the desired object was not being achieved, this group believed, it was proper and admissible to resort to what might euphe-
mistically be described as "other methods." By nature, Suharto was
inclined to seek consensus and harmony and, to achieve this, he relied on the liberal use of the carrot and the limited use of the stick.
His preference was always to use carrots to bring people around.
The president appeared to believe that every man had his price, and
by means of the strategic distribution of patronage he had shown that
it was possible to buy off or coopt much of the opposition. The
stick--which was only brought out when the carrot had failed--ran
the gamut from intimidation, intervention, and arrest to the sometimes
spiteful and vindictive denial of "facilities."

Much of this could be described as standard political practice.
What set Suharto--or at least his chief lieutenants--apart was that

30.   For details, see Crouch, *Army and Politics*, pp. 309-17.

they appeared to have few, if any, scruples about relying on covert intelligence operations to discredit and destabilize their political opponents. The principal aim of the Suharto inner circle was the enhancement or at least the maintenance of the military's dominant position in society. And insofar as political Islam was seen by them as a dark and malevolent force in society, a force that was manipulated by those bent on the creation of an Islamic state, then it was fair game for those who not only had the necessary instruments at hand but who believed that their use was both desirable and necessary.

Such efforts were invariably taken in the name of upholding the principles of the Pancasila and the 1945 Constitution. Moreover, they were taken for the most part by men who genuinely believed that one had to use all methods at hand, and at times cut a few corners, in the interest of serving the greater good of society as a whole. The pragmatists, believing, perhaps with good reason, that the forces of stability and development might not command the unswerving support of the populace in any fair fight under the inherited political system, had seen fit to intervene extensively in the activities of various political groupings in society. This had been done to ensure that these groupings, discredited but with deep roots in Indonesian society, did not reassert themselves and thereby jeopardize what the ruling group sought to build. However, being only marginally more certain of a satisfactory result even after such steps had been taken, they reserved the right to continue their use of covert means to counter their opponents.

In short, the pragmatists took the view that the end justified the means. They believed that the intelligence services should, and indeed must, manipulate the political processes in order to achieve the desired result—a stable and prosperous Indonesia. And, having identified political Islam as the major threat to such a society, they felt justified in employing all the means at their disposal, including the resources of the state intelligence services, to divide and discredit the Muslim groupings. In doing so, they seemed to have the full support of the president.

Suharto had, over the years, been well served by his more pragmatic advisers, in particular by Ali Murtopo. In the efforts to end Confrontation with Malaysia, to ensure a favorable Act of Free Choice in West Irian, to neutralize the political parties, and so on, Murtopo had proved himself a loyal and useful assistant. However, on the domestic front at least, these "achievements" had been bought at a high cost. In the words of an Indonesian social scientist, Ali Murtopo and his advisers "have done the country a great disservice because of the very great fears they have engendered in others of Islam. Once you embark on that policy it becomes a self-fulfilling prophecy. Your fear of Islam creates a situation which makes your fears come true."[31]

---

31. Confidential communication, August 8, 1978.

In fact, it might be argued that this group had done the country a double disservice. They had not only fed and fashioned an exaggerated fear of Islam. They had, in manipulating the democratic processes so extensively and in resorting to "black operations" to discredit their opponents, greatly eroded the government's credibility and engendered a deep-seated cynicism about the sort of things the armed forces were prepared to do in order to remain in power. This, combined with a Javanese disposition to find a *dalang* (literally, puppeteer) behind every event--however improbable--had led people to see the hand of Ali Murtopo in almost everything that appeared to enhance the short-term interests of the government. As a result, trust in the government's goodwill and good faith had been seriously impaired.

The "principled" group, though not suggesting that ABRI withdraw to the mountain top, wanted to see less military involvement in society. Its members tended to be less suspicious of political Islam--although this suspicion ran deep in the armed forces--and felt there should be an essentially legal and predictable system of government, one that was less corrupt, less free wheeling, and less inclined to misuse the powers at its command, particularly those of the intelligence services.

There was also another aspect. The pragmatists, by and large, tended to be more action-oriented; they were "doers," few of whom seemed to have much interest in abstract thought. The more principled officers tended to be better educated and more reflective, more inclined to measure actions by fundamental moral considerations of what was right and wrong. The more pragmatic officers of the inner circle, intent on maintaining a state of affairs in which the military exercised an all-pervasive influence in society and in which Islam was kept well at bay, tended to be largely indifferent to arguments based on moral considerations. They were inclined, by nature and training and experience, to fall back on what their opponents saw as "Machiavellian" means to achieve their ends. And when, as happened from time to time, those methods were exposed, they tended to shrug off any suggestion of wrongdoing by saying in effect: "That's politics. What do you expect?"

Those inclined towards a more principled approach, while just as keen to see that the armed forces acted as the *dinamisator* and *stabilisator* of society, believed not only that there were necessary limits to military involvement but that there were moral constraints that should govern their actions. In the view of these critics, Suharto had extended ABRI's involvement beyond all reasonable limits and had compromised the military's integrity by allowing it to give its wholehearted backing to Golkar in two successive elections. Those associated with the "reform" movement advocated a return to the "pure" ideals of the TNI, as outlined at the second army seminar in Bandung in August 1966, a reduction in the level of corruption, and a less confrontational approach to Islamic groups.

CHAPTER TWO

THE STRUCTURE OF ARMY DOMINANCE

I know this man [Suharto] very well. He is not feeling
safe. He has got concrete power, the weapons, in his
hands and he won't permit any argument. As he said at
that time [1948] in Yogyakarta, "My politics are at the
end of the bayonet."

--Retired General[1]

Pak Harto is a plain soldier, you see. He's only protecting the Pancasila in his own way.

--General Sumitro[2]

The New Order leaders had, from the very start, committed
themselves to an adherence to Pancasila, including the principle of
popular sovereignty, and to the 1945 Constitution, with all that that
implied about a Parliament elected through a free and secret ballot.
This, it was felt, was essential if the New Order was to maintain its
legitimacy. However, as Donald Hindley has observed, neither Suharto nor those around him "envisioned the sharing of real power
with the political parties, let alone its transfer to them."[3] The parties were seen as discredited patronage machines, staffed by oppor-
tunists and serving narrow sectional interests. An even more fundamental concern, key members of the Suharto group have argued, was
that the two major surviving political parties--the traditional (and
traditionally accommodative) Nahdatul Ulama (Muslim Scholars' Party)
and the pro-Sukarnoist Partai Nasional Indonesia (PNI)--contained
powerful elements that were bent on changing the Pancasila and the
1945 Constitution.

In the late 1960s, Suharto had adopted a more conciliatory
approach to the political parties than the socalled "New Order radicals," officers like Maj. Gen. (later Lt. Gen.) H. R. Dharsono and
Maj. Gen. (later Lt. Gen.) Kemal Idris, who displayed an undisguised

---

1. Confidential communication, November 10, 1981.

2. Interview with General Sumitro, December 12, 1981.

3. Donald Hindley, "Indonesia 1971: Pantjasila Democracy and the
Second Parliamentary Elections," *Asian Survey* 12 (January 1972): 57.

contempt for the existing political groupings and who sought the immediate use of the army's power to force through rapid modernization.
Suharto feared that the radicals' desire for utmost haste, backed up
if necessary by coercion, would only exacerbate the existing divisions
and hostilities within Indonesian society,[4] an assessment which was
almost certainly correct. Nevertheless, Suharto remained wary of
political parties in general and of the PNI and the NU in particular.
Once he felt he was in a position to proceed, he took steps to ensure
that neither party would again pose what he saw as a threat to the
very foundations of the state. According to General Sumitro, Suharto
was "obsessed" that the Pancasila and the 1945 Constitution were in
danger. "Until the introduction of the Political Parties Law in 1975,"
the former Kopkamtib commander said in 1981, "he was still doubting
the stance of the political party organizations."[5]

According to close military associates, Suharto was convinced
that the NU and the PNI were not content with the Pancasila as it
was. The NU, he believed, wanted the "Pancasila plus"--meaning the
Pancasila plus the Jakarta Charter.[6] Suharto saw Muslim leaders'
continuing preoccupation with the Jakarta Charter as proof that important elements within the Islamic community were still bent on the
creation of an Islamic state, something to which the army remained
unalterably opposed.

According to members of the ruling group, Suharto believed the
PNI was likewise insisting on a "Pancasila Plus," their demand being
for the Pancasila plus the word Marhaenism (a reference to the political philosophy elaborated by the late President Sukarno) or Pancasila
plus *kerakyatan* (popular sovereignty). Sukarno had frequently made
the point, New Order leaders noted, that Marhaenism was Marxism
applied to Indonesian conditions, and this notion was, in their view,
totally unacceptable.[7] "About 80 percent of the [former] PNI mem-

---

4. Donald Hindley, "Alirans and the Fall of the Old Order," *Indonesia* 9 (April 1970): 57.

5. Sumitro interview, December 12, 1981.

6. See above, p. 7.

7. Feith has described Marhaenism as a philosophy of "proletarian
nationalism." However, the term is misleading. Sukarno, concerned
above all with the forging of national unity, rejected in the 1920s the
argument of the Indonesian Communists that the proletariat was the
most powerful force that could be marshalled against the Dutch,
partly because the proletariat was too small, but more significantly
because he feared that this would lead to class struggle rather than
national struggle. The term Marhaenism, which took its name from a
small farmer Sukarno claimed to have met near Bandung, was more
embracing. The proletariat, Sukarno argued, could be included in
the Marhaen ranks and might in fact be the most revolutionary group.
But it was not *the* force to be singled out.

bers are influenced by the Communists," the minister of religion, Lt. Gen. Alamsjah Ratu Perwiranegara, a key member of the Suharto group in the late 1960s, claimed in 1982.[8] In theory, there could be no such objections to the PNI's use of kerakyatan, a term which enjoys a place of honor in both the Pancasila and the preamble to the 1945 Constitution. But within the ruling councils of the New Order, the kerakyatan of the PNI was seen as "a different kerakyatan," one built on the dangerous sands of mass action and allowing for the unbridled expression of the popular will. "Their kerakyatan," Alamsjah argued, "is the kerakyatan according to the doctrine of socialism. And that is still a danger."[9]

In the 1960s, this political theory became complex and confused, and Sukarno himself did define Marhaenism as Marxism applied to specific Indonesian conditions. On the origins of the Marhaenist doctrine, see Bernhard Dahm, *Sukarno and the Struggle for Indonesian Independence* (Ithaca: Cornell University Press, 1969), pp. 143-55. I am indebted to Ruslan Abdulgani for his comments on the evolution of Marhaenism.

8. Interview with Lt. Gen. Alamsjah Ratu Perwiranegara, March 24, 1982. Crouch has argued (personal communication) that Alamsjah's view of the PNI does not necessarily represent that of the Javanese generals, many of whom are related to PNI figures by blood or by marriage. Although Alamsjah is non-Javanese, I would suggest that the Javanese officers around Suharto take essentially the same view, even when they have family links to the PNI. Sumitro was a case in point.

9. Alamsjah interview, March 24, 1982. Many of these suspicions remain, particularly those having to do with the role and ambitions of political Islam. In his National Day address in 1981 Suharto said that "we do not need to cover up the fact that . . . threats to Pancasila indeed do exist both from extreme left and extreme right views. And up to this very day we cannot yet say that these threats to Pancasila do not exist any longer." Only when Pancasila was truly "acculturized" and reflected in the practices of daily life would its pursuance be guaranteed.

> Meanwhile, I need to remind us all that we may not be lax and feel self-satisfied. There are still dangers for Pancasila and they can come from both without and from within. The dangers from without stem from other ideologies or other ideas that do indeed want to be enforced on our nation. Dangers can come from within if we ourselves do not, in the fullest sincerity, practice Pancasila in our personal lives and in our common life.

See Address of State by President Suharto to the DPR, August 15, 1981. State Secretariat, 1981, p. 5.

There is not much in this explanation which is persuasive. The fear of the power of political Islam certainly ran deep in the thinking of the New Order generals, a point of central importance in any understanding of contemporary Indonesian politics. But it is doubtful that the New Order leaders were all that concerned by the PNI and Marhaenism, or for that matter by the majority of the NU. Their concerns centered on some NU and ex-Masyumi radicals. What seems likely is that the allegations that the PNI wanted "Pancasila Plus" were intended to make more "even-handed" the attack on Islam's "Pancasila Plus," which was the real target.

It is almost certainly true, as a number of observers have suggested, that these concerns were manipulated by Suharto's principal lieutenants, most notably Ali Murtopo, for short-term political purposes. It is also almost certainly true that the activities of men like Murtopo were undertaken with at least the tacit approval of Suharto himself. However, it would be wrong to interpret the talk of "threats to the Pancasila" as nothing more than the manipulation of an integrative symbol by men bent on maintaining and furthering army rule. The concern was genuine enough, even if the manipulation carried out in the name of protecting the Pancasila often tended to obscure that fact.[10]

Suharto's answer to this dilemma--which involved a drastic restructuring of the political landscape--centered on the transformation of a loose coalition of army-backed "functional groups" into a full-

---

10. In some ways, Suharto was himself open to the charge of seeking to change the Pancasila. For Sukarno, the Pancasila was not only based on the unity of the Indonesian nation but strongly anticolonial in nature. If Communists and Muslims were prepared to accept the basic tenets of the Pancasila and were anticolonial in outlook then Sukarno was content to let them pursue their various goals in the political arena. Only when he saw their actions as a threat not only to himself but to the state as well did Sukarno ban the Muslim Masyumi political organization. Significantly, the other Muslim groupings were left untouched. For Suharto, the "threat" often appears to be Islam as a whole. Though nominally Muslim, Suharto is deeply influenced by kebatinan and he has sought to give the Pancasila an infusion of ethical values stemming from Java's pre-Islamic past. In this sense, Suharto is seeking, consciously or unconsciously, to "Javanize" the Pancasila. The essence of the Pancasila, he believes, is to be found in traditional Javanese precepts. This being so, there is no need in his view for Islam to come with "new" ethical values. For my understanding of the way in which the president views the Pancasila, I am indebted to Ruslan Abdulgani, General Sumitro, Lt. Gen. Sutopo Juwono, and Lt. Gen. Alamsjah. The material in this section is drawn in large part from the following interviews: Ruslan Abdulgani (March 24 and March 26, 1982), General Sumitro (December 12, 1981), Lt. Gen. Sutopo Juwono (March 22, 1982), and Lt. Gen. Alamsjah (March 20 and March 24, 1982).

blown government political "party," and the systematic undermining of existing political institutions. In the late 1960s, Suharto's military associates began transforming Sekber Golkar, the Joint Secretariat of the Functional Groups, into a fully-fledged political grouping. Through manipulation, intervention, and obstruction, those same aides were able to circumscribe the power of all major political parties save the NU, the leaders of which had shown themselves to be as amenable to the wishes of the new ruling group as they had to those of the old.

Even so, the parties still had deep roots in Indonesian society and the ruling military officers could not be at all sure that Sekber Golkar would command a majority of votes in the forthcoming 1971 general elections. Sumitro, who was at that time a key member of the ruling group, believes that Golkar (as the group later became known) would not have had a chance on its own: "If you had left it to Golkar in 1971, without any interference by ABRI, the Muslim parties would have won. I can assure you of that! Oh yes! Seventy One! Seventy Seven! Without the help of ABRI, PPP [Muslim Party] would have won. And won a majority!"[11]

In order to achieve the necessary victory for the functional group, Suharto's aides resorted to widespread intimidation and coercion, as a result of which Golkar achieved a decisive electoral victory, carrying off 62 percent of the votes.

Suharto thus sought to maintain the outward trappings of democratic rule while at the same time ensuring that an expression of the popular will did not "jeopardize" either the Pancasila, the 1945 Constitution, or, more particularly, the stability of military rule. This, the ruling group was convinced, was the only realistic way to proceed. The result was that the government went through the motions of upholding the letter of the Constitution while steadfastly ignoring its underlying principles and intent. The president went to great lengths to present himself as a strict constitutionalist and provided all the formal trappings of popular sovereignty, as specified in the Constitution. There was a People's Consultative and a People's Representative Council (Dewan Perwakilan Rakyat, DPR). There were periodic elections and secret ballots. The president was "elected" by the MPR, and his ministers and senior officials made routine appearances before DPR committees to report back to the people's representatives and answer questions about government policy. All of this meant little. The legislative branch lived very much in the shadow of the executive; in the MPR of 1978-83, 86 percent of the 920 representatives owed their positions in one way or another to their selection by bodies that were largely under the influence of the president or his chief lieutenants.[12] What is more, Suharto never reported back

---

11. Interview with General Sumitro, December 12, 1981.

12. When Suharto was seeking a third five-year term in 1978, there were times when the MPR resembled a chamber of mirrors in which a

to the particular MPR which "elected" him; he reported instead to the new one--and *after* reelection. It is also worth noting that no legislative body under the New Order had ever passed a law "of its own."

"The governing elite," writes Allan Sampson, "perceived the appropriate role of political participation to be that of passive approval or legitimation through controlled symbolic acts."[13] The election amounted to no more than the "organized ratification" of the rule of a military regime.[14] However, as Benedict Anderson has pointed out, "the government's very success in using the polls to serve its purposes created the first serious divisions in the 1965 coalition, as well as foreclosing the possibility that parliamentary institutions" would broaden the coalition base by incorporating new elements into it. "For by 1971, Suharto's policies were beginning to create grievances as well as satisfaction, but the engineering of the elections--which were intended to demonstrate support for the Suharto regime--was such that grievances would find neither expression nor resolution in the bodies they created.[15]

The former defense minister, General A. H. Nasution, who watched these developments from the parliamentary sidelines, has provided an illustration of the sort of thinking that went into the making of the Golkar victory in 1971.

> During the first election, I was still chairman of the MPRS [Provisional MPR] and participated in some talks. At that time, they calculated that if Golkar had 35 per-

---

man comes face to face with his own image everywhere he turns. No sooner had Suharto delivered an 18,000 word report to the Congress than Maj. Gen. Amir Murtono, chairman of the Golkar grouping and a man who had been Suharto's aide in Yogyakarta in 1948, rose to support all that Suharto had said, endorse the Suharto-inspired GBHN (Broad Outlines of State Policy), and nominate the president, his former commanding officer, for another five-year term. Murtono was followed by General Surono, deputy commander of the armed forces and spokesman for the powerful military faction in the MPR. He too accepted the account given by Suharto and called on the Congress to vote the president back for another term. After that came Maj. Gen. Sunandar Prijosudarmo, the Suharto-appointed governor of East Java and spokesman for the regional representatives' faction. His remarks were similar to those of his colleagues. Together, these three generals spoke for 86.1 percent of the 920-man MPR. The only discordant notes came from the two political parties, particularly the PPP.

13. Allan Samson, "Indonesia 1972: The Solidification of Military Control," *Asian Survey* 13 (February 1973): 127.

14. Benedict Anderson, "Last Days of Indonesia's Suharto?" *Southeast Asia Chronicle* 63 (July-August 1978): 7.

15. Ibid.

cent of the vote it's enough. It is enough to have a majority in Parliament and the MPR, because with the wide
powers of appointment they would have everything well in
hand.   But then some generals within the ruling elite
were thinking more about this. You had to give the impression you were a majority. So then it became more
than 35 percent. And after, more than 50 percent.
Then came the problem that you can change the Constitution if you have a two-thirds majority. It's not necessary
because of the appointments. But then people said in
unofficial talks that they needed two-thirds of the membership. And the Minister of Home Affairs was in charge
of this and he said to the people "80 percent." You
know it is A.B.S. [Asal Bapak Senang--"As long as the
boss is happy"]. So if you go lower, the villages have
maybe 95 percent in some areas. And that is the whole
problem. From 35 percent to more than 50 percent, to
two-thirds and then by the people working on the project
it is becoming more than 90 percent.[16]

Golkar, which had entered 1971 as a largely paper entity, was not
without its attractions to many Indonesians and had come by many of
its votes honestly. Golkar, says Hindley,

> represented those people who had destroyed the PKI [In-
> donesian Communist Party], unseated Sukarno, and
> brought about an unprecedented degree of political sta-
> bility and economic improvement. In addition, the gov-
> ernment was reasonably humane to all but Communists,
> reasonably tolerant of and responsive to constructive crit-
> icism, at least verbally concerned with the plight of Indo-
> nesia's impoverished millions, and dedicated to "25 years
> of accelerated modernization and development" while safe-
> guarding Indonesian-ness. And the government seemed
> irremovable.

> Under these circumstances, it appears that tradition-
> alism brought Golkar millions of votes; traditionalism in
> the sense of obeying the non-costly wishes of "the au-
> thorities," in opting for what one knows, if it is not too
> bad, rather than risk the unknown.[17]

It was also true, as Hindley noted with delicate irony, that the
government had not merely waited for its record and its promise to
attract votes; steamroller tactics had been employed to ensure that

---

16. Interview with General Nasution, July 14, 1981.

17. Hindley, "Indonesia 1971," p. 59. The first part of this statement is not entirely accurate. Golkar represented *some* of those
people who had destroyed the PKI etc.

nothing was left to chance. On the other hand, there had in 1971 been some reason for believing, as a number of Indonesian intellectuals had in fact believed, that Golkar might develop into something worthwhile, might become a force in its own right, not just an instrument in the hands of the army, a body with no more life of its own than the various *badan kerjasama* (cooperation boards) that Nasution set up in 1958-60.

By the mid-1970s, these initial hopes for Golkar had begun to dissipate. The distinguished independents who had lent their names to the organization had started to drift away. Golkar, having won the election for the army leaders, had been put back on the shelf, a lifeless instrument with no real role in the parliamentary process. Now, as the 1977 poll drew closer, it looked very much as though the government intended to bring Golkar out for another "organized ratification" of military rule.

In theory, Suharto did not have much to worry about as the nation approached the 1977 general election; the machinery that would ensure his continuing dominance of the legislative branch was in place, well oiled and incapable of failing to achieve the desired results. In 1973, the ruling group had forced nine existing political parties to fuse into two new groupings. The four Muslim parties which had contested the 1971 election were merged into the Partai Persatuan Pembangunan (United Development Party or PPP), while the five remaining Christian and nationalist groupings had been forced under the umbrella of a new, and seriously divided, Partai Demokrasi Indonesia (Indonesian Democratic Party or PDI). Riven by internal dissension and with no clear identity of their own, the new groupings were not expected to pose any significant threat to Golkar.

Through a system of appointments, made in accordance with powers acquired from Sukarno on March 11, 1966, and through the Kopkamtib decree, the president and his chief lieutenants, were able virtually to hand-pick 61 percent of the 920 members who sat in the MPR, the body that would put its stamp on the GBHN (Broad Outlines of State Policy) and elect a new president.[18] The "election" was to fill 360 of the 460 seats in the DPR (the other 100 were also appointed), meaning that only 39 percent of the full MPR was chosen by direct vote.

At the same time, the executive branch had the power to "screen" candidates for the MPR--weeding out those it deemed unsuit-

---

18. Of the 100 members of the DPR appointed by the president 75 represented the armed forces, whose members were not allowed to campaign or vote; the other 25 represented Golkar. (The other 360 members were elected.) The remaining 460 seats in the full Congress were occupied by 135 regional delegates, 118 Golkar and political party delegates, and 207 additional government members--155 from the armed forces and 52 from Golkar. This gave the armed forces 230 (exactly one quarter) of the 920 Congress seats, not counting the military men who sat as regional delegates.

able. This task was in the hands of two bodies, one headed by a four-star general who was a member of the president's inner circle, the other headed by Suharto himself. The first of these two bodies was Bakin, a nominally civilian institution which was headed by General Yoga Sugama, a trusted Suharto associate from the Diponegoro military region. Yoga's deputy was Ali Murtopo, another long-time associate of the president and the man who had formerly been the presidential assistant for political affairs. It was Ali Murtopo who was widely credited with the intervention that had emasculated the political parties in the late 1960s.

The other body involved, at the operational level, was Kopkamtib, headed by the president himself, and with Admiral Sudomo, another member of Suharto's inner circle as its chief of staff.[19] Not surprisingly, the screening affected the two political parties more than Golkar. At the national level, Golkar lost only 5 percent of its nominees, while the PPP lost 16 percent and the PDI 19 percent.[20]

There were other constraints as well. In 1975 the government had submitted to the DPR bills on political party organization and election procedures. "The chief intent of both bills," says Liddle:

> was to further restrict the parties' ability to compete with Golkar. The parties' bill attempted to prevent civil servants from joining a party (but not Golkar), to limit the parties' choice of ideological foundation to Panca Sila and the 1945 Constitution (thereby making both parties indistinguishable from Golkar, a special handicap to the Islamic PPP), and to prohibit party organization below the level of district (an area of roughly half-a-million people in populous parts of Java and Sumatra, further divided administratively into subdistricts and villages). The general election bill was designed to maintain the leverage of the 1971 election, when the government was able to exercise broad discretionary powers concerning campaign rallies, the placing of polling booths in government offices, the political activities of military officers, the screening of candidates and so on.[21]

The government was later to compromise on the three controversial provisions in the parties bill but no change was made in the election bill. "In effect," says Liddle, "the parties at the end of

---

19. Kopkamtib also had the power to screen candidates standing for the provincial and district legislatures. Suharto resumed command of Kopkamtib in May 1974 following the fall of General Sumitro. He held the post until April 1978, when it was transferred to Admiral Sudomo.

20. Liddle, "1977 Indonesian Election and New Order Legitimacy," p. 127.

21. Ibid., p. 126-27.

1975 seemed to be about where they had been at the beginning of the 1971 campaign."[22]

Other constraints included a provision, similar to the one in 1971, that former members of the Communist party and its mass organizations were not permitted to take part in the elections and a set of four campaign "don'ts" which severely curtailed the parties' freedom to operate. These "don'ts," which were elaborated by Admiral Sudomo on the eve of campaigning, were broadly similar to those which governed the 1971 poll. At that time, candidates were

> prohibited to reason about or discuss Pantja Sila Prin-
> ciples and the 1945 Constitution, to slander, show con-
> tempt or disrespect of the government or government offi-
> cials, individuals, groups, organizations, or a foreign
> country, or to commit any other acts/activities contrary
> to the ethics/moral code of Pantja Sila Principles.[23]

Sudomo's four "don'ts" were: don't intimidate your opponents; don't offend the dignity of the government and its officials; don't disrupt national unity; and don't criticize the policies of the government.[24] These rules effectively prevented any discussion of substantive issues and provided the government with a sweeping set of headings under which it could take action against those who threatened the outcome of a "successful" election.

Finally, and most importantly, the government was able to count on the loyalty of its own administrative structure--and in particular on the Departments of Defense and Home Affairs--to ensure that the election was a success. This gave it an infinite advantage over its political opponents. Ostensibly, these two departments were "the neutral organizers and safeguarders of an open electoral process."[25] In practice, their resources were used in the most partisan fashion. The ministers of defense and home affairs, who, like Yoga Sugama and Ali Murtopo, were members of Suharto's inner circle--and who were, as well, members of the Dewan Pembina (Control Board) of Golkar--presided over parallel vertical structures which, reaching down into almost every village, had an all-pervasive influence on Indonesian political life. The government was playing with heavily loaded dice.

The most important of these instruments of control and influ-ence was the army's "territorial" structure, through which the ruling group could exert political pressure at every level of society. This was to prove crucial in 1977, just as it had in 1971. The TNI, unlike

---

22. Ibid., p. 127.

23. Quoted in Hindley, "Indonesia 1973," p. 58.

24. Quoted in Liddle, "1977 Indonesian Election," p. 128.

25. Anderson, "Last Days," p. 8.

a conventional Western army, is deeply involved in *sospol* (social-political) affairs. The *panglima* (commander) of each regional military command (Kodam) presides over not merely a regular operational force but a "territorial" organization which is considered of at least equal importance. This territorial structure, which is seen in its most developed form on Java, corresponds broadly with the various tiers of the civilian administration of the Department of Home Affairs and forms a parallel "shadow government" which is intimately involved in nonmilitary functions. Territorial officers are supposed to monitor political and social developments and "prod" their civilian counterparts where necessary. But their influence goes far beyond this. Because it is necessary to secure military permission to travel, to organize meetings, to deliver sermons, or to issue any publication, the territorial structure has come to dominate local politics.[26]

Immediately under the Kodam commanders, who report directly to the Department of Defense and Security on territorial matters, are a number of Military Resort Commands (Korem). These generally correspond to the old position of Residency in the civilian administrative structures. One tier further down and corresponding generally with the Kabupaten (Regency) is the Kodim (Military District Command). At another level below this and roughly equivalent to the Kecamatan (subdistrict) is the Koramil (Military Rayon Command). Below the Koramil is the Babinsa (Bintara Pembina Desa), an NCO, who, together with two or three men, represents the army at the *desa* (village) level.

In the normal course of events, the tour of duty of an up-and-coming officer will be arranged so that he "zig-zags" up through the system, moving between operational and territorial responsibilities. And in an army which places so much emphasis on the territorial apparatus, there has been a natural tendency to see territorial assignments as "more senior" and more desirable than troop commands. Troop units are involved in training and little else; the territorial system is what makes the country run. Thus it is that the best battalion commanders tend to be appointed as Kodim commanders. Like-

---

26. Hamish McDonald, *Suharto's Indonesia* (Melbourne: Fontana/Collins, 1980), p. 94. In accordance with its "Territorial Warfare" doctrine, which grew out of its guerrilla experience during the revolution, the army seeks to "integrate itself with the people." See Crouch, *Army and Politics*, p. 222.

The size of the regular force unit varies from one Kodam to another. Each of the three large Java commands (Siliwangi, Diponegoro, and Brawijaya) have three brigades at their disposal, each of about 2,500 men. The smallest Kodam (Kodam XV/Pattimura in Maluku) has only one battalion, or about 600-700 men. This operational force can venture anywhere in the province; it can also be used outside the Kodam at the discretion of the commander of the armed forces. As and where necessary, the territorial force would assist the operational force with intelligence and support.

wise, the best brigade commanders tend to become Korem commanders. (A Kodim commander, having performed his tasks satisfactorily, may be rewarded with an appointment as chief of staff of a brigade. A Korem commander who succeeds in his appointment may be assigned, if he is a graduate of both Akabri [Military Academy] and Seskoad, as chief of staff to a Kodam outside Java. Alternatively, he may be assigned to staff officer duties, serving in either a Kowilhan [Regional Defense Command] or as a head of section [kepala bagian] to one of the six assistants to the army chief of staff.) Assignments given to officers who have completed the course at Seskoad reflect the preeminent position of the territorial apparatus. While the top ten or twelve graduates may be selected by the intelligence service to serve as military attachés, those immediately below them are generally given Korem commands. "The challenge for the individuals at Seskoad was to get enough brownie points to get a territorial assignment," one foreign student observed.[27] "There is a tendency to select the best for territorial. The reaction of people when they heard they had been posted to a territorial slot was great pleasure." (As part of their course work, mid-career officers at Seskoad study the mounting of a territorial intelligence exercise during the run-up to a general election. They decide the groups to target and what sort of psychological or intelligence operations should be launched against them. This is known as Opsgalangan, or "Guidance Operations."[28]

---

27. Confidential communication, November 9, 1981. At the time of the Semarang congress of the PNI in April 1970, Kodim commanders in East Java summoned PNI branch delegates before their departure and demanded assurances that they would vote for Hadisubeno, Ali Murtopo's preferred candidate for party general chairman. See Ken Ward, *The 1971 Election in Indonesia: an East Java Case Study* (Melbourne: Monash University Centre of Southeast Asian Studies, 1974), p. 145.

Another attraction of a territorial assignment is that officers in this stream have control over quite substantial sums of money. Korem, Kodim, and Koramil commanders are charged with the task of raising funds from the community. Ostensibly, money is raised to cover such things as "security operations" to secure the elections or to celebrate some important event, be it Youth Day, Independence Day, or the anniversary of the local Kodam. In practice, there is virtually no accounting for the sums raised or the purposes for which they are spent; large amounts are known to have been used "improperly." These forced levies, in which a small businessman might be put down for a "contribution" of Rp 50,000 (the equivalent, perhaps, of a month's income) are highly unpopular and contribute significantly to ABRI's bad name in society.

28. A contraction of the words *Operasi Galangan*. There is an obvious "contradiction" between this aspect of the Seskoad course work and the emphasis that is placed in other courses on ABRI's role as an upholder of the 1945 Constitution.

Invariably in these exercises, the political parties are listed as targets, with special attention being paid to which members of these groups are of particular interest. The "targets" also include informal leaders in the community--a man who stands up and commands attention at the local mosque, a student leader, and so on.)

Under this system, there is an equation, even at the village level, between the army territorial structure and the civilian administration. And the interaction between military officers in the territorial organization and the officials in the Home Affairs hierarchy is very close. This is particularly so when the governor, *bupati* (regent), *camat* (subdistrict officer), or *lurah* (village head) is an ABRI man serving in a kekaryaan (nonmilitary) capacity. Thus a military man serving as a provincial governor will keep in close touch with the local military commander (Panglima Kodam, or Pangdam). A bupati will coordinate his programs with the local Kodim commander (Kommandan Kodim, or Dandim). In some cases, the distinction between the two hierarchies becomes completely blurred, as is the case where a Kodim commander is moved across, prior to his retirement, to become bupati in the area where he has already been serving, or a sergeant who has served as Babinsa is moved across to become lurah in the same village.

This structure gives the army leaders great capacity to influence the outcome of a general election; with army men resident in almost every village, most village heads find it prudent to follow their suggestions. And that, in most cases, is all that is needed; if the village head comes out for Golkar, he can often deliver the whole village to the ruling group. The "suggestions" of the local military officials are, of course, backed up by the "suggestions" and inducements of the civilian officials. Thus, a village head who proves malleable can be reasonably certain that development funds will continue to be allotted to his area. One who proves obstinate might find that such funds rapidly dry up.

While the territorial structure allowed the regional military commander to monitor political and social developments in his bailiwick, his four other hats tended to reinforce a bias in favor of the ruling "functional group," at the same time providing him with extensive ancillary powers to deal with those who might upset the outcome of the poll. Prior to 1978, the military commander was nearly always chairman of Golkar's Dewan Pembina Daerah (Regional Control Board), and also chairman of the Dewan Kekaryaan Daerah (Regional Functional Affairs Board). In this latter capacity, he was able to select those officers and NCOs who would serve as bupati, camat, and lurah in his domain--officials who played a crucial part in Golkar strategy and were themselves part of the Golkar "team." (Although in theory the Department of Home Affairs had the final say on these appointments, recommendations "from below" were almost always approved.) In his further capacity as chairman of the Muspida (Provincial Leadership Council), the military commander had all manner of back-up powers, and could, if necessary, issue instructions to the governor, the

Table II. *Parallel Regional Bureaucracies and Their Interaction*

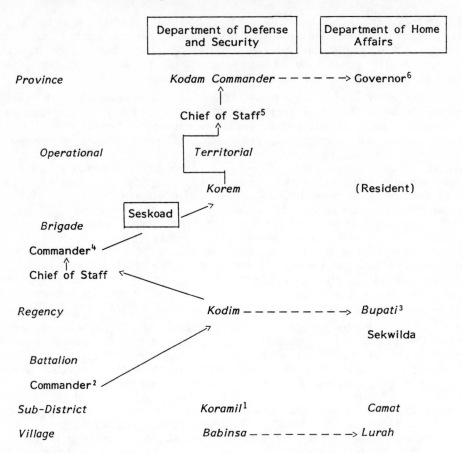

1.   Recent Akabri (Military Academy) graduates may be appointed, under plans now being discussed, as Koramil commanders.

2.   The best battalion commanders generally become Kodim commanders.

3.   Older Kodim commanders may be appointed bupati prior to retirement.

4.   The best brigade commanders generally become Korem commanders.

5.   An outstanding Korem commander may be appointed chief of staff to a Kodam outside Java, or become staff officer in Army Headquarters if he is a graduate of both Akabri and Seskoad. In some cases, the chief of staff of a Kodam may be given command of his "own" or some other Kodam.

6.   Nineteen of Indonesia's twenty-seven governors are military men.

NOTE: The above table is diagrammatic in the sense that an officer would not spend his entire career in one area but would have tours of duty in various Kodams.

police chief, and the public prosecutor. In most cases this was un-necessary, for these officials were themselves members of the armed forces or the civil service (and thus Golkar) and so answerable to superiors who were Suharto loyalists. Finally and most importantly, in his capacity as Laksusda (Special Executor) of Kopkamtib, the Kodam commander had the power to arrest or detain anyone who might threaten the "success" of the general election.

The Department of Home Affairs--the other great bastion of Suharto's rule--was of equal importance in any Golkar victory. Pre-sided over by the blunt-speaking Amir Machmud and with an influence which extended down to virtually the village level, it was dominated by military men serving in kekaryaan roles. The minister was a gen-eral and so too were all but one of his seven principal assistants--the secretary general, the inspector general, and four of the five direc-tors general. This gave the military 89 percent of the top slots in Home Affairs (up from 29 percent in 1966 and 71 percent in 1971), well above the percentage in any other department outside Hankam and an indication of the importance with which the ministry's work was viewed.[29] In 1977, twenty-one of the twenty-seven--that is, 78 percent--of provincial governors were army men.[30] In Java, four of the five provinces or special territories had military governors, the one exception being the Special Territory of Yogyakarta. According to Nasution, there were three kinds of governors--"Suharto gov-ernors, Amir Machmud governors, and Hankam governors." The most important were the governors appointed at the behest of the presi-dent. "The Java governors," Nasution said, "are all Suharto gov-ernors."[31] In May 1977, the month of the general election, more than half (155) of Indonesia's 294 bupati and mayors were ABRI men.[32] In

---

29. For a detailed study of military penetration of the upper levels of Indonesia's central government bureaucracy, see John A. MacDougall, "Patterns of Military Control in the Indonesian Higher Central Bureaucracy," *Indonesia* 33 (April 1982): 89-121.

30. In January 1978, following a reshuffle which involved the ap-pointment of eight new governors, there were nineteen ABRI and eight civilian governors. The two provinces that went from military to civilian governorships were Southeast Sulawesi and Bali.

31. Interview with General Nasution, March 2, 1981.

32. See *"Jumlah Anggota ABRI Yang Ditempatkan diluar Bidang Hankam/ABRI"* in *"Pejuang dan Prajurit: Konsepsi dan Implementasi Dwi Fungsi ABRI,"* ed. Nugroho Notosusanto (Jakarta: Sinar Harapan, n.d.) [the so-called "Hankam paper"], pp. 378-79. This figure had fluctuated over the years. By 1969 the number of military bupati and mayors had risen to 147 out of 271 throughout Indonesia, or 54 percent. After the 1971 elections the proportion reached about two-thirds. (See Crouch, *Army and Politics*, p. 244.) In November 1983, approximately 45 percent of the nation's bupati were karyawan ABRI. (Minister of home affairs, Gen. Supardjo Rustam, private communication, November 16, 1983.)

many cases, the Sekwilda (Regency Secretary) was also an ABRI man, particularly if the bupati was a civilian. In Java, according to an estimate by a former panglima, half of the lurah were or had been military men.[33]

During the 1977 election campaign, the Golkar chairman, Maj. Gen. Amir Murtono, was to make great play of the fact that all of the governors, bupati, and camat were on the Golkar team, to the general amusement of those attending his rallies and the mild embarrassment of those whose ostensible neutrality was so damagingly compromised.[34] And if there was some doubt about the commitment of the lurah to Golkar in 1977, they were to come under increasing pressure after the passage of the government's Draft Bill on Village Administration in October 1979. Under that legislation, the bupati was given authority to appoint the village secretary after consultations with the village head and the camat. The camat, in turn, was given the authority to appoint the heads of various branches of the village government (including, for example, the officials in charge of the maintenance of village roads, irrigation, and other communal projects) after consultation with the village head. The addition of this new level of officialdom, it was estimated, would create an additional 500,000 village officials. Although the ostensible aim was greater efficiency, many saw the law as an attempt to bring Indonesia's 62,875 villages more directly under the sway of the Department of Home Affairs, and feared that the government would use this leverage for partisan political purposes in future elections.[35]

In October 1979, 65 of the 132 bupati and mayors in the Kowilhan II region (Java, Madura, and Nusa Tenggara) were ABRI men. See statement of Brig. Gen. Purwosasmito, chief of staff of nonmilitary affairs of Kowilhan II, in *Sinar Harapan*, October 17, 1979.

33. This estimate was given by Lt. Gen. Dharsono in an interview on November 12, 1981.

34. To reinforce his message that Golkar was the party of power and patronage, Amir Murtono, at numerous rallies during the 1977 campaign, listed the names of prominent leaders connected with the functional group. "*Bapak* Presiden Suharto" was the "Pembina Utama" (Chief Controler) of Golkar, he stressed. "Sri Sultan" (Vice President Sultan Hamengku Buwono IX) was also Golkar. "Mendagri [Interior Minister]?," he would ask rhetorically, and then answer: "Golkar!" And so it went on. "Menteri Pasar [a slang expression for Trade Minister]?" "Golkar!" "(Menteri Widjojo [the Minister of State for the Economy]?" "Golkar!" In Bali, this not-so-subtle reminder that Golkar and the government were virtually one and the same was taken a step further. Murtono, standing before a crowd of perhaps 80,000 people, asked who the camat were for. Predictably enough, the crowd roared back: "Golkar!" The *pedanda* [high priests]?" "Golkar!" the crowd answered, greatly enjoying the joke.

35. Confidential communication, 1979.

In practice, it would have been unrealistic to expect the Departments of Defense and Home Affairs to remain above the political fray. Not only were the departmental heads--not to mention all civil servants--personally committed to a Golkar victory, the functional group had in fact been constructed largely from these two bureaucracies. At the central level, Golkar was dominated by Suharto and his close military associates. In 1977, the president was the Chief Controller (Pembina Utama) of Golkar, with the power to select the other members of the Control Board (Dewan Pembina), the decision-making body of the organization. The minister of defense, General Maraden Panggabean, was the chairman of the Dewan Pembina and the minister of home affairs, General Amir Machmud, was shown in functional group documents at the head of the list of ordinary members. Other members included Lt. Gen. Darjatmo, the chief of staff for functional affairs, Lt. Gen. Ali Murtopo, Lt. Gen. Sudharmono and Maj. Gen. Amir Murtono. The secretary general of the DPP was Brig. Gen. Sapardjo. The seventeen-man Central Executive Board (Dewan Pimpinan Pusat) was likewise dominated by members of the ruling group. The general chairman, Maj. Gen. Amir Murtono, had served as Suharto's aide in Yogyakarta in 1948 and was known to carry out all instructions to the letter. Four of the eleven secretaries (Jusuf Wanandi, Cosmas Batubara, Pitut Suharto, and David Napitupulu) were members of the Ali Murtopo group. The second deputy chairman (and one of the most active members of the DPP), Maj. Gen. A. E. Manihuruk, was head of the State Personnel Administration Board (Badan Administrasi Kepegawaian Negara, BAKN), a government position which gave him control over all civil service promotions and pensions. (This office came directly under Lt. Gen. Sudharmono and the State Secretariat.)

Military dominance of Golkar was equally apparent at the provincial level. There were in the mid-1970s twenty-six Regional Control Boards (Dewan Pembina Daerah--Tingkat 1, or Wanbintu), responsible for policy making at the province level. As we have seen, the panglima were, almost without exception, the chairmen of the Wanbintu. Moreover, most of the members were themselves military men. (The members of the Muspida, which, as we have seen, was itself dominated by military officers, were members of the Wanbintu, along with other tokoh-tokoh daerah [prominent local figures], including perhaps a rector and one or two civilian intellectuals.) Golkar also had twenty-six Regional Executive Boards (Dewan Pengurus Daerah, or Wanbinda) and these bodies, which were responsible for the execution of policy, were also dominated at this time by active military officers. The chairman of the executive board was, in every case, an active officer appointed by the chief of staff for functional affairs (Kaskar). In theory, the chairman was answerable to the Kaskar and the Golkar Central Executive Board (DPP) in Jakarta. In practice, he was answerable to the local military commander (in the latter's capacity as chairman of the regional supervisory board of Golkar), via the assistant VI (Territorial Affairs) of the Kodam. This left the provincial Golkar policy-making and policy-executing boards very much under the sway of the military and administrative hierarchies. Shortly before the 1977 elections, it is true, the government announced that active officers would not be permitted to take part in any election activities. This, however, was no setback for Golkar. Most of the key officers in the functional group were at, or close to, retirement age and were able to retire and continue their activities on behalf of Golkar with barely any interruption to their schedules. Mingling with members of the local Golkar organs during the 1977 election campaign, one might just as well have been attending a meeting of the Muspida or the governor's council, so strong was the sense that Golkar in the provinces was staffed by, and was an extension of, the ruling military and civilian elite. Golkar gave every sign of being the party of the government, with few, if any, roots in society.

What this all meant was that a situation had been created in which the president's key assistants--all of whom were high-ranking military officers--enjoyed extraordinary power to influence the outcome of any election. These powers were not separate and diffuse but overlapping and mutually reinforcing. Moreover, because no clear-cut distinction was ever made between the actions taken by senior officials in their separate ministerial and functional group capacities--there was, in fact, some valiant obscurantism on this point--an election result could provide no more than a very qualified indication of the degree of support for the ruling group.

Given this capacity to influence the outcome of a general election, it might be supposed that the government could have afforded, in the period before the 1977 poll, to rest easy. This was not the case. The Suharto group, when it had "simplified" the party system in 1973, had assumed that the four Muslim parties, so different in their outlook and objectives, so disputatious and faction-ridden, would dissipate their energies in internal squabbling and thus neutralize one another. As Anderson has observed:

> The government's political strategists, most notably General Ali Murtopo, had calculated that the forced fusion of parties traditionally in rivalry with one another and with well-established popular identities would fatally weaken them, both internally and externally. It was expected that the rivalries would continue and even intensify as the different parties' leaderships struggled for pre-eminence in the new entities, thereby paralyzing their electoral energies and sapping their morale and organizational coherence. . . . In fact, the government's strategy worked perfectly in the case of the Indonesian Democracy Party. Without a coherent image or program and rent by internal incompatibilities it achieved no more than 8.6 percent of the vote. In the case of the PPP, however, the strategy was an almost complete failure.[36]

---

36. Anderson, "Last Days," pp. 13-14.

That may overstate the case somewhat. The leaders of the various factions in the PPP had not, by the mid-1970s, been able to compose their more functional differences. Nevertheless, they had recognized--and made the most of--the obvious electoral benefits to be reaped by campaigning under the one Islamic banner.

As the nation approached the run-up to the 1977 general election, the government was in the invidious position of having to keep the PDI from being run off the road. More serious still, it had to come to terms with the fact that the Islamic political grouping had emerged as the main opposition group in society, largely as a result of the government's tactical blunder in fusing the various Islamic groups into one stream. This was to make electioneering particularly difficult. The government, having brought these disparate groups under one Islamic umbrella, had to counter a political party which had Islam as its base without being seen to attack Islam itself. And the Muslims, though rent by internal rivalries, had it within their power to put up a very tough fight. The PPP had forced the government to back down over the controversial Marriage Bill in 1973 and was to confirm many of the ruling group's worst fears when, in early 1978, it walked out of the MPR over one issue and forced a vote, the first in that body in almost twenty years, over four other controversial issues.

By the mid-1970s there were indications that the government, for all its power to command the support of the largely appointive MPR, might face a serious upset at the polls, with the Islamic party cutting deeply into the Golkar vote. An increase in the Muslim vote at the expense of Golkar would in no way have threatened Suharto's hold over the Parliament nor affected his reelection for a third five-year term in 1978. However, it would have been viewed--both in the Palace and outside--as a loss of face for the ruling group and its powers to command the forces of harmony.

In view of this, some of Suharto's political opponents in the PPP have suggested, the government took steps to add yet another weapon to the military's already significant armory. The main opposition to Golkar was coming from the Muslim party, the government thinking allegedly ran. Therefore, steps should be taken to undermine the party by depicting it as connected in some unstated way with political extremism in general and the dream of an Islamic state in particular. This, it is alleged in Muslim circles, is what lay behind the preelection revelations of an antigovernment conspiracy calling itself the Komando Jihad (Holy War Command). Events were to show that the Komando Jihad leaders were connected with Ali Murtopo--although not, he would allege, in the way people thought-- and in the view of many Indonesians there was little doubt that the Komando Jihad was an instrument fashioned by Murtopo with the specific aim of putting Islam on the defensive.

And by the mid-1970s too popular disenchantment with Golkar, meant that it was now seen as a hollow shell, as Jusuf Wanandi, a Murtopo strategist, was ready to concede following the 1977 poll:

We simply can't go on like this. Golkar has been directed
too much from the top. It looks just like a government
department--the Social Participation Department. What we
need is a real people's movement, growing from the
grassroots. There must be a new leadership, one that
enjoys a real status with the people.[37]

The role of the government had been so overwhelming, Wanandi
complained, that Golkar had had to take a back seat. The political
parties had been given "considerable freedom" to develop, but Golkar
had been kept in the background. The answer was for the functional
group to be given a greater degree of autonomy. "We must become a
strong party with grassroots support," Wanandi declared, "or we will
have no chance in the 1982 election"[38]

To some extent, that had become a familiar refrain of the
Murtopo group, a reflection of their long-thwarted aim to build Golkar
into a mass party that would provide Ali Murtopo with the independent power base he had always lacked. Even so, there was genuine
room for official concern that Golkar was no more than a hollow shell.
Now, in the mid-1970s, the government was to receive independent
confirmation of the fact that Golkar might not fare as well as was
hoped in a relatively free contest with the PPP.

---

37. Jusuf Wanandi (Liem Bian Kie), May 1977. Suharto had been
careful not to allow Golkar to fall under the sway of any one group,
and the Golkar leadership reflected a balance between key power
groups. To some extent, Wanandi's remarks may have been due to
the frustration of the Ali group to gain sufficient leverage over
Golkar to shape the organization to their own ends. However, his
feeling that Golkar could not go on indefinitely in the same fashion
seemed to be genuinely held.

38. Ibid.

CHAPTER THREE

MOUNTING INTRAMILITARY TENSIONS

> . . . the only national property that is still whole
> and unchanging notwithstanding all sorts of chal-
> lenges and changes is the . . . Indonesian National
> Army.
>
> --General Sudirman, August 1949[1]

In 1972, President Suharto gave the late Lt. Gen. M. R. Kartakusuma, the secretary general of the National Defense and Security
Council (Dewan Pertahanan Keamanan Nasional, or Dewan Hankamnas)[2]
the task of gathering materials for the GBHN (Broad Outlines of State
Policy), which was to be put before the MPR in 1978. To do this,
Kartakusuma and his associates traveled widely and held hearings
with various organizations, including the Indonesian Ulama Council
(Majelis Ulama Indonesia, MUI), the teaching staff at a number of
universities, and provincial and local leaders. These visits to the
provinces revealed widespread dissatisfaction with the government in
general and with the military in particular. Not long before the

---

1. The late General Sudirman, Commander-in-Chief of the Indonesian
Armed Forces during the revolution, used this phrase in a letter
which he wrote (but was persuaded not to send) to President Sukarno
in August 1949. (The letter is published in A. H. Nasution, *Sekitar
Perang Kemerdekaan Indonesia* Vol. 2, *Diplomasi atau Bertempur*
[Bandung: Disjarah-AD, 1977], pp. 349-50.) In the years since
1953, when Nasution first made the Sudirman letter public in his book
TNI, it has become common for ABRI personalities to quote Sudirman's
words about ABRI being *hak milik nasional* (national property) as a
declaration of the Father of the TNI.

2. The Dewan Hankamnas (National Defense and Security Council)
was established on August 1, 1970, to assist the president determine
policies in the field of national defense and security. Chaired by the
president, the council consisted of seven members, including the vice
president and five key ministers; Lt. Gen. Kartakusuma, the first
secretary general of the council, was installed in November 1970. As
originally conceived, the Dewan Hankamnas was to be a high-level
body that would, amongst other things, prepare the draft GBHN for
the MPR. It is said that in setting up the body, the government
aimed, quite consciously, at bridging the civilian-military gap, by
bringing together people from both fields.

anti-Japanese and antigovernment Malari riots of January 1974, Dr. Ruslan Abdulgani and another member of the Dewan Hankamnas team attended a performance of a W. S. Rendra play in Yogyakarta. The audience, which had braved the rain at an open-air theater, appeared to be "totally anti-Golkar and antimilitary."[3] In Jombang, a staunchly Muslim center in East Java, members of the Kartakusuma team were surrounded by a hostile throng of students who were equally anti-Golkar and antimilitary. The same sentiments were evident in Malang on the day before Malari. Everywhere, said Ruslan Abdulgani, there seemed to be "opposition to the military establishment, to the dictatorship of the bureaucracy, and to the manipulation of so many things."[4] (At Tanjung Karang in South Sumatra, local businessmen jumped to the conclusion that, if members of the "*suku Jakarta*" [Jakarta tribe, or ruling elite] were in town, it must be because they had inside knowledge about a new development project and wanted to buy up land in the vicinity of the project, a practice identified in their minds with military men and civilian officials from the capital; hoping to participate in the anticipated windfall, they badgered the visitors night and day.)

It is not known what Kartakusuma reported to the president after these visits.[5] However, the Dewan Hankamnas secretary general was then given the additional task of making an informal evaluation of the likely outcome of the 1977 general election, looking particularly at the prospects for Golkar. The findings, which were presented in 1974 or 1975, could not have been especially pleasing to Suharto. According to the Dewan Hankamnas team, Golkar would be lucky to get 50 percent of the vote in the forthcoming elections and would only get about 45 percent if the contest was completely fair and above board.[6] According to General Nasution, certain members of the Kartakusuma group were of the opinion that it would be difficult for Golkar to win a clear-cut mandate in the elections in the absence of a "special situation."[7] This opinion appears to have been shared by a

------

3. Interview with Ruslan Abdulgani, March 14, 1982.

4. Ibid.

5. Interviews with General Nasution, May 10-11, 1979, and June 23, 1980, and with Ruslan Abdulgani, March 24, 1982. Although Nasution does not know exactly what Kartakusuma reported to the president, he says he was told of the overall conclusions of the report by former officers who were at that time assigned to Kartakusuma. Nasution, like many other prominent retired officers, received regular and detailed information about contemporary events from former subordinates.

6. Ruslan Abdulgani interview, March 14, 1982.

7. Interview with General Nasution, July 24, 1981. Certain members of the Centre for Strategic and International Studies (CSIS), the "think-tank" set up by Maj. Gen. Ali Murtopo in 1971, have suggested that the Kartakusuma tour of the provinces was really no more

good many others. Pepabri, the association of ex-servicemen, had taken similar--albeit informal and less comprehensive--soundings and come to virtually the same conclusion.[8] General Sumitro, the former commander of Kopkamtib, felt the same way, having come face to face with popular disenchantment with the regime during a tour of university campuses late in 1973.

It was against this background, many retired officers believe, that the ruling group decided it would have to create a "special situ-

---

than a "junket," a not particularly taxing assignment for an aging general who had been put out to grass. These sources speak disparagingly of Kartakusuma in his declining years and dismiss the contention that his opinions counted for anything. Interview with Jusuf Wanandi [Liem Bian Kie] and Harry Tjan Silalahi, July 22, 1981. While statements like this clearly reflect the anti-Dewan Hankamnas bias of those at CSIS, the observations are not without some foundation. On the other hand, there were important members of the Kartakusuma group, in particular Ruslan Abdulgani and the late Oejeng Suwargana, who did take detailed political soundings in the regions. Interviews with Ruslan Abdulgani (March 24, 1982) and General Nasution (July 24, 1981). Nasution had had a long association with both Kartakusuma and Oejeng Suwargana and these two men were themselves close. Oejeng Suwargana had been one of Nasution's closest friends at the Teachers Training School in Bandung in the years 1935-38, and it was mainly because of Nasution's influence that Oejeng joined the Royal Military Academy's Reserve Officers' Training Course in 1941. (See Susan M. McKemmish, "A Political Biography of General A. H. Nasution" [MA thesis, Monash University, 1976], p. 14.) Nasution had joined the academy a year earlier. In the late 1950s, Nasution sent Oejeng Suwargana to the Netherlands to hold informal meetings with the Dutch as part of an Indonesian effort to sound out the possibilities of a peaceful solution to the West Irian dispute. (Ibid., p. 214.) In these efforts, Oejeng Suwargana worked closely with several Indonesian military attachés in Western Europe, among them Kartakusuma who was stationed in Paris. (Oejeng was also widely regarded as Nasution's contact with the CIA.) In the late 1970s, Oejeng Suwargana was a member, as was Nasution, of the Yayasan Lembaga Kesadaran Berkonstitusi (Foundation for the Institute of Constitutional Awareness). Nasution had been especially close to Kartakusuma when the two men were officer cadets in Bandung in 1940. In 1945, when Nasution was chief of staff of the TKR for West Java, Kartakusuma was a member of his staff. According to Nasution, Kartakusuma's role in the 1975-77 provincial visits was mainly of a "protocol" nature; however, Oejeng Suwargana was present on each of Kartakusuma's trips around the country and participated "very actively." (Interview, July 24, 1981.) This is confirmed by Ruslan Abdulgani.

8. Ibid. General Nasution had been told of this by Lt. Gen. Suprayogi and Admiral Nazir, both of whom were members of the central administration of Pepabri.

ation." The "issue" that it came up with, they say, was the security threat allegedly posed by the Komando Jihad. There is, of course, no easy way of establishing whether or not the Komando Jihad was a product of the government's own making. But the timing of the announcement--the commander of Koptamtib, Admiral Sudomo, revealed details of the alleged conspiracy a few weeks before the election campaign on February 14, 1977--and a general sense of cynicism engendered by earlier "black operations" mounted by the various intelligence agencies gave rise to widespread suspicion. As Liddle has noted, Sudomo stated explicitly that there was no connection between the Komando Jihad and the PPP. But party leaders were certain the move was designed to provide Kopkamtib "with a ready excuse to arrest any Islamic politician not to its liking and more broadly to remind political Muslims of the armed forces' view of them as fanatical proponents of an Islamic state."[9]

Those familiar with the Indonesian intelligence services and the philosophy of the group around Suharto believe it is quite possible that the Komando Jihad movement was indeed an electoral ploy and little else. According to the former head of Bakin, Lt. Gen. Sutopo Juwono, there were "certain people" who were always thinking along these lines.

I don't know if the government was behind the Komando Jihad; I was not here. But if you talk about the possibility, thinking like that, it is possible. So create the problem, a special issue, something like that. . . . This is not always true, of course. It's possible but not always true. But somebody is thinking about such things like that. The reason is simple. Even in the intelligence in my period there were two streams. One group said that if we talk about Pancasila, for instance, or about the Constitution we have also to act accordingly. Otherwise we can't talk about the Constitution. But another group of the intelligence is saying that we are still developing so nobody can give an assurance that if we act like this we will win. So I think that winning is the first aim of this group. And the other group is more or less saying that morality is more important than winning. "Yes, we have to win, but according to the rules, according to moral values." But this group is not. So from this group it is possible that we had better create a special

<hr>

9. Liddle, "1977 Indonesian Election," p. 128. Sudomo always took pains to emphasize that the plot was in no way connected with Murtopo, almost to the point of protesting too much. In March 1981, while setting out the background to unrest in Jember, East Java, Sudomo said that Muslim MPs might choose to suggest that the unrest had been organized by the government "like in that case of the Komando Jihad. We are accused of that. It's nothing to do with Ali Murtopo." Interview with Admiral Sudomo, March 3, 1981.

issue. But I can say for sure that I am at the time belonging to this second group. And, you know, in 1969, I
think, I created an intelligence doctrine for Indonesia
based on moral values. And it's very strong. I think
it's still existing and is actually still valid but I don't
know whether or not it's used in practice.[10]

This doctrine had been designed to cover all the activities of
Bakin. But there had been another stream.

Ali Murtopo is belonging to this group. So, for instance,
you talk about Komando Jihad. It's not a new issue.
From the beginning on he has this opinion. I had to stop
that at the time. He had the opinion that we must create
issues. He said, "One time we will have to use this" and
so on and on. Let's say it's always in his mind. I tried
to stop him. But I can't stop that because he's always
going to the president. He had his own Opsus [Operasi
Chusus, Special Operations section].[11]

Many in Indonesia share this suspicion, and take the view that
the Komando Jihad was an operation mounted by Murtopo to discredit
the Muslims. Former prime minister Mohammad Natsir, a prominent
Muslim leader, claimed in 1978 that Ismail Pranoto, a Komando Jihad
leader who was sentenced to life imprisonment in September 1979, was
"an *agent provocateur* run by Ali Murtopo."[12] People at the grassroots were dissatisfied with conditions, Natsir argued, and were
easily led. Murtopo's agents had planted rumors about the Communist
comeback and had promised former Darul Islam activists weapons to
fight the leftist "threat." The leaders of the Komando Jihad--Ateng
Jailani, Abu Darda (a son of S. M. Kartosuwirjo, the original Darul
Islam leader), Danu Subroto, Zainal Abidin, Ismail Pranoto, and
Kadar Salihat--were former Darul Islam leaders who were "now in the
control of Ali Murtopo and his group. . . . From the start they got
help from the Ali Murtopo group, not from the military as a whole.
That is his special hobby. Even the West Java commander, [Maj.
Gen.] Himawan [Sutanto], knows it is a fabrication, but no one can
say it. He knows it. He was furious that everything is blamed on
[West Java] as a center of the Darul Islam."[13]

According to members of the Ali Murtopo group, the Komando
Jihad leaders did indeed have links with Murtopo,[14] but they

---

10.   Interview with Lt. Gen. Sutopo Juwono, July 23, 1981.

11.   Ibid.

12.   Interview with Mohammad Natsir, December 12, 1978.

13.   Ibid. A number of army officers expressed an almost identical
opinion during interviews.

14.   Interview with Harry Tjan Silalahi and Jusuf Wanandi, July 22,
1981.

"misused" this link, with the result that people had come wrongly to suspect Ali. Murtopo, it was pointed out by his associates, had long been a master of the unexpected. In the mid-1960s he had used former members of the 1958-61 PRRI-Permesta rebellion, most notably Des Alwi, an Indonesian of Arabic descent, to pioneer the ending of Konfrontasi with Malaysia. He had also been largely responsible for the release in 1966 of prominent army officers who had taken part in the rebellion, including Col. Maluddin Simbolon, Lt. Col. H. N. V. Sumual, and Lt. Col. Ahmad Husein. In the same year he had helped arrange the release from military prison of a number of Masyumi leaders, including Natsir and former foreign minister Mohamad Roem, both of whom had been detained by Sukarno. Although Ali had fought the PRRI-Permesta, it was explained, he was not vindictive towards his former enemies. He had an open mind and wanted to make use of the people who were available, while at the same time giving those people a chance to do something for the nation.[15] The Komando Jihad leaders, according to this explanation, were a group of ex-Darul Islam supporters whom Ali, in his capacity as deputy head of Bakin, had "wanted to use." As one of the civilian intellectuals associated with the Murtopo group put it: "Ali wanted to contact them and give them a chance of going back to [President] Suharto. They asked for such a chance and Pitut [Suharto, a member of Opsus] was taking care of that."[16]

---

15. Interview with Jusuf Wanandi, March 5, 1982. Barbara Harvey has noted that many of the former TNI officers who returned with Maj. (later Lt. Col.) Daniel Julius Somba's Permesta group were given positions in "army intelligence [Bakin]" (sic), amongst other places. In 1971-72, Somba was a lieutenant colonel on the staff of Bakin. See Barbara S. Harvey, *Permesta: Half a Rebellion* (Ithaca: Cornell Modern Indonesia Project, 1977), pp. 151 and 159. Although its senior positions are held by military figures, Bakin is in fact a civilian agency.

16. Harry Tjan and Jusuf Wanandi interview, July 22, 1981. In June 1977, Admiral Sudomo announced that 700 people had been arrested in connection with the Komando Jihad movement. In reply to a question, he said that the movement was organized in Aceh, North Sumatra, Riau, South Sumatra, Lampung, Jakarta, West Java, Central Java, and East Java. The movement, he said, had a "war commander" and a "Messiah." Members of the movements were "sworn." According to Sudomo, the long-term aim of the movement was to form an Islamic state. The short-term aim was to make trouble by engaging in terrorist activities against other groups and religions and by discrediting the government. He dismissed reports in some newspapers that the Jihad Command movement had been manufactured by the government expressly to face the 1977 general election. At the time of the crackdown, Sudomo said, the movement was limited to cells or groups which were later to have been developed more widely. See *Kompas*, June 8, 1977. (United States Embassy translation service, henceforth USE.) During his trial in Surabaya, Haji Ismail Pranoto

However, according to this version, these people "misused their position, misused the loyalty Ali had given them, and misused Ali's name to do things that were detrimental." When the security forces clamped down, it is said, some of the group had insisted that they were together "because Ali asked us." This led to rumors that Ali had created the Komando Jihad to oppose the Muslims."[17] Many Indonesians, a number of prominent military officers among them, find this "explanation" unconvincing. "It is a manufactured account," one general insisted. "Pitut did not misuse his authority. He did exactly what he was told to do. He was an agent provocateur seeking to fan the flames."[18] Whatever the truth about the Komando Jihad, the government was clearly motivated by a desire to contain the PPP within very narrow limits.[19] In a series of special meetings, the army leaders instructed their subordinates to throw their full weight behind Golkar, just as in 1971.[20]

If the government was preparing to climb into bed with Golkar yet again, then the policy did not enjoy the unquestioned support of the officer corps. At the time of the 1977 general elections, there were conflicting views within the armed forces about the TNI's proper role in an electoral situation. Some officers, those who shared the basically "pragmatic" outlook of the officers close to Suharto, tended

---

bin Suleiman, or "Hispran" as he was more commonly known, was described as the "deputy war commander of Java-Madura." A former Darul Islam/Tentara Islam Indonesia member from Brebes, Central Java, he was said to have visited East Java to propagate his ideas and find new followers. According to the prosecution, he had installed "Jihad Commands" at Bojonegoro, Tuban, Blitar, and Lamongan and was in the process of swearing in a number of Komando Jihad leaders at the time of his arrest on January 8, 1977. During his trial, Hispran requested the presence of Ali Murtopo and Pitut Suharto as defense witnesses. The request was turned down by the trial judge. Hispran was aged 58 at the time of his arrest. See *Antara*, February 1, 1978, *Merdeka, Angkatan Bersenjata, Berita Buana*, and *Kompas*, April 6, 1978.

17. Harry Tjan-Jusuf Wanandi interview.

18. Confidential communication, March 1982.

19. Liddle, "1977 Indonesian Election." Although the discovery of the "plot" may have provided the government with a convenient excuse to crack down on political Islam, there was never any possibility of Suharto losing control of the MPR; as we have seen, 61 percent of the 920 MPR members were appointed. The reasoning may have been that there was a danger that the PPP might eat into the 62 percent of the popular vote secured by Golkar in 1971. This would have occasioned considerable loss of face for the government.

20. Reference was made to such instructions by Nasution in an interview on July 27, 1981. Sumitro confirmed as much in an interview on December 12, 1981.

60

to accept the necessity and desirability of taking certain steps to ensure a "successful" election and the maintenance of stability. Golkar,
in this view, was a creation of the armed forces, and it was only natural for them to lend support to the grouping. A smaller faction,
whose outlook was similar to those described earlier as being of a
more "principled" cast of mind, took the view that the support that
was being asked of ABRI was not consistent with the pure identity of
the TNI. If ABRI were to back Golkar, this group felt, its actions
would not be in accordance with the doctrines of the late General
Sudirman who had stressed that the armed forces were not the property of any one section of society but of the nation as a whole. This
concern found what was perhaps its fullest expression amongst a number of prominent members of the teaching staff of the four service
staff and command schools in Bandung.[21] But it was also present in
the thinking of officers at Lemhannas (the National Defense Institute)
and among a number of prominent retired officers; it found adherents
also within the upper echelons of the army leadership.

The Seskoad Initiative

　　　Each of the four service staff schools included a Departemen
Juang (Struggle Department), and the teaching staff from each of
these institutions had been meeting privately since 1976 on the initiative of members of the Air Force Staff and Command School (Seskoau)
to review the implementation of the military's dual role. In order to
help resolve differences of opinion on this matter, participants from
the various staff schools decided that it would be helpful if General
Nasution, the former minister of defense and the founder of the dwifungsi doctrine, came to Bandung to answer questions about the
army's proper role in such a situation.

　　　As a preliminary, an officer from the teaching staff at Seskoad
called on the former minister to advise him informally of the planned
invitation. However, before the Sesko's could send any official invitation, officers within the intelligence section of the Defense Ministry,
took steps to ensure that Nasution was not invited.[22] Instead, the

21.　The four staff and command schools in Bandung are: Seskoad
(Army), Seskoau (Air Force), Seskopol (Police), and at a more ad-
vanced level, the Combined Armed Forces Staff School (Seskogab).
The Seskoal (Navy) is in Jakarta.

22.　According to Nasution, this was not the first time that Hankam
intelligence had intervened in this way. During the annual meeting
between the older and younger generation of Siliwangi officers in
1977, the assistant I (Intelligence), Maj. Gen. Benny Murdani, had
turned up with members of his staff although his name had not been
on the original invitation list. The following year, the annual meeting
was canceled by the Siliwangi on instructions from Jakarta. Nasution
had already received his invitation and was preparing his speech.

government sent the secretary general of the Department of Home Affairs, Maj. Gen. R. Suprapto, to Bandung to explain what it was doing during the election campaign. But Suprapto was unable to satisfy the teaching staff or the students with his answers to the questions raised. A military bureaucrat with a somewhat narrow focus, he could not explain the fundamental concept behind the dwifungsi; he seemed out of his depth when asked to comment on anything but operational or administrative aspects of the electoral process.[23] The government tried again. This time it sent General Darjatmo, the chief of staff of functional affairs, to Bandung. He also failed to satisfy the teaching staff, being unable or unwilling to answer the sort of questions that were asked of him. As a result, the government was left with an unresolved problem.

In these circumstances, members of the teaching staff at the four staff schools in Bandung went ahead on their own and put together a lengthy paper on the dual function of ABRI.[24] This paper, which ran to forty-three pages and which was completed nine months after the election, was largely theoretical in nature and reflected much of the thinking of Nasution, the ban on the general's visit to Seskoad notwithstanding. There were two reasons for this. As a former Siliwangi commander, Nasution made regular visits to Bandung and had, on various occasions, been approached informally for his views on the subject. Secondly, the Seskoad paper was essentially the work of the deputy commander of Seskoad, Colonel (later Brig. Gen.) Abdulkadir Besar, a man who had been close to Nasution for many years.[25] Abdulkadir was responsible for the courses on ide-

There have been no meetings of Siliwangi seniors since then. The reason, according to one retired officer, is "because we are talking politics." (Interview, March 23, 1982.) Early in 1978, the leadership of Pepabri, the association of retired military personnel, sent a number of retired senior officers, including Nasution, an invitation to discuss problems likely to be faced by the country in the future. Some time after he had received his invitation, Nasution was sent a letter of cancellation. He was later told, in an informal way, that the cancellation was made at the behest of the Defense Department. At about the same time, the former defense minister was prevented from publishing an article which had been requested by the editors of the magazine *Purnawiraan* ("Retirement"). The article contained an evaluation of the efforts of the New Order up to the end of 1977 and included suggestions about possible corrections.

23. A Western diplomat in Jakarta was fond of describing Suprapto as "an absolute zero," adding that this was "one reason why the department (Home Affairs) does not work." Communication to author, February 2, 1980.

24. Confidential communication to author, May 1979.

25. Born in Magelang, Central Java, on November 11, 1926, Abdulkadir Besar was a graduate of the Military Academy in Yogyakarta

ology and the state constitution at Seskoad, and his paper concerned itself largely with the areas in which there had been "excesses" in the past. This paper reflected the consensus of the teaching staff and had also been discussed by students at the various Sesko's.

The Seskoad Paper

During the first half of 1977, Abdulkadir Besar had reformulated ABRI's Hankamrata (Total People's Defense) Concept, following essentially the existing doctrine but setting it out in what he felt was a more systematic way. He began work on the "Seskoad Paper"--a green-covered document entitled "Dwifungsi ABRI"--in mid-1977 and completed it in February 1978.

Written with a frequent disregard for the niceties of grammar and weighed down with a good deal of sociological jargon, the Seskoad paper does not always make easy reading. Nevertheless, the thrust of the argument is clear. After a brief introduction, the paper sets forth the notion, central to Adbulkadir's thinking, that Indonesian cultural values are posited on the notion that every member of a family has a responsibility for the welfare of the entire family. From this flows the idea that an ABRI man is responsible not just for the defense of the state but for developing, inter alia, its economic, cultural, and political life. Should a member of a family experience dif-

---

and the Military Law Academy in Jakarta. In the early 1960s, when Nasution was defense minister, Abdulkadir served as a lieutenant colonel in the army's internal security department. The two men worked together closely between 1967-72 when Nasution was chairman of the MPRS and Abdulkadir its secretary general. In 1973, after Nasution had issued a "White Paper" critical of the national leadership, the government, unable to strike directly at him, took out its displeasure on Abdulkadir Besar. The MPR secretary general was interrogated by Kopkamtib from 8 a.m. till 5 p.m. every weekday for four weeks. Abdulkadir was a member of the teaching staff at Seskoad from 1972 to 1975 and deputy commandant of the staff school from 1976 to 1979. At that time, after seven years at Seskoad, he was named assistant for internal political affairs to General Maraden Panggabean, the coordinating minister for political and security affairs. Although obliged by this move to give up his position as deputy commandant of Seskoad, he continued to head the Departemen Juang at the staff school and to lecture there. In the view of a civilian academic who lectured at Seskoad, Abdulkadir might well have been appointed secretary of state had Nasution ever become president. Instead, he remained a one-star officer. "Many of these bright guys from Seskoad are still putting their views," this source noted in an interview (July 15, 1980). However, in the political field, Suharto had adopted the policies of the Ali Murtopo group, not the Seskoad group. As a result, many of the Seskoad people had become a focus of opposition to Suharto.

ficulties or fail while fulfilling his function, the paper says, "the other members [of the family] will assist [not take over]." Likewise, should ABRI, as a member of the large Indonesian family whose particular duty it is to defend the nation, have a relative who, in implementing his duty in the economic, cultural, or political field, experiences difficulties or fails "then ABRI has the right to and is responsible for assisting this troubled family member."[26]

In a section dealing with ABRI's dwifungsi, the paper suggests that the dual function principle does not involve "the creation of a new system"; instead, it merely recognizes that it is legitimate for military men to exercise the normal constitutional rights guaranteed to all citizens. "In a state based on family principles a citizen who enters military service does not undergo a change in status; because of that, the principles of 'civilian supremacy' and 'civil-military relations' are unknown and invalid."[27] In the following section the paper makes a careful analysis of the meaning of the word "function." In a normal management situation, it says, the word has a clear and accepted meaning. In the case of ABRI's dual function, however, the scope of management is potentially so wide that it is necessary, in order to ensure that the dwifungsi is kept within "its true and real limits," to interpret the dwifungsi according to the Sapta Marga, the seven-point pledge, "here explained as being *dharma* [duty]."

In a section dealing with the identity of ABRI, the paper argues that just as human personality is influenced by culture, so ABRI's dual function is a product of Indonesian culture. Because of that, it claims, ABRI's dual function is a cultural reality for the Indonesian people. ABRI's personality was formed during its early years and is expressed in the Sapta Marga. To prevent a change in ABRI's personality, that is, a change from a Sapta Marga personality to something else, each member of ABRI needs to recall the original, pure personality, "that is, the personality of Sapta Marga whose implementation is expressed as the dual function of ABRI." The Sapta Marga made it clear that an ABRI man saw himself as a citizen, patriot, knight, and soldier; the virtues embodied in the Sapta Marga had been distilled from the revolutionary experience. In a section headed "Emotional Response," the author goes on to suggest that various cases of military "intervention" in the political processes can be understood in terms of ABRI's adherence to the principles of the Sapta Marga. The emotional response which was expressed by the armed forces during the revolution was manifest in the statement of General Sudirman that "With or without the government, the TNI goes on with the struggle." (*Met of zonder pemerintah, TNI jalan terus mempertahankan kemerdekaan.*) A similar response was apparent, the paper suggests, when army leaders urged Sukarno to dissolve the "liberal" Parliament in October 1952 and when they pushed for a re-

---

26. Abdulkadir Besar, "Dwifungsi ABRI," mimeographed (Bandung [?]: Seskoad, 1978), p. 3.

27. Ibid., p. 30.

turn to the 1945 Constitution in 1959. The dissolution of the PKI in 1965 and the creation of the New Order were likewise examples of a response which had its roots in an adherence to Sapta Marga. ABRI's rationale was: That which is best for the people and the state is that which is best for ABRI. In developing the theme that an ABRI man is not merely a soldier but a citizen, patriot, knight, and soldier, the paper accepts that this gives ABRI members a responsibility which is "broad and complex."

The section on ABRI's credentials is unusually blunt. "We can indeed imagine," the paper states, "the dangers [of] an armed force participating in politics along with other social forces which are unarmed." An armed force such as this could degenerate into a political party that was armed, which would tend to use its weapons or the threat of its weapons to attain its political goals. The liberal democracies had avoided this danger by formulating guidelines concerning correct civil-military relations. The danger arose, in a country without such guidelines, if the armed forces possessed *their own political aims*. If, on the other hand, the armed forces had no such aims the danger would automatically disappear. "The question that arises is: does ABRI possess its own political aims outside the political aims of the state?" The answer, as formulated by the Seskoad paper, was that, according to the first three marga of the Sapta Marga, ABRI did not possess its own political aims: ABRI men were citizens who believed in and supported Pancasila, were patriotic defenders of the state ideology, and were warriors who defended honesty, truth, and justice. What prevented ABRI from having its own political aims? None other than the basic principle that had guided ABRI since 1945--that "the Constitution is the basis and politics of the army." And this really provided the credentials of ABRI before the Indonesian people. Without these credentials it would be impossible for the people of Indonesia to allow ABRI to participate in politics, impossible that they would allow ABRI to implement its functions as a social force. The document continued:

> We must contemplate the opposite case, namely, should ABRI at some moment go against its own credentials, that is if the politics carried out by ABRI were no longer those of the '45 Constitution but the politics of a certain group i.e.: another group towards which ABRI were sympathetic, or ABRI as a group, a small group within ABRI, then immediately ABRI would lose its philosophical and sociological basis to carry out its function as a social force. And if while breaching its credentials, ABRI still carried out its functions as a social force, then these activities would no longer be called dual function but would change to "*dwiporsi*" [dual portions] . . . its decline to dwiporsi would result in plunging the state and the people into endless suffering. Because of this, the purity of ABRI's credentials must be guarded; to that end,

ABRI circles must set up control mechanisms which have authority and which are effective.[28]

Out of the dwifungsi concept had come nine principles that had to be upheld in the implementation of ABRI's dual function. These nine principles were interrelated so that, should even one principle not be carried out, still less breached, the significance of the dwifungsi would change. Such a change in significance could, in turn, result in a situation in which ABRI's identity was no longer that of Sapta Marga.

In introducing the first of the nine principles, the document said that, because ABRI as an instrument of Hankam was a power instrument of the government (*alat kekuasaan pemerintah*), its position was equivalent to that of the government; that is, it was above all groups in the community. From this line of reasoning, it said, came the first principle--"the politics carried out by ABRI are those of the 1945 Constitution, not the politics of a group or the politics of ABRI as a group." In this context, the author noted that the 1945-50 Commander-in-Chief, General Sudirman, had set out three guiding principles. The first was that "the State Constitution is the basis and politics of the army." The second was that "the army knows no political view except that of the state and because of this the army will defend the state and the state's political views." The third was that "in defending the state and its politics the army will not compromise."

Before setting out the second principle to be upheld in implementing ABRI's dual function, the paper noted that, as ABRI had a position in both the "political superstructure" and the "political infrastructure," its activities in realizing its function as a social force had to remain proportional. Were this not the case, the political system of family principles (*kekeluargaan*) could become dictatorial. From this line of reasoning came the second principle--that "in attaining its political goals ABRI must use neither its weapons nor the threat of its weapons; neither can it abuse its power as a participant in the political superstructure."

The document went on to note that Indonesia possessed a democratic political system. One condition of such a system was that it was necessary to use legitimate methods of persuasion in implementing political activities. From this, the third principle was born--that "in carrying out political activities ABRI must use methods of persuasion and constitutional methods and must not resort to force." Fourthly, the essence of ABRI's participation as a social force was its participation in defining the direction of the state. This participation could only be implemented through the institution that gave expression to the sovereignty of the people and in the legislative body--that is, in the MPR and the DPR. The fifth principle was that ABRI's participation in the executive branch of government was "only carried out

_____
28. Ibid., p. 37.

within the framework of stabilizing and/or dynamizing that branch."
The principal force in politics was that of public opinion, the paper
said, and this did not manifest the sort of rigidity or hierarchy
found in the military system. From this came the sixth principle,
that "in carrying out its political policy ABRI does so through deliberations between the leadership and a number of ABRI members who,
based on their experience and capabilities, are considered capable of
forming objective opinions, not opinions fashioned according to the
desires of the leadership." The seventh principle was that ABRI's
nonmilitary function must be executed in accordance with the following
notions: that authority is not based on power; that tension should be
broken without using force; of winning without defeating; and that
wealth should come not from material objects. Power, the paper went
on, always tended towards the center and tended to commit errors.
Because of this, power had to be restrained in both extent and time.
To avoid a decline in ABRI's authority in the implementation of the
dwifungsi, an eighth principle had been formulated: "Leadership is
founded on greatness of spirit and must be realized in word, attitude, and action." Finally, there was the ninth principle: "So long
as a function can be carried out by another institution or individual
with good results then it should be looked after by the institution or
individual."[29]

In a section on ABRI's role as a stabilizer and dynamizer, the
Seskoad paper stressed that ABRI was above all groups in society.
If, in implementing the dwifungsi, ABRI departed from the nine principles already alluded to, the people's recognition would be erased
and ABRI's position "will degenerate to the level of other groups in
society."

In this document, one hears closely the voice of the officers of
a principled cast of mind, a group committed above all to the notion
that ABRI's behavior should be posited on certain moral values, a
group concerned by the apparent backsliding and decline in standards
that had taken place under the New Order leadership. At the time,
the Seskoad paper was to go almost unnoticed. Before long, however, it would become the basis of an important restatement of army
principles, a restatement that brought elements of the army leadership
into a direct confrontation with Suharto and his principal lieutenants.

The Role of the Retired Officers

In the meantime, initiatives for change were coming from another quarter--retired army officers who shared a growing concern
about the political directions of the Suharto government. Indonesia,
these officers felt, was in the political doldrums. The armed forces
had established a virtual stranglehold on society and there was no
sign that they were inclined to ease their grip. Such views had been

---

29. Ibid., pp. 38-40.

present to some extent since the founding of the New Order. But they came to be heard more frequently in the mid-1970s, and they found expression at a series of *keluarga* or *rumpun* (literally, "family") meetings of retired officers from the former Brawijaya, Siliwangi, and Diponegoro divisions in 1977. Among those participating were Lt. Gen. G. P. H. Djatikusumo, Lt. Gen. R. Sudirman, Lt. Gen. Mohammad Jasin, Maj. Gen. Subiyono, Brig. Gen. Agus Prasmono, and Col. Chandra Hasan from the Brawijaya; Maj. Gen. Brotosewoyo, Maj. Gen. Iskandar Ranuwihardjo, Maj. Gen. Munadi, Maj. Gen. Muamil Effendy, Brig. Gen. Broto Hamidjojo, and Brig. Gen. Sroehardojo from the Diponegoro; Lt. Gen. A. J. Mokoginta, Lt. Gen. Sugih Arto, Lt. Gen. Kemal Idris, Maj. Gen. Achmad Sukendro, Brig. Gen. Daan Jahja, Col. Alex Kawilarang, and Col. Sukanda Bratamenggala from the Siliwangi. Brig. Gen. Abimanju, who had served in each of the three big Java divisions, also took part in these deliberations, as did Maj. Gen. Harun Sohar, a "ring in" from South Sumatra's Sriwijaya military region.[30]

These were names to conjure with. Djatikusumo, a prince of the royal court of Solo, the son of Paku Buwono X, one of the most glamorous sultans of Solo, was a former army chief of staff who had served as commandant of the Military Academy in Yogyakarta and of the Staff and Command School in Bandung. Sudirman--not to be confused with the late Commander-in-Chief of the same name--was a former commander of the Brawijaya (East Java) military region, a very distinguished officer, with a good reputation, clean and capable, albeit somewhat straightlaced. Jasin, another former Brawijaya commander, was an officer who had gone on to serve as deputy army chief of staff. Daan Jahja and Alex Kawilarang had each served as commander of the prestigious Siliwangi (West Java) military region. Kemal Idris had commanded Kostrad, the army strategic reserve, and been commander of Kowilhan IV, the unified command for East Indonesia. Munadi was a former governor of Central Java (1966-74), Sugih Arto a former attorney general (1966-70). Mokoginta had been the Sumatra interregional commander during the years 1964-67, Sukendro the assistant for intelligence to the army chief of staff.

Many of these men had links with one another dating back to the revolution, if not earlier; they had participated together in the crucial early years of the struggle. The young Abimanju had been the first adjutant to the late General Sudirman, had slept in the same room with him for six months at one stage in 1945-46. The young Mokoginta had been ADC to General Urip Sumohardjo, the former

---

30. Interview with Maj. Gen. Sukendro, March 3, 1982. Although frequently listed as such, Djatikusumo was not in fact from the Brawijaya, which was only formed in 1948. He had headed the Ronggolawe division which operated in the Semarang-Tuban north coastal area in 1945-47--which spans parts of today's Diponegoro and Brawijaya territories--before going on to head the Military Academy in Yogyakarta.

KNIL major who, with Sudirman, provided the dominant army leadership in the early days of the Republic. Although a year behind cadets like Nasution, Simatupang, and Kawilarang when he was accepted into the Royal Netherlands Military Academy in Bandung in June 1941, Mokoginta had known Kawilarang--both were from North Sulawesi-- since that time; later he had served as Nasution's chief of staff in the Siliwangi division during the first Dutch attack against the Republic. Abimanju, the son of a low-level government official, had known Djatikusumo and the other, East Java, Sudirman, since the three had graduated together as company commanders at a Japanese-run course in Bogor in 1943.

The meetings of the socalled "Brasildi" group--Brasildi was an acronym derived from the names of these three Java-based divisions --were held in the period between the general elections of May 1977 and the presidential elections of March 1978. Initially, the concern of this group of retired officers had been theoretical in nature. However, when the government sent troops in to occupy university campuses and secondary schools in early 1978 the debate assumed a new urgency.

One difficulty was that there was no formal body through which the views of retired "seniors" could be channeled to the army leadership. In earlier years, it had generally been accepted that, if the government were contemplating any actions touching on army matters, it was only right and proper that it should consult not just the army commanders but prominent retired officers as well. This, according to Djatikusumo, had been the practice throughout the Sukarno period, and it was something that had carried over into the early years of the New Order.[31] Thus in 1968, when General Panggabean was Pangad (army commander), a group of twenty-three semiretired army officers, all but five of them brigadier generals, were brought together in an advisory body, the Team Poleksos, ostensibly to provide an input to the army commander on nonmilitary affairs.[32] A semioffi-

---

31. Interview with Lt. Gen. G. P. H. Djatikusumo, March 9, 1981. Sukendro believed, however, that it would be more correct to say that this was the practice during the *later* years of the Sukarno period. Interview, July 11, 1981. In 1960, when Sukendro was the officer in charge of "special duties," the army had an informal body of this kind. In the regions there were meetings between active and retired officers during the anniversary celebrations of the various Kodams. This was the only formal communication between the retired and active officers and there was generally a frank exchange of views. Many retired officers retained considerable influence, as active members of the armed forces were frequently their former subordinates.

32. For details about the establishment of the Team Poleksos, see "Surat - Perintah, Nomer: Prin - 243/5/1968," signed by Gen. Panggabean in his capacity as Panglima Angkatan Darat on May 27, 1968. A copy of this document was made available to the author.

cial body chaired by the Kaspri Pangad (chief of staff of the Personal Secretariat of the army commander), the Team Poleksos consisted of three subcommittees; a Kelompok Politik (Political Group) under Maj. Gen. Dr. Satrio, a Kelompok Ekonomi under Maj. Gen. Achmad Sukendro, and a Kelompok Sosial under Brig. Gen. Sujatmo.[33]

It is difficult to escape the conclusion that the Team Poleksos was simply a convenient dumping ground for officers unwanted by the Suharto group, and it seems unlikely that the leadership took much, if any, notice of its advice. Strictly speaking, the members of the team were neither retired nor nonactive. In practice, they were very much in a half-way house--prominent in the army, but not enjoying the sympathy of the new ruling group around Suharto, and to all intents and purposes inactive.[34]

The early meetings of the Team Poleksos were chaired by Brig. Gen. Abdul Karim Rasyid, who served as Kaspri Pangad between 1967 and 1970.[35] The conclusions were sent, by way of the army com-

---

33. The membership of the three subcommittees was *Kelompok Politik/Team Poleksos*: Maj. Gen. Dr. Suhardi, Brig. Gen. Ibnu Subroto, Brig. Gen. Brotosewoyo, Brig. Gen. Mas Isman, Brig. Gen. Wijono, Brig. Gen. Djuhartono and Brig. Gen. J. Singedekane. *Kelompok Ekonomi/Team Poleksos*: Brig. Gen. Sukendro (chairman), Brig. Gen. Sunitioso, Brig. Gen. Njak Adam Kamil, Brig. Gen. Harun Sohar, Brig. Gen. R. MD. Sudarman, Brig. Gen. Muljosudjono, Colonel Brori Mansjur, and Colonel Sudarto. *Kelompok Sosial/Team Poleksos*: Brig. Gen. Sujatmo, Brig. Gen. Pirngadi, Brig. Gen. Suprapto, Brig. Gen. Sardjono, Brig. Gen. Sujono Ongko, Brig. Gen. Rahardjodikromo, and Colonel A. Batubara. For further details see "Surat - Perintah, Nomer: Prin - 244/5/1968," signed by Panggabean on May 28, 1968. There are some odd names in this group. The Kelompok Politik included a number of "populist" Sukarnoist officers; Djuhartono may even have been under arrest for a time in 1966. The Kelompok Ekonomi also included at least one officer (Sukendro) who had been under arrest in 1967-68 for apparent Sukarnoist leanings, and at least two officers (Sudarman and Sudarto) who were widely thought to have been involved in questionable business dealings. In the membership of the Kelompok Sosial were several other officers of the Old Order period, including Pirngadi, Suprapto, and Rahardjodikromo. I am indebted to Prof. Ben Anderson for making this point.

34. Interview with Maj. Gen. Sukendro, July 11, 1981.

35. Born in Batang Kapas, West Sumatra, in 1914, General Rasyid had spent much of his career away from Indonesia. He served as a teacher in Malaya between 1932-41 and, having risen to the position of chief of staff of a Peta unit during the Japanese period, served as military attaché in Bangkok and Rangoon 1951-56. He was chargé d'affaires (and later ambassador) in Cambodia from 1957 to 1965 and ambassador to the Philippines in 1965-66. See O. G. Roeder and

mander, General Panggabean (and subsequently by way of the army chief of staff, General Umar Wirahadikusumah) to President Suharto.

In the early 1970s, however, following the 1969 restructuring of the armed forces, the body was dissolved. Djatikusumo, who had joined in 1970 after serving as ambassador to France, proposed to the then chief of staff of the army, Umar Wirahadikusumah, that, if it was only a matter of reorganization, the body could be transferred to the Defense Ministry and the other services brought in. But it appeared that the group was not regarded favorably, and the government seemed content to let it die.[36] According to Sukendro, who was chairman of the Kelompok Ekonomi, the body was disbanded in 1971 or 1972.[37]

Late in 1977, however, the government did an abrupt about-face on this issue, thus paving the way for the reemergence of an association of retired generals. This was a result of two separate but interrelated developments. The first centered on Sukendro, an ex-Siliwangi officer who was to emerge as a central figure in the Fosko (Forum for Study and Communication) leadership. Sukendro, a man of swaggering self-assurance, flamboyant and sarcastic, was regarded by many of the New Order generals as an incorrigible intriguer, a reputation which stemmed from his time as assistant I (Intelligence) in the late 1950s and his involvement in such organizations as the Liga Demokrasi (Democratic League) in the early 1960s.

Born in Banyumas in 1923, Sukendro had played an active--and sometimes controversial--role in army politics. In 1959, while serving as Nasution's intelligence chief at army headquarters in Jakarta, he had been linked with a smuggling scandal at Tanjong Priok, the main port of the capital city. Army-sponsored smuggling and barter operations had mushroomed in the regions in the period after a state of war and siege was declared in 1958, not least in Central Java, where the Diponegoro commander, Col. Suharto, and his intelligence chief, Lt. Col. Ali Murtopo, were helping to devise new methods of collecting revenue, and army headquarters was not slow in following suit. This development was to lead to a temporary setback for Suharto--who was quietly relieved of his command and sent to attend a special course at SSKAD, the Army Staff and Command School in Bandung--and public embarrassment for Sukendro and other senior officers in Jakarta. The smuggling activities of the headquarters group, organized by Sukendro and Col. Ibnu Sutowo, then deputy chief of staff for operations, ran afoul of an investigation undertaken by the civilian attorney general, Gatot Tarunamihardja SH. As the scandal

---

Mahiddin Mahmud, *Who's Who in Indonesia*, 2nd ed. (Singapore: Gunung Agung, 1980), p. 225.

36. Djatikusumo interview, March 9, 1981.

37. Sukendro interview, July 10, 1981. According to Sukendro, the idea to set up such a body "came from our side" and was approved by the Menpangad.

unfolded, an attempt was made on Gatot's life, leading to suggestions that Sukendro had been involved.

The following year Sukendro emerged as an active backer of the Liga Demokrasi, an organization established to resist Sukarno's plans to curb the power of Parliament. When the league was banned in 1961, the staunchly anti-Communist Sukendro was dismissed from his position and sent abroad. Sukarno brought him back from virtual exile in late 1963, and in September 1964 appointed him minister of state for the Supreme Command for Economic Operations (Kotoe). Sukendro, very surprised to be recalled, felt that Sukarno may have wanted him in the cabinet to "balance" Njoto, a key PKI leader who had been appointed the previous month as one of three ministers seconded to the Presidium and whose importance would soon grow when he became a senior aide to the president. This is entirely plausible. However, it has also been suggested that Sukarno wanted Sukendro to keep an eye on the smuggling and intelligence activities of Kostrad, the Army Strategic Reserve Command, now headed by Suharto, with Ali Murtopo as his intelligence officer, the idea being that Sukarno was working on the principle that one should set a thief to watch a thief. This too is possible. There were more than superficial similarities between Sukendro and Ali Murtopo, and to some extent the former served as "Nasution's Ali Murtopo." Both men had had long careers in army intelligence and both were viewed as devious and unscrupulous. Both had been involved in smuggling activities in the late 1950s and both were involved in putting out secret feelers to the Malaysian government over Confrontation, Sukendro on behalf of Sukarno, Ali Murtopo on behalf of Suharto and, indirectly, the army commander, General Yani. (In the end, Ali Murtopo's efforts in this area were crowned with success, while those of Sukendro failed, although Ali's success doubtlessly owed much to the fact that he had more freedom of manoeuver than Sukendro, whose mission was merely to explore the possibility of a new summit meeting.)

When Sukarno was eclipsed by Suharto, Sukendro's days were obviously numbered, and in fact the former intelligence chief was arrested in mid-1967 and jailed for nearly nine months. In the view of some senior officers, the ebullient Sukendro was an unreconstructed Sukarnoist, a suggestion which is not entirely persuasive given his implacable opposition to Sukarno's Nasakom concept in the late 1950s and his subsequent exile abroad. In any event, Sukendro certainly had no time for either Suharto or Ali Murtopo, and his appointment as head of the economic grouping within the Team Poleksos can only be seen as a crumb thrown his way by Suharto's New Order associates.

During the 1970s, Sukendro's business interests prospered and he became in time the president of the holding company of a number of enterprises run by the Central Java provincial government. Members of the ruling group, however, were never entirely sure that Sukendro was confining himself to the business sector and, knowing that Sukendro had no time for them and that he still had the capacity to cause considerable mischief if he chose, tended to see his hand in every manifestation of opposition to their rule. Sukendro, in the words of a close associate of Ali Murtopo, was "always a subversive."[38] A Western military attaché who had known him for many years took a wry--but not altogether different--view. "He's so tricky," he said, "he couldn't lie straight in bed. He was always an intelligence man and people always wonder what he is up to. You could offer him a nine-to-five job and he wouldn't take it. He'd rather be doing his own thing."[39]

Though he seemed genuine enough in his expressions of concern about the constrictiveness of New Order policies towards the democratic processes, the rigidity of the Suharto group's interpretation of Pancasila, and the constraints imposed upon Islamic groups, Sukendro also gave the impression at times that he was an old fox who liked to be out, leading the Hankam hounds a chase, for the sheer pleasure it gave him. There was a certain whimsy in his behavior, a savoring of the minor irritations his group of "seniors" were able to cause those in power. Aware of how the Suharto generals viewed him, he tended nonetheless to be philosophical, choosing to interpret their suspicions as a consequence of his success as an intelligence officer in the late 1950s. Indeed, General Sumitro is said to have assured him that this was the case.

> According to Sumitro, it is due to my achievements in the past in the intelligence field. So they always consider that whatever the event, whether it be riots or anything else, there must be a connection with Sukendro. That's what Sumitro told me. He added about my achievements: 'There is no intelligence officer up to now who is greater than you.' That is why I am always suspected.[40]

By 1977, Sukendro's activities had become a matter of considerable concern to the government, and Lt. Gen. Widodo, the commander of Kowilhan II, was instructed by Kopkamtib in Jakarta to find out what the former army intelligence chief was up to; Sukendro, Widodo was told, was involved in "many actions against the government."[41] In the course of his preliminary enquiries, Widodo asked the governor of Central Java, Maj. Gen. Supardjo Rustam, about Sukendro. (Sukendro, in his capacity as the head of the *perusahaan daerah* [regional enterprises] of the Central Java government, commuted frequently between Jakarta and Semarang.) Supardjo suggested that it would be better if Widodo contacted Sukendro directly, a course of

---

38. Interview with Jusuf Wanandi, June 7, 1979. On another occasion (June 7, 1980), Wanandi observed that Sukendro was "always a schemer."

39. Confidential communication, January 9, 1980.

40. Interview with Maj. Gen. Sukendro, July 30, 1981.

41. Ibid.

action which Widodo duly followed. Not long afterwards, on November 24, 1977, Widodo "invited" Sukendro to his home in Semarang for a talk. ("You could consider it an interview or an interrogation," Sukendro recalled with some amusement.) Whatever the format, the meeting apparently proved useful to both men. Sukendro had first met Widodo in the tense days of January 1966 when, as a brigadier general, he had been accompanied on an inspection of the student situation in Semarang by Lt. Col. Widodo.

Although Widodo told his visitor that the Suharto group had received information that Sukendro was involved in numerous activities against the government, the meeting, which ran for nearly three hours, appears to have been cordial. Sukendro, aware that Widodo was being spoken of as the next chief of staff of the army, found this a useful opportunity to present his views on the current situation, and suggested to his host the usefulness of a "forum" for communication between retired officers and the current military leadership. Widodo, he felt, was close to Suharto, and, as it had also been his experience that Widodo was always receptive to new ideas, he felt that he might be able to "sell" some of his social-political thoughts to the leadership via this channel. Widodo, he says, agreed on the need for a study group of the kind proposed, and promised that he would in fact set up such a forum if he were to become Kasad.

In some ways, Widodo was well placed to serve as a lightning rod for the discontent of retired officers, notwithstanding the fact that he had, in earlier years, been very much eclipsed by some of the senior officers with whom he would now come in contact. He shared a number of these officers' concerns and privately acknowledged, as Murdani, Yoga, and others of that ilk refused to do, that the armed forces had become altogether too dominant and that this was not healthy for Indonesian democracy. But it would be wrong to see Widodo as no more than an honest broker between active and retired officers. At the time, the Kowilhan II commander was widely seen as an up-and-coming figure in the armed forces and even spoken of in some quarters as a possible future president. He was a man of many facets, authoritarian, ambitious, and with intellectual pretensions, and his motives were almost certainly more complex than they appeared. It is entirely possible that he saw himself as someone who had a chance to be the next president, and that he was looking for political support and a "new image" as open-minded in the pursuit of this objective, in much the same way that General Sumitro had sought to polish his image in 1973. Certainly it was felt by others that he was cultivating a constituency, not least by Ali Murtopo and Benny Murdani, who always insisted, perhaps correctly, that Widodo's only claim to fame was his long association with Suharto, and that without the president's backing he would never have reached such heights in the first place. In the end, Widodo's efforts would prove counterproductive. He failed to persuade many people of his new-found intellectualism--the surpassing mediocrity of the inputs from his Gajah Mada "think tank" did not help--and his much-vaunted interest in a more puritanical approach and a clean officer corps dedicated to serving the people not only rang hollow in view of his own business interests in Yogyakarta, but was perceived as indirect criticism of the president and his family.

The son of a retired, low-ranking retainer in the Yogyakarta kraton, Widodo had trained as a platoon-leader under the Japanese in Bandung before being assigned to a unit of the Peta in Yogyakarta. In 1945 he was the leader of one of the five companies which took part in the celebrated attack on the Japanese garrison in Kotabaru under the command of Suharto, then a Lt. Colonel. Unlike many of his contemporaries, Widodo rose very slowly through the ranks. He remained a captain for no less than eleven years--from 1945 to 1956. In 1957, after eighteen months as a student at SSKAD, he was appointed an SSKAD instructor, a position he held for eight years (1957-63). Among those he taught was his former battalion commander, Suharto. He served under Suharto once again in 1962, when he was appointed by the late Gen. Yani as chief of staff of the paratroop task force undertaking operations in West Irian as part of the Mandala Command. After two stints in the United States--at the infantry school at Fort Benning in 1960 and the Command and General Staff College at Fort Leavenworth in 1963--Widodo was assigned to Central Java. The plan was that he would serve as regimental commander in Yogyakarta. But when he reported for duty, the general staff of the Central Java military command in Semarang, an area in which the PKI wielded considerable power, refused to accept him. As a compromise, Widodo was assigned as a member of the staff of the local military commander, with special orders from Yani to report to Jakarta on Communist activities in Central Java. Widodo is said to have acted with initiative and despatch during the 1965 coup attempt, taking bold actions at a time of great uncertainty and at a time when the Diponegoro commander faltered. In the years since then he had progressed steadily, if unspectacularly, through the ranks.

The Growing Unrest on Campus

The other developments had taken place on the student front. Indonesian university students had been generally quiescent since the Malari crackdown in January 1974, but by mid-1976 they were showing signs of a new restlessness. What is more, there was an astringency in their criticism that had earlier been lacking. In 1970, the student movement had been concerned primarily with government corruption; its tone, as Rocamora has noted, was "moralistic and almost apolitical."[42] By the time of Malari, the area of student concern had expanded to include economic nationalism and the activities of Suharto's personal assistants. Now, it was Suharto himself who was under di-

---

42. See Joel Rocamora, "Excerpts from the 1978 Student White Book," Editors Note, *Southeast Asia Chronicle* (July-August 1978), p. 20.

rect attack. Campus parades mocked the corruption and greed of those in high office, the first family in particular, and student leaders called into question the whole basis of the president's development strategy. Early in 1977 there had been open student agitation on behalf of the PPP. Now, in mid-1977, Dipo Alam, former chairman of the University of Indonesia Student Council, thumbed his nose at the Suharto government by publicly "nominating" former Jakarta governor Ali Sadikin as the new president. "As each incident goes by unpunished," one commentator noted at the time, "the students become increasingly emboldened. They are very rambunctious at the moment and are really ready to do something. They are seeking the outer limits of dissent and they haven't found them yet. They are a little surprised by that."[43] Initially, the government did not seem particularly troubled by these developments, although Widodo noted in a speech at about this time that "a culture stressing opposition" was being created in society.[44] However, student discontent, so long bottled up, was something that could not be ignored very much longer.

In August, the minister of research, Dr. Sumitro Djojohadikusumo, led a team of seven technocrats in the cabinet on a campus "safari" aimed at explaining the government's long-term development goals. The plan was to establish a "dialogue" with the students, but this quickly backfired. The first round of talks between the Sumitro group and students, held at the University of Indonesia on August 3, set the tone for what was to be a series of noisy confrontations. Students concentrated on the abuse of power, unequal distribution of wealth, illegal levies, city bus fares, social injustice, the Pertamina affair, and the so-called commercialization of public office.

The situation was not much better in Yogyakarta five days later. About 1,000 students attended the meeting and grilled the ministers about the dual role of the armed forces. They also wanted to know why many civilian posts were staffed by nonprofessionals and why Kopkamtib had not been disbanded.

However, the worst setback came when the ministers went to the Pajajaran University in Bandung on August 13. Dr. Sumitro had just finished his introductory remarks when the students, instead of asking questions, read out a statement entitled "Attitude of Stupefaction." This said, among other things, that the students would not join the discussion because the dialogue would not ensure the settlement of what the general public sensed to be the real problems. The dialogue seemed designed to silence restlessness, they said, and as such would not solve any problems or eliminate any discontent.

The students then outlined conditions that would have to be met before they would agree to participate in any dialogue. These in-

---

43. See David Jenkins, "Stirrings on the campus," *Far Eastern Economic Review*, July 15, 1977.

44. Ibid.

cluded a guarantee that there would be a jointly written conclusion on every problem discussed, a subsequent evaluation of the steps taken by the government to execute the joint conclusion, and a provision for further meetings. Adding to the overall sense of confrontation were large posters, one of which proclaimed: "Eradicate corruption entirely--change the Government."

By mid-August, it was clear that the dialogues had been a failure, and had only served to highlight the depth of student discontent. Recognizing their failure, the government shelved its plans for further government-student meetings in Surabaya, Ujung Pandang, and at two centers in Sumatra. "The government is willing to have an open dialogue with the students," Dr. Sumitro said later, "but if they try to force their will as a starting point for political movements, the government will have no other alternative but to deal with them sternly."[45] This sentiment was echoed by President Suharto in his National Day speech the following day. Given the circumstances, it was probably unrealistic to imagine that the government-student dialogue could be productive. The students understood from the start that no real "dialogue" was intended by the government, and many felt that Sumitro's abrasive and arrogant personality only underlined this.

In November, the president was subjected to stinging student criticism over allegations that his family was spending US$9.6 million on an elaborate mausoleum on a royal burial hill in Central Java. At a student rally in Jakarta, ostensibly to mark National Heroes' Day, antiriot troops seized sixty-eight banners and placards on the grounds that they were "not in line with the spirit of the Heroes' Day celebration." One placard read: "The people are hungry and the boss prepares his grave." Another said: "Heroes, look at the result of your sacrifice." A third asked Admiral Sudomo, who was at that time conducting a well-publicized antigraft campaign, when "the boss" would be hit. At a similar rally in Bandung, one poster said pointedly: "It is not the ideal of a hero to buy a mountain." In Surabaya there was a placard which proclaimed: "The State is not the property of Auntie Sun," an obvious tilt at the first lady, Madame Tien Suharto, who had been accused of questionable business dealings and who was often likened to the avaricious, nouveau riche "Auntie Sun" featured in a popular song of the time.

The day after the demonstrations, President Suharto summoned top military and civilian leaders to the palace for a three-hour review of the security situation in the country. He instructed the officials to be "alert and prepared," especially because of the actions of "a small part of the population lately."[46] There was no direct mention

---

45. See David Jenkins, "Campus 'gibberish' halts dialogue," FEER, September 2, 1977.

46. See David Jenkins, "A chorus of critics for Suharto," FEER, December 9, 1977.

of the students, but the president was known to have been deeply stung by the taunts about the family mausoleum; several days later a detailed rebuttal of the charges was published by Antara, the national news agency. According to Antara, the development of the mausoleum was being carried out by a private foundation and not by the presidential family. The cost was not US$9.6 million, it said, but "only" US$1 million.[47]

Towards the end of November, the president addressed himself personally to the question of student demonstrations. In a meeting with sixteen university rectors, Suharto said that student actions were "still within the limits of propriety" but cautioned that freedom of speech could only exist if people acted responsibly and within limits.[48] He then asked the rectors to explain to the students that the mausoleum was not his private property and gave them each a booklet on the Mausoleum Building Foundation and its work. He also denied publicly that his son Sigit had bought a US$3.3 million Jakarta mansion from wealthy Indonesian businessman Hasyim Ning, described as a "fishing mate" of the Head of State.

This was the sixth time in as many years that the president had felt constrained to deny allegations of personal or family wrongdoing, and some people were concerned that the continuing student attacks, which were getting bolder and increasingly personal, might drive him into a corner. In 1971, the president had thrown away his prepared notes at the dedication of the new Pertamina hospital in Jakarta and threatened to bring down the full weight of the armed forces against students who continued to demonstrate against the controversial Mini Indonesia project being built by Madame Suharto.

A New Wave of Criticism

If the student criticism was bad, there was worse to come. Four days after the Heroes' Day marches, Lt. Gen. Alamsjah, the deputy chairman of the Supreme Advisory Council (DPA), delivered a speech which was unusually critical of the New Order regime. Speaking in Menado on behalf of the twenty-seven-man council, Alamsjah said that it was necessary to acknowledge that efforts to fulfill revolutionary aspirations were far from realized. Constitutional life remained unstable and law reform had not been carried out. Each year, said Alamsjah, the workforce increased by 1.4 million people. Yet development efforts during two five-year plans had not provided any significant hope. The social gap was still widening, "particularly since the start of the development efforts."

"This imbalance is not only between the rich and the poor but also between urban and rural, between the capital and the regions,

---

47. *Antara* (November 1977).

48. *FEER*, December 9, 1977.

and between the regions." Foreign and domestic investment had struck at the businesses of the little man and the middleman and the question of land ownership had become acute. There were food shortages in areas which had long been known as major granaries. There was rampant crime in certain areas, scandals and manipulations, smuggling, bribery, credit blockages, and misuse of authority. Indonesia was importing commodities such as corn, soyabeans, copra, and sugar, which it once exported. The country was supposed to have been self-sufficient in rice in 1973 but it was feared that by 1985 it would be importing five million tons a year.

It was not surprising, Alamsjah said, that students, the young generation, political parties, and community leaders were expressing unrest and discontent. Political education was neglected and every day one could see inequalities in the way the government upheld the law.[49]

In the past, individual members of the DPA had made similar criticisms of Government policy. But this was a collective broadside, delivered in the name of the council as a whole, and it gave rise to intensive speculation. Much of this centered on Alamsjah, who was said to have become disenchanted with Suharto. The statement about the widening gap between rich and poor, it was suggested, indicated this. In his National Day speech in August, the president had gone out of his way to say that the gap was being narrowed. Now, in a speech which reflected the thinking of some of the nation's most distinguished elder statesmen, came an observation directly to the contrary. Some people, it was suggested, were preparing to leave the sinking ship.

There is, in fact, little evidence that this was the case. Alamsjah and Suharto had been friends since early 1960 when the former, a lieutenant colonel who had recently arrived in Jakarta from South Sumatra, was an assistant to Brig. Gen. Suharto, at that time deputy I (Research and Development) to the chief of staff/army commander. The friendship, based partly on the fact that Suharto and Alamsjah were both "outsiders" who felt they were treated with condescension by better-educated fellow officers at army headquarters,[50] had strengthened in the years that followed. And although Alamsjah had had his ups and downs, his loyalty to Suharto had never been in question. Alamsjah was, by his own account, well aware that the content of the speech was sensitive, and says that for this reason he had reported to Suharto before Menado and received his permission to make the speech. "I am a military politician," Alamsjah said. "I

---

49. The Alamsjah speech, which was a cut-and-paste version of the annual DPA report to President Suharto, was delivered at the national conference of the Association of Indonesian Social Scientists (Himpunan Ilmiawan Pengetahuan Sosial, or Hipis) in Menado on November 14, 1977.

50. Interview with Lt. Gen. Alamsjah, March 20, 1982.

knew the situation. There were many issues that could be used against him [Suharto]."[51] The president, he says, gave his permission for him to raise these matters and was not angry or upset by the speech.

Be that as it may, both men seem to have been taken aback by the reaction to the speech. According to one account, Alamsjah subsequently told members of the DPA that the incident had been blown out of all proportion, and that "the Christians" were conspiring against him; the speech had only been intended for social scientists and yet it had been reported virtually in its entirety by the Jakarta daily *Sinar Harapan*, a paper associated with the Protestant Church.[52] In fact, the coverage given to the Menado speech probably had more to do with the vagaries of journalism than with any attempt by the Christians to undermine Alamsjah. Very much surprised by the critical tone of the address, the deputy chief editor of *Sinar Harapan*, Sabam Siagian, sent a full report to his office in Jakarta, along with a request to the front page editor of the morning (Outer Island) editions to put a restrained headline on the item. This was done, but the editor of the main afternoon editions of the paper, with an eye on street sales, ran the item under a banner headline reading: "Alamsjah di Menado--Gap Sosial Melebar" ("Alamsjah in Menado--Social Gap Widens"), which is said to have prompted an angry Suharto to instruct State Secretary Sudharmono to find out just what Alamsjah was saying.[53]

At the same time, it is possible that Alamsjah, knowing that the speech was bound to attract attention and having his eye on a position in the soon-to-be-formed Third Development Cabinet, used the occasion as a way out of reminding Suharto, boldly but not too boldly, of his presence. If this interpretation is right, then Alamsjah played his cards well. At 11 p.m. on March 23, 1978, barely four months after the Menado speech, Alamsjah was summoned by Suharto and offered the Religious Affairs portfolio. According to this interpretation, Alamsjah was known well to Suharto, Ali Murtopo, Sudomo, and Yoga as a man who was ambitious, not particularly bright, not scrupulous, and not dangerous. If the president wanted to put an army man and a Suharto man into the Religion Ministry, it is suggested, the only other plausible candidate would have been General Mohammad Jusuf, at that time minister of industry. As events were to show, Suharto had Jusuf in mind as minister of defense. By appointing Alamsjah to the post, it is argued, the president was able both to silence him effectively *and* tighten his own grip on the Religion Ministry in a difficult year.[54]

---

51. Interview with Lt. Gen. Alamsjah, March 24, 1982.

52. Confidential communication, April 1982.

53. Ibid.

54. I am indebted to Prof. Ben Anderson for making this point. It has been suggested in some circles that Suharto offered Alamsjah the religion portfolio simply to "buy him off." This seems unlikely.

Meanwhile, Muslim youth groups were joining the campaign against the alleged shortcomings of the regime. Placards called on the security forces to "investigate the Rupiah 4,500 million (US$10.85 million) grave" and spoke of "hell for the greedy" when a large religious rally was held in Jakarta late in November.[55] These criticisms were well covered in the local press. Unable to say the sort of things the students were saying, the papers took a vicarious delight in reporting fully and faithfully the mounting attack on the honesty and probity of the Head of State. At one stage it almost seemed as though government-controlled newspapers were doing some sniping of their own. Two days after the Heroes Day demonstrations, an article in *Angkatan Bersenjata*, the official armed forces daily, made a forceful, if elliptical, plea to Suharto and the army leadership to wind up the period of rule of the 1945 Generation and hand over honorably to their successors in the next few years. *Angkatan Bersenjata* was generally a vehicle for news about army promotions and laudatory features about the achievements of the army-backed government. But in this carefully argued "think piece," the writer, who used the *nom de plume* Abu Firman, dealt publicly with political succession, generally considered a "taboo" subject.

The theme of the article was that it was most important for anyone finishing an enterprise, whether a painting, their life, or the work of a generation, to get the finishing touch right. This could only be done if the person or group concerned listened to the advice and opinions of others and was aware of his or their own faults. The author applied this generalization to the 1945 Generation. Although the situation was still calm, the people were dissatisfied with their leaders and, if one was honest, one could see the people's deep restlessness and worry. Some of this restlessness had been engineered for political purposes but most of it was genuine concern (for the good of the country) and based on altruistic motives.

At the meeting with Suharto on March 23, Alamsjah says, Suharto, looking somber, made the observation that religion was the biggest problem facing the nation and that he, Alamsjah, knew the government's policies and was the only man who could do the job. Suharto reportedly said that Alamsjah not only had his trust as president but also had the trust of, and was acceptable to, "the largest religious group." He was, moreover, an armed forces man. Interview with Lt. Gen. Alamsjah, March 24, 1982.

Well before the Menado speech, Suharto seems to have decided that Jusuf should serve as minister of defense/commander of the armed forces in the next cabinet. According to Jusuf, the president first sounded him out about this job in August 1977, a good seven months before the new cabinet was announced. He is said to have mentioned the idea again in November 1977 and in January 1978. Interview with General Jusuf, July 25, 1979.

55. *FEER*, December 9, 1977.

The 1945 Generation should cleanse themselves prior to the early 1980s and their handover to their successors. They had a tendency to want to see physical evidence of their efforts to develop the country, and this tendency could be understood and praised. But if their efforts to promote physical development were accompanied by the pursuit of personal interests, this was a disgrace. "The moral patterns of the Constitution and Pancasila have been brought into disrepute," the article said. "It is always dangerous when the leaders appear to enjoy their power."

There was a lesson to be taken from the Bharata Yudha, the article continued, where King Abiyasa of Astina Pura, who was not entranced into enjoying his power, handed it over to his two sons, Destarata and Dewanata, and took on the role of "wise elder," respected by all because he had been clean and scandal-free during his reign. King Abiyasa was contrasted in the article with King Duryudana whose practices were bad and whose decisions were dictated by greed. Civil war became inevitable, and the Pandawas, although his cousins, fought him to defend justice and truth. They won because right was on their side. Thus King Abiyasa was capable of putting the right finishing touch to his reign, but King Duryudana could not do so and was destroyed by his cousins. The article finished with the sentence "let us take note of this."[56]

That rather pointed parable, with its allusions to the contemporary political scene, not unnaturally drew a good deal of comment. This was not the first time that *Angkatan Bersenjata* had published an article along these lines. But with the presidential elections just over the horizon and critics zeroing in on the actions of the president and his family it raised many eyebrows.[57]

In the midst of these developments, troubling enough in themselves for those in the government, Suharto received a bizarre report that "some brigades" were behind Nasution and were ready to back the student leaders. The details of this affair are not entirely clear.[58] However, it appears that a deputation of student leaders

56. *Angkatan Bersenjata*, November 12, 1977. It is interesting to note that exactly the same proposal was put to Sukarno in early 1967. See Crouch, *Army and Politics*, p. 215.

57. The identity of "Abu Firman" was never revealed. However, a senior member of the newspaper staff told the author that Abu Firman was a name used by a number of individual writers. (Interview, May 3, 1980.) There were no articles by Abu Firman for some months after the King Abiyasa story although the column eventually reappeared; there had been a number of columns under this name in the preceding period.

58. The following account is based on a report in *Merdeka* on December 22, 1977, and interviews with Nasution on March 2, 1981 and November 10, 1981.

from Bandung--including Iqbal, the acting chairman of the Bandung Institute of Technology (ITB) Students Council--allegedly told a secret student meeting at the Surabaya Institute of Technology (ITS) that Nasution had informed them that "some brigades" were behind him, and that he was sure these troops were prepared to assist the student cause. An informer in the student ranks reported on this development to the commander of the Brawijaya military region, Maj. Gen. Witarmin, and he in turn informed the army chief of staff, General Makmun Murod. On November 20, when Nasution arrived at Yogyakarta to address a gathering at Gajah Mada University, he was surprised to find the local Korem (Military Resort Command) commander, Colonel Sitorus, waiting to meet him at the airport. Also present was the assistant I (Intelligence) of the Diponegoro (Central Java) military command, another colonel. These two officers, who represented the panglima (commander) of the Diponegoro, presented the former minister of defense with a copy of the official history of the Diponegoro. Then, in a discussion with him in the airport VIP room, they told him of the report from Surabaya and said they would like to know more about the matter. Nasution says he was surprised by the report, which had no basis whatsoever. Because the conversation was being followed by students who were clustered around the open door of the VIP room, Nasution says, he took the opportunity of pointing out, in a voice loud enough for them to hear, that he could never condone the idea of ABRI troops giving such an undertaking. He had always taught, he said, that, under the Sapta Marga, a military man did not fight for any individual but for ideals and principles. The two Diponegoro colonels seemed satisfied by this explanation and the meeting ended amicably.

Suharto, however, was not at all satisfied. While Nasution was still traveling in Central and East Java the president summoned Makmun Murod and the members of the Army General Staff to Bina Graha, the presidential office block. At the meeting, Suharto demanded to know how far it was true that some brigades were loyal to Nasution. Makmun Murod assured the president that this was out of the question and that he knew nothing that would justify such a conclusion. Suharto insisted that this was what the intelligence report had said. When Makmun Murod gave a guarantee that the report could not possibly be accurate, Suharto apparently accepted the fact. However, he made the point that several army colonels were still attached to Nasution, an officer who had been pensioned off and who no longer had any official function. Suharto ordered Makmun Murod to withdraw these officers at once, stressing that Nasution "has no right to have army men there." This order was carried out immediately. When Nasution returned to Jakarta he received a visit from a colonel sent by the assistant I (Intelligence) of the army, Maj. Gen. Harsoyo, informing him of the meeting between the president and the senior army officers and of the discussions that had taken place concerning the report about his alleged remarks to the students. The director of personnel at Hankam also called on him to inform him about the implementation of the president's order concerning his secretary.

Later, in mid-December, Nasution received a third official visit, this one from Maj. Gen. Himawan Sutanto, the commander of the Siliwangi. Speaking as "a son to a father,"[59] Himawan told Nasution of a new intelligence report, this one concerning a discussion by representatives of all Indonesia's student councils in Bandung in connection with Youth Pledge Day. According to the Siliwangi commander, a student leader from Parahiyangan University had reported to the intelligence section that Nasution had expressed the people's dissatisfaction and had said that ABRI was similarly dissatisfied with the present situation, and that part of ABRI might be joining the students' actions. Himawan indicated, respectfully and obliquely, that it would be helpful if everyone were to remain within acceptable limits. Nasution responded that the intelligence report, like the one he had been told of in Yogyakarta, was without foundation and came as a complete surprise to him. In comments published by *Merdeka* on December 22, he said that he had been framed twice recently.[60]

On top of all this, rumors had begun to circulate that General Surono, the deputy commander of the armed forces, was mounting some sort of challenge to Suharto and encouraging the students in their endeavors. A year earlier, Surono had, unbeknownest to himself, been implicated in the socalled Sawito Affair, a bizarre plot by Sawito Kartowibowo, a retired official and part-time mystic, to force Suharto from office. In documents drawn up by Sawito, Surono was listed as one of four advisers who would assist the former vice president, Dr. Mohammad Hatta, run Indonesia after Hatta had received a transfer of authority from Suharto. The fact that Surono's name had been included among Sawito's advisers, although kept secret at the time, may have accounted for some of the more persistent rumors about Surono now.[61] The new rumors were not particularly persua-

---

59. Interview with General Nasution, March 2, 1981. The account of Suharto's meeting with Makmun Murod was given by General Nasution in an interview on March 2, 1981 and in written comments on November 14, 1981. Nasution based this account on what he was told by the colonel sent by Maj. Gen. Harsoyo and by other sources.

60. *Merdeka*, December 22, 1977. Details of the various meetings with ABRI officials were outlined by Nasution in written comments on November 14, 1981.

61. During his interrogation, Sawito said that his group had been hoping for the support of certain generals. When asked which generals, he answered, "Surono." There was no suggestion then or at any other time that Sawito had contacted Surono or that the deputy commander of the armed forces had any sympathy for his efforts. Sawito's reference to Surono was passed on to Suharto, without any effort being made to ask Surono whether in fact he was involved. Surono was hurt and embarrassed at the apparent lack of trust in him that this evinced. (Confidential communication, March 23, 1982.)

There is some (not very persuasive) evidence that at about this time Suharto may have viewed Surono as a possible successor. After

sive--Surono was viewed by his colleagues as a straightforward military man who was genuinely apolitical--but the talk about growing splits in the military ranks, with all the memories that invoked of the Malari riots, was enough to persuade Suharto that something had to be done.

The Official Response

Stung by the gathering criticism and by the report about the two brigades, the president called in the defense minister, General Maraden Panggabean, the army chief of staff, General Makmun Murod, and other top military aides and let them know, in oblique but unmistakable fashion, that he would appreciate a show of support.[62] At the meeting, Suharto reminded his generals that he had not sought the presidency. However, he said, he had been given the task and would carry it out to the best of his ability. The recent criticism, if allowed to continue unchecked, would weaken the office of the presidency and make things difficult for whoever followed him in the job.[63]

---

he had completed his term as Governor of West Java in 1975, Lt. Gen. Solichin settled on a farm south of Sukabumi. One of his early visitors was Suharto, who complimented him on the way he had handled himself after retirement. Suharto expressed the wish to be a farmer himself soon, after his retirement. He confided to Solichin that Surono was being groomed as heir apparent. According to Solichin, who gave this account to an old friend, Suharto sounded genuine. This incident occurred in 1976. (Confidential communication, March 25, 1982.)

62. Interview with Jusuf Wanandi, December 1977.

63. Ibid. There were persistent rumors at the time that a number of senior army officers were reconsidering their support for Suharto. The evidence suggests that these rumors were not entirely unfounded. Although nothing was said openly, there were informal discussions about the possibility of a change in the leadership. At the same time, the author has been able to find no senior officer, active or retired, who puts any credence on suggestions that Surono might have mounted a challenge to Suharto at the time. (In 1980-1981, when his name was sometimes put forward as a possible compromise army candidate for the presidency should anything happen to Suharto, the general feeling was that Surono would not be interested, and would prefer to see someone else take the job.) Nasution says that the army leadership had agreed at the Commanders Call *before* the 1977 general elections that Suharto and the vice president, Sultan Hamengku Buwono IX, would stand again. (Interview, May 10, 1979.) The Sultan, of course, withdrew at the eleventh hour as a result of his own private disenchantment with Suharto.

Taking his cue from this, Panggabean summoned the nation's top military leaders to a meeting at the Defense Ministry on December 13. The group emerged forty-eight hours later with a pledge that the army would take strong action against anyone threatening the "national leadership."[64] Initially, the meeting had been restricted to senior service officers in ABRI. But after two hours of talks, these men decided to call in fellow generals serving in a kekaryaan (nonmilitary) capacity in the cabinet. Among the newcomers were the minister for home affairs, General Amir Machmud, and the minister for industry, General Mohammad Jusuf, the two surviving "kingmakers" who had persuaded President Sukarno to transfer authority to Suharto in March 1966.[65] Now a gathering of twenty-five generals, the meeting ran for another six hours until a basic agreement was reached on policy. The following day, the service officers continued alone, hammering out matters concerning the implementation of the policies drawn up. Then, after a final discussion with the president, Panggabean called a press conference to announce what Suharto was later to describe as a "brotherly warning."[66] (Significantly, Widodo was among those who felt there was no need for ABRI to give any such "warning" to the populace.)[67]

With the conference over, Panggabean invited a number of prominent retired generals to Hankam, with the aim, apparently, of giving the impression that these officers were somehow in agreement with the policy statement that was being issued.[68] However, the re-

64. A retired army officer who spoke to one of the participants was told that the pledge had more the characteristics of a "command decision." Confidential communication, July 27, 1981. At the time, there was a good deal of speculation over the wording of this statement, some analysts concluding that the pledge of support for the "national leadership" was a rebuff to the president, who was not referred to by name. This was not necessarily the case. Senior army officers argue, quite plausibly, that their loyalty is to the system and the institutions, not to any individual.

65. These two officers had been promoted to full general several months before the meeting. Some prominent army leaders, including General Sumitro, were forceful opponents of the procedure of awarding military promotions to officers serving in a nonmilitary capacity.

66. *Kompas*, December 17, 1977.

67. Interview with General Widodo, November 17, 1981.

68. According to a booklet issued by members of the "ex-Fosko" group in 1980, "the original idea of a communications forum came up at the time when General M. Panggabean held a briefing on December 14, 1977, concerning the plans of the ABRI leadership to face up to the flare-up in the populace, particularly among the students. At the time it was suggested that it was important to have a communications forum, especially between retired senior officers and those who

tired generals refused to be a party to this. Having had no opportunity to help shape the statement, they were in no mood to give it
their automatic endorsement. There had been no participation by retired army officers, Sudirman and several others told Panggabean,
and no consultation.[69]

Faced with truculent "seniors" and evidently feeling a need to
placate this group and have them on side, Panggabean agreed to set
up a suitable channel of communication. Not long afterwards, General
Darjatmo called Sudirman and suggested that a forum be set up to improve communication between serving and retired officers. Sudirman,
who felt that this was a good idea, discussed the suggestion with
Sukendro who had only recently put such an idea to General Widodo.
Sukendro, he found, was also in agreement.

Sudirman accepted Darjatmo's view that Pepabri, the association
of retired military personnel, would be an appropriate vehicle for this
communication--but only on condition that certain changes were made
in its structure. Later, with Panggabean's approval, discussions
were arranged with Colonel (retd.) Iskandar Widyapranata, the general chairman of Pepabri. Before this meeting took place, however,
five retired officers--Sukendro, Lt. Gen. Jasin, Brig. Gen. Abimanju, Col. Alex Kawilarang, and Brig. Gen. Agus Prasmono--met at
Sudirman's home to discuss the matter. (Lt. Gen. Mokoginta, although invited, was unable to attend.)[70] At this meeting it was decided that Pepabri should not be used as a vehicle for communication
as long as it remained in its existing form. Pepabri had, at that
time, been a member of the *keluarga besar Golkar* (big Golkar family)
for more than a year, and the retired officers wanted to express
their views through an open and independent body. Another reason
why this initiative did not succeed was because Pepabri was more
concerned with the social problems of retired military men. The

were still active. General Darjatmo, who was at that time still serv-
ing as Kaskar, was very much in agreement with this idea." *Apakah
Forum Komunikasi dan Studi Purna Yudha Itu?* (Jakarta: Sekretariat
FKS Purna Yudha, 1980) henceforth *Fosko Brosur 1980.*

69. Born in East Java in 1913, Sudirman had been panglima Brawijaya (1952-56) and later commander of Seskoad in Bandung. A devout Muslim, he was active in his retirement in the *Perguruan Tinggi
Dakwah Islam* (Islamic Mission of Higher Education). The PTDI was
established by Nasution as an army-backed counter to the People's
Universities (*Universitas Rakyat*, UNRA) which had been set up by
the PKI at the kabupaten level. See: *The Indonesian Military
Leaders: Biographical and Other Background Data*, 2nd ed. (Jakarta:
Sritua Arief Associates, 1979), pp. 264-65.

70. In an interview (March 15, 1982) Maj. Gen. Sukendro said that
Lt. Gen. Djatikusumo was present at this meeting. However, Brig.
Gen. Abimanju is emphatic that Djatikusumo was not there. (Inter-
view, March 7, 1982.)

reform-minded officers were anxious to deal not just with social problems but with political, economic, cultural, and legal ones as well.[71]
Finally, Pepabri included pensioned members of the KNIL (Royal
Netherlands Indies Army) that the TNI had taken over in 1950, and
there were those who could not accept these people as fighters
(*pejuang*).

In the meantime, the ruling group had had second thoughts
about using Pepabri as a communications channel. Widyapranata,
having received the green light from Hankam, had invited about
eighty retired military officers to submit their views at a special session of the Pepabri.[72] However, a dispute broke out when Widyapranata said he could not follow a Hankam instruction that he control
the direction of the debate of the retired seniors and ensure that
their conclusions were in line with guidelines provided by the Ministry. "I cannot do this," Widyapranata told an officer from Hankam.
"They are my seniors."[73] Because of this, Hankam cancelled the
meeting.

As the efforts to set up a communications channel continued, a
storm broke over a speech in which Lt. Gen. H. R. Dharsono, the
former commander of the Siliwangi (West Java) military region and at
that time secretary general of the five-nation Association of Southeast
Asian Nations (ASEAN), had called on the armed forces to be more
attentive to public unease. Addressing members of the Generation of
'66 in Bandung in mid-January 1978, Dharsono said that the most important thing was for the armed forces leaders to listen to the aspirations of the common people. If they continued to rely on military
power and strength, he said, people would obey out of fear, not
love. The people were growing restive and their recent appeals suggested that there was something improper in their relations with
ABRI. The New Order had diverted from its original ideals and
needed redirecting.[74] Although Dharsono had stressed that he was
speaking in a private capacity, his criticism was too much for the
ruling group. Furious at this outburst, Panggabean summoned the
three-star officer and demanded that he apologize, as had other nonactive officers, including Lt. Gen. Kemal Idris, who had voiced simi-

71. There is no relation between the Veteran's Association (LVRI)
and Pepabri. All retired military men are, by law, veterans. However, not all of them become members of Pepabri.

72. Although invited, Nasution had not intended to go himself. Interview with General Nasution, May 10, 1979. In the event, the
meeting was cancelled by either Hankam or Kopkamtib.

73. Interview with Nasution, March 11, 1982. Mrs. Yani, widow of
the former army chief of staff, General Achmad Yani, was among
those invited to participate. She was angry when the government
cancelled the meeting.

74. *Antara*, January 17, 1978.

lar criticisms. When Dharsono refused, the government decided that he should be removed from his ASEAN position, a decision which entailed mounting a significant lobbying campaign amongst fellow members of the association. In the midst of these developments, the government decided to take swift and decisive action against its critics. On January 20 it closed down half a dozen leading newspapers and sent troops into university campuses to round up some of its more outspoken political opponents. This was seen by many as an over-reaction to the problem but was deemed necessary by armed forces leaders, who argued that, unless something were done to nip the growing unrest in the bud, the nation might be faced with another Malari-type disturbance.

As criticism of the government had mounted, the value of a communications channel for retired officers became increasingly apparent. And though Pepabri had been ruled out as a forum, the momentum already built up was not lost, neither the government nor the retired officers being anxious to see the failure of attempts to set up such a body. At a meeting with Sudomo on January 31, 1978, members of the new grouping delivered a report concerning the formation of a provisional forum. This body consisted of retired senior officers from the Brawijaya, Siliwangi, and Diponegoro military regions, together with some other "seniors" from outside Java. It was known, perhaps inevitably, as the "Brasildi Plus" group. Officially, it was for all retired army officers. In reality, it was for ex-members of the three big Java "divisions."[75]

Sudomo was strongly in favor of such a body.[76] But the real push, once the organization was off the ground, was to come from Widodo, who, as expected, had moved up from Kowilhan II to become army chief of staff. On April 12, 1978, Widodo announced the official existence of a "TNI Forum for Study and Communication," or, as it was more popularly known, "Fosko TNI-AD"[77] This was to be a sub-

---

75. Nasution interview, May 10, 1979. Strictly speaking, there had been no Siliwangi, Diponegoro, or Brawijaya "divisions" since 1948. These evocative names had been retained, however, when in the period 1957-1959 the seven Tentara dan Territorium (TT), or Troop and Area Commands, were transformed into seventeen regional military commands (Kodam). At that time TT III (West Java) became Kodam VI Siliwangi. TT IV (Central Java) became Kodam VII Diponegoro and TT V (East Java) became Kodam VIII Brawijaya. (Part of the former TT III was hived off to become Kodam V Jaya (Greater Jakarta.) A new staff and command structure ensured that younger officers were no longer identified with a particular "division" as an earlier generation had been. In the early 1970s, the South and Central Kalimantan Kodams were merged, reducing the number to sixteen.

76. See *Fosko Brosur 1980*, p. 8.

77. TNI-AD, i.e. Tentara Nasional Indonesia-Angkatan Darat (Indonesian National Army).

organization of the Yayasan Kartika Eka Pakci, an army foundation which was chaired by the chief of staff.[78]   In the months that fol- lowed, Widodo was to play a central role in coordinating and develop- ing the views of both the serving officers at Seskoad and the retired officers in Fosko.[79]   Widodo had been installed as chief of staff on January 26, 1978, six days after the Suharto government's crackdown on the opposition.   It was a tense and difficult time and the govern- ment actions had focused further attention on the question of ABRI's proper role in society.   And Widodo, though he won the respect and trust of those who sought to purify the system, may well have paid for this; when he was replaced as chief of staff barely two years later, there were many who felt that his involvement with Fosko had played at least some part in his downfall.

---

78.   *Fosko Brosur 1980*, p. 8.   See also "Surat Keputusan No.: 060/YKEP/1978," of the Yayasan Kartika Eka Pakci, Jl. Merdeka Utara 2, Jakarta, concerning the "Inauguration of the Organisational Struc- ture and Composition of the Board of the Forum for Study and Com- munication of the TNI."   This document was signed by Widodo in his capacity as chairman of the Dewan Pengurus, YKEP, on July 20, 1978.   When Nasution was pensioned in 1972, the chief of staff, Gen- eral Umar Wirahadikusumah, offered him the job of heading the YKEP with the aim of helping take care of the welfare of former TNI men in the widest sense.   However, Nasution declined.   (Interview with Gen- eral Nasution, July 27, 1981.)

79.   Ibid.

CHAPTER FOUR

THE CALL FOR PURIFICATION: FOSKO AND THE LKB

This effort achieved momentum with the appointment of Gen. Widodo as Kasad [army chief of staff]. Widodo tried diligently to provide a communications forum for retired officers.

--Gen. A. H. Nasution[1]

With official recognition and the sympathetic ear of the army chief of staff, Fosko blossomed. On July 21, 1978, Widodo sent a two-page letter to the newly installed minister of defense, General Mohammad Jusuf, reporting on the formation of the Forum for Study and Communication TNI and on developments to date.[2] In this letter, the chief of staff noted that, on being appointed Kasad, not only had he become responsible for the "organic" military but he had become chairman of the Kartika Eka Pakci Foundation (YKEP) as well. This foundation, which had been set up in August 1972 and which consisted of all former army chiefs of staff, had the task of making recommendations to the Kasad on "the maintenance of the ideological struggle of the army."[3] It was already managing the Achmad Yani Technical Academy, and Widodo noted that it had been considered appropriate for it to serve as a channel for the conveyance of social and political problems that might arise, both now and in the future. To this end, he had set up Fosko-TNI. All financial needs would be taken care of by funds from the YKEP but most of the personnel would be "senior Pati" TNI.[4] Although the forum had only been es-

---

1. General Nasution, in a written communication, July 27, 1981.

2. Letter from Kasad, General Widodo, to Menhankam/Pangab, Gen. Jusuf, No: 314/VIII/1978, July 21, 1978. Widodo was installed as chief of staff on January 26, 1978, just as Fosko was being organized. Jusuf was named defense minister on March 29, 1978.

3. Interview with General Widodo, November 17, 1981. The foundation counted many prominent generals among its members, including Umar Wirahadikusumah, Surono, Panggabean, and Suharto. According to Widodo, the members of the foundation met very infrequently --"maybe once in three years or once in five years." It was "very difficult to collect them" all in one place at one time.

4. Pati, an acronym for *Perwira Tinggi* (Senior Officers), meant officers of brigadier general rank upwards.

tablished a short time, he reported, it had already been able to send him reports in the form of working papers. "In my opinion," Widodo wrote, "the results are quite good and have been very useful to me in carrying out my duties as Chief of Staff."[5]

Considering that social-political developments occurred very quickly, Widodo said, he had authorized the Fosko group to contact the minister of defense; Lt. Gen. A. J. Mokoginta (retd.) had been appointed as the contact officer on behalf of the group, and had in fact held several meetings with the minister, one of which took place on June 8, 1978. In conclusion, Widodo said that he would like to report officially to Jusuf that the activities of the senior officers whose names were attached were valid according to law. It was necessary, he felt, to raise this matter so that in practice none of the people involved would encounter any difficulties or obstacles.

If Fosko had some high-level active officers among its supporters, its membership list also included the names of some distinguished, if sometimes prickly, former army leaders. The Fosko presidium consisted of Lt. Gen. G. P. H. Djatikusumo, Lt. Gen. Sudirman and Maj. Gen. Achmad Sukendro. The secretary general was Lt. Gen. H. R. Dharsono, who had come into the grouping almost immediately after being dropped as secretary general of ASEAN. The "political sector" consisted of Mokoginta and Brig. Gen. Daan Jahja. Lt. Gen. Mohammad Jasin was a member of the "economic sector" and Lt. Gen. Sugih Arto a member of the "legal sector." Col. Alex Kawilarang was one of the ordinary members.[6] Apart from Dharsono, who was new, the eighteen-man Fosko central leadership reproduced almost unchanged the membership of the loosely organized Brasildi discussion groups, the one notable exception being Brig. Gen. Abimanju, who had reservations about the political orientation of a number of the key retired officers in Fosko and who declined to join.

Given that Fosko was soon making some rather far-reaching, albeit discreet, suggestions to the ruling group about the need for more democracy and a reduction in the role of the armed forces, it should be said at once that none of the Fosko leaders had ever carved out a reputation as a flag-bearer of participatory democracy or advocate of a lower military profile while still in uniform. Most had been deeply involved in military politics for more than thirty years, and some of the more prominent leaders had earned themselves reputations as authoritarian men who brooked little or no interference in their affairs. Dharsono had been prepared to use the army's power to dragoon the political parties in West Java into two groups in the late 1960s. Jasin had been more than happy to take stern measures against the PNI and other parties in East Java in 1967. Mokoginta

---

5. Widodo letter, July 21, 1978.

6. See *Susunan Pengurus: Forum Studi dan Komunikasi TNI* (Jakarta, Yayasan Kartika Eka Pakci - Forum Studi dan Komunikasi TNI, [July 20], 1978).

had been known as a tough, even brutal, CPM (Military Police) man and had been very repressive when serving as interregional commander in Sumatra in the early New Order period. Sukendro, as we have seen, enjoyed a reputation as a devious and conspiratorial man with few moral scruples.

It should also be acknowledged that some of these retired officers were disenchanted with the ruling group for one reason or another, a factor which, some would later argue, cast doubt on their credibility as critics of government policy. As we have seen, Sukendro had little or no time for the Suharto group. Nor had Jasin, who had been passed over as army chief of staff in 1973 and who was offended by the government's refusal to do anything about the high level of corruption. Nor had Dharsono, who was still smarting from the humiliation he suffered when the government engineered his removal as secretary general of ASEAN. These factors notwithstanding, it would be wrong to take an overly cynical view of the calls for reform that were soon being put forward by the retired senior officers in Fosko. These men, whatever their past actions and present dislikes, gave every appearance of being genuinely concerned about the need to reform the system and in time they were able to persuade others, including a number of prominent, but skeptical, civilians, of their sincerity.

Certainly they wasted no time in getting down to business. Meetings were held at least once a week, and it was not long before recommendations from the Fosko presidium in Jakarta were arriving on Widodo's desk. In a letter to the army chief of staff on March 28, 1978, Djatikusumo, as chairman of the four-man Fosko daily board, forwarded an eight-page "memorandum" regarding a meeting of the senior officers with Widodo on March 9.[7] This Fosko memorandum

---

7. Letter of Djatikusumo to Widodo, March 28, 1978. This was the first of five "Working Papers" (*Kertas Kerja*) forwarded to Army Chief of Staff Widodo, henceforth cited as *Kertas Kerja I–V*. In Djatikusumo's letters to Widodo and in the Fosko working papers, the president was referred to as *Rekan* (comrade or colleague)--not as president, not as general, not even as *kawan*, the genuinely friendly word for "friend." "Rekan" here is rather chilly--almost "colleague"--and something of a putdown. Djatikusumo's use of the term *"Saudara"* in addressing Widodo is polite and "army-brotherly." Sundhaussen is wrong in suggesting that it would have been more "correct" to use the term "Bapak." Djatikusumo is significantly older, the son of a Javanese king, a distinguished revolutionary era commander and former army chief of staff, on every dimension Widodo's superior. Sundhaussen's statement that Djatikusumo could remind Widodo "of their common service in the Diponegoro division" is also incorrect. (See Sundhaussen, "Regime Crisis in Indonesia: Facts, Fiction, Predictions," *Asian Survey* 21 (August 1981): 827). Djatikusumo headed the Ronggolawe division which operated in the Semarang-Tuban north coastal area in 1945-47 before he went to head

noted that, although Suharto had been unanimously reelected for a third five-year term on March 23, the MPR session had taken place in an "atmosphere of war." The Fosko members hoped that their memorandum would be considered and would prove useful in reinstating the army's authority.

The major thrust of the memorandum was that the atmosphere of confrontation should be changed to a more normal atmosphere, from the top to the bottom, by eliminating feelings of fear, hatred, restlessness, apprehension, and so on. To do this would require high moral courage. At the same time, the memorandum noted, it was necessary to listen to what members of the younger generation were saying, especially those who had been active and vocal in disseminating "negative images." Once again, high moral courage was necessary (a) to face and talk with these people, (b) to acknowledge that which was true in what they were saying, and (c) to correct them by teaching them where their concepts were wrong. As the rector of the Bogor Institute of Agriculture (IPB), Prof. A. M. Satari had said, "in confronting the happenings that are now being faced by our schools of higher education we must display a mature attitude. It is not proper if we are carried along merely by emotions and frustration." Finally, it would be best, the Fosko document said, if the activities at the "Laboratorium Widodo" could begin, so that in the shortest period possible the restoration of the TNI-AD could be started scientifically.[8]

On May 20, 1978, less than two months later, Djatikusumo sent Widodo a thirteen-page "Second Working Paper" entitled "TNI and its Dual Function."[9] This document, perhaps the most important produced by the retired senior officers in Fosko, made three main points. First, it declared that while the dwifungsi had in principle been conceptually sound during a certain period in the national struggle, it should be studied and reviewed. Its realization needed immediate corrections, meaning that it should be adapted to the people's development. Second, political life in Indonesia should be disciplined, based on fundamental democratic principles, particularly equal opportunity for all groups to pursue their political ambitions. Finally, the TNI should be freed from involvement in the political parties and groups. It should return to its original position, one parallel to all the other groupings of national fighters in society, and not part of any one of those groups. Moreover, it was to be hoped that, because of its moral values, the TNI would remain above all groups (berada diatas semua golongan). In 1965 the PKI had not succeeded because the TNI still thought, acted, and had an attitude based on Sapta Marga and was not only a tool.

---

the academy in Yogyakarta. I am indebted to Ben Anderson for clarifying this point.

8. *Kertas Kerja I*, May 20, 1978.

9. Djatikusumo letter to Widodo, May 20, 1978.

The Fosko working paper concluded with three suggestions. First, the authors hoped that within the next year or two, by the end of 1979 at the very latest, the implementation of the dwifungsi principle would be corrected so that it went back as far as possible to its base. This would open the opportunity for the dwifungsi to continue to be merely a latent function of the TNI, implemented only as and when necessary. Second, the authors said that the current leadership should not force policy outlines and the values included in those outlines onto the new generation. Rather, it was to be hoped that an open, two-way dialogue with the future leadership generation would achieve a reciprocal understanding that could be used to bridge the generation gap and lessen tensions between generations. Finally, political life in society should be directed in a correct way so that political parties were not forced to function in a conformist fashion according to the desires of those in power.[10]

The issues raised in the May 20 Fosko paper--the need to review the dwifungsi doctrine and its implementation, the stress on the importance of democratic principles, and the reminder that ABRI should be above all groups in society, not siding with one group or another--are strikingly similar to those set forth in the Seskoad paper drawn up by Abdulkadir Besar. However, this was not a case of one group taking up and developing the ideas of another. Rather, it was an instance of different groups independently giving expression to ideas already abroad in the community. The Fosko paper was written by Dharsono, Sukendro, and Mokoginta, with Daan Jahja also playing a role. Yet Dharsono says that neither he nor his colleagues had seen the Seskoad paper at the time they put down their own views on the dwifungsi.[11]

Fosko's third working paper, which Djatikusumo forwarded to Widodo on September 14, was a twelve-page document which addressed itself to "The Functional Group and Its Problems/Issues" (*Golongan Karya Dengan Permasalahanya*).[12] Drawn up on the eve of Golkar's Second National Congress (MUNAS II) in Bali in October 1978, it developed themes that had been introduced in the second working paper and made a ringing call for the armed forces to abandon their active support for Golkar and stand above all groups in society.

In his covering letter, Djatikusumo wrote that Fosko was sending the working paper in view of the fact that the MUNAS II of Golkar was about to be held. "We strongly hope," he wrote, that the meeting would produce "decisions that can support the development of the MPR in March 1978, particularly in MPR decree No. IV/78 concerning the GBHN."

---

10. *Kertas Kerja II*, May 20, 1978.

11. Interview with Lt. Gen. Dharsono, November 12, 1981.

12. Djatikusumo letter to Widodo, September 14, 1978.

In a section dealing with ABRI's role as a social-political force, the paper said that it was necessary to review the message of the late General Sudirman that the only national property that was still whole and unchanging, notwithstanding all sorts of challenges and changes, was the TNI.[13] It was the responsibility of all those associated with ABRI--active ABRI employees, karyawan ABRI, retired servicemen, other members of the big ABRI family, ABRI wives, veterans, and so on--to ensure that the validity of the above declaration existed not only during the life of General Sudirman but also "today, tomorrow, and in the future." It was necessary, the paper said, to ask oneself two questions: Whether the TNI was still the only national property that was still intact and unimpaired? And whether the TNI still stood above all groups?[14] If the answers to these questions were negative, "then, in a soldierly way we must have the courage to make corrections in order to achieve 'the unity of ABRI and the people' [manunggaling ABRI dengan Rakyat]."

In the period leading up to the birth of the New Order, the paper said, the TNI had had very many experiences and had certainly emerged as a determining political force. The dwifungsi had been formally accepted and legalized, and this had consolidated the role of the TNI/ABRI as a "dinamisator" and "stabilisator." At the same time, one had to admit there had been excesses. There was suspicion and dissatisfaction and, of late, estrangement; so much so, in fact, that a student poster had said, "Bring ABRI Back to the People." Drawing on a Maoist analogy often quoted (usually without attribution) by senior army officers, the document said that relations between the TNI/ABRI and the people could be likened to that of a fish in water. The TNI/ABRI as both a defense and security force and a social force must at all times strive for the unity of the armed forces and the people and must stand above all groups. In order that the people could freely estimate that the armed forces were taking measures to unify themselves with the people and stand above all groups, the TNI/ABRI must in an honest way make self-corrections and self-criticisms. The armed forces should not cultivate (membina) Golkar, as in reality Golkar was just like a political party and functioned in the same way. The term "golongan" (group) was used to describe Golkar, but in actual fact it was a political party. The term "political party" was used to describe other institutions, but the institutions thus described were not in fact political parties. It was said that members of the armed forces were prohibited from becoming members of political parties, but in reality individuals and personalities of ABRI occupied positions as members of the Control Councils (Dewan Pembina) of Golkar, both in Jakarta and in the provinces. "As a conclusion from the above," the paper stated, "it is clear that 'The TNI as a social-political force must be above all groups.'" The guidance, leadership, management, and so on of Golkar within the

---

13. *Kertas Kerja III*, September 14, 1978.

14. Ibid., p. 9.

framework of the implementation of the dwifungsi should be entrusted to the big ABRI family--that is, the organization of ABRI wives, retired servicemen, veterans, disabled veterans, Hansip (Civil Defense), Hanra (People's Defense), and so on. From among TNI members who were still active, there should be selected those who in the opinion of the leadership had potential for work within the world of politics. These servicemen should be released from their military duties and placed within the Golkar organization, Golkar itself having severed its ties with the government and Hankam; Golkar, it was to be hoped, would at the same time be restructured and become a proper political party.

In a subsequent section, the paper said that, in order for ABRI and the people to become one, it was necessary for the armed forces to embrace all of the people, whether they were within a political organization or not. Because of this, it was not right that ABRI should side with one group and be active in its development so that other groups appeared to be inappropriate: "ABRI must be above all groups. [*ABRI harus berada diatas semua golongan.*] With the placing of ABRI officials in Golkar's Dewan Pembina it becomes a fact that ABRI is siding with one social-political force. Does this not appear to obstruct the aim of creating unity between ABRI and the people?"[15] ABRI officials, the paper suggested, should resign from their positions as members of the supervisory council of Golkar, particularly the chairmanship.

In a section dealing with the weaknesses of the Golkar organization, the paper made two specific points. First, it said, Golkar had not yet shown maturity in its organization. It depended too much on, and accepted too much help from, the government apparatus and ABRI; it lacked resolution in cadre-formation, with the result that the abilities that were needed from the cadres were not available; it was not rooted sufficiently in society as a whole; and the construction of the group's organization, as well as its operational field activities, was still department-oriented and bureaucratic. Second, Golkar was still weak in political activities. The leaders of the functional group did not communicate or consult with others; they did not show sensitivity towards the people or to those who had elected them; they were not sufficiently capable or militant in facing their competitors, particularly in the social-political field; nor were they consistent in implementing their political struggle.

By now, clearly, Fosko was warming to its work. Having stressed the importance of the notion that ABRI should be "above all groups" and "close to the people," the September working paper zeroed in on the hypocrisy inherent in the heavy military involvement in Golkar affairs, being specific to the point of bluntness about just where the changes should be made.

Fosko's fourth working paper, a thirteen-paper document which Djatikusumo forwarded to the army chief of staff on January 5, 1979,

---

15. Ibid., p. 11.

was entitled: "Some Notes Concerning the Consolidation and Control of TNI/ABRI; TNI/ABRI as a Social Force: Uniting ABRI With the People; and Dynamic National Stability."[16] It was, in many ways, a reworking of the themes that had been developed in paper No. III. Two months later, on March 5, 1979, Djatikusumo sent Widodo Fosko Working Paper No. V, a thirteen-page study dealing with equity and development.[17]

In the space of twelve months, the retired generals in Fosko had produced five papers, all of them warning that, unless the government made adjustments, there would be a widening of the gap between the people and the army. At the same time, Fosko had warned that, if things continued as they were, people would lose faith in the Pancasila and the Constitution.

By May 1979, Fosko was getting too bold for the government's liking, and a decision was taken to sever its official links with the army. This stemmed from the organization's participation in a controversial commemoration of National Awakening Day. At a meeting in Jakarta on May 7, the leaders of twenty-one groups, including Fosko, came to the conclusion that there had been a vacuum in political life over the preceding ten years. It was necessary, these groups felt, to make a profound study of why the sense of national awareness had weakened. To this end it was decided to make the commemoration of the May 20 National Awakening Day the starting point for a "Program of National Awareness."[18] The National Awakening Day committee's list of advisers included such figures as Vice President Adam Malik, former Vice President Dr. Mohammad Hatta, the coordinating minister for people's welfare, General Surono, and the ambassador to Japan, Lt. Gen. Sajidiman. The general chairman was Maj. Gen. Achmadi of the Angkatan 45, an odd appointment given that he had been in prison for many years. Dr. Jusuf Ismail, the chairman of Leppenas, the Malik "think-tank," and a former ambassador to Japan and West Germany, was one of the first vice chairmen. General Sukendro was the other.[19] The secretary general was Imam Waluyo, a former stu-

---

16. *Kertas Kerja IV*, January 5, 1979.

17. *Kertas Kerja V*, March 5, 1979.

18. *Tempo*, June 9, 1979.

19. Interview with Dr. Jusuf Ismail, December 5, 1979. The twenty-one groups, many of them with a somewhat oppositionist coloring, were as follows:

DHD-45 DKI Jaya; Fosko TNI-AD; Soksi (Sentral Organisasi Karyawan Sosialis Indonesia); Kosgoro; GMNI; GMKI; Wirakarya Indonesia; Gema MKGR: G. M. Kosgoro; Yayasan 17-8-45; LSS Dewan Hankamnas; Yayasan Idayu; Sekr. Darmo 49; Leppenas; PSA; Yayasan Gedung Bersejarah; LPEP; Indonesia Muda; LBH; DKJ; HIPKI. See *Daftar Panitia Bersama Peringatan Hari Kebangkitan Nasional 1979*. (Copy made available by Jusuf Ismail.)

dent activist who had been detained in the wake of the Malari riots of 1974, and who later became a director of Leppenas.

The week-long commemoration program, which included a series of lectures by such New Order figures as Ali Murtopo, as well as a panel discussion, did not raise any difficulties. However, a speech delivered by Adam Malik at the closing session so angered the government that its wrath fell on all those who had taken part. Speaking extemporaneously, the vice president said that the floods, wereng pests, earthquakes, volcanic eruptions, and diseases which had recently struck the country "are really a warning from God to us." "We have all sinned," said Malik. "We have pledged to be loyal to and apply and practice the Pancasila and the 1945 Constitution but the vows were often not fulfilled by deeds. This is our sin. This is a fundamental problem and the major cause of the jams in government operations." According to the vice president, some government officials were simply "stooges," who listened but did not understand, who saw but did not observe. These people, he said, did not care about Pancasila, the 1945 Constitution, or the fate of the common man. A few weeks earlier, Malik had warned that, if things continued in the present way, the highest leaders in the land would be "hanged." Now he added a curious rider to his remarks that only seemed to make matters worse. No matter how wrong the situation was, no matter how big the fault of the New Order government, there was still a way to make corrections. "Our people are not fond of coups," said the vice president. "Our people are not that stupid." In Indonesia, where criticism tends to be veiled and elliptical, the Malik speech--like the Alamsjah speech of 1977--had an immediate impact. Malik was known as a man who liked to speak his mind, but many in the government, including prominent military figures, felt that he was going altogether too far.[20]

In making his observations, Malik seemed to be identifying himself with some of the more outspoken critics of the regime. His deliberate use of powerful Javanese court imagery about signs of decay in society was hardly calculated to win the sympathy of Suharto, a Javanese ruler who set considerable store by such omens. Indeed, two days after Suharto returned from a working visit to Japan, Malik issued a "clarification," in which he claimed his words had been misinterpreted. Malik, in fact, considered that there was no need for a clarification. He told reporters the speech had been "a small thing" and that it had been blown up out of perspective. Asked why he had to give an explanation, he shrugged and said: "Apparently they needed a clarification, so I gave one." The response was classic Malik, glib and seemingly accommodative. But while it showed a nice regard for the political realities, it did not really do justice to the

20. For a more detailed account of this rather extraordinary speech, see David Jenkins, "Adam's Heavenly Warning," FEER, June 29, 1979, p. 30. The Malik speech was delivered on June 1 at the Graha Purna Yudha (Veteran's) Auditorium.

vice president's true feelings. For some time, Malik had felt that things were going wrong in Indonesia, particularly in areas that fell within the competence of the Western-trained technocrats. This, combined with a certain frustration at having been moved from the center of decision making, a tendency to shoot from the hip when speaking without notes, and, no doubt, a calculated assessment that he could probably deliver himself of a few well-chosen barbs and get away with it, gave the speech its astringency. Not surprisingly, the observations were given full coverage in the local press. The nationalist daily *Merdeka* saw it as a sign of progress that government officials were now prepared to criticize themselves and their leadership. *Tempo* found Malik's remarks rather "sensational" and refreshing." Even *Angkatan Bersenjata*, the official newspaper of the armed forces, found the speech of importance, devoting 500 words to it under the headline: "Natural disasters a warning from God."

As a direct result of the National Awakening Day affairs, the army chief of staff "froze" the Fosko TNI-AD, the decision to take effect from May 26.[21] A release of the Army Information Service said that the measure was taken because there were elements within the Fosko TNI-AD who had used the name of the organization for political activity and thus harmed the good name of the army. This, it said, could create an assumption that the army stood behind these people.[22] In a follow-up move on June 21, Widodo, in his capacity as chairman of the YKEP, announced that henceforth the Fosko TNI-AD would be known as the "FKS Purna Yudha." In all future activity, it was said, the body would not be permitted to reveal itself to the outside world. By talking "outside" at this time, Widodo observed after his retirement several years later, the Fosko leadership had made things "very difficult" for him as chief of staff. The president himself had been displeased by this affair.[23] Nevertheless, Widodo served as the lightning rod of official displeasure and the affair proved a fairly minor setback for the retired generals in Fosko. Although the name of their organization had been changed, their work continued. "Actually it was no change at all," Sukendro said later. "Only the name!"[24] In December 1979, six months after the incident, FKS leaders were still seeing Widodo regularly.[25]

The aim of the FKS was to see the system changed, to work for a "better political infrastructure."[26] To this end, the body organized

---

21. See *Merdeka*, June 2, 1979, and *Tempo*, June 9, 1979.

22. *Tempo*, June 9, 1979.

23. Interview with General Widodo, November 17, 1981.

24. Interview with Maj. Gen. Sukendro, December 22, 1979.

25. Ibid. "I can see Widodo any time," Sukendro said in December 1979. "I see him regularly." See also "*Surat Keputusan* No: 059/YKEP/1979," June 21, 1979, of the Yayasan Kartika Eka Pakci.

26. Sukendro interview, December 22, 1979.

a limited "dialogue" between retired TNI members. This was held in Semarang on November 9, 1979.[27]

Appointment in Semarang

On November 10 (Heroes Day), 1979, President Suharto was to travel to Akabri, the Armed Forces Academy in Magelang, Central Java, in the company of Jusuf, Widodo, and a large group of others, to unveil a statue of the late General Sudirman. Widodo, who, as we have seen, had gone to some lengths to make himself available to the retired army generals of the "Fosko" group, felt this would be a good opportunity for prominent retired generals to meet the president to discuss contemporary issues. To this end, he invited members of the FKS daily board to attend the ceremony. He also made an effort to persuade Nasution to attend. Maj. Gen. Slamet, the SPRI (personal assistant) to Widodo, visited Nasution to invite him, as a former army chief of staff, to be present at Magelang as Widodo's guest. Three prominent retired generals--Maj. Gen. Munadi, Lt. Gen. Mokoginta, and Maj. Gen. Sukendro--made separate and consecutive visits to Nasution to persuade him to accept the invitation. Lt. Gen. Sudirman telephoned him to make the same plea. Each time, Nasution declined. His "excuse" was that a formal meeting with the president would not amount to a "struggle dialogue" (*tidak akan berarti dialog perjuangan*). Only a meeting as fighters with a fighter (*pejuang-pejuang dengan pejuang*), disregarding everyone's position, could succeed.[28]

The retired officers in Fosko had no such qualms about a meeting with Suharto, and accepted Widodo's invitation. Then, deciding they could kill two birds with one stone, they took the opportunity to hold a meeting in Semarang, sixty-five kilometers north of Magelang, on November 9, to confer with retired officers who were outside Fosko and to inform them about Fosko and what it was planning to do.[29]

The "Fosko" generals stressed later that this was in every sense a "legal" meeting, Lt. Gen. Sugih Arto, the former attorney

---

27. See *"Kata Pengantar Dialog Antar Para Purnayudha TNI/ABRI Terbatas*, pada tgl. 9 November 1979 di Semarang." Also interview with Maj. Gen. Sukendro, January 30, 1980.

28. General Nasution, written communication, November 14, 1981. In this note, Nasution said, "I remember Nasser's method during the first years, all the officers of the revolution conferred each year before the anniversary of the revolution as one fighter with another fighter."

29. The account of the Semarang meeting is based on a joint interview with Lt. Gen. Dharsono and Maj. Gen. Sukendro on July 10, 1981. Among those who sat in on part of the interview were Lt. Gen. Jasin, Lt. Gen. Sudirman, and General Hugeng.

general, having already informed Admiral Sudomo of the plans and received his approval to go ahead. Among those invited to the meeting
was retired Maj. Gen. Suryosumpeno, a former commander of the
Diponegoro (1964-66) and at that time chairman of the Central Java
Pepabri.[30] Also invited was Maj. Gen. Munadi, the former governor
of Central Java (1966-74) and a founding member of the Fosko TNI-
AD, who had of late drifted away from the group. A number of
prominent serving army officers were also invited, including the
Siliwangi, Diponegoro and Brawijaya commanders and the commander
of Kowilhan II, Lt. Gen. Widjojo Sujono. However, these officers
failed to attend. The governor of Central Java, Maj. Gen. Supardjo
Rustam, also sent his regrets.

In all, about twenty-one retired army officers attended the
meeting, most of them traveling down from Jakarta by train. On the
morning of November 9 the group met at the home of Maj. Gen.
Munadi at Ungaran, a small town about twenty kilometers south of
Semarang. In the evening they continued their deliberations at the
Sky Garden Hotel in Semarang. At this point, according to Dharsono
and Sukendro, Hankam received a report that the retired generals
had gathered in Semarang to make preparations for some kind of
"takeover" when Suharto visited Akabri the following day. Although
this all sounds decidedly odd, the report is said to have been taken
very seriously. As a result, unusually tight security measures were
enforced at the Military Academy on November 10 and the presidential
itinerary is said to have been altered at the last minute. Instead of
having lunch with the cadets as originally planned, Suharto, Jusuf,
and a number of cabinet members in the official entourage, left immediately after the ceremony. Widodo was the only important member of
the group to stay behind. (Although reluctant to discuss the affair
in detail, Widodo dismisses the notion that any "coup" was in the air;
that, he says, was due to "a false intelligence report." The retired
officers did not intend to "make a coup" but merely wanted to convey
their views to the president.[31] As in 1977, when there had been the
bizarre report that "several brigades" were "for Nasution," the leadership was to prove unusually sensitive to the danger, however remote, of alleged plots and manoeuverings from outside. In any
event, Nasution remains convinced that he did the right thing in declining the invitation to attend the Magelang ceremony. "My guess
was right," he noted. "Evidently the president did not hold that
meeting. They did not even shake hands."[32]

---

30. Suryosumpeno had served as military secretary to President
Sukarno in 1966-67 before being appointed inspector general of the
Ministry of Home Affairs. See Sritua Arief, "*The Indonesian Military
Leaders*," 2nd ed. (Jakarta: Sritua Arief Associates, 1979), pp.
334-35.

31. Interview with General Widodo, November 17, 1981.

32. Nasution, written communication, November 14, 1981.

"Separate Roads in the Same Direction"

Fosko, as we have seen, limited its membership to retired senior army officers and dealt only with matters touching on the TNI and its relations with society. However, the wave of concern that had brought forth Fosko also produced a similar but more broadly based organization--the Foundation for the Institute of Constitutional Awareness (*Yayasan Lembaga Kesadaran Berkonstitusi, YLKB*). Set up at the initiative of Nasution, this body made a point of including representatives of all elements of the nation. The general chairman was Dr. Mohammad Hatta, the first vice president and Co-Proclamator of Independence, and the membership list was notable for the fact that it brought together an almost unique combination of retired generals and "retired" politicians. The military members of the LKB, as it was more commonly known, including Lt. Gen. Ali Sadikin, the popular former governor of Jakarta; Maj. Gen. Azis Saleh, a former minister of people's industries; General Hugeng Imam Santoso, the former chief of the national police; Lt. Gen Mokoginta; Maj. Gen. Munadi; and Admiral Nazir, one of the founders of the Indonesian navy and navy chief of staff between 1946 and 1949. Among the civilians were Mochtar Lubis, a well-known journalist and writer; Oejeng Suwargana, a publisher and long-time acquaintance of Nasution; Dr. Anwar Haryono, an ex-Masyumi leader; Prof. Sunario, an old PNI leader and former foreign minister; Slamet Bratanata, a former minister of mines; Nurbani Yusuf, a lawyer and former film star; Prof. Achmad Subardjo, a onetime foreign minister; Drs. Frans Seda, a onetime finance minister; Nuddin Lubis, head of the PPP *fraksi* (grouping) in the DPR; Sanusi Hardjadinata, a member of the first New Order presidium and general chairman of the PDI; Sabam Sirait, secretary general of the PDI; and Drs. Chris Siner Key Timu, a lecturer at the Atma Jaya University. The leadership of the LKB, it was sometimes pointed out, thus combined all the main "generations"--Dr. Hatta from the Generation of '28, Nasution from the Generation of '45, and Drs. Chris from the Generation of '66. Students associated with the Kampus Kuning group sat on a number of LKB committees.[33] Nasution was officially the adviser (*penasehat*) to the institute.

---

33. The *Kampus Kuning* group consisted of student activists detained in the wake of the January 1978 military crackdown. The phrase was coined by Col. (now Maj. Gen.) Eddy Nalapraja, at that time assistant for intelligence at the Jakarta military command, and now a deputy governor of metropolitan Jakarta, and referred to the detention center where the activists were held--a newly completed barracks with a yellow fence. Among the more prominent members of the kampus kuning group were Arif Rachman, a lecturer in English at the teachers college, Rawamangun, Jakarta, Dipo Alam, former chairman of the students' council of the University of Indonesia, and Zulkarnain Jabar, chairman of the students' council of the Syarif Hidayatullah Islamic State University in Jakarta.

If the idea was to bring together a number of "big names," then one initial obstacle was Hatta's lingering distrust, if not dislike, of Nasution. Hatta looked on Nasution as the man who had paved the way for military intervention in Indonesian politics, and had never really forgiven him for this. (Once, when the former minister of mines, Slamet Bratanata, asked how it was that the military had come to dominate the political stage so thoroughly, Hatta's answer was brief to the point of rudeness. "Don't ask me," he said impatiently, "Ask Nasution!"[34] Hatta, aware that Nasution was the force behind the proposed institute, was wary about its aims. However, not long after the MPR session in March 1978, Admiral Nazir arranged for the two men to meet at a house outside Jakarta. (It is not clear why the meeting should have taken place on "neutral ground." Nasution, who respected Hatta, says he was quite prepared to call on the former vice president at his home. "I said I will go anywhere.")[35] There, in the presence of Nazir and Admiral Kamal, the two men talked for three hours. When Nasution outlined his proposals for the *lembaga* and invited Hatta to be the first signatory, the older man agreed immediately. When Nasution later showed him the preamble for the LKB, Hatta did not change a word.[36] This change in Hatta's attitude--from skepticism to support--was not only central to the fortunes of the LKB. In a broader sense, it typified the sort of reappraisal that was being made at the time by prominent civilians, many of whom had hitherto shown a marked distrust of the military as a whole. In the late 1970s, a number of civilian leaders came to accept that significant groups within the larger military establishment were working essentially towards the same kind of goals, and doing so not simply because they were members of an "out" group but because they were concerned about the way in which Indonesian society was being shaped.

At about the same time as the Hatta-Nasution meeting, feelers were put out to the Sultan of Yogyakarta, who in March had stood down as vice president. The Sultan was disenchanted with Suharto, partly because he had been excluded from the decision-making pro-

---

34. Interview with Ir. Slamet Bratanata, March 25, 1982. Nasution, who had a high regard for Hatta, offers a different explanation for this attitude. "I did not have good relations with Hatta because of the PRRI. He was on the other side [i.e. in the government debate on how to handle the rebellion]." At the same time, Nasution is well aware of Hatta's strong antimilitary feelings. When Fosko was set up, Nasution says, there were some people who argued that this body was more important than the LKB because everything depended on the TNI. "Always the TNI! And people like Hatta couldn't listen to such talk. They said, "It's up to the people!" Interview with General Nasution, March 11, 1982.

35. General Nasution interview, March 11, 1982.

36. Ibid.

cess during his term as vice president but even more so because he wanted to see civilians enjoying much greater authority in the government. Initially, the Sultan may have been attracted by the idea of lending his name to the proposed LKB. Mochtar Lubis, who called on him twice in the period after the MPR session, found him very much in agreement with the aims and objectives of the institute, as did Azis Saleh, who also discussed the matter with him at this time. However, in the end there were two reasons why the Sultan felt he could not join. One problem was that it might appear unseemly if he were to join such an association immediately after stepping down as vice president. More importantly, he is said to have felt, as a good Javanese, that one should not confront openly. "In the Javanese context," he told Mochtar Lubis, "it would amount to an open declaration of war against Suharto, and I don't think that will profit anyone--not Suharto, not the lembaga, not the country." All the same, the Sultan was "full of sympathy" for the aims of the LKB.[37]

Built around a Hatta-Sultan-Nasution axis, the LKB would have been an especially influential body, one that brought together the country's first two vice presidents as well as the most prominent retired military officer. But even without the Sultan it carried a good deal of weight, the participation of Hatta ensuring it both attention and respect.

Founded on June 1, 1978, barely six months after Fosko, the lembaga maintained close links with the grouping of ex-army "seniors." At the time Fosko was established, Sudirman had talked with Nasution about whether he would join or not. Likewise, when the LKB was started, Naustion asked Sudirman whether or not he would join. The aims were the same, but Fosko limited itself to the TNI while the LKB had to include all elements of the nation. It has been suggested that "longstanding personal animosities between Nasution and some members of Fosko" were one of the factors preventing a merger between Fosko and the LKB.[38] This was not the case. Fosko had been set up by the army chief of staff and was obliged to limit its membership to senior army officers. Nasution wanted a broader approach. Moreover, he reasoned--correctly as it turned out--that, if Fosko had been set up by a government agency, then it could be disbanded by the same body. There was little, if any, animosity between members of the two groups. "Our formula," Nasution says, "was 'gescheiden samengaan' [separate roads in the same direction]."[39] There were, it is true, differences of a sort over tactics.

---

37. Interview with Mochtar Lubis, February 29, 1984.

38. See Sundhaussen, "Regime Crisis in Indonesia," p. 827. This suggestion was emphatically rejected by General Nasution (March 11, 1982), Lt. Gen. Mokoginta (March 25, 1982), and Maj. Gen. Sukendro (March 3, 1982).

39. General Nasution, written communication, November 14, 1981. Maj. Gen. Sukendro, in an interview on March 3, 1982, disputed

Sudirman and those associated with him in Fosko believed that it was best to zero in on the army leadership because that was where power was held; Nasution wanted a national--and not merely a military--approach. (Although there was an "understanding" that there would be no overlap in Fosko and LKB membership, Mokoginta was, from the start, a member of both organizations. By late 1980, membership distinctions had become blurred and it was common to find members of the LKB, particularly Hugeng, Slamet Bratanata, and Air Vice Marshall Suyitno Sukirno, at meetings of what was, by now, the "ex-Fosko" group.)

In keeping with its name and its proclaimed goals, the LKB hammered repeatedly at the theme of constitutional propriety. In August 1978, the then chairman of the LKB, Azis Saleh, met General Darjatmo, by now the Speaker of Parliament, to discuss the current political and social situation in the country. He was quoted afterwards as saying that some discontent was present in the community because of the lack of understanding of the Constitution. Darjatmo suggested to Azis Saleh that the institution should hold a similar dialogue with the government. In October, a group of LKB members met at Ali Sadikin's house to listen to a speech of Dr. Hatta on the objective of the organization, which was to make people aware of the Constitution and, by implication, the government's departure from it in many areas. "We not only have a Constitution," Dr. Hatta said, "but also have a consciousness of having a Constitution."[40] The LKB presented no concrete program, but it reportedly intended to confine itself to holding dialogues and publishing periodicals.

On January 27, 1979, Dr. Hatta was to be the keynote speaker at a panel discussion on the implementation of Article 1 of the 1945 Constitution, which declares that sovereignty is vested in the hands of the people. However, the man who had jointly proclaimed that Constitution on August 17, 1945, was not able to give his address; several days before the symposium the Jakarta police asked the LKB to "postpone" the gathering.[41] Two weeks later, two leaders of the institute, Dr. Azis Saleh and General Hugeng, called on Admiral

---

Nasution's suggestion that Fosko was set up by the government. "We were set up by ourselves," he said, adding that Fosko had the link with Widodo because it was looking for an "umbrella." If Widodo had not agreed to sponsor such a body, the retired officers would have gone ahead on their own, as they did after the forum was "frozen." Widodo did not form Fosko, said Sukendro, he just provided the umbrella. There is something to be said for both the Nasution and Sukendro explanations.

40. See Leo Suryadinata, "Indonesia under the New Order: Problems of Growth, Equity and Stability," in *Trends in Indonesia II*, ed. Leo Suryadinata and Sharon Siddique (Singapore: Singapore University Press, 1981).

41. *Pelita*, January 25, 1979.

Sudomo to discuss the ban. They were told the permission to hold the meeting would be withheld indefinitely because "the situation does not allow" such a discussion.[42]

Despite this setback, the LKB became increasingly active in 1979. At the commemoration of the institute's first anniversary in June, Nasution said "there are many things which are not democratic and against Pancasila under Pancasila democracy."[43] The following month, five leaders of the group (Sunario, Sadikin, Mochtar Lubis, Nazir Lubis [a businessman close to Nasution], and retired Admiral Kamal) called on both the PDI and the PPP factions in the DPR as part of a program to gather views about the application of the Constitution. Leaders of the group had already met Dr. Hatta, former DPA chairman Wilopo, and General Nasution, who, though serving as an "adviser" to the institute seems to have chosen a role of "leading from behind." The journey to the Parliament provided the group with a convenient--and "constitutional"--forum to take issue with the constitutional shortcomings of the Suharto government. In the meeting with the PDI faction led by Usep Ranuwidjaja, Ali Sadikin observed: "Our Republic is sick from head to foot." The situation was so serious, he said, that "we do not know what to do, where to begin doing things, and how to end it." Noting that the general election law was one of the keys to the Indonesian political structure, the former Jakarta governor asked why the law (which was at that time before the Parliament) still had to be "perfected." "Perfected for whom?" he asked rhetorically. "Perfected so that the victorious party will be even more victorious?" In the opinion of Sadikin, there were many "political prostitutes" in the political parties. These people were in a formal sense party members but essentially they obeyed others.[44] At the same meeting, Sunario claimed that the government had violated Article 11 of the Constitution concerning foreign loans and debts. Every loan agreement had to be known to or ratified by the DPR. It was not enough for the president to say that he was not selling the state by contracting foreign debts. Article 11 seemed to be irrelevant, Sunario claimed, and if in fact it were not needed any more it should be removed from the Constitution.

The LKB delegation was received the same day by PPP faction leaders Rachmat Mulyomiseno, Amin Iskandar, Syufri Helmi Tanjung, and Jamaluddin Tarigan. At this meeting, Rachmat Mulyomiseno observed that in 1966 everyone had been talking about the faithful implementation of the 1945 Constitution; now, all of a sudden, it was

---

42. *Kompas*, February 7, 1979.

43. *Pelita*, June 2, 1979. At this meeting, the general chairman of the LKB, Azis Saleh, said LKB representative offices and groups had been set up in Medan, Padang, Bogor, Bandung, and other cities.

44. *Merdeka*, August 22, 1979. USE.

said that the past ten years, the period of Repelita I and II, were a period of "transition."[45]

In September 1979, a delegation from the LKB returned to Senayan to meet the DPR leadership, including the Speaker, General Darjatmo, and deputy Speakers, Mashuri, K. H. Masykur, and Mohammad Isnaeni. The discussion centered on two topics--democracy and ABRI's dual function. Regarding the problem of democracy, the LKB spokesman, Mokoginta, warned that, while the form of democracy in Indonesia was already perfect from the formal legal aspect, "we also know that our democracy does not work." According to Mokoginta, what was working at that time was "the mechanism of a current from the top to the bottom." Since nobody objected, this was regarded as democratic. But this was not so. If the people did not say anything, the reasons might be that they were afraid to express themselves or because they were "inarticulate." In his view, the fighters who struggled for independence aspired for a democratic republic in which the sovereignty of the people in the shape of aspirations and ideals could be realized by the leaders. The style of democracy did vary from country to country, Mokoginta noted. But what the democracies had in common was that the system was able to give form to the aspirations of the masses of the people. Pancasila democracy could be judged by whether or not the aspirations of the people had been realized. To underscore this point, he cited the example of the election of a bupati or a governor; often, he said, these candidates were "dropped from above." During the dialogue, Ali Sadikin asked whether the DPR and the government could not create a mechanism which, while permitting ABRI's dual function to work, prevented people from regarding ABRI as being dominant everywhere, in the political and in other fields. Mokoginta said that, when it was formulated at the first and second army seminars, ABRI's dual function was meant to bring the people to maturity in living in a constitutional state and then restore this responsibility to the people. The dual function was not intended as a device to enable ABRI to remain in power through "artificial" domination; that would not involve bringing people to political maturity but "gagging."[46]

This round of activity by the LKB drew some sniping from the secretary of the Golkar faction, Ir. Sarwono Kusumaatmadja. When the LKB critics had been in power, Sarwono claimed, they "did not fully use the opportunity to improve things related to the establishment of democracy." Generally, he said, they had been too occupied with safeguarding their own spheres of power "and now they have retired they are awake and sorry and talk about democracy."[47]

That sort of carping, while it may have had some basis in fact, was hardly sufficient to deter the LKB leaders. At a five-hour meet-

45. *Berita Buana*, August 23, 1979. USE.

46. *Kompas*, September 25, 1979, USE.

47. Ibid., September 29, 1979.

ing with the Golkar faction six days later, retired officers continued their criticism. A number of matters were raised, amongst them a complaint by the former police chief, General Hugeng, that Kopkamtib was unconstitutional and that police powers were not in the hands of the police alone but also in the hands of the military police, the Koramil (Military Precinct Command), and so on. However, it was Ali Sadikin's criticism of the implementation of ABRI's integration with the people which drew most comment. "If it is true that ABRI is united with the people and stands above all groups," Sadikin asked, "why is there still the Big Golkar Family comprising Korpri (Civil Servants Corps), Golkar, and ABRI?" It was not stated in the Seven Pledges or in the Soldier's Oath that ABRI belonged to the Big Golkar Family, he said. ABRI's dual function had become too extensive; if the dual function was to be continued, he stated, it must be confined to areas where military involvement was truly necessary. With the expanding notion of the dual function, the excesses, too, were expanding. Now, it seemed, there were two classes, ABRI and non-ABRI, a situation that had not existed during the revolution.[48] If all this was very much in line with the thinking of the institute's adviser, Nasution, so too were Sadikin's observations on the electoral system. A general election based on party symbols did not make the elected members feel dutybound to be responsible to their voters, Sadikin charged. "We had better use the district system so that individuals will be elected and so that when there are problems people can meet them and demand an account."[49]

Six days later, the LKB held another five-hour meeting at the DPR, this time with leaders of the ABRI faction. At this encounter, Sadikin restated his belief that the concept of ABRI as an instrument of the state and as a social force were overlapping and had caused various excesses. It was necessary, he said, to discard the statement that ABRI was a member of the Big Golkar Family. ABRI should not side with any one group in society.[50] During this encounter, Azis Saleh made the point that the 1971 and 1977 elections had been neither free nor secret, neither fair nor clean. "I have spoken with competent people on this subject who said that there were dirty tricks in the past general elections," he said.[51]

At yet another meeting with members of the PPP faction at the end of November, LKB leaders elaborated on their earlier criticisms. According to Azis Saleh, the existing general election law and the procedures for forming the consultative and legislative bodies did not yet meet the requirements of the 1945 Constitution, in particular Article 1 which states that "sovereignty is in the hands of the people."

---

48. Ibid., October 12, 1979. USE.

49. Ibid., and *Suara Karya*, October 12, 1979.

50. *Merdeka*, October 18, 1979. See also *Pelita*, and *Berita Buana* of same date.

51. *Kompas*, October 18, 1979. USE.

Table III. *Susunan Pengurus "Forum Studi dan Komunikasi TNI" 1978*

(All of these officers were retired)

Presidium:	1. Lt. Gen. G. P. H. Djatikusumo
	2. Lt. Gen. Sudirman
	3. Maj. Gen. Drs. Achmad Sukendro
Secretary General:	Lt. Gen. H. R. Dharsono
Political Department:	1. Lt. Gen. H. A. J. Mokoginta
	2. Brig. Gen. Daan Jahja
Economic Department:	1. Lt. Gen. M. Jasin
	2. Brig. Gen. Agus Prasmono
Social Department:	1. Maj. Gen. Munadi
	2. Maj. Gen. Drs. Iskandar Ranuwihardjo
Cultural Department:	1. Maj. Gen. Brotosewoyo
	2. Brig. Gen. Broto Hamidjojo
Legal Department:	1. Lt. Gen. Sugih Arto
	2. Maj. Gen. Muamil Effendy S.H.
Members:	1. Col. Alex Kawilarang
	2. Col. Chandra Hasan
	3. Maj. Gen. Harun Sohar
	4. Col. Sukanda Bratamenggala

SOURCE: *Susunan Pengurus: "Forum Studi dan Komunikasi TNI."*

Improvements had to be sought without let-up, and this was the task of the DPR. "If the DPR can do nothing," said Mokoginta, "they had better pack up and go home."[52] If in the past appointments had had to be made because there had not yet been a general election, Azis Saleh said, then the notion of appointments had become institutionalized. In accordance with Articles 1 and 27 of the Constitution, there should be no discrimination or special rights in a general election or in obtaining seats in the DPR/DPRDs (provincial representative assemblies); all members should be elected. The candidates of the TNI as a social force, he said, could always participate in a general election under the district system.

Anxious to establish their legitimacy, the New Order leaders had gone out of their way to stress a fundamental commitment to the 1945 Constitution. At the same time, they had been compelled by political realities to ignore and ride roughshod over many fundamental provisions of the Constitution and to go on doing so over a sustained period. Nasution, who had pushed for a return to the 1945 Constitution and who found much to criticize in Suharto's government, was not slow in making the most of this contradiction. The Lembaga Kesadaran Berkonstitusi he created had the advantage of being able to attack the government and its constitutional shortcomings and to do so in a constitutional--and therefore "acceptable"--manner, thus making it difficult for the government to retaliate.

Although Nasution was listed merely as an adviser to the LKB, he was, in fact, very much more than this. Nasution was the focal point for those associated with the institute, and the membership list included the names of a number of his friends and associates. Oejeng Suwargana was a long time close associate of Nasution;[53] Dr. Azis Saleh and Admiral Nazir had been the first two Indonesian military officers to achieve cabinet rank when, on Nasution's initiative, they had been appointed minister of health and minister of navigation respectively in the 1957 Karya Cabinet (Work Cabinet) of Ir. Djuanda Kartawidjaja. In 1954, Azis Saleh had been one of the founders of the League of Upholders of Indonesian Independence (*Ikatan Pendukung Kemerdekaan Indonesia*, IPKI), the political "movement" set up on Nasution's initiative. The writings of Nasution, Oejeng Suwargana, Azis Saleh, and Nazir were especially prominent in the booklets and pamphlets issued by the LKB and reflected a similar outlook on constitutional questions.

It is tempting to see a connecting thread running from the activities of the IPKI of the late 1950s to the LKB of the late 1970s and there is more perhaps than a superficial resemblance between the two bodies. Founded at a time when there was growing disenchantment over the corruption and ineptitude of the political parties, IPKI brought together a number of fairly prominent officers and civilians.

52. Ibid., November 30, 1979. USE.

53. See above ch. 3, n. 7.

According to a manifesto of the grouping, Indonesia had experienced one crisis after another in the years since independence and the aspirations of the people had not been realized. The solution, the manifesto said, was a return to the spirit of the Proclamation and the 1945 Constitution. IPKI sought a stronger form of government, but one which would allow for greater regional autonomy and find an enlightened solution to the problem of continuing regional disturbances, the simplification of state agencies, the elimination of corruption, and a greater degree of army autonomy.[54] As Sundhaussen has pointed out, Nasution saw IPKI drawing its electoral support essentially from military men and their families, veterans, West Java, and the Outer Islands. Some such support was forthcoming: in West Java, the Outer Island military commander, Col. Alex Kawilarang, provided transport and even money for IPKI campaigners. However, the group's manifesto alienated ethnic Javanese, and IPKI, coming face to face with an obstructionist government, fared dismally in the 1955 elections.[55] Although IPKI had played a fairly significant role in paving the way for Guided Democracy, most of its leaders later came to oppose what they saw as Sukarno's attempt to eliminate democracy altogether. In March 1960, largely on the initiative of IPKI, a Liga Demokrasi (Democratic League) was established, ostensibly to protest against the dissolution of Parliament and to demand the preservation of the parliamentary system, but more particularly to counter the growing power of the PKI. The driving force behind the Liga Demokrasi was Nasution's intelligence chief Col. Sukendro, a Siliwangi officer who, as we have seen, would later play a central role in Fosko, an organization with parallel aims to those of the LKB. Although Nasution had remained at arm's length from the league (if only to avoid Sukarno's wrath), he is thought to have lent active support to Sukendro at that time.

There were important differences, however, between IPKI and the LKB. For one thing, Nasution and the other officers who had participated in IPKI were now retired and in no position to bring anything other than moral pressure to bear on issues. For another, the LKB was in no sense a political party, with a manifesto, programs, and candidates; it was a foundation which merely sought the "pure" application of the 1945 Constitution.

As we have seen, the LKB brought together a wide range of people and a broad spectrum of political opinion. This made for odd bedfellows, the mingling of ex-Masyumi figures and army officers who had crushed the 1958 rebellion being in itself unique. On one level, this could be--and was--presented as evidence of an impressive and growing alignment of forces opposed to the Suharto government. At another level, however, it could be seen as a brittle and essentially temporary alliance. The members of the LKB were indeed drawn from a wide range of groupings. But while they might agree on the sort

---

54. See Sundhaussen, *Road to Power*, pp. 89-90 and p. 125.

55. Ibid., p. 90.

of things they opposed, their weakness was that they remained as divided as ever over the sort of government they would like to see in
Indonesia.

CHAPTER FIVE

ARMY PROPOSES, PALACE DISPOSES

It is appropriate to distract the people's attention from political problems and ideological exclusiveness to efforts of national development. For that reason it is necessary to limit the activities of the political parties to the district level only.

Lt. Gen. Ali Murtopo (1972)[1]

No government is as strong as this one. It controls everything, from below to the highest levels. The question is whether we continue like this in the future or whether we make improvements. I think improvements are necessary--to make the system more democratic. We should reduce ABRI's involvement, give more chance to the people. The situation at present is not good. I have always recommended to the president that he make an improvement.

General Widodo (1981)[2]

Soon after his installation as army chief of staff in January 1978, Widodo called for a copy of the Seskoad paper. The sentiments he found therein were very much in line with his own thinking, and within a short time he had set up a committee, under his deputy, Lt. Gen. Poniman, to discuss the matter in detail with all groups in the army. The ostensible aim of the exercise was to produce a paper on the Hankamrata (Total People's Defense) Concept. However, the committee's more immediate task was to formulate clearly the dwifungsi doctrine of the army.[3]

The Widodo paper, like the Seskoad paper before it, was written in its entirety by Brig. Gen. Abdulkadir Besar. And, not surprisingly, it reflected the sort of thinking that had emerged during

1. Ali Murtopo, "Some Basic Considerations in 25-year Development," *The Indonesian Quarterly* 1 (October 1972): 20.

2. Interview with General Widodo, November 17, 1981.

3. Ibid. Widodo noted in this interview that the paper gave equal attention to the Hankamrata and the dwifungsi. However, he conceded that the section dealing with the dwifungsi was more important.

the Seskoad deliberations on this topic. However, the Widodo paper naturally carried a lot more weight. The Poniman committee included not only members of Seskoad but representatives from all other elements in the army as well. Officers from the intelligence, operational, and territorial branches sat in on the committee sessions and were asked for their opinions. The governor of Lemhannas (National Defense Institute), Lt. Gen. Sajidiman Surjohadiprodjo, and his successor, Lt. Gen. Sutopo Juwono, also contributed to the document.[4] Widodo, playing a crucial "brokerage" role, also sought--and listened to--the views of the retired officers in Fosko. At the same time, he sought the views of a number of prominent civilians, in particular academics from the University of Indonesia, the Bandung Institute of Technology, and Gajah Mada University in Yogyakarta.[5] During this process, Abdulkadir was obliged to accent some aspects and play down others. But the underlying principles remained the same.

As we have seen, Abdulkadir had, during the first half of 1977, reformulated the "Hankamrata Doctrine," an exercise that involved gathering together the existing material on this topic and setting it out more systematically. During the second half of 1977 and the early part of 1978 he had written the Seskoad paper on the dwifungsi. The Widodo paper was essentially a fusion of these two documents, with perhaps 80 percent of the material being incorporated without change. After a two-page preface and some introductory remarks of equal length, the army paper incorporated six closely typed pages of material from the Seskoad dwifungsi paper.[6] This included the section, centrally important to Abdulkadir's argument, asserting that Indonesian cultural values are posited on familial principles and that an ABRI man is responsible not just for the defense of the state but for developing, inter alia, its economic, cultural, and political life.[7] The army paper discarded a six-page discourse in the original paper concerning "The Position of Man in Pancasila." But the following twenty-page section was taken over, with only minor rewording and rearrangement, from the earlier study. A new three-page section

---

4.   Interview with General Nasution, July 7, 1980. Lt. Gen. Sajidiman and Lt. Gen. Sutopo Juwono had views that tended to be in harmony with those of the teaching staff at Seskoad and the retired officers in Fosko and the LKB. They were, in this sense, more broadly in sympathy with those in the "principled" group. Interview with Lt. Gen. Sutopo Juwono, July 23, 1981. Sutopo Juwono, who had been appointed ambassador to the Netherlands in 1974 following the Malari Affair, returned to Indonesia in September 1978. He took up his new post as governor of Lemhannas in November 1978.

5.   Interview with General Widodo, November 17, 1981.

6.   See *Dwifungsi ABRI: (Kensep 1979)* (Departemen Pertahanan Keamanan, Markas Besar, Tentara Nasional Indonesia Angkatan Darat), pp. 5-11. (Henceforth "Widodo paper.")

7.   Ibid., p. 6.

was added setting out "Seven Principles Concerning the Implementation of ABRI's Dual Function," as was a page on "ABRI's Mission as a
Social Force."

Although the earlier sections of the army paper focused on the
philosophical basis of the dwifungsi, the seven principles outlined in
the new section implicitly limited the scope of a doctrine which might
otherwise have been thought to have sanctioned an almost unre-
stricted military involvement in nonmilitary affairs. The first of the
seven principles was that "the attitude and behavior of ABRI in all
situations must always reflect a populist [kerakyatan] and knightly
[kesatriaan] nature."[8]

A populist orientation was defined as one which, while taking
account of ABRI's aims, was directed towards the achievement of the
aspirations of the people. A knightly nature meant that, during the
struggle to shape the aspirations of the people, ABRI "dares to admit
its own mistakes and dares to admit the correctness of others." The
second principle was that "ABRI has always to be one [manunggal]
with the people." The moment that this was no longer the case ABRI
would lose its identity as an army of fighters and with that its moral
basis for acting as a social force as well as its basis as the core of
the Hankamrata. To guarantee the oneness of ABRI and the people,
ABRI had unhesitatingly to put into practice a third principle. This
was that "what is best for the people is best for ABRI."[9] In order
to be aware of the people's aspirations members of ABRI had to live
in the same way as the people. Hence the fourth principle, that
"ABRI must desire and be able to live according to the living conditions of the people." If members of ABRI lived more luxuriously than
the people, the armed forces would become divorced from the people
and lose their strength. The fifth principle was that the "Sapta
Marga rejects the notion that ABRI is a dead instrument [of the
state], just as it does not permit ABRI to become a dictator." The
sixth principle was that "ABRI is above all groups in society"
(mengatasi segenap golongan yang ada dalam masyarakat). Only in
such a position, the document said, could ABRI function as a stabilizer and dynamizer of the life of society and the state. A seventh
principle, said to derive from the idea of a state based on familial
principles (negara kekeluargaan), was that "in solving the problems
of society and also of defense and security ABRI has to use the integrative method of thinking."

In the second of these two additions the paper made the point
that the mission of ABRI as a social force is to give selflessly of its
social capacity and ability in the struggle to realize the national aspirations, as outlined in the preamble to the 1945 Constitution. This
struggle, it said, is not implemented by ABRI alone but by various
other social forces, including political parties, functional group

8.   Ibid., p. 30.

9.   Ibid., p. 31.

organizations, provincial groups, professional groups, and other people's organizations. "Therefore ABRI is merely one social force *among so many others* that fights for the realization of the national aspirations. This means that all social forces are in the same position as a political infrastructure." (italics added)[10] The next five pages, including sections on "ABRI's Credentials" and "The Nine Principles of the Implementation of ABRI's Function as a Social Force," were taken straight from the Seskoad document.

A lengthy section on "ABRI as a Defense Force," which spans nearly thirty pages, incorporated Abdulkadir's original paper on the Hankamrata. The only change was the inclusion of an additional point to the original "Six Principles Concerning the Implementation of ABRI's Role as a Defense Force."[11] The addition, suggested by two Fosko leaders (Djatikusumo and Sukendro), is as follows: "The government must be capable of providing for the welfare of the people, which includes the provision of social justice for all the Indonesian people."[12]

This sentence expressed the feeling among certain retired officers in Fosko that people would go to war to defend the state if they felt that the government was committed to their welfare and was doing all it could to guarantee social justice. Abdulkadir, who shared this opinion, made this the first of the seven principles in his revised formulation.[13] (The wording of the sentence, it might be noted, is strikingly similar to that introduced by the Committee on Army Doctrine in 1958; Mokoginta, a prominent member of Fosko, had served as chairman of the earlier committee.)

After incorporating some additional material from the Seskoad paper, the army document set out an important new section on "The Future of ABRI's Dual Function." This not only foresaw a progressive withdrawal of ABRI members from the executive branch of the government but suggested that this process must be realized during the 1980s.

ABRI's dual function, the paper declared, is an integral part of the system of the participation of the people within the "familial state," and in essence its existence is fully guaranteed. In its capacity as a social force, the document said, ABRI participates in determining the nation's course. This meant that ABRI shares political responsibility, and, as a defense and security force, is unable to carry out coup d'etats or create military juntas. With this concept, it said, the continuous existence of a democratic political system is guaranteed. The document then referred back to the fourth and fifth principles on the realization of ABRI's function as a social force.

---

10. Ibid., p. 33.

11. Ibid., p. 65.

12. Ibid.

13. Interview with Brig. Gen. Abdulkadir Besar, March 12, 1982.

One of these principles is that the "principal" participation of ABRI as a social force--and this, it stressed, is a role that is everlasting--is within the institutions giving expression to the people's sovereignty and within the legislative bodies. The second is that ABRI's participation within the executive branch of government is only to stabilize and dynamize that branch, and can only be justified, the document suggested, if one were to estimate that the Indonesian political system would gradually become stable in the future, with each of the various parts fulfilling its own function. Under increasingly stable conditions, it said, the political system "no longer needs the help of the stabilizing and dynamizing efforts of ABRI."[14] ABRI's dual function, it added, could automatically adapt itself to a changing situation.

In the first decade of the New Order, the document continued, the role of ABRI as a social force was very prominent. This was only natural as that was a time of transition from a "totalitarian" life during the Old Order to a democratic life with aspirations to follow Pancasila and the 1945 Constitution. During this transition period ABRI had been called on to carry out the role of stabilization and dynamization; "If the New Order succeeds in this decade, then it can be estimated that in the second decade, from the early 1980s onwards, the social function of ABRI will only be realized within the institution possessing the people's sovereignty and in the legislative institution."[15]

In the future, it said, ABRI saw itself more as a defense and security force, dedicating itself to maintaining the territory and all its contents in the context of total defense. The result of this--national security--automatically contributed to elevating the people's welfare. This did not mean that ABRI's social function was erased or ignored, because the duty to build the territory, a duty that had become ABRI's responsibility in its capacity as a social force, was realized through those institutions which gave expression to the people's sovereignty and through the legislative bodies, both at the national and regional levels.

The basic theme of the Widodo paper, then, was that ABRI, in accordance with an historical process, had emerged from the people and that the people were the source of its power and inspiration. More important still, the paper stressed that the armed forces were based on the Pancasila, and that they were pledged to uphold the letter of the Constitution. The armed forces, the paper said, must never ally themselves with only one group in society, but must embrace the entire population. If the TNI relied on any single group in society it would endanger both its unity and its identity. (This in a sense was a triumph for Nasution's ideas; it would be hard to imagine a formulation that more closely resembled his political thinking.)

---

14. "Widodo paper," p. 74.

15. Ibid., p. 75.

Equally important the paper envisaged a great reduction in ABRI's involvement in nonmilitary affairs during the 1980s, with civilians regaining effective control over the executive branch of government. This was a major departure from the thinking of those around Suharto. At the time the paper was written there were more than 20,000 ABRI men serving in a kerkaryaan capacity, the bulk of them in executive rather than legislative positions. Although a number of officers associated with the ruling group accepted the need to reduce the number of military men serving outside the Defense Ministry, there was nothing to suggest they favored such a wholesale cutback. In this sense, the Widodo paper addressed two central issues in the emerging debate over the army's role in Indonesian society: the question of ABRI's relations with other social and political groups, and the question of the extent of military involvement in nominally civilian institutions.

In the course of a number of committee meetings during the year, particularly in the last two of September and October 1978, various officers pointed to the political difficulties that would inevitably flow from any attempt by the army to play a purely neutral role. On one occasion, a general who was a member of the committee made the point that, if the government were to adhere to the principles set forth in the document, the army could not fulfill its "mission" to make Golkar win the 1982 general election. The answer, as formulated by a key member of the "principled" group, was, in effect, "That's not our problem. Our job is to safeguard the identity of the TNI and, through that, the Constitution and the ideas of the Revolution."[16] When a similar objection was made in the final meeting, another general said that it was up to the people--not the army--to decide who won the election.[17] While some of the more "pragmatic" officers were arguing that it would be electoral suicide for the army to stand above all groups, Widodo was of the opinion that the existing system only served to repress legitimate political expression. As he noted after his retirement: "You must give the political parties a chance to take part in the system. Also the people. You must give them a chance to take part in the system. Otherwise there are more people outside the system. It is very dangerous."[18] Criticisms were coming from the people and from intellectuals, and eventually the intellectuals would have their roots in the people: "I think we must listen to the voices."[19]

This, it need hardly be said, did not reflect the thinking of those in power. Indeed, the suggestion that the army would endanger both its unity and identity if it relied on any one group in society was a barely veiled criticism of the policies of Suharto and his

---

16. Interview with General Nasution, May 10, 1979.

17. Confidential communication.

18. Widodo interview, November 17, 1981.

19. Ibid.

associates. Eventually, someone decided that things had gone far enough. In October 1978, shortly before the last meeting of the committee (one chaired by Widodo himself), an anonymous single-page pamphlet was circulated at Hankam and Seskoad. This claimed that the ultimate aim of the reform-minded group—it mentioned Abdulkadir as the *"konseptornya"*—was the abolition of the dwifungsi doctrine, a fairly bizarre claim in view of his well-known attachment to the views of Nasution. Because the pamphlet went on to note that Abdulkadir had been the secretary general of the MPRS at the time Nasution had been the chairman of that body, it gave rise to speculation that the principal target of the attack was Nasution himself. According to Nasution, it is inconceivable that anyone but "the security people" could have circulated such a pamphlet.[20]

Abdulkadir reported the existence of the pamphlet to Widodo at a meeting at the latter's house on the night of October 16. He claimed, inter alia, that its author was "against the original identity of the army" and was speaking on behalf of those with a vested interest in the status quo. Widodo shared this opinion and told Abdulkadir not to worry about the claims.[21] At this meeting, Abdulkadir warned Widodo that, although the committee he had established was engaged in an internal discussion about army matters, it was necessary, given the prevailing political atmosphere, to be clear about the way these actions would be viewed in certain quarters; the ruling group, he pointed out, were not likely to take kindly to the implementation of the doctrines formulated by Widodo. The army chief of staff responded that that did not matter: "Those who are unwilling to discuss the dwifungsi of ABRI scientifically," he said, "are people who misuse the dwifungsi to preserve their own power." Abdulkadir agreed with this and noted that "as a staff officer I have warned you that it is a political deed."[22]

The Widodo paper, which ran to seventy-five pages, was approved the following day at a complete plenary session of the army general staff. Among those present were a number of prominent "outsiders," both active and retired. These included Sajidiman, Sutopo Juwono, the four-man Fosko "daily board" (Djatikusumo, Sudirman, Dharsono, and Sukendro), plus Mokoginta and Daan Jahja, both of whom were ordinary members of Fosko.[23] Following an expo-

20. Nasution interview, May 10, 1979. The role of the intelligence section was confirmed by a confidential source.

21. Interview with Brig. Gen. Abdulkadir Besar, March 5, 1982. Although Widodo took a "strong" line in supporting the document, Nasution believes, he also had "good tactics." The document, the chief of staff had argued, was not made by him personally but had grown from within the army itself. Nasution interview, May 10, 1979.

22. Abdulkadir Besar interview, March 5, 1982.

23. Interviews with General Widodo (November 17, 1981), Maj. Gen. Sukendro (July 25, 1981), Lt. Gen. Dharsono (November 12, 1981),

sition by Abdulkadir, a lively discussion took place about ABRI's role in society. At one stage, Sajidiman raised the question of whether the armed forces were a tool of the government or a component of the state. If they were a tool of the government, he said, they would be obliged to follow every dictate of the government of the day. The unanimous answer of those present was that ABRI was a component of the state, not a tool of the government.[24] The truth of this assertion, Abdulkadir felt, had been borne out by experience. History had shown that on four occasions the TNI had been loyal to the ideals of the state, not to the government of the day, a point made in both the Seskoad and Widodo papers.[25] In December 1948, after the capture of the Republican leaders by the Dutch, General Sudirman had said that "with or without the government, the TNI goes on with the struggle." At the time of the October 17 Affair in 1952, the army leaders had reacted against what they had seen as an attempt by Parliament--a Parliament which included representatives of the "puppet states" created by the Dutch--to send them back to the barracks, a course that was against the aspirations of the army. In 1959, the army had pushed the government to return to the 1945 Constitution. Finally, in 1965 Suharto had refused to subject himself to President Sukarno when the latter, contrary to the wishes of the TNI leadership, had sought to defend the PKI. The purist might well object that this was a fairly dangerous sort of doctrine, one which left it up to the army leadership to decide when and how to obey the orders of the government of the day. And it was fitting perhaps that the men who endorsed this notion--and these were, after all, those of a more principled cast of mind, not the Suharto hard-liners --should have done so on the 26th anniversary of the incident in which Nasution's troops trained their guns on the presidential palace.

In any event, at the October 17 meeting it was agreed that the army owed its loyalty to the state, not to the government of the day. This established, Sajidiman asked what ABRI's attitude should be if the PPP or the PDI were to emerge victorious at the next general election. The answer, as formulated by Mokoginta and endorsed by the gathering, was that it did not matter which group won the election; if either of the "opposition" political parties won, it was simply a consequence of the democratic process. There needed to be a national consensus, Mokoginta said, that ABRI would be loyal to whichever group came to power, the only caveat being that the Republic of Indonesia must continue to be based on the 1945 Constitution and on the Pancasila. If anyone sought to change the philosophical basis of the state, he said, the army must take prompt action against it.

---

and Brig. Gen. Abdulkadir Besar (March 5, 1982). Widodo invited the nonactive officers to his office on two separate occasions--once to discuss the army's role in society and once to discuss the Hankamrata concept.

24. Interview with Brig. Gen. Abdulkadir Besar, March 5, 1982.

25. See "Seskoad paper," p. 35, and "Widodo paper," p. 27.

At the end of the meeting, late on the afternoon of October 17, Sudirman expressed the hope that "with this conception we can restore the original dwifungsi."[26] Widodo was in complete sympathy with the views outlined in the army paper and with those expressed at the meeting. "We cannot afford to sacrifice the dignity of the army," he said, "because if we do the army will be undermined."[27]

It is interesting to note--and understandable perhaps--that the key "military professionals"[28] who had been dismissed or displaced in the wake of the Malari Affair in 1974--Sumitro, Sutopo Juwono, Sajidiman, and Charis Suhud--believed, albeit with varying degrees of enthusiasm, that ABRI should return to its "pure" ideals. "When I read the draft [of the Widodo paper]," Sutopo Juwono noted in an interview, "I absolutely agreed with what was written there. This, in my opinion, is what we call the pure ideal of the dwifungsi, of the role of the armed forces."[29] As we have seen, Sajidiman felt precisely the same way. Charis Suhud, according to his close associates, shared these views, although as chief of staff for functional affairs he was in no position to express them. (Instead, Charis Suhud personified the dilemma of many senior New Order officers, being caught between the demands of his conscience and the need to implement the orders he received from his superiors.) Sumitro's position was more complex and was, in fact, something of a "working compromise" which fell between these two poles. On the one hand, Sumitro was concerned about a number of the "excesses" of military rule. He claimed that he had urged Suharto, as early as 1971, to dissolve Kopkamtib[30] and said that he felt that the government could afford to scale back on the number of officers serving in a kekaryaan (nonmilitary) capacity. On the other hand, Sumitro had many of the characteristics of a New Order "pragmatist." Though less rigid in his thinking than Suharto, he was very much the "commander" type

---

26. Ibid.

27. Interview with General Widodo, November 17, 1981.

28. The term "military professionals" was introduced by Crouch. See *Army and Politics in Indonesia*, p. 317.

29. Interview with Lt. Gen. Sutopo Juwono, July 23, 1981.

30. Interview with General Sumitro, February 28, 1981. In an interview (March 4, 1981), Admiral Sudomo refrained from either confirming or denying that Sumitro had been keen in the early 1970s to see Kopkamtib disbanded, although, in stressing that he (Sudomo) had always felt that such an approach was ill-considered, appeared to concede that the suggestion had been made. Such a suggestion is not as implausible as it may sound. Although Kopkamtib was an important Sumitro power base, he also enjoyed considerable influence in his capacity as deputy commander of the armed forces. At the time, he was actively seeking to disengage himself from day-to-day Kopkamtib business and involve himself more in his more purely army activities.

and saw the need for strong and effective government; he might have been expected to maintain many of the practices of the Suharto group, at least in the short run, were he to be in a position to make key decisions. What set these former "military professionals" apart from some of their more outspoken retired colleagues was that they were still playing (or, in Sumitro's case, hoping to play) a role in the government, albeit in a somewhat reduced capacity. In view of this, they were in no position to air publicly any misgivings they may have had. Besides, they still felt themselves bound by certain ties to the ruling group. Whatever the reservations of men like Sutopo Juwono, they still considered themselves *setiakawan* (bound by a feeling of solidarity) with the New Order leaders. According to Sutopo Juwono: "Up to now, the situation is not like 1965. President Suharto, besides his shortcomings, also has his achievements. . . . And even if we don't like Suharto personally or something like that our moral is setiakawan. This spirit of friendship is still existing because we are from the same generation and we had also experiences between life and death and so on. It's still existing in our mind."[31]

Partly because of this and partly because they did not favor the idea of ABRI airing its dirty linen in public, these officers tended to be circumspect in their comments, to criticize, if they criticized at all, in an oblique and Javanese manner. They were, in some ways, in a half-way house, in contrast to Sukendro and Sudirman, who had never been members of the New Order, and Nasution and Dharsono, who had not belonged to the group around Suharto. Sumitro, Sutopo Juwono, and the others had been key members of this group in the early years of the New Order and had only been pushed aside after their clash in the early '70s with the "political" and "financial" generals around Suharto, most notably Ali Murtopo. Now, in the early 1980s, Sutopo Juwono and Sajidiman were once more aligned, at least in spirit, with those who put principle above pragmatism. However, Suharto and the pragmatists around him--Ali Murtopo, Benny Murdani, Amir Machmud, Sudomo, and Yoga Sugama-- commanded the heights of the political system and, though not especially numerous, they were solidly dug in.

What was even more significant was the degree of support for "principled" thinking amongst senior officers who were not only on the active list but occupying some of the most important command positions. As we have seen, the army chief of staff believed there was a need to reduce ABRI's involvement in society and make the system more open and democratic. These views were shared by the minister of defense, General Jusuf, who, since his appointment in March 1978, had been making repeated reference to the importance of ABRI-people unity and to the fact that ABRI must stand above all groups in society. Later, as we shall see, some doubts came to be expressed about Jusuf's commitment to the sort of fairly fundamental reforms he so frequently espoused, or at any rate to his willingness

31. Interview with Lt. Gen. Sutopo Juwono, July 23, 1981.

to endanger his position by pushing openly for such reforms in the face of Suharto's somewhat inflexible views on the matter. Nevertheless, his statements in the late 1970s had a ring of conviction to many people and, when in May 1979 he issued every member of the armed forces with a small blue pocket book on the military's role in society, the doctrines he set forth could hardly be faulted by those committed to reform. (Perhaps the only exception was a statement that ABRI's relations with the political parties, Golkar, the Veterans' Association, and other social forces should be implemented on the basis of the eleven principles of ABRI leadership, one of the most important of which was *tut wuri handayani*. As Crouch has noted, this Javanese phrase refers to the guidance given by a parent to a child learning to walk, where the parent does not actually support the child but is always ready to save him from falling.[32])

---

32. See *ABRI Sebagai Kekuatan Sosial dan Pokok-Pokok Kebijaksanaan Dalam Rangka Memelihara dan Meningkatkan Kemanunggalan ABRI Dengan Rakyat* (Jakarta: Departemen Pertahanan Keamanan, 1979).

The Jusuf "blue book" was divided into two sections. Part One, written by Brig. Gen. (Hon.) Nugroho Notosusanto, the head of the ABRI History Department, at the behest of Lt. Gen. Charis Suhud, the chief of staff for functional affairs, dealt with ABRI as a social force and made a number of interesting points. One was that as a social force "ABRI is in the same position as political parties and Golkar, neither being higher than the other." ABRI always regarded the political parties and Golkar as fellow freedom fighters and would always work shoulder to shoulder towards the success of development efforts to create a solid and dynamic national stability, as well as promote national resilience. ABRI was responsible for guiding and developing Pepabri, the association of ex-servicemen, the document went on, and also had a responsibility to guide (individual) veterans. As noted, the booklet said that ABRI's relations with the political parties, Golkar, and other social forces should be implemented on the basis of the eleven principles of ABRI leadership, the most important of which were *tut wuri handayani, ing ngarsa sung tulada*, and *ing madya mangun karsa*. The "blue book" also devoted some attention to the question of kekaryaan ABRI, the appointment of military men to nonmilitary positions, and stressed the measures that should be taken to avoid excesses in this area. Amongst other things, it said the placement of ABRI *karyawan* (functionaries) should always be done selectively, according to qualitative requirements, and not be just a channelling of personnel into comfortable positions. Part Two of the Jusuf "blue book," which dealt with the matter of ABRI-people unity, was prepared by a committee chaired by a former deputy assistant for territorial affairs.

Suharto used the phrase *tut wuri handayani* in this context in a speech on Armed Forces Day, 1974. See Crouch, *Army and Politics in Indonesia*, p. 272.

As we have seen, "principled" thinking also existed amongst members of the teaching staff at the various service staff and command schools and enjoyed the support of both the outgoing and and incoming governor of the National Defense Institute. There is evidence that the commander of Kowilhan II (and later chief of staff of Kopkamtib), Lt. Gen. Widjojo Sujono, shared these views, and that General Surono Reksodimedjo, although not in any sense politically minded, felt much the same way. Even General Darjatmo, in the view of some of his senior colleagues, was of a similar opinion, although in his case an overriding loyalty to Suharto worked against this to some extent.[33]

This was, in a sense, the first formal reassessment of the army's position since the third army seminar in Bandung in 1972.[34] However, the paper formalized by Widodo was different, insofar as it emerged not from a seminar but from official general staff meetings. It was also different in that it focused on broad philosophical questions; the accent in the two post-Sukarno army seminars, particularly the second army seminar in 1966, had been more on political affairs.

The Widodo paper provided striking proof that the army "body" was not necessarily in agreement with the policies that were being pursued by the Suharto/palace/intelligence community "head." That this should have occurred while Widodo, a longtime associate of Suharto, was chief of staff made the development all the more awk-

---

33. Confidential communication. General Darjatmo retired in 1980. Other reform-minded generals, it was said, included Lt. Gen. Solichin G. P.; Maj. Gen. Achir, the inspector general of the army; Maj. Gen. Slamet Danusudirjo, deputy chairman of Bappenas (National Planning Agency) for planning, program, and implementation; and Lt. Gen. Sarwo Edhie Wibowo, the inspector general of the Department of Foreign Affairs. A number of officers closely associated with General Jusuf, including the chief of the national police, General Awaluddin Djamin, were likewise interested in purifying the existing system.

34. Abdulkadir, according to Nasution, "was also the key personality in that seminar." Interview, July 7, 1980. As we have seen, three major army seminars have been held over the past twenty years. At the first seminar, which was chaired by the late General Yani in April 1965, the army produced a doctrine that declared, inter alia, that the armed forces had a dual role as both a "military force" and a "social-political force." As a "social-political force," the army's activities covered "the ideological, political, social, economic, cultural and religious fields." (See Crouch, *Army and Politics in Indonesia*, pp. 24-25.) However, the army doctrine at that time was closely interwoven with the political thinking of the late President Sukarno. At the second army seminar in 1966, there was a "total correction"; all vestiges of Sukarnoism were wiped from the slate, and the army returned, in theory at least, to its original doctrine. The third army seminar was held in Bandung in 1972 at a time when General Umar Wirahadikusumah was army chief of staff.

ward for the ruling group. (There were, of course, two sides to this coin. It was precisely because Widodo had been close to Suharto that he was able to speak frankly to the president.)

In theory, the army was obliged to be loyal to the principles set forth in the Widodo paper. In practice, the document had little impact. The position of army chief of staff, all powerful during the first two decades of independence, had been emasculated by the restructuring of the armed forces in 1969. All real power now lay with the president and with the ruling generals at Hankam. And with the possible exception of Jusuf,[35] they were not persuaded by the argument that the army should return to the barracks. The Widodo paper was distributed to commanders with an instruction from the chief of staff to be loyal to the principles contained therein. But in reality, as Nasution noted in July 1980, "you also have other instructions."

> There is a dualism in the standpoint of the military man. On the one hand there is the paper of General Widodo and the blue booklet of General Jusuf--to be above all groupings, that ABRI is of the whole nation. On the other hand, there is the statement of the president himself that the army is still part of the big Golkar family. These are two strong poles. One is from the line of command and the other is from the government. Really, they are contrary. But [in Indonesia] if there is a contradiction you usually keep smiling and don't talk directly about it.[36]

In theory, the Widodo paper had had a free run from the time it was issued on October 17, 1978, until the president signalled a very different approach in his speech at Pekanbaru in March 1980. In practice, Admiral Sudomo had, almost since the beginning and almost certainly at the president's behest, been effectively undermining the sort of things that Jusuf and Widodo had been saying. On October 17, 1979, on the first anniversary of the Widodo statement, Sudomo, having first discussed the matter with Suharto, held a secret meeting with Golkar leaders in which it was agreed that ABRI was

---

35. According to Nasution, the formulation of the "Widodo paper" was completely in accordance with the views of Jusuf, Widodo and Jusuf having discussed the matter at some length. Interview with General Nasution, May 10, 1979. Widodo, whose relations with Jusuf were anything but warm, implicitly concedes that his views and those of Jusuf were similar on this subject. However, Widodo criticizes Jusuf for not having the "courage" to implement the ideas he proclaimed. Interview with General Widodo, November 17, 1981. According to Dharsono "this initiative from General Widodo was a result of [an] assignment by Jusuf . . . to prepare that kind of paper on . . . the role of ABRI." Interview with Lt. Gen. Dharsono, November 12, 1981.

36. General Nasution interview.

"absolutely Golkar" and "part of the big Golkar family." This is a matter which will be pursued in a later section. In the meantime, it is worth noting the observation of Sukendro; "It seems to me," he said in July 1981, "that they don't use this [Widodo] paper at all."[37] Indeed, within three days of officially accepting the Widodo paper the regime had casually brushed aside one of that document's key proposals--that ABRI stand above all groups in society--when Suharto had Golkar brought still more directly under his personal control and that of the dominant military men in his circle. A week in politics is truly a long time.

Golkar Chooses a Chairman

> Rarely had any institution been so totally the lengthened shadow of a single man.[38]

That observation, made by Arthur M. Schlesinger, Jr. about the FBI under J. Edgar Hoover, could, with equal accuracy, have been applied to Golkar under Suharto in the late 1970s. Suharto and his lieutenants had fashioned it into an effective electoral machine in the late 1960s and had steered it thereafter to two successive legislative victories. The Suharto circle was totally committed to Golkar, and the ruling councils of this "functional group" were so dominated by the president's military associates that, though nominally independent, it was in most respects a carbon copy of the government and all that for which it stood.

At the First National Congress (MUNAS) of Golkar, held in Surabaya in September 1973, Suharto had been confirmed in his position as chief controller (Pembina Utama) with the power to select the other members of the Central Control Board (Dewan Pembina Pusat, or Wanbinpus), the decision-making body of the organization.[39] (ABRI's influence was clearly apparent at the Surabaya meeting. Half of the 660 delegates were said to be military men and during the con-

---

37. Interview with Maj. Gen. Sukendro, July 1981.

38. Arthur M. Schlesinger Jr., *Robert Kennedy and His Times* (New York: Ballantine Books, 1979), p. 263.

39. Leo Suryadinata, "Golkar of Indonesia: Its Origins and Development," Unpublished monograph (Singapore: Institute of Southeast Asian Studies, 1981), ch. 4, p. 15. The term "Pembina Utama" was first used in mid-1971. I am indebted to Dr. Suryadinata for this information.

The use of acronyms like Wanbinpus is an obvious pointer to army influence. "Membina" and "Pembina," Ben Anderson notes, are part of a peculiar army terminology dating from the early 1960s. "Pembina" conveys a sense of "shaper," "moulder," or "controller" (in the intelligence sense). (Private communication, February 2, 1984.)

ference the Golkar general secretary, Brig. Gen. Sapardjo stated in quite explicit terms that Golkar consisted of three important components, one of which was ABRI.)[40]

In October 1978, barely three days after the promulgation of the Widodo paper, the Second National Congress of Golkar (MUNAS II) was held in Bali. At this gathering, the post of Pembina Utama was abolished. However, Suharto was chosen as the chairman of the forty-five-member Control Board (Ketua Dewan Pembina). As such, he wielded untrammeled control over the functional group. The Central Control Board is the "Politboro" of Golkar, and Suharto had the power not only to appoint members of the twenty-five-member Central Executive Board (Dewan Pimpinan Pusat, DPP)--the "Central Committee" of the organization--but the power to veto any policies of that body. He also had the power to suspend the DPP.[41] In the event of any such freeze, the DPP's functions were to be taken over by the Control Board.[42] At the same time, the Dewan Pembina was authorized to convene a special congress of the organization to elect and appoint the members of the Control Boards at the provincial and kabupaten level.[43] These new powers not only enhanced Suharto's ability to control the selection of any eventual successor as president; they also gave him more day-to-day involvement in Golkar affairs. "As chairman of the board," a member of the executive board noted at the time, "he will always have the last say."[44]

The post-Bali membership of the Central Control Board was dominated by military officers and civilians associated with Suharto. Amongst the military representatives were General Panggabean, General Darjatmo, General Amir Machmud, General Surono, Lt. Gen. Sudharmono, Lt. Gen. Ali Murtopo, Lt. Gen. Alamsjah, Maj. Gen. Mudjono, Maj. Gen. Bustanil Arifin, Lt. Gen. Sunandar Prijosudarmo, Lt. Gen. Charis Suhud, Maj. Gen. Sudjono Humardhani, and Brig. Gen. Sapardjo. Among the civilians were Dr. Widjojo Nitisastro and half a dozen other prominent technocrats from the cabinet (Drs. Radius Prawiro, Dr. J. B. Sumarlin, Prof. Sudarsono Hadisaputro, Dr. Emil Salim, Dr. Purnomosidi Hadjisarosa and Drs. Harun Zain). A number of other present and former cabinet ministers were also

40. Suryadinata, "Golkar of Indonesia," ch. 4, p. 14. According to Dr. Suryadinata, Sapardjo was the first official to make this point in such strong terms. (Private communication.)

41. The terms "politburo" and "central committee" were used by Jusuf Wanandi, a member of Golkar's Dewan Pimpinan Pusat and a deputy treasurer of the organization. Interview, October 24, 1978.

42. Suryadinata "Golkar of Indonesia," ch. 7, p. 28.

43. See Julian M. Boileau, "Golkar: Functional Group Politics in Indonesia" (M.A. thesis, University of Auckland, 1980), p. 129.

44. Interview with Jusuf Wanandi, October 20, 1978.

included. President Suharto was both chairman and a member of the Dewan Pembina.[45]

The Control Council's eleven-man daily executive committee (Presidium Harian), the body through which the president was said to exercise direct control over Golkar, reflected a similar composition. Seven of the eleven members were prominent generals (Panggabean, Darjatmo, Amir Machmud, Surono, Sudharmono, Ali Murtopo, and Alamsjah); there were three technocrats (Widjojo, Radius Prawiro, and Sumarlin), and one former cabinet minister (Mashuri). The chairman of the body was General Panggabean, coordinating minister for political and security affairs.[46] (It is interesting to note that the Murtopo-CSIS group did not come out of the MUNAS II as well as they had expected. They had supported the idea of the president becoming chairman of the Dewan Pembina, but despite his indifferent health, Ali Murtopo is said to have had his eye on the job of chairman of the daily executive board. There was, however, considerable opposition to this and Suharto may have preferred to keep Murtopo at arm's length, placing Panggabean there instead.[47])

By the time of the MUNAS II, Golkar had gone some way towards "demilitarizing" itself. Prior to its first national congress in 1973, the Golkar leadership, both at the center and in the regions, had been almost completely in the hands of active military officers. The panglima was in almost every case the chairman of the provincial Golkar Control Board (Dewan Pembina Daerah), and Korem and Kodim commanders served concurrently as chairmen of the functional group's Control Boards at the kabupaten and kecamatan levels. (In some areas outside Java, where a Kodam might cover two or three provinces, it was possible for a Korem officers to serve as the chairman of the Golkar *provincial* Control Board.) The Golkar executive boards at the national, provincial, kabupaten, and kecamatan levels were likewise dominated by active military officers. In 1973 the government took the first tentative steps towards "demilitarization," when territorial officers were informed that they had to choose whether to remain within the territorial structure or become full-time Golkar officials. This "change," however, was more apparent than real. For example, a Korem commander who opted to stay on as chairman of a Golkar Control Board was simply transferred to kekaryaan duties; he was still on active duty and still answerable to the Defense Ministry. This could hardly be said to have lessened military influence over Golkar. As a karyawan, such an officer was answerable to the chief of the

---

45.   See *Keputusan Ketua Dewan Pembina Golongan Karya Nomor 02/DP-Golkar/1978 tentang Susunan Personalia Dewan Pembina Golongan Karya*, Jakarta, December 28, 1978. This document was signed by President Suharto in his capacity as chairman of the Dewan Pembina Golongan Karya.

46.   Ibid.

47.   Confidential communication, July 16, 1981.

functional affairs staff (*Kaskar*) in Jakarta (rather than the assistant for territorial affairs), and at the same time, to Golkar headquarters in Jakarta, itself very much in the hands of senior military officers. What is more, the local panglima was still, in almost every case, the chairman of the provincial Golkar Control Board, with considerable influence (via his assistant VI/territorial) over the affairs of the functional group at the local level.

Shortly before the 1977 general elections the Suharto government took a further--and more significant--step towards the "demilitarization" of Golkar when it introduced a ruling that active military officers could not be members of the functional group. The main impact of this decision was felt in the renamed Regional Assessment Boards and the Regency Advisory Boards, the Golkar control bodies at the provincial and kabupaten levels.[48] These bodies, as we have seen, had largely been under the influence of serving military officers, which meant that they were particularly responsive to the wishes of the military and administrative hierarchy. However, the decision to "demilitarize" also affected Golkar's provincial and kabupaten-level *executive* boards. There were twenty-six of the former and roughly 300 of the latter, and the proportion of military officers on these bodies was still quite high.[49] In all, it was said, the decision would result in about 300-400 active military officers giving up their positions in the Golkar regional structure over a six-month period.[50]

To some extent, this second round of civilianization was also more apparent than real. Most of the officers who were obliged to resign were at or near retirement age anyway, and all but a handful were immediately reelected to their former positions. Given their long connection with the armed forces, their status as favored members of the "new class" in the towns and cities of Indonesia, and the influence exercised over them by the ruling organs of Golkar in Jakarta, the so called "demilitarization" was not calculated to produce many upsets.

The rapid transformation of many key Golkar functionaries from territorial officer to karyawan to retired officer in the space of five years was insufficient to still a "more autonomy" debate among certain

---

48. The name Regional Assessment Board (Dewan Pertimbangan Daerah) was introduced under the Golkar constitution of 1978 in place of the former Regional Supervisory Board (Dewan Pembina Daerah - Tingkat I, or Wanbintu). The name Regional Advisory Board (Dewan Penasehat Daerah) took the place of the old Regional Supervisory Board--Regency Level (Dewan Pembina Daerah--Tingkat II, or Wanbindu). This change appears to have been aimed at removing misunderstanding over the use of the word pembina. As of 1978, the Dewan Pembina in Jakarta was the only body to use this term.

49. Interview with Jusuf Wanandi, October 24, 1978.

50. Ibid.

disaffected members of the ruling group. In the period leading up to the MUNAS II in Bali, the leaders of the socalled Trikarya group, the three ex-*kino* (groupings) which had been the major components of the original Sekber Golkar in 1964, voiced wide-ranging criticisms of Golkar as part of an attempt to regain influence in the organization. In the view of the Trikarya leaders--Maj. Gen. (retd.) Suhardiman of Soksi, Maj. Gen. (retd.) Mas Isman of Kosgoro and Brig. Gen. (retd.) Sugandhi of MKGR[51]--Golkar had lost contact with the mass of the people. The organization, they felt, was too bureaucratic and too dependent on the backing of ABRI and Korpri. Not long before the Bali congress, Mas Isman held a meeting of former members of the Seventeenth Brigade of student soldiers at the home of Brig. Gen. Sugandhi. Though all those in attendance were members of Golkar, they opted for less army involvement in the affairs of the functional group and more grassroots input. As a power play, the Trikarya move failed. The Suharto group quite easily crushed an attempt by Mas Isman to contest the Golkar leadership during the Bali meeting; the Mas Isman group, it was said, was able to muster the support of no more than seventy-five of the 1,200 delegates.[52] On the other hand, the conference did at least adopt a resolution giving verbal recognition to the need to ensure that Golkar was more strongly rooted amongst the people.

---

51. The full names of these *kino* was as follows:

Soksi (Sentral Organisasi Karyawan Sosialis Indonesia) or Central Organization of Indonesian Socialist Karyawan; Kosgoro (Koperasi Serba Usaha Gotong Royong) or All-Purpose Mutual Help Cooperatives; MKGR (Musyawarah Kekeluargaan Gotong Royong) or Family Mutual Help Association.

52. Prior to the Bali meeting a number of senior officers, including Lt. Gen. Solichin Gautama Purwanegara, Brig. Gen. Sudarto, Maj. Gen. Mas Isman, and Rear Admiral Djambir Pardjaman, visited Yoga Sugama, Sudomo, and Mohammad Jusuf, all of whom expressed support for the initiative for less army and more grass-roots support in Golkar. According to these three senior generals, Suharto was also receptive to the idea. (At one stage, Sudomo is said to have made the point that Maj. Gen. Amir Murtono, the chairman of the Dewan Pimpinan Pusat of Golkar, was unfit to lead the organization.) If Suharto ever had shared these views, he had changed his mind by the time of the Golkar congress in Bali. According to one account, Lt. Gen. Ali Murtopo made the point (via an editorial in *Merdeka*) that, if the army withdrew from Golkar, it would leave a vacuum which would be filled by forces bent on challenging Suharto. At this stage, it is suggested, Suharto decided that he would lead Golkar himself. Confidential communication, March 25, 1982. Whatever the truth of that account, there is the odd fact that General Panggabean interrupted his stay in Bali to fly back to Jakarta to confer with the president. He returned with the message that Suharto would lead Golkar himself.

If the 1977 changes meant that Golkar was becoming more ci-vilianized, then the Catch 22 to the proposition was that the "civil-ians" concerned were mostly retired military officers. As this devel-opment coincided with the retirement of many members of the Genera-tion of '45, the move could be seen not so much as a "demilitariza-tion" as a device to ensure, at the central level at any rate, the con-tinued dominance of the functional group by those around Suharto.

"Demilitarization" did not mean any substantive changes in Golkar's central leadership or policy. Indeed, it indicated that the Generation of '45 leaders maintained their control over the functional group. At the provincial level, Golkar's "civilianization" was likely to have more impact; but here too the key positions would be filled by retired military men. Golkar strategists argued at the time that this was a significant step, if only because it severed the direct link be-tween official duty and service on the Golkar regional policy-making boards. Retired military men, it was said, would not have any offi-cial backing and would have to rely on their own standing and au-thority in the community to bring influence to bear on their bodies; they could not simply issue orders and insist that these be obeyed. There was something to this assertion. Experience had shown that Hankam's hold over an officer often began to "fade" once he was on the retirement list. However, if the government leaders were worried that they tended to lose control over retired ABRI men, critics charged that the community would still look on these men as *baju hijau* (green shirts), a valid concern in many regions.

Moreover, it could hardly be said that the government had abandoned all control of the provincial Golkar boards. Though these boards might no longer be under the thumb of the Ministry of De-fense and Security, they were very much under the control of Golkar's Central Executive Board, which was itself beholden to the Central Control Board. And that amounted to much the same thing: the leadership of Golkar and the government was interchangeable.

Why did Golkar "demilitarize" itself? The answer would appear to be that the move was forced upon it. Many officers were uncom-fortable with the idea of helping the government political grouping in such an overt and obvious way. Moreover, the presence of military men on Golkar boards was hardly conducive to the notion of Golkar as an independent entity. Times were changing, and an adjustment was necessary. The solution to the problem typified the approach of the New Order rulers. Though changes were made--some cosmetic, others more substantive--the bottom line was the same; power re-mained where it had always been--in the hands of the president and those around him.

Whatever the long-term consequences of MUNAS II, Suharto thus emerged from the conference with his hold over Golkar greatly enhanced. This, in its own way, helped set the stage for the show-down that was looming over the military's role in society. At a time when the army chief of staff was responding to calls that the military stand above all groups in society, the president was tightening his

Table IV. *Golkar: The Structure and Distribution of Power*
(as of 1978)

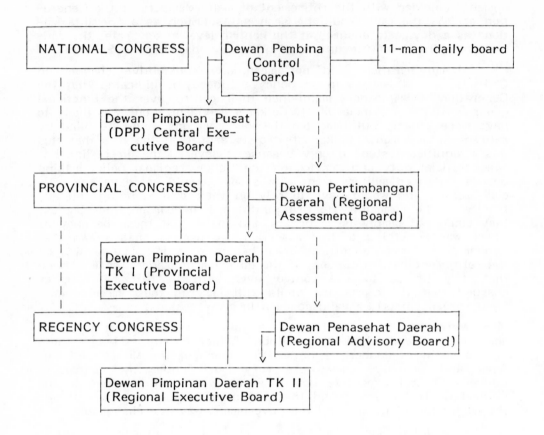

SOURCE: The above diagram was adapted from that prepared by Dr. Leo Suryadinata in his study "Golkar of Indonesia: Its Origins and Development."

Chaired by President Suharto, the 45-member Dewan Pembina was the "Politburo" of Golkar. Day-to-day power was in the hands of an 11-man "daily board" headed by General Panggabean. The DPP was the "Central Committee" of Golkar. After MUNAS II in 1978, seven of the 11 members of the Dewan Pembina's daily board were senior generals, all of them longstanding associates of Suharto.

grip on Golkar with the almost certain intention of ensuring that the functional group would maintain its preeminence in the 1982 general elections. There were still a number of acts to be played out. The "ABRI-above-all-groups" line was only just being taken up by the new minister of defense, General Jusuf. However, it seems beyond doubt that Suharto had always intended that when it came to the crunch, ABRI would weigh in on the side of the political grouping over which he himself presided.

CHAPTER SIX

BOTH SIDES AGAINST THE MIDDLE

We are still being shadowed by the feudal system.

General Sumitro[1]

If you know the tradition in the court of the sultans, the kraton, there is the king, the Sultan, and you have the princes. If the princes come to the Sultan it is always: "You are alright." Maybe three or four princes have different opinions but in their talks it is always one to one, not together. "You are alright!" But if the princes are going to fight, ya, you can fight and the one who wins is the right man. It's more or less the same today, not 100 percent.

General A. H. Nasution[2]

Suharto will never use only one person. He will balance these people, the one controlling the other, for his purpose. And everybody feels Suharto likes him.

Maj. Gen. Sukendro[3]

Sometimes we ask ourselves whether this rivalry problem is not just created by the president himself.

Lt. Gen. Sutopo Juwono[4]

Domo is a watchdog.

General Widodo[5]

When a new presidential office block was nearing completion in Jakarta in the late 1960s, it was known initially as the "KISS" build-

---

1. Interview with General Sumitro, July 18, 1981.
2. Interview with General Nasution, June 23, 1980.
3. Interview with Maj. Gen. Sukendro, July 17, 1981.
4. Interview with Lt. Gen. Sutopo Juwono, July 23, 1981.
5. Interview with General Widodo, November 17, 1981.

ing, this being an abbreviation of the words describing the key functions that were to be performed there--Koordinasi, Integrasi, Stabilisasi, and Sinkronisasi. But the cynics, knowing the way Suharto liked to summon his chief lieutenants and play them off against one another, were soon suggesting that KISS was an acronym derived from the words "Ke Istana Sendiri-Sendiri." ("To the palace one by one.") It was an apt observation. Suharto, though he enjoyed enormous power by virtue of his position as president and Commander-in-Chief of the armed forces (not to mention his position as the dominant influence in the all-powerful armed forces) adopted a style of rule that was at times decidedly patrimonial.

Suharto was highly skilled at playing one "prince" off against another. And the structures he had erected, particularly in the army, his choice of men for top military positions--in which loyalty was preferred over application and aptitude--along with a highly unorthodox "doubling up" of key military functions, allowed him enormous scope to play just this game, the system thus created serving admirably his own immediate ends, if not necessarily those of the armed forces or the nation as a whole. As we have seen, Suharto believed in the need for a "creative tension" between those who served around him, and adopted a style of divide-and-rule under which the position of potential rivals was effectively weakened while his own position was effectively enhanced.

Suharto, having been thrust on to the center of the political stage by the events of 1965, had spent the years since then systematically extending and defending his power base. The result was that the institutionalization of the military within the bureaucratic polity was virtually complete, and the position of Suharto virtually unassailable. Through an elaborate and extensive command system, in which power and responsibility were often parallel and overlapping, and through the judicious appointment of trustworthy Javanese and/or Christians and Outer Islanders, Suharto had been able to ensure that the power and influence of any one of half a dozen of the key powerholders was always counterbalanced and neutralized by the power and influence of at least one or other of his colleagues.

Nowhere was this more apparent than within Hankam. In the early 1980s, General Jusuf was the minister of defense and the commander of the armed forces. Admiral Sudomo was the deputy commander of the armed forces and, in theory, answerable to Jusuf on military matters. But Sudomo was also the commander of Kopkamtib. Acting in this capacity, he was able to go "above" Jusuf to the president and "below" him in the sense that he had direct access to and commanded the loyalty of the commanders of each of the military regions. The pattern was repeated throughout the system. Yoga Sugama was not only chief of Bakin but was, for two years, chief of staff of Kopkamtib as well. Benny Murdani was not only assistant 1 (intelligence) at Hankam but head of Kopkamtib intelligence and deputy chairman of Bakin. He was, at the same time, head of Pusintelstrat (Strategic Intelligence Center) and would in an emergency have had day-to-day command of all Kopassandha (Red Beret) units,

the "praetorian guard" of Hankam. The commander of the Kopassandha, Maj. Gen. Yogie Suardi Memet, doubled as commander of the
Siliwangi (West Java) military region. By this device, patently
"illegal" in the eyes of a number of retired officers, Suharto concentrated extraordinary power in the hands of half a dozen of his most
trusted aides. At the same time, he ensured that his position remained paramount by dispersing power among officers who, while loyal
to both himself and the armed forces, were divided by interpersonal
rivalries and suspicions. These interpersonal rivalries were, in fact,
a key feature of the group of ruling military officers around Suharto,
and there is a good deal of evidence to suggest that they were actively encouraged by the president. For example, Ali Murtopo (and
the institutions and groups over which he presided) were largely an-
tagonistic to Amir Machmud and the powerful Ministry of Home Affairs
over which he ruled. (Murtopo had earlier been a bitter rival of
General Sumitro and was suspected in some quarters of having engineered Sumitro's downfall.) Jusuf was wary of Murtopo, contemptuous of Panggabean, his predecessor as minister, and had no time for
Widodo, the 1978–80 army chief of staff. Murdani shared Jusuf's feelings about Widodo and enjoyed a fairly testy relationship with Yoga
Sugama. Yoga remembered Sumitro with hostility. Nor were those
rivalries confined to military circles. Murdani and the civilian foreign
minister, Dr. Mochtar Kusumaatmadja, were often felt to be competing
for influence on foreign policy matters, each confident that he enjoyed the full backing of the president. Indeed, Suharto had been
known to use Murdani and Mochtar on the same problem, sometimes
sending them out to accomplish opposite goals, thereby exacerbating
personal, institutional, and also civilian-military rivalries.[6]

This system had been used to good effect in the past and, if it
had played a part in fanning the uniquely destructive Sumitro-Ali
Murtopo clash in the early 1970s, it had at least kept most of the loci
of power in rough balance and in harmonious orbit around the president. Now, as Suharto was forced to consider the question of ABRI's
increasing estrangement from society, there is considerable evidence
that he fell back on the old device of not letting the right hand know
what the left hand was doing. In 1979, the two most senior officers
in Hankam--Jusuf and Sudomo--were sent in different directions and
apparently encouraged to make contradictory statements about the role
that ABRI would play in society, the more "positive" remarks being
delivered in public by Jusuf, while the more "pragmatic" and conventional observations were made by Sudomo in private meetings with
senior military commanders. (There were, however, a number of
cross-currents running at this time and, while the evidence suggests
that Suharto played one key aide off against another, it would be

---

6. When Vietnamese foreign minister Nguyen Co Thach puzzled aloud
over the fact that Murdani and Mochtar had come to Hanoi on different occasions and said very different things, an Indonesian editor
had said, "Yes, and you must remember that both were sent by the
same man!"

wrong to see the events of this period solely in terms of presidential manipulation. To some extent, Jusuf may have been a willing partici- pant in the game that was being played.)

When Jusuf took up his post as defense minister in March 1978, there was already considerable concern about the widening gap be- tween the armed forces and the people. Late in 1977, students in Jakarta and Bandung had stressed that "ABRI should be returned to the people."[7] In mid-January 1978, Lt. Gen. Dharsono had called on the armed forces to be more attentive to public unease and not base everything on military power and strength.[8] In March, the PPP had felt that the situation was serious enough for it to put forward a pro- posal in Commission A (Defense and Security) of the MPR that "ABRI stand above all groups in society."[9]

None of these pleas had received a particularly sympathetic hearing. The student call, being so closely interwoven with the in- creasing student criticism of the president and his family, was either rejected out of hand or treated as some sort of subversive manoeu- ver. Dharsono's call, critical of the New Order and made in the presence of the very students and others who had criticized Suharto, had so angered the president that he insisted that the unrepentant Dharsono be removed from his post at ASEAN.[10] Nor had the PPP met with any success. The faction, which had differed on a number of issues with other groups in the MPR, particularly the combined factions of Golkar, ABRI, and the Provincial Delegates, saw this proposal, like most of its others, turned down.

Change was in the air, however. As we have seen, the ABRI leadership had felt at the time of the December 1977 meeting that they needed to get prominent retired generals on side--and one of the major concerns of the retired "seniors" had been this very estrange- ment. It was perhaps not coincidental that the theme of the 1978 Commander's Call, held in Jakarta in February, was "To step up vigi- lance, alertness, *and the integration of ABRI and the people* to safe- guard and make a success of the 1978 MPR General Session" (italics added).[11] Widodo, installed as army chief of staff on January 26, 1978, had been working hard to get Fosko off the ground and had taken steps, almost immediately on entering office, to set up a com- mittee to redefine the army's position. Widodo's early public state- ments on this question were cautious and seemingly noncommittal. In

---

7. David Jenkins, "The generals flex their muscles," *FEER*, Febru- ary 3, 1978.

8. "The second time around," Ibid., February 3, 1978.

9. *Tempo*, March 25, 1978.

10. David Jenkins, "Exit outspoken Dharsono," *FEER*, February 24, 1978, and "Last broadside from Dharsono," Ibid., March 3, 1978.

11. See *Berita Buana, Merdeka, Suara Karya, Pelita,* and *Angkatan Bersenjata*, February 22, 1978.

April 1978, he talked of the "estranged relations" between ABRI and a section of the community. "ABRI is reduced in its genuine worth in the eyes of the people," he noted elliptically, "and is said to be socio-politically no longer above all groups."[12] In June, speaking in Medan at the 27th anniversary of the Bukit Barisan (Kodam II) Command, Widodo stressed that the people were an inexhaustible source of strength for the armed forces, and should not be neglected on any pretext. Uniting the people and the armed forces, "as urged by President Suharto," should be carried out by ways of corrective and educative contacts, not by coercion and pressure.[13] In Jakarta two days later, the army chief of staff reiterated his appeal for unity between the people and ABRI "as urged by President Suharto some time ago."[14] By October 1978, Widodo--and the army general staff--was not only stressing the need for ABRI-people unity but had come out in favor of ABRI playing a less central role in the political process. In his Armed Forces Day speech on October 5, Suharto had himself taken up this call.[15]

Jusuf, no less concerned about this state of affairs than Widodo, had known of the existence of the Seskoad paper and had, soon after his installation as minister of defense in March 1978, asked for a copy of it. Initially, his staff at Hankam had sought to deflect him by writing an entirely new paper.[16] However, this attempt did not prove successful. Jusuf was able to obtain a copy of the Seskoad document and this, it is said, influenced him and reinforced his own belief that there was a very great need to bolster ABRI-people unity. When Jusuf unveiled his program for ABRI in mid-1978, one of its three central pillars was the need to bridge the gap between the armed forces and the people. (The other goals were improving the welfare of the ordinary soldiers and increasing the quality and combat readiness of the Indonesian forces. This was an astute blend of objectives; in the wake of ABRI's poor performance and heavy losses in East Timor, many professionally oriented officers were said to have blamed this on the military's neglect of its "true" role while it concentrated on the politico-economic aspects of its dual function in the years since 1966.[17] Jusuf's program ministered to these concerns while stressing ABRI's oneness with the people, an essential prerequisite if ABRI were to continue to be effective as a social-political force. At the same time, his great popularity among Muslim groups

---

12. *Antara*, April 1978.

13. Ibid., June 22, 1978.

14. Ibid.

15. See speech by President Suharto, October 5, 1978.

16. Interview with General Nasution, May 11, 1979.

17. See Barbara S. Harvey, "Indonesia: The Search for Stability, the Inevitability of Change," *Dyason House Papers*, 2 (October 1977): 1.

helped break down the impression that ABRI and Islam were somehow bound to be more or less permanently at loggerheads.)

To help bridge the ABRI-people gap, Jusuf gave top priority to what he called "territorial cultivation"--the improvement of the all-important territorial structure. His aim, he said in the second half of 1978, was to send specially qualified territorial officers to key posts, presumably at the Korem and Kodim level; until they were ready, a team of social scientists was to be assigned in each Kodam to assist the territorial officers. In keeping with the new policy, the minister took steps to curtail the activities of ABRI officers, some of them very highly placed, whose ostentatious lifestyles were a matter of notoriety. As part of the new emphasis on austerity and simple living, he withdrew the armed military guards that had been posted around the clock at the homes of cabinet ministers, senior bureaucrats, and high-ranking military officers. Jusuf's policies thus had something for everyone; they stressed the need to improve the training and performance of ABRI's operational units while at the same time tending to the needs of the territorial "leg."

There was, as we have seen, considerable ill feeling between Jusuf and Widodo; neither man had any time for the other, a fact that worried a number of senior staff officers. However, the two men did discuss the matter of the army's role in society at some length and were in broad agreement about what that role should be.[18] The "Widodo paper," which was endorsed by the army chief of staff six months after Jusuf became minister, is said to have been "completely in line with Jusuf's views."[19] Jusuf, like all other senior officers, was committed to the notion of the army having a dual function in society. But, like Widodo, he wished to see certain limits on this role. In July 1979, Jusuf was asked whether the military had not "gone too far" with the dwifungsi. "I would not use the term 'going too far'," he answered, "but we should be much more moderate."[20]

During his first ten months in office, Jusuf's statements on this topic had been of a rather general nature. However, in February 1979, he squarely addressed the question of the army's relationship with the political groupings in society. During a tour of West and South Sumatra, Jusuf ordered all ABRI echelons not to interfere in, or busy themselves with, the internal affairs of the political parties and Golkar. In briefing all ranks of Kodam IV/Sriwijaya in Palembang and Kodam III/17 August in Padang, Jusuf said repeatedly that ABRI should let the political parties and Golkar alone to learn and attempt to grow and become mature on their own strength: "Don't be suspicious instantly when you assume that people are of the United Party or the PDI, that's not good and that's wrong. As ABRI members you must be fair and accommodate their aspirations. Don't defend one

---

18. Nasution interview, June 23 1980.

19. Ibid.

20. Interview with General Jusuf, July 25, 1979.

while you do all sorts of things with the others, that's not good. You must remember this well and note it well."[21]

Although certain themes were always stressed in his public utterances, Jusuf had the politician's knack of keeping his ear close to the ground and addressing particular problems and grievances as they were brought to his attention. His observations on ABRI's role in society, which were to receive so much attention in the months to come, may have been triggered to some extent by purely local developments. Before his statements in Padang and Palembang, the minister had received a report from the Kodim commander in Tanjong Pandan and Belitung, Lt. Col. Ali Masahwa, on the split in the PDI in the region. Jusuf, according to one account, gave an order on the spot that, true to the basic principles that it was a protector and guardian of society, ABRI must not side with only one group. He ordered ABRI members to stop interfering in disputes in the political parties or Golkar unless those disputes created a problem of security and order.[22] Jusuf noted that the ABRI territorial apparatus had often "meddled" in local government affairs. If this continued, he said, it would obscure the rights, tasks, and authority of "another department." Accordingly, he ordered the territorial apparatus to stop the practice. "Up front, ABRI must be an example," he said, "and in the rear it must be a stimulus for society's progress. . . . If ABRI does not wish to be the target of a policy of playing it off against others, then you must by no means engage in intrigues to get people to fight against one another. That's extremely dangerous. I warn you from now on that it must be stopped." Jusuf observed that almost every matter--even the loss of a chicken--was reported to Kopkamtib. This, he said, was mistaken; that was not Kopkamtib's task. It was the "stimulus and mover" in case there was stagnation in the mechanism of the government organization: "I have said to Admiral Sudomo, 'When can you ever take a rest when all matters in the life of this nation are reported to Kopkamtib?'"[23]

The account of Jusuf's observations in Sumatra would seem to suggest that the defense minister was drawn into this matter almost by accident. However, even if that were the case, it must be assumed that Suharto very soon gave this line his blessing. It is inconceivable that Jusuf made it such an issue without Suharto's express backing; indeed, the minister always went out of his way to emphasize that he was acting in the name of the president.

In his Padang and Palembang speeches, Jusuf noted that there were certain standards by which one could judge the progress of the parties. There was progress if they were developing strong roots in the community, and thus serving as the real channel of the community's political aspirations. There was progress if, besides devel-

21.   *Pelita*, February 6, 1979.   USE.

22.   Ibid.

23.   Ibid.

oping and struggling for the interests and the aspirations of their own groups, they were also developing national aspirations under which group interests and aspirations were subordinated. There was progress if members of the parties and Golkar were freer in electing their leaders at all levels according to their own organizations' constitutions and by-laws. Political development in the past ten years, he said, had concerned the orientation, culture, and restructuring of organizations. Party and Golkar functionaries had often been the target, approached in all ways, from persuasion and pressure to direct intervention. Now this period was considered to have passed. The time had come to permit the parties and Golkar to function from below.[24]

Jusuf's speech, so at variance with what had until then been considered the government view, brought an immediate response. "The statement is very encouraging," observed Sabam Sirait, the PDI secretary general.[25] According to Ridwan Saidi of the PPP, the Jusuf statement was a fresh stimulus for the sociopolitical groups to come of age and function as they should. "The democratization process has got an encouraging stimulus."[26] H. M. Munasir of the PPP and Hardjanto of the PDI fully supported the defense minister's instruction that ABRI not interfere in the internal affairs of the parties. The reaction from Golkar was a little more subdued. Ir. Sarwono Kusumaatmadja, secretary of the Golkar grouping in the DPR, welcomed the minister's statement but said that, if the sociopolitical groups refused to comply with the rules of the game in their own organizations, this would automatically invite the intervention of outsiders. Moreover, so long as ABRI did not yet trust 100 percent the commitment of these sociopolitical forces to Pancasila and the 1945 Constitution, it would continue to interfere. The Jusuf statement, he said, was a signal that the "intensity" of ABRI's interference would be "regulated" as time went on. However, no one should dream that ABRI's interference would automatically disappear.[27] As it turned out, this sort of skepticism was not misplaced.

From Sumatra, Jusuf flew to Irian Jaya, where he again called on ABRI to refrain from interfering in the internal affairs of the political parties and Golkar.[28] The following week he emphasized that ABRI did not give precedence to or favor any one group, faction, party, or Golkar because ABRI was from and for all the people. ABRI must neither let itself be pitted against others, nor pit one

---

24. *Kompas*, February 7, 1979. USE.

25. Ibid., February 12, 1979. USE.

26. Ibid.

27. Kompas, February 8, 1979. USE.

28. Ibid.

group against another. ABRI must not take steps that could "make a muddle" of its authority in the country's constitutional life.[29]

The Jusuf message, which the minister continued to spell out in speeches across the country, attracted increasing support. *Pelita*, the paper associated with the PPP, recognized the obvious benefits that would accrue to the political parties if the policy were enforced.

> The late General Sudirman once said that soldiers were those who joined the TNI not because of wanting to get a bowl of rice but because of the call of *"ibu pertiwi"* [another word for *"tanah air"* or fatherland]. Sudirman did not use the word "tanah air." His intention was none other than to indicate that ABRI is the people's own flesh and blood. . . . Considering General Sudirman's dictum, the stipulation of the preamble of the 1945 Constitution, and Article 30 of the state's Constitution, we underscore and welcome the statement of General Jusuf . . . that ABRI as an instrument of the state shall protect all layers of the populace and that the people should be involved in the defense of the country and state.[30]

As Jusuf continued, his message became clearer and more explicit. Speaking in East Java at the end of April, he said that ABRI was not the defender of a group of people but the defender of all groups of people; ABRI did not defend a part of the country but all parts of the country. ABRI was not an instrument of a group, a political party, or an individual, but an instrument of the nation and state.[31] This, of course, was precisely what the Widodo paper--and many retired ABRI "seniors"--had been saying. What is more, Jusuf made a point of being available to these people. As he noted in July 1979:

> I see them all the time, these people. Kawilarang! Adjie! They all know me well from the days when I was a young officer. I said, "Whenever you have anything you want to say, you come and see me before you go screaming it out. If you don't get anywhere with me, you can scream it out all over the world." But I said, "If you scream it out *before* you see me, then I will push you down to the very bottom of the ocean. And I won't push you in the back. I will push you face to face."[32]

---

29. Ibid., February 15, 1979. USE.

30. *Pelita*, February 19, 1979. USE.

31. *Angkatan Bersenjata*, April 28, 1979. USE.

32. Interview with General Jusuf, July 25, 1979.

Late in August, the defense minister told an "informal gathering" of senior government and ABRI officials in South Sulawesi that the role demanded from ABRI to be the dynamizer of the people's political awareness did not mean that ABRI must interfere in the internal affairs of the political parties. Let the political parties as a social institution grow normally in Indonesia's political life, he said. "Let the political parties elect their own chairman. Don't interfere in their internal affairs." ABRI had to stand in the middle, not side with any one group, in accordance with the message of the late General Sudirman and the 1945 Constitution.[33]

Meanwhile, Jusuf's initiatives continued to receive widespread support--particularly from retired senior officers. Early in October, Lt. Gen. Ali Sadikin observed in an interview with *Merdeka* that during the physical revolution "ABRI and the people were indeed like fish and water."[34] But at the time of the 1977 election, Sadikin said, people had been shocked by the statement of a high government official, headlined massively in the newspaper, that ABRI was a member of the big Golkar family. "And now General Jusuf wishes to restore ABRI to its true position as the property of the people, of the PPP, the PDI, and Golkar, in accordance with the law, the nation's philosophy, the Seven Pledges, and the Soldier's Oath." According to Sadikin, the concept of ABRI being a sociopolitical force needed to be questioned again. What were ABRI's politics? In his opinion, ABRI's politics were to safeguard Pancasila and the 1945 Constitution. In essence, the aspiration of ABRI's dual function was to protect Pancasila and the 1945 Constitution, and the political emphasis had to be placed there.

> ABRI's dual function must be interpreted as meaning that ABRI comes when needed to improve the situation. After the situation has returned to normal, ABRI must restore the non-ABRI apparatus. The dual function must be interpreted as a mission, not as a placement means. As a channel, non-ABRI components tend to be treated as being incompetent, untrustworthy. The channel tends to break spirit and initiative, the sense of belonging and responsibility.[35]

Domination was "extremely dangerous" as the people might be pushed to abandon ABRI, to be indifferent and apathetic. Speaking of his experience as governor of Jakarta, Sadikin said,

> I assigned ABRI men to the post of mayor only when it was necessary. Out of the five mayors only two were ABRI men. I thought if all the mayors were ABRI

33. *Kompas*, August 27, 1979. USE.

34. *Merdeka*, October 2, 1979. USE.

35. Ibid.

people, civilians would at most reach the position of secretary to the camat [subdistrict chief]. And I feared
that this would be a blow to the dignity, self-respect and
hopes of the civilian employees. If we fly into a rage
when accused of upholding a military government, we
must show that the charges are unfounded and that most
government positions must be filled by civilians.[36]

If the Hankam leadership wished to convince the people that
ABRI stood above all groups and that ABRI was not the property of
only one group, then "the political ambition" must inevitably be curtailed: "If the political ambition is too big, it will encourage the ambition for power and this power ambition tends to treat non-ABRI
parties as political enemies. I think the campaign of ABRI's integration with the people will face a test, for example, in the coming general election."[37] ABRI, Sadikin said, should leave the parties and
Golkar alone. It should protect these three sociopolitical forces so
long as they remained within the framework of Pancasila and the 1945
Constitution, and should only act when one of them should prove to
have deviated. In his opinion, civilians were not stupid. They were
experts in their various fields. But they were submerged, as conditions and environments denied them any opportunity.

When I arrived in the context of the dual function, I offered a leadership and conditions that created the climate
to restore their confidence and self-respect. That, for
example, the man responsible in the village is the lurah
and not the Babinsa [village noncom], that in the subdistrict the camat is responsible and not the Koramil,
that in the municipality the mayor is responsible and not
the Kodim and that in Jakarta the governor is responsible
and not the Kodam. And responsibility cannot possibly
be upheld if the person responsible is himself cowardly.[38]

Similar sentiments were being voiced by General Sumitro, now
making his first public pronouncements since his retirement in 1974.
In an interview in the same issue of *Merdeka*, the former Kopkamtib
commander called for change in essentially two main areas—ABRI's relations with other social-political groups, and the appointment of ABRI
men to nonmilitary functions.[39] The ABRI-people unity that was being promoted by Jusuf, Sumitro said, should be followed up by a
"normalization" program. This program should cover a phased reduction in ABRI's involvement in practical politics, and the public should
provide support by making suggestions for the program, because it

---

36. Ibid.

37. Ibid.

38. Ibid.

39. *Merdeka*, October 2, 1979. USE.

was time ABRI "returned to its old position." "As the political parties made a mistake, ABRI too, had confessed likewise, and now the
important thing is that we should work together." Golkar, Sumitro
said, must stand on its own. "Its cadres must be able to produce
new ideas, new concepts, and be able to solve social and state problems." Golkar, the PDI, and the PPP were equal in position and
Golkar should no longer be asking ABRI for help. ABRI engaged in
politics "only at the strategic level between strategic leaders." As
Sumitro saw it, the political parties and the functional group should
become mass organizations; at present, he felt, they tended to be
cadre organizations. According to Sumitro, ABRI's involvement in
"practical politics"--by which he appeared to be referring to the appointment of karyawan--had stemmed from its desire to prevent any
revival of the PKI. In this process, he noted, many military men had
become bupatis, directors-general, governors, and ambassadors.
This involvement "has now gone too far and this has given rise to
unnecessary weaknesses." What was needed was a process of "disas-
sociation." However, such a process must run smoothly so as not to
create a vacuum. The home minister, Sumitro thought, was obliged
to prepare civilian leaders for these jobs.

In May 1979, the principles that had been enumerated by Jusuf,
including, inter alia, those dealing with the role of ABRI as a social
force, had been set out in a pocket-sized, 110-page "blue book."
With regard to the relationship between ABRI and the political parties
and Golkar, this affirmed that ABRI as a social force had a position
equal to the political parties and Golkar; there was no subordination
and none should feel superior to the other. ABRI, the blue book
stressed, always regarded the political parties and Golkar as partners
in the struggle, and worked side by side with them in making a success of the development program, creating a steady and dynamic national stability and promoting national resilience.[40] The chief of staff
for functional affairs, Lt. Gen. Charis Suhud, made exactly the same
points when addressing mid-career officers at Seskoad on August 11,
1979.[41]

By October 1979, those principles had apparently gone by the
board. ABRI had climbed into bed with Golkar yet again and had
confirmed that it was in fact a member of the "big Golkar family."
The story of how this happened provides some telling insights into
the way Indonesia was governed in the late 1970s.

Suharto, it seems clear, had recognized the need to bridge the
gap between the armed forces and the community and had given his
blessing to Jusuf's attempts to present a new-look ABRI. However,
the president was enough of a realist to know that, while there were

40. See *ABRI Sebagai Kekuatan Social*, p. 34.

41. See *Ceramah Kaskar Hankam Tentang Kekaryan ABRI* didepan
Siswa Peserta Seskoad pada tanggal 11 Augustus '79 di Bandung
(Departemen Kejuangan, Seskoad, 1979).

obvious benefits to be gained by such an approach, there were potential dangers as well. In Suharto's view, ABRI and Golkar appear
to have been indivisible and, if Jusuf were to run too far with the
"ABRI-above-all-groups" ball, it would almost certainly undermine
Golkar's position at the 1982 elections.

On the evidence available, it appears that Suharto resolved this
dilemma by being all things to all men--at least in the initial stages.
He gave his backing to Jusuf and let him make the running about the
role that ABRI would play. At the same time, he covered his bets by
having Sudomo privately reassure senior officers that nothing had
really changed, and that in the next election government policy
would, in effect, be "more of the same." Long before the October
1979 meeting at which it was affirmed that ABRI was "absolutely
Golkar," the evidence suggests, Suharto employed Sudomo to undermine Jusuf.

At the Rapat Gubernur (governors' meeting) in January 1979,
Jusuf stressed that governors were civilian officials within the Department of Internal Affairs. Although a governor might be a military man, the defense minister said, he was not to treat the job as a
military position; civilians working in the governor's office should be
brought into things and made to feel part of a team, and there should
be no military-type parades at provincial government offices. Later
the same day, Sudomo addressed the conference and provided an "explanation" of the ABRI position which, in the opinion of many of
those present, was directly at variance with that of the minister of
defense. Returning the next morning, Sudomo sent all civilian officials from the room and "clarified" Jusuf's statement in even stronger
terms.[42] Such a policy, it is suggested, had two attractions. On
the one hand, it allowed the government, the army, and the president
to benefit from the considerable goodwill that Jusuf was generating,
while in no way threatening the outcome of the 1982 election. On the
other, it would leave Jusuf, whose popularity was by now quite extensive, highly vulnerable when the wind eventually changed, as it
was bound to.

Jusuf and Sudomo, Suharto's two principal instruments in this
endeavor, were very different from one another, although both were
Suharto loyalists and both owed their positions to Suharto. Jusuf, a
member of the Buginese nobility, had been one of the three offi-
cers--in his view the principal officer--who had persuaded Sukarno to
sign the March 11 (Supersemar) Order of 1966 which transferred
authority to Suharto. He had been considered a loyal member of the
Suharto team ever since. His appointment as minister of defense/
commander of the armed forces, which had come as a complete surprise in the army, had been a reminder not only that Suharto rewarded his most loyal lieutenants and chose key ABRI officers from
among them but that he still wielded extraordinary power over the
armed forces. It was in almost every way an artful political move.

---

42. Confidential communication, December 27, 1979.

Jusuf had always been a loner; he had never been a member of any particular clique, and he had neither a strong divisional background nor an independent power base. He was, moreover, an Outer Islander and a devout Muslim. Long before his arbitrary command style and his sublime disregard for paperwork had antagonized many senior staff officers at Hankam, it had been apparent that Jusuf was unlikely ever to pose any sort of a threat to Suharto. In that sense, his appointment had been a master stroke; from Suharto's point of view, it was all pluses and no minuses.

Sudomo was a very different kind of officer. First associated with Suharto in 1961, when he was commander of the naval forces assigned to Suharto's Mandala Command for the liberation of West Irian, he had polished up his pro-Suharto credentials during his term as chief of staff of the navy between 1969 and 1973, disposing of whole concourses of leftist and pro-Sukarno officers, and doing it with such singlemindedness and despatch that it had become something of a joke amongst those in the Suharto group that, if Sudomo did not stop soon, the Indonesian Navy might be left with a number of ships but no officers to command them. (By his own count, Sudomo "disposed of" 1,500 naval officers at this time.) He had been rewarded with the post of chief of staff of Kopkamtib under General Sumitro, and, despite a shaky start during Malari, had held on to the position after Sumitro's fall. In 1978, his loyalty and responsiveness to the presidential will established beyond question, he had assumed the mantle of Pangkopkamtib (commander of Kopkamtib) from Suharto. Sudomo was a Suharto man through and through, with no political ambitions of his own. (In fact, by the late 1970s Sudomo was making it plain that he wanted to retire; it was Suharto who, needing Sudomo as part of his grand design, insisted that he stay on.) And even if he had had ambitions, his religion—he had converted to Christianity in order to marry—and his service affiliation would have made it impossible for him to move any higher in an environment that was dominated by the army and that was at least nominally Muslim. At first glance, Sudomo struck many people as bland, affable, and good-natured, if perhaps a little shallow. Some retired senior officers, particularly those out of favor with the ruling group, spoke of him disparagingly and made him the butt of their private jokes. (Ali Sadikin, who had once been Sudomo's commanding officer and who was a lieutenant general long before Sudomo received his third star, tended to look on the admiral as a derisory figure and make unkind comments about his competence.)[43] But Sudomo was loyal, hard-working (when Jusuf was off on his travels Sudomo regularly signed 200 of the most important Hankam documents a day), powerful, and, above all, "pragmatic." If Suharto had decided fairly early in the piece that it would be necessary to keep a rein on Jusuf and ensure that the talk about ABRI's neutrality did not jeopardize the electoral interests of Golkar, then Sudomo would have been an ideal instrument

---

43. Confidential communication, June 4, 1980. Several other retired officers made the same point.

for his purposes. In his capacity as deputy commander of the armed forces, Sudomo was subordinate to Jusuf. But as the commander of Kopkamtib, he had direct access to Suharto and could, in fact, meet the president at any time he wished. Equally important, he had direct access to the all-important Kodam commanders in their capacity as regional executive agents of Kopkamtib. As we have seen, each Kodam commander was chairman of the Muspida (Provincial Leadership Council) and, until the late 1970s, chairman of the local Golkar Control Board. Moreover, with Jusuf away so often and disinclined to immerse himself in paperwork, Sudomo, as deputy commander of the armed forces, was in an ideal position to "remind" senior officers that one had to be realistic, to emphasize that, whatever Jusuf might be saying in public, there was no intention on anyone's part in Jakarta to ignore the wellbeing of Golkar.

In 1983, after he had taken up a new position as minister for manpower, Sudomo confirmed that he had indeed played such a role. By and large, he said, his actions could be described by the Javanese word *ngemong*--he had sought to avoid any confrontation in his relations with Jusuf. But sometimes he would take a more conventional "military management" approach and point out privately to the minister that he had made a mistake in a certain statement; on these occasions, Jusuf would quite readily allow him to clarify the remark. At other times, he would just go ahead and correct the mistake anyway. "I considered all the time my position at Kopkamtib," Sudomo said. "Because I am not under him at Kopkamtib; I'm under the president." At times, Sudomo would actually raise a Jusuf statement with the president, who would say: "You have to change that!"[44]

By their very nature, these differences took place out of public view. But at the end of 1979 a document surfaced which brought the contradictions in the Suharto approach to light, an embarrassing development for the ruling group. This document recorded details of a secret meeting Sudomo had held with the Golkar Central Executive (DPP) on October 17, 1979 after meeting with the president earlier that morning. Twelve months to the day after Widodo had endorsed a document in which it was affirmed that the army would endanger its unity and identity if it relied on any one group in society, Sudomo here made it perfectly clear that ABRI was "absolutely Golkar" and a key member of "the big Golkar family."[45] Copies of this secret Golkar memorandum were later to find their way into the hands of various opposition figures, much to the embarrassment of the government. If the document was genuine--and it seems beyond doubt that it was--then it suggests that the ruling group was capable of a quite extraordinary degree of cynicism and duplicity.

---

44. Interview with Admiral Sudomo, August 6, 1983.

45. See *Hasil Pertemuan DPP Golkar dan Wapangab Pangkopkamtib* (Jakarta: Dewan Pimpinan Pusat, Golongan Karya, Sekretariat Jendral, Jl. Majapahit 29, October 17, 1979). The document is signed by the secretary general of the DPP Golkar, Sugianto.

The Golkar document, which ran to four pages and a little over 1,000 words, was typed on paper bearing the Golkar letterhead and with the signature and "chop" of the Golkar secretary general, Sugianto. According to it, the meeting between Sudomo and an eleven-man Golkar DPP delegation was held between 8 and 9:30 a.m. on October 17, at the Ministry of Defense building, with Sudomo reportedly speaking for and on behalf of the Ministry of Defense and Security. The Golkar delegation included the general chairman, Maj. Gen. Amir Murtono, the four deputy chairmen (Brig. Gen. Sugandhi, H. Moch. Tarmudji, Lt. Gen. Sugih Arto, and David Napitupulu), and Sugianto.

The document indicated that at the meeting, an agreement was reached to form a forum for periodic consultations between Hankam/ABRI and the DPP Golkar both at the central and provincial levels. The regular liaison officers were to be Sukardi, representing the DPP Golkar, and Col. Harisugiman, representing Hankam.[46] At the central level, these consultations would be held between the DPP Golkar and Hankam, which would be represented by Sudomo.[47] At the province level, the consultations would take place between the Dewan Pimpinan Daerah (DPD, Provincial Executive Board) and the military region commander acting in his capacity as Laksusda (special executor of Kopkamtib). These forums, which were to be limited and closed, would seek the optimal syncronization of actions taken within "the big Golkar family." It had been agreed, the document said, that in the near future Sudomo and members of the DPP Golkar would make unannounced visits to the regions. The aim, amongst other things, was to explain the relationship and position of Golkar within the three-lane framework of the big Golkar family (Golkar-Korpri-ABRI) in efforts to ensure a Golkar victory in the 1982 general elections. The document continued: "In this meeting it is affirmed that ABRI is absolutely Golkar. This is in line with President Suharto's affirmation to the same effect in the meeting with the deputy ABRI commander/Kopkamtib commander at 7 a.m. on Wednesday, October 17, 1979."[48]

If that document suggested that ABRI and Golkar were getting together again despite Jusuf's assurances to the contrary, then there was more to come. A three-and-a-quarter page "draft memorandum" allegedly hammered out by Golkar officials between October 18 and 20 seemed to force an already sensitive issue by deliberately juxtaposing Jusuf's words with Sudomo's purported statements. The problem facing the Golkar leaders was the apparent "contradiction" to which Ali Sadikin had referred only one week earlier. "If ABRI is really one with the people and does not side with any one group," Sadikin had asked, "why is there a Big Golkar Family which is composed of

---

46. Ibid. Harisugiman was the Spri (personal assistant) to Admiral Sudomo.

47. There was no mention in the document of Jusuf.

48. See *Hasil Pertemuan DPP Golkar dan Wapangab/Pangkopkamtib*.

Korpri, Golkar, and ABRI?"[49]   The "Draft Memorandum on the Internal Mechanism of the Big Golkar Family" came up with a novel answer
to this question.

It made plain that the Golkar leaders felt that they were dealing
with a matter of fundamental importance to the future development of
their organization.   Golkar had been established fifteen years earlier
as a joint secretariat with the aim of enforcing the unity of the sociopolitical forces in confronting the dominating role of the Communist
Party.   After the coup attempt, the memorandum said, Golkar had become the mainstay of the sociopolitical forces supporting the New
Order.   In 1975 the existence of Golkar and the two restructured
political parties had been formally recognized, and Golkar had then
been able to form a majority in both the MPR and the DPR, and had
participated in drawing up the Broad Outlines of State Policy.   The
growth and development of the Golkar family, of which Korpri and
ABRI were "supporting components," was positive, as these two components were not sociopolitical forces in their own right.   At the same
time, the document quickly added, "the organization of relations within the body of the Big Golkar Family is totally an internal issue of
Golkar, which has formal legal status as a sociopolitical force."   Because Golkar was recognized as a sociopolitical force and because
Korpri and ABRI did not possess this function, the memorandum went
on, problems had arisen regarding the relationship between Golkar
and these two components.[50]   Many complications had arisen, result-
ing in the lack of development of Golkar's role as the biggest sociopolitical force.   Meanwhile, Golkar's other two components were "increasingly holding prominent roles."   Such a state of affairs could
lead to overlapping and "defunctionalization" in Golkar and open the
way for an abuse of authority by irresponsible parties.   The statements of the minister of defense about ABRI-people unity and the importance of ABRI remaining above all groups must be interpreted as
meaning that, as a *stabilizer*, ABRI must indeed stand above all
groups but that, as a group which implements its dual functions
through the kekaryaan system, ABRI was still a functional group and
a component of Golkar and would develop and grow as one of Golkar's
three elements.   The memorandum concluded by saying that the All-
Indonesia Golkar Leadership Conference was of the opinion that the
matters outlined in the document should be submitted to the chairman
of the Golkar Supervisory Board (Suharto) in order that he might organize the best coordination possible.

Several things can be said about this memorandum.   The first
is that the legalistic hairsplitting about ABRI having a role to play at
two levels was unlikely to have any practical effect.   It was hardly a
sufficient argument to convince such critics as Sadikin, and many
even within Golkar in fact dismissed it, particularly the hard-nosed

49.   *Kompas*, October 12, 1979.

50.   See "Rancangan Memorandum Tentang Mekanisme Intern Keluarga
Besar Golongan Karya" (unsigned), Jakarta, October 20, 1979.

pragmatists of the Ali Murtopo group, a sure indication, it might be noted, that it was the brainchild of a rival power center, perhaps the one associated with Amir Murtono. And, more important still, this sort of argument was not likely to have much impact on Suharto, the man to whom the issue was being conveyed for further action. Suharto, of all people, was little interested in abstract arguments about such matters. His concept of power was essentially Javanese, one in which these niceties had little relevance. Besides, if Korpri and ABRI were flexing their muscles to the detriment of Golkar, then it was the president who had allowed this to happen. All the same, it is interesting to see the efforts that were being made by some in Golkar to come up with answers to the criticisms that had been launched against the existing system.

When photocopies of the October 17 ABRI-Golkar document began to surface barely a month later, it led, not surprisingly, to an immediate political storm. "I have an authentic document that ABRI and Golkar are not going to part company," Lt. Gen. A. J. Mokoginta, a member of the LKB (Lembaga Kesadaran Berkonstitusi, Institute of Constitutional Awareness) said in a hearing with the PPP grouping (F-PP) late in November: "ABRI is still included in the big Golkar family. In that case, what is the 1982 general election going to be like? If ABRI does not stand above all groups, the next general election in 1982 is not going to be far different from the previous general elections."[51] Anwar Nurris, an F-PP member, replied that he too had a copy of the document, and asked rhetorically, if it was true that ABRI was still included in the big Golkar family, what sort of implementation could one expect of Jusuf's statement that ABRI must stand above all sociopolitical forces. The document's existence, said Nurris, caused his grouping rather to doubt Jusuf's statement.[52] An editorial in *Pelita*, the pro-PPP daily, took up the matter. "Is It True That ABRI is Taking Sides?" asked a headline over an editorial in the paper on December 4. The editorial went on to note that "there is an indication, which had its source in the general public, of a new form of relationship between ABRI and Golkar, namely ABRI is absolutely Golkar within the framework of the three-lanes big family to win the 1982 general elections."[53]

In an interview, Mokoginta said that ABRI as an organization must have the principle of not taking sides. It was natural for ABRI, which consisted of ordinary human beings, to tend to sympathize with a certain group. But "even though for instance, 99 percent of the ABRI members sympathize with Golkar, it cannot be offi-

51. See "Wednesday Morning Commitment," *Tempo*, December 15, 1979. USE.

52. Ibid.

53. *Pelita*, December 4, 1979, as quoted in *Tempo*, December 15, 1979. USE.

cially included in the big Golkar family."[54]   Mokoginta admitted that
Golkar was "born" of ABRI in a pressing situation.   In the second
army seminar of 1966 which he had attended, the ABRI leaders had
seen the need for increasing the groups that did not want PKI and
other political parties.   However, when it had grown up, the child
that had been brought to birth by ABRI should be left to live on its
own.   Golkar's two absolute victories in the general elections showed
that it was time for ABRI to leave Golkar on its own.   "Let Golkar
develop on its own," said Mokoginta.   "Leave Golkar alone so that in
the next general election in 1982 we'll see where the people's sympathy is."[55]

Faced with an outcry over the document, Hankam and Golkar
felt obliged to issue "denials."   A close examination of these statements reveals, however, that the "denials" were in fact something
less than that.   Sukardi, a retired ABRI officer who, according to
the document, was to represent Golkar as a liaison officer, was the
most unequivocal in his wording; "As chairman of the Golkar DPP I've
never heard or read such a written commitment.   I fully support the
statement of General Jusuf that ABRI is not taking sides with any
group.   ABRI is to take sides with all people, as ABRI is a fighter
that should become one with the people."[56]   Sukardi conceded, however, that ABRI, in its struggle, would seek a partner, a phrase
that would be given the presidential imprimatur six months later.   "I
believe," he said, "ABRI in its impartial position will support the
sociopolitical forces that have the 1945 Constitution and Pancasila as
their aim of struggle."   All the sociopolitical forces in Indonesia had
nearly the same aim but it was "up to ABRI to choose which sociopolitical forces . . . are closest to its aims of struggle."[57]   Sukardi's
statement may have helped get Golkar off the hook, but it was, on
the most generous interpretation, designed to mislead and deceive.
And while it is true that Sukardi had not been present at the October
17 meeting at Hankam, it seems difficult to believe that he had
neither heard of nor read the document.

The Hankam spokesman, Brig. Gen. Gunarso, phrased his comment with a good deal more care.   According to Gunarso, the principle articulated by Jusuf that ABRI was not taking sides with any one
group would always be adhered to by the entire armed forces.   It
was true that on October 17 a meeting had been held between the
Golkar DPP and Sudomo.   "All persons can meet with the deputy
ABRI commander," he said.   "But this doesn't mean they will then
make a policy deviating from the regulations of the defense and secu-

---

54.   Ibid.

55.   Ibid.

56.   Ibid.   During the independence struggle Sukardi is said to have
worked for the Dutch army as an auto mechanic.   He was not highly
regarded by members of Fosko.

57.   Ibid.

rity minister. The community should not let itself be influenced by such an issue."[58]

Sudomo, finding himself in an invidious position, was decidedly ill-at-ease when asked during an interview for a categorical denial that there had been any secret agreement with Golkar, his apparent discomfort being shared by Gunarso and his deputy, both of whom were present. After repeatedly sidestepping the question, he came out with a flat denial. "There was no agreement between me and Golkar," he said. "With this fake document, certain people are trying to separate General Jusuf and me and to separate Golkar and the armed forces. They want to put Jusuf in a corner."[59] In the interview, Sudomo suggested that, while certain matters had been discussed during the meeting, Sugianto had failed to record the deliberations accurately. General Jasin, who had been Sugianto's commanding officer in East Java, found this suggestion intolerable: "He [Sugianto] was wakil asisten I [deputy assistant for intelligence] in East Java. I know him. He is very clever. He cannot make a mistake (about something like that).[60]

Another source, while disputing Jasin's suggestion that Sugianto was clever, conceded quite readily that the document contained a faithful record of the October 17 meeting. According to this official, Sudomo had said that no one except his secretary was to take notes. However, Sugianto had asked Awan Karmawan Burhan SH, one of the three deputy secretaries of Golkar, to make notes. Awan, who was from West Java, had sent a copy to the West Java governor's office thinking, correctly but somewhat disingenuously, that this was an important development. "Pretty soon everyone had a copy," said this official with some despair. "You know in this country not even two people can keep a secret. Photocopying is only Rp 30 (5c)!"[61] The document drawn up by Sugianto contained a complete and accurate record of the October 17 meeting, according to this official. Sudomo, exasperated at Sugianto's ineptitude, had said, "I don't want to set eyes on that man again!"[62] That, however, was the extent of the concern; government and Golkar leaders were embarrassed that news of the secret agreement had leaked out, but none suggested that the agreement should not have been made in the first place. In an interview eight months after the October meeting, one official dismissed criticism of the Golkar-Hankam deal in language typical of that

---

58. Ibid.

59. Interview with Admiral Sudomo, December 17, 1979.

60. Interview with Lt. Gen. Jasin, May 23, 1980.

61. Interview with a member of the Dewan Pimpinan Pusat Golkar, July 3, 1981.

62. Ibid.

used by the "pragmatists."   "What do they expect?" he asked.
"That's politics."[63]

Put Not Your Trust in Princes

If Suharto and Sudomo had put paid to any notion that ABRI
would stand above all groupings in future, what then of Jusuf?
Where did he stand and was it possible that he too was a party to the
deception?   At least one Indonesian political scientist seems convinced
that he was--at least to some extent.   In May 1980, Dr. Juwono
Sudarsono of the Faculty of Social Sciences at the University of Indonesia maintained that there was a "tacit agreement" between Jusuf and
Suharto.   "All along, Jusuf has been playing the game of accommodation with Islam," Juwono said.   "But I think he'll conveniently drop
the platform in the run-up to the '82 election."[64]

This sort of skepticism may have been warranted to some extent.   In an interview nine months earlier, one senior general had
claimed that it would be wrong to put too much weight on Jusuf's assurances about ABRI being above all groups.   "Jusuf may say something like that in public," this officer said, "but he says something
else to me and [my colleagues] in private.   So (in 1982) we will do
the same things.   I can assure you that at the polling booth it is
99.9 percent honest.   It is beforehand where we give our support for
Golkar."[65]

Jusuf, it is true, had earned a reputation as a somewhat devious and duplicitous man.   "Jusuf was very good at manoeuvering,"
according to a source familiar with his early career in South Sulawesi.
"He got rid of layers of officers above him by getting them involved
in the rebellion and he came out, if not smelling like a rose, then at
least looking pretty good."[66]   It is significant, according to this
source, that both Jusuf's admirers and his detractors often make the
point that he has no loyalty to his family or to people who have
helped him in the past.   Jusuf, it is said, makes his decisions in
terms of the present and the future; this is proffered as a criticism
by some and as praise by others.   Another criticism of the defense
minister was that, despite all the talk, he had never shown any pronounced democratic leanings.   He had, his opponents conceded, a
certain populist air, a certain flair and plausibility.   But his ap-

---

63.   Ibid.

64.   *Asiaweek*, May 9, 1980, p. 21.

65.   Confidential communication, August 1979.

66.   Confidential communication.   Jusuf was No. 57 on the list of
Permesta officers who rebelled against the central government in 1957.
However, he sided with Jakarta soon afterwards and later became
very close to Sukarno.

proach had always been essentially paternalistic and authoritarian, one of "noblesse oblige."

On the other hand, it would be wrong to see Jusuf as a malleable instrument in Suharto's hands. Jusuf gave the impression of feeling in no sense inferior to the president, unlike so many others who seemed to go out of their way to defer to the Head of State. There was in Jusuf's manner a calm self-assurance, a sense of hubris almost, an inner certitude and aloofness that bordered at times on arrogance. Intensely proud of his Buginese origins, conscious of his elevated social status and his preeminent position as one of the three officers--*the* officer, as he told it--who had arranged the transfer of authority from Sukarno to Suharto, he was not inclined to be swept into anyone else's orbit unless it was on what he considered to be his terms. Suharto might be president but Jusuf did not seem to be particularly overawed by that. (He had, according to one account, been present in Makassar in 1950 when Colonel Alex Kawilarang struck Lt. Col. Suharto for some blunder committed by the latter's troops--and had not forgotten the scene.)[67]

Jusuf had a private catalog of complaints about the style and substance of Suharto's rule. He disapproved of the corruption and greed of many of those in power and was openly contemptuous of those leaders who had used their public position to enhance their private wealth. He appeared to have little time for the first lady or those in her circle. More importantly, he disliked the way Suharto put so much trust in the technocrat ministers, despite (perhaps because of) the fact that he had served so long as the only military minister in an essentially "technocratic" department. He disliked the technocrats for their apparent obsession with plans and programs and macro thinking, for their apparent disregard for the rakyat (people). (In this, he had something in common with Adam Malik.) He disliked them for what he saw as their overdependence on institutions like the World Bank and the IMF, a dependence which, in his highly nationalistic view, undermined Indonesia's pride and self-identity.

Jusuf did have a vision of the sort of Indonesia he wanted to see, and at times it seemed to have more in common with the vision of men like Widodo, Sutopo Juwono, and the retired generals in Fosko, than it did with that of Suharto. But he seemed no more capable of achieving it than did any of the others. Jusuf's shortcoming was not that he made statements with a cynical disregard for their meaning. It was more that he did not have the opportunity--and, some of his fellow officers felt, the courage--to do what he would have liked to do. And it was this which was to prove so disappointing to those who expected more of him.

Jusuf, who seemed incapable of building up a team of his own --he wanted, said Nasution, to kick all the goals himself--had, with

---

67. Kawilarang denies that he struck Suharto but concedes that it was necessary to admonish him. Interview with Col. A. E. Kawilarang, November 7, 1981.

whatever reservations, gone along with all that Suharto had done. Nasution had put great store on his early actions, seeing in them an inevitable return to a "purified" military role. But by 1981 he had become disenchanted with his former subordinate. Suharto had cracked down on dissent in a hard-hitting speech at Pekanbaru and dismissed complaints made in a petition signed by fifty prominent people, but Jusuf had done nothing.

> He said the army has to protect people, give them the chance and so on. You have the problem of the *Petisi* and so on. And people, students, come to see him, and he refuses to receive them. So there are no deeds behind the words. And I think it's characteristic. I know when he was a younger officer [there were] these problems also. You cannot change your personality. He has always been on [the side of] what is safe. He takes the safe approach. He doesn't take risks.[68]

Widodo spoke even more bitterly. Jusuf, he said, should have implemented all that he had said about ABRI standing above all groups. Jusuf had spoken every day about the need for change. But his actions had not been consistent with his words. He may have believed what he said, but he did not have the courage to fight for it: "I criticized him, 'You don't have the courage.' I think that if he talks with the president he does not have the courage to advise the president."[69] Jusuf talked, said Widodo, but there was "no action." These sentiments were echoed by Dharsono. "Most of us are disappointed," he said. It was hard to tell whether Jusuf had ever meant what he had said--"we are not quite sure ourselves. . . . We had quite a lot of respect for him when he became the Menhankam because of the statements he made about a new life in the army and so on. Later on we were not quite sure whether he was really willing to carry out what he had been saying. So for me personally he is still a question mark, a big one . . . after the Petisi 50 we never had the chance to see him anymore. I had quite easy access to him before."[70] Jusuf had become distant, Dharsono said. At the same time "perhaps at this moment he is the only man who can change the attitude of the army--if he wants to."[71]

It may have been that Jusuf, recognizing the hopelessness of further struggle after Pekanbaru, had decided to lie low. Widodo had tried and failed and was now on the sidelines, and it was necessary to remain in power if one sought to change the system. The danger with this course of action, as Jusuf must have been well aware, was that the chance to do something might never present itself again.

---

68. Interview with General Nasution, July 24, 1981.

69. Interview with General Widodo, November 17, 1981.

70. Interview with Lt. Gen. Dharsono, November 12, 1981.

71. Ibid.

CHAPTER SEVEN

THE STORM OVER PEKANBARU

> . . . two-thirds of the members [of the MPR] can, if
> they wish, change the Constitution. [But] ABRI does
> not wish to have a change, and if there is a change, it is
> its duty to use weapons. . . . Rather than using weap-
> ons in facing a change of the 1945 Constitution and
> Pancasila, we had better kidnap one out of the two-thirds
> who wish to make the change, because two-thirds minus
> one is not valid according to the 1945 Constitution.

--President Suharto, March 1980[1]

If Sudomo had confirmed in the October 17 meeting that ABRI
was part of the big Golkar family then it only remained for Suharto to
put the presidential imprimatur on such an understanding. This he
did in March 1980. Speaking extemporaneously at the RAPIM ABRI
(Armed Forces Commanders' Meeting) in the central Sumatran oil town
of Pekanbaru on March 27, the president hit out at political opponents
and offered some fairly controversial thoughts about the army's role
in society. "Before the New Order was born," he said "we saw and
sensed that our national ideology was submerged by various existing
ideologies, whether it was Marxism, Leninism, communism, socialism,
Marhaenism, nationalism, or religion."[2] Groups which adhered to
these various ideologies had sought, once they considered themselves
strong enough, to impose their will on other groups by force. "And
so there were unending rebellions," all of which had been obstacles to
the creation of a just and prosperous society based on Pancasila.
"Hence the determination of the New Order to make a total correction
of deviations from Pancasila and the 1945 Constitution."[3] According
to Suharto, there was a certain "party or group which does not yet
trust Pancasila 100 percent." ABRI had to make a success of its dual
function in society, he said, and "so long as we cannot succeed in
bringing [this group] to their senses we must always step up our
vigilance, choose partners, friends who truly defend Pancasila and

---

1. President Suharto's speech at Pekanbaru, March 27, 1980. See
Tempo, June 14, 1980. USE.

2. A transcript of this speech was published in *Kompas*, April 8,
1980.

3. Ibid.

have no doubts whatsoever in Pancasila."[4] Although the president did not specify which party he meant, he did refer to the "walk-out" during the MPR discussion of the P-4 (Guide to Understanding and Implementing Pancasila) problem. Another walk-out had occurred when Parliament was finishing its deliberations on the General Elections Bill. As the PPP (and, more specifically, the NU faction of the PPP) had been the only party involved in these actions, it was not hard to guess which group the president had in mind.

Given the political outlook of those in power, the basic theme of the president's remarks came as no surprise. But Suharto, by casually adding socialism, Marhaenism, nationalism, and religion to the list of discredited philosophies, managed to raise the hackles of just about every important political or social group in the country. He upset the socialists, upset the secular nationalists, upset the Muslims. Even some who were genuinely apolitical were stunned at his passing swipe at nationalism. "What does he mean?" asked retired Air Vice Marshall Suyitno Sukirno, a former ambassador to Australia. "He mentions nationalism in his speech. It is crazy. We are all nationalists. I was a nationalist at the age of sixteen before the word Pancasila had even been coined."[5]

At the same time, Suharto's no-nonsense warning that ABRI would once again have to "choose friends" who supported Pancasila (in other words throw its weight behind Golkar in the 1982 general election) offended those who had believed Jusuf's assurances that ABRI would in future stand above all groups.

What was the significance of this outburst at Pekanbaru? What prompted Suharto to speak out in such uncharacteristically forthright language? First, it seems clear that he was genuinely angry and aggrieved that the NU had walked out of the discussion on the P-4 and the election bill. That action was like a red rag to a bull; it was proof, in Suharto's eyes, that there were elements within the Islamic political movement who were not to be trusted. More than anything else, the Pekanbaru speech gave expression to Suharto's underlying concern, his obsession almost, that there were groups seeking to change Pancasila. The president, although he sought assiduously to project the aura of a traditional Javanese king--patient, restrained, even-tempered, and judicious, a man of inner calm and effortless self-control--was given to periodic emotional outbursts in which he would lash out, almost blindly, at those who had crossed him. The March 27 speech was one such occasion. (Two weeks before Pekanbaru, Suharto had shown signs of irritation over the constant sniping that was coming from the retired "seniors." At a meeting with the Golkar "Central Committee" at his home in Jalan Cendana on March 14, he described these officers as "renegades." It was the government's duty to talk with them, to appeal to them, he said. But,

---

4. Ibid.

5. Interview with Air Vice Marshall Suyitno Sukirno.

if they did not change their ways, the government would be entitled to write them off as "traitors.")[6]

Secondly, Suharto was making it abundantly clear that, whatever Jusuf might have been permitted to say, ABRI and Golkar were still virtually one and the same. Indeed, according to General Sumitro, the president was "a little bit angry, upset actually" by a speech Jusuf had made at Pekanbaru stressing the now familiar theme that the armed forces should be above all groups.[7] In the view of those around Suharto, it was "unrealistic" to argue--as Jusuf, Widodo, Sutopo Juwono, and the retired generals were arguing--that ABRI should stand above. If ABRI did that, Sumitro had noted, the PPP would win the election. And if that happened, "ABRI will hit again."[8] At Pekanbaru, Suharto seemed to be making it fairly clear that the campaign was on, not just for the 1982 general election but for the 1983 presidential election as well, and that he was off and running for a fourth five-year term. In his speech, the president established the need for his own continuing presence. Islam was identified as the threat and ABRI as the one force that could safeguard the Pancasila.

It was also possible to detect an added self-assurance, a cockiness even, in Suharto's approach. "It has been so long now since he had any opposition in the government," the senior editorial writer of one of the nation's leading dailies noted three weeks before the Pekanbaru speech. "There is no one like Sumitro anymore, no one like Ibnu Sutowo." Ali Murtopo had been on the sidelines since his heart attack in 1978. "He [Ali] does nothing. Can you imagine the old Ali Murtopo at a time like this? He would be involved in everything."[9] Suharto's willingness to chance his hand on the US$850 million Dumai hydrocracker project in which his personal cukong (financier), Liem Sioe Liong, acted as an intermediary in what would normally have been a Pertamina project, could be seen as an example of the president's heightened self-assurance, in this view. "It is a very Javanese thing. You are very cautious at first. Then you get overconfident."

There is much to commend this view. In the fifteen years since he had come to power Suharto had changed quite considerably. He had become more rigid, more authoritarian, more feudalistic, more mystical, more cynical, more corrupt, very much less inclined to listen to criticism.[10] In his early years as acting president and then

---

6. Confidential communication, April 1980.

7. Interview with General Sumitro, December 12, 1981.

8. Ibid.

9. Confidential communication with Indonesian editorial writer.

10. I am indebted to Ben Anderson for drawing my attention to this point and to both Adam Malik and Mochtar Lubis for their observa-

president, Suharto had relied to a quite considerable degree on his civilian as well as his military advisers, and in particular on Sultan Hamengku Buwono IX and Adam Malik, the two other members of the initial ruling triumvirate. He always sought—and listened to—their advice. Before long, that began to change. Increasingly confident of his ability to handle his new responsibilities and with the close support and advice of military associates like Ali Murtopo, he began showing signs of irritation at the advice being proffered by men like Malik and the Sultan. Once he had made a decision, it was impossible to persuade him to change his mind, even if it could be shown that the decision was wrong. At the same time, there were factors at work that made such a change almost inevitable. Suharto may have emasculated the political parties, may have muzzled the press, clamped down on the students, and thrown many of his opponents in-to jail. But he had also achieved much in his years as president. The economy was moving ahead, oil and timber revenues were pouring in, rice production had doubled, new schools were going up and new roads being built all over the archipelago. Almost every other day, the president was cutting the ribbon at yet another US$800 million oil refinery or hydrocracker plant, opening yet another provincial airport or hospital or highway or port facility. Confronted wherever he went by this physical evidence of Indonesia's successful development, by the new dams and aluminum projects, generators turning, power har-nessed for the good of the nation, he can only have become increas-ingly convinced that Indonesia was locked onto the correct course, that he knew what was needed, what worked, and that the carping of his critics was not worth considering. The great deference with which he was treated by his most senior advisers and cabinet minis-ters, and not just the Javanese amongst them, can only have rein-forced his sense of conviction about the wisdom of his own policies and his irritation at the occasional discordant note sounded by men like Adam Malik.

As his power continued to grow, the president became increas-ingly preoccupied by "threats" to the Pancasila and to the 1945 Con-stitution, threats which many felt were greatly overstated. Increas-ingly, he sought to erect structures that would ensure that no change would be made to either the state philosophy or to the Consti-tution. And in the final analysis, ABRI was to be the guarantor that there would be no such changes.

Three weeks after the Pekanbaru speech, in off-the-cuff re-marks delivered at the 28th anniversary of the Kopassandha at Cijantung, West Java, Suharto lashed out again. The targets this time were "university students and housewives" who spread rumors that his wife Tien Suharto was receiving commissions and determining who would win tenders, and who said that he, Suharto, had taken a

---

tions about the way in which the president's actions began to change in the late 1960s. Interview with Adam Malik, March 1, 1984 and Mochtar Lubis, February 29, 1984.

well-known actress as his paramour. The president said these rumors were aimed at removing him from office. However, those who spread them were forgetting that if they eliminated him others would appear --citizens and soldiers of the ABRI--who would always thwart their schemes, especially if they wished to substitute another ideology for Pancasila and change the 1945 Constitution.

Suharto's speech at Pekanbaru clearly put Jusuf in an invidious position. For more than a year the minister of defense had been stressing that ABRI would stand above all groups. Already undercut by Sudomo's secret agreement with Golkar, Jusuf's promises were now dealt a humiliating blow by the president. Publicly, Jusuf seemed inclined to play down any appearance of a rift between himself and the president. Immediately after the Pekanbaru speech he told a group of Indonesian editors that Suharto had sought his opinion about the speech he had been about to make, and he (Jusuf) had encouraged him to go ahead and deliver it.[11] Speaking in private, Jusuf took a very different tack. When the governor of the National Defense Institute, Lt. Gen. Sutopo Juwono, spoke to Jusuf not long after the Pekanbaru speech, he sought the minister's opinion about what Suharto had said. Jusuf replied, "That is not according to what the army represents." If he had to talk about this question in future, Jusuf said, he intended to stress what the president had said in his Armed Forces Day speech on October 5, 1979. According to Sutopo Juwono, Jusuf "has the same idea as us actually. And he said 'If I have to talk about this I will always base my speech on what the president said before, on October 5. I will take that as my opinion, not the Pekanbaru opinion but his opinion *before* Pekanbaru.'" [Italics added.][12]

If Jusuf was taken aback by Suharto's outburst then so too were many other Indonesians, including some of the more prominent retired officers. On April 18, Lt. Gen. Mokoginta sent a nine-page letter to Jusuf voicing concern at Suharto's remarks at Pekanbaru.[13] On May 2, the FKS Purna Yudha sent a letter, in even stronger terms, to the new army chief of staff, General Poniman.[14] The let-

---

11. Confidential communication with Indonesian editor.

12. Interview with Lt. Gen. Sutopo Juwono, July 23, 1981.

13. Letter from Lt. Gen. Mokoginta to General Jusuf, April 18, 1980.

14. See Letter of May 2, 1980, from "FKS Purna Yudha," Number 141/FKS/V/80 to General Poniman. The final sentence of the letter read, "It is to be hoped there will not be any more speeches which can create restlessness" [Mudah-mudahan janganlah sampai ada pidato-pidato lagi, yang dapat menimbulkan keresahan]." A copy of this letter was sent to General Jusuf. Poniman had been installed as army chief of staff on April 17, 1980, two years after Jusuf became minister of defense. Widodo, by now out of favor with the ruling group, was offered a job as ambassador to Australia but declined it. Interview with General Widodo, November 17, 1981.

ter, which was signed by Dharsono and Sudirman, prompted Poniman, acting on the written instructions of Sudomo, to sever the last links between the army and the FKS; this was done on June 1.[15]

However, the most damaging attack was yet to come. On May 13 a group of fifty Indonesians, including a number of respected elder statesmen, presented a one-page "Statement of Concern" (*Pernyataan Keprihatinan*) to the DPR.[16] In this document the group expressed "the heartfelt disappointment" of the Indonesian people with the Suharto speeches. The document bore the names of two former prime ministers--Mohammad Natsir and Burhanuddin Harahap; the head of the revolutionary emergency government, Sjafruddin Prawiranegara; along with those of Generals Nasution, Ali Sadikin, Hugeng, Mokoginta, and Jasin. The names of several former cabinet ministers and various Muslim and student critics were also attached.

The petition claimed that the president's speeches made the assumption that a polarization existed between the idea of "preserving Pancasila" on the one hand and "replacing Pancasila" on the other; this, the petitioners feared, would breed fresh conflicts among social groups. The petition said that Suharto had falsely interpreted Pancasila in his two speeches so that the state ideology could be used as a tool to attack his political enemies, whereas the founders of the Republic had intended it as a tool to unite the nation. The signatories claimed that the president's speeches invited ABRI to take sides, to choose friends and enemies on the basis of the arbitrary evaluation of the authorities alone, and not stand above all community groups. They claimed that the speeches gave the impression that there were those who considered themselves personifications of Pancasila, so that "every breath of opposition" to them was interpreted as an anti-Pancasila attitude. As voters, they called on the representatives of the people in the DPR and MPR to respond to the two speeches. This petition, it is clear, contained some rather pointed criticism of the president. However, it had been artfully worded and delivered in a constitutional way, making it difficult for the authorities, however angry, to respond.

Like many of the signatories, Nasution was concerned about the way the president had zeroed in on Muslims: "Ninety percent of the Indonesian people are Muslims. It was our mutual understanding from the start that having Islamic aspirations does not mean that one doubts the Pancasila; indeed, with a religious mind the followers can understand the ethics and morals of Pancasila. Bung Karno and Bung Hatta explained this clearly on many occasions."[17]

---

15. Interview with Lt. Gen. Dharsono, November 7, 1981, and interview with Admiral Sudomo, March 4, 1981.

16. See *Penyataan Keprihatinan* (1980)," the "Statement of Concern," otherwise known as the Petition of Fifty.

17. Interview with General Nasution, June 17, 1980.

Chalid Mawardi, an NU politician who was deputy secretary general of the PPP, echoed this view. The PPP, he said, held that Pancasila and Islam were identical; they were not contradictory but in fact complemented each other. Amin Iskandar, a PPP faction leader in the DPR, added that no leader of the party and no politician from among the party circles had any ambition to change Pancasila as the foundation of the state and substitute for it the foundation of an Islamic state.[18] The walk-out over the P-4, said Muhammadiyah general chairman H. A. R. Fachruddin, was performed "not in the anti-Pancasila framework but in the framework of democracy."[19] According to K. H. Anwar Musaddad, the deputy Rois A'am (general chairman) of the NU Supreme Advisory Council, the walk-out of the PPP faction at the 1978 MPR session and by the NU group in the adoption of the general election law was merely a difference of opinion which was guaranteed by Pancasila and the 1945 Constitution. "Must all people be yes-men according to Pancasila?" he asked.[20] (It is interesting to note that, while Suharto's ire had been aroused by the actions of NU traditionalists, the prominent Muslim political figures who signed the petition were modernists associated with the former Masyumi. Natsir, Burhanuddin, and Sjafruddin had all held high office in the Masyumi. In 1957-58, these three men had joined the PRRI rebellion in West Sumatra.)

When, subsequently, a delegation from the "Petisi 50" group was received by various factions in the DPR, Natsir explained that a speech by any Head of State was important and nowhere more so than in Indonesia, where such utterances always had a certain value, whether as law or instructions or orders. Because of this, he said, the group of fifty had been very much concerned by the speeches made by the president in front of army commanders and members of an elite army command. The speeches, Natsir said, were not wise and that was why the group was asking the Parliament to consider the matter. A speech like that at Pekanbaru could endanger national unity.[21] When Natsir had concluded his remarks, several other sig-

---

18. See *Merdeka*, April 3, 1980. USE.

19. See *Tempo*, June 14, 1980. USE.

20. Ibid.

21. The group, which included Muslims, Catholics, secular nationalists, retired officers, and members of both the younger and older generations, were received by the DPR leadership and by each of the main political groupings. (The meeting with the DPR leadership and the F-PP took place on May 13, the meeting with the PDI grouping on May 14, and the meeting with the F-KP [Golkar] on May 16.) The ABRI faction, which had some initial qualms about meeting a delegation which included civilians, eventually received the group on May 13, having decided that ABRI was already *manunggal* with the people. This meeting lasted three hours (despite an initial time limit of one hour) but was in no sense a dialogue. Suyitno Sukirno read the ini-

natories made the point that, following the end of the Darul Islam rebellion and the crushing of the PKI, the Pancasila was no longer a
problem. All were Pancasilaists; the problem was how to execute the
Pancasila.[22]

The Jasin Attack

If the men who signed the so-called "Petition of Fifty" had
chosen to lock horns with the president over the Pancasila issue,
there was more to come. When Lt. Gen. Jasin joined the delegation
delivering the protest petition to the DPR in mid-May, he took along
a seven-page document of his own which carried the criticism well beyond anything in the petition proper. In this document, Jasin lashed
out at what he labeled the hypocrisy and corruption of the Suharto
government, backing up his charges with what he asserted was a
blow-by-blow account of the way the Head of State had come by his
720-hectare cattle ranch south of Jakarta. "If we tolerate, permit, or
accept the hypocrisy and corruption [of Suharto's New Order govern-
ment]," said Jasin, "we sin against ourselves and the Indonesian nation."[23]

In a subsequent interview, Jasin explained that his objective in
submitting the report to Parliament was to change the Indonesian
democratic system. "Given the character of the present president
you cannot expect any change. He will make ABRI a strike force to
help Golkar win the election in 1982. My aim was to wake the people
up, to raise the temperature."[24] Suharto, he said, might be as
thick-skinned as an elephant. "But if you give an elephant an injec-
tion every day you can eventually make him weak." If weakening the
president and lowering his credibility was Jasin's aim, he seemed to

---

tial statement to the faction, whereupon a representative of the ABRI
faction read from a prepared statement of his own. This said in essence that the government had already provided a Parliament in which
people could express their views, and that if anyone had political ambitions they could express them through the political parties. The
government had already made the rules and it would be better if
everyone adhered to them. In response, Suyitno Sukirno said that in
1966 the slogan of the New Order was "Dinamisator, Catalisator,
Stabilisator." Now, there were so many other "tor's"--an oblique
swipe at "koruptors" and "manipulators." The representatives of the
group of fifty were there with the *Orde Baru* (New Order) spirit, he
said, and wanted a return to the original ideals of the New Order.
The F-PP, like the Fraksi ABRI, had been instructed to avoid a dialogue with the group. Interview with Suyitno Sukirno, June 5, 1980.

22. Ibid.

23. Statement by Lt. Gen. Jasin, May 9, 1980.

24. Interview with Lt. Gen. Jasin, May 23, 1980.

have some initial success. This was the strongest public attack made against Suharto by a onetime member of the ruling army group and, despite a domestic press blackout on the affair, news of Jasin's stinging rebuke spread rapidly through the country. Only hours after Suharto's security officers had telephoned editors with instructions to ignore the story, the Jasin document was being run off on copying machines and distributed on university campuses across the nation.

In one sense, the Jasin document contained little that Indonesians had not already known or suspected. Several dozen retired generals--and a host of civilian critics--had been saying much the same sort of thing in private for the past ten years or so. But there was a strong sense of cohesion and esprit de corps among serving and retired ABRI officers and, until this time, no one had broken ranks and put the blame so squarely on the president. Suharto, though still the undoubted master of the Indonesian political scene, was now being openly attacked on the highly sensitive corruption issue--the Achilles heel of his regime.

In a country in which criticism of the *bapak* (father, boss) was invariably muted and elliptical, the Jasin document came like a slap in the face. The retired officer began his attack by saying that he had made his attitudes and opinions about the national leadership clear in a letter he had sent to Jusuf on February 27. In that letter, he said, it had been clearly and explicitly stated that the nature of the Suharto leadership was *kemunafikan* (hypocritical), and that this had consequences which influenced all state decisions. Jasin said he realized that the authorities were likely to claim that he was speaking out because he was anti-Pancasila, anti-1945 Constitution, antidevelopment, frustrated, no longer in an official position, no longer able to get facilities, or just plain disloyal. But, he added, his criticism was justified. To back up this claim, the general detailed events which, he said, proved that Suharto had been hypocritical in both the political and the economic field. In the political field, the president had agreed with Jusuf that ABRI had to stand above all political groups and acknowledged that it should not take sides. Yet on October 17, 1979, Suharto had instructed Sudomo to map out a joint strategy with Golkar for another Golkar win in the next election. Jasin's claims about hypocrisy in the economic field were even more pointed and were underpinned by what seemed a considerably body of expert evidence. Suharto, Jasin said, had claimed on various occasions that he and his son Sigit were only honorary consultants in the company PT Tiga "S," which operated two cattle ranches in the foothills behind Bogor, forty miles south of Jakarta. "What is the truth? The people ask themselves because, according to natural and simple logic, this is not possible."

Because he was daring, the general went on, he had sought information on the two ranches among people in competent positions. One such person, he said, was a former governor of West Java.[25]

---

25. Although Jasin did not name the former governor, he was known to be referring to Lt. Gen. Solichin, governor of West Java from

This man had stated that Suharto had called him in and said that he wanted a place to relax, as it was always busy in the city. In Jasin's opinion, the presidential palace at Bogor was large enough for Suharto's recreational purposes. But, he added, the governor had admitted that he provided Suharto with land certificates for 720 hectares where former land rights had expired--almost enough on Java, Jasin noted, for an entire village.

Jasin, who served as secretary-general of the Department of Public Works in 1973-74, added that a former minister of public works had told him that the construction of roads and irrigation works on the property had been carried out, at Suharto's request, by the Public Works Department.[26] An admiral had told him that the cattle on the property had been brought from Australia on navy ships: "Now comes the big question. How is it that Mr. Sigit Suharto, as a private citizen, is able to issue orders to the following: a governor a minister, and the navy? The answer, according to very simple logic, is that it is impossible."[27]

What was surprising, said Jasin, was that all this could be done. "And here we come to the core of the hypocrisy in the national leadership of Suharto." There was constant talk about having to take action against the commercialization of office, yet this did not apply to Suharto himself and the talk of him acting as an honorary consultant was "an absolute lie." In the statement, Jasin said he clearly remembered the words of General Darjatmo, the speaker of the MPR and the Parliament, when he, Jasin, had met him in his office on September 10, 1979. "How can a battalion commander take action against his subordinates," Darjatmo had asked, "if he himself is dishonest?" According to Jasin, all true nationalists were now asking who was the battalion commander of the state of Indonesia. The Indonesian people admired and valued development policies being imple-

---

1970-76. According to Murdani, Solichin had been asked about this matter by the president and had replied that he had not spoken to Jasin for seven years. Interview with Lt. Gen. Benny Murdani, July 3, 1980. (It was possible, of course, that Solichin had told Jasin of this prior to 1973.)

26. Although Jasin was equally unforthcoming about the identity of the former minister of public works, this was known to be Sutami, who held this position from 1965 to 1978. In the view of senior officers of the ruling group, it had been quite wrong of Jasin to involve the former minister in this fashion. "Sutami is dead now," one officer said. "In this country it is very unacceptable to use someone who is dead." This officer, who had received the first of the Jasin interrogation reports the previous day, claimed that Jasin had said: "Saya disuruh Dharsono." ("I was ordered/commanded by Dharsono.") Confidential communication July 1980. "If there is evidence, we will charge him [Jasin]," this officer said. "It's libel."

27. Jasin statement.

mented by the New Order government led by Suharto. "But how can we, the Indonesian people, including ABRI, tolerate or permit or accept the hypocrisy and corruption of the New Order led by President Suharto?"[28]

Jasin, as we shall see, had got off a few sighting shots against Suharto in earlier letters to Jusuf and other senior officers. But his public broadside in Parliament made unprecedented use of vitriol. Many senior military leaders had been prepared to listen to the sort of statements that had been made in the Petition of Fifty, even if that too had sorely angered the president. But many were appalled by the vituperation of the Jasin attack, which seemed to them out of keeping with the Javanese character. Not even the students who had attacked the president in 1977 over his US$1 million mausoleum had used such bitter language. "We don't mind about the others," one senior general said at the time, "but we really feel that Jasin did not behave in the correct way. . . . We [staff officers] know all about Tapos. But it's nothing. The president is a farm boy. He likes to get his hands in the dirt. He didn't take the land, [he] just leased it for twenty-five years. It's pretty useless hill land anyway. And if [Australian Prime Minister] Malcolm Fraser sends him a bull he crossbreeds it and sends the cattle around to other areas."[29] Two weeks later, this officer added: "A lot of people know how Pak Harto got it. He didn't spend a single penny on it."[30]

In the wake of these developments the shutters suddenly came down. Indonesian editors were instructed not to mention the petition or the Jasin document, and there were reports that the government was planning to close down the local office of Radio Australia which had carried the items in both its English and Indonesian news bulletins.[31]

On June 3, General Yoga Sugama and Admiral Sudomo summoned the chief editors of the nation's leading newspapers and magazines to explain and justify the government's actions. However, their comments only seemed to add fuel to the fire. The petition, Yoga announced, had been a "constitutional coup d'etat" and the key signatories were now under constant surveillance.[32] Moreover, the govern-

---

28. Ibid.

29. Comments made by a senior Indonesian general in a conversation with Warwick Beutler, June 14, 1980. Communication with Beutler, June 15, 1980.

30. Confidential communication, July 1980.

31. The Radio Australia correspondent, Warwick Beutler, was unable to renew his visa and left the country in mid-1980. His virtual expulsion was the culmination of a number of events.

32. Information provided by a senior Indonesian journalist, June 4, 1980. Yoga made the point "about ten times" that Jusuf was fully behind the government. "You should not just think it is [the two of]

ment had evidence of a plot to assassinate sixty-seven people, starting with Suharto. To back up this claim, Yoga produced a document
which purported to be the work of the retired generals from the ex-
Fosko group.

In the twenty-eight-page document, which made illegal use of
the army crest on its front page, it was said that Fosko had begun to
take steps to change the national leadership because this could not
wait until 1982. The minister of defense, it said, should urge the
president to hand over the reins of government to a presidium led by
the minister of defense and consisting of prominent national figures of
his choosing. On the next page, the document mentioned Jusuf by
name. There was no date when the presidium should take over and
no indication of the size of the presidium. However, Sudomo is said
to have mentioned August 17, Indonesia's National Day, as the date
the alleged plotters had in mind, and to have spoken of a council of
six.

The document was a patent forgery—as some government
leaders, crestfallen and embarrassed, later privately admitted—and it
is hard to believe that Yoga ever took it very seriously. Certainly
the editors did not. At the briefing, the talk of a constitutional
coup—which smacked of a contradiction in terms—was met with scorn
and derision. The suggestion that men of the stature of Nasution,
Hugeng, and Natsir were somehow connected with a plot to assassinate government leaders was dismissed as an absurdity. Nasution,
deeply offended by the government's tactics, described the claims as
fitnah (defamation).

> At the funeral of General Yani [after the coup attempt in
> 1965] I said the Communists had committed fitnah against
> us in the military leadership, by claiming that we had
> been planning to overthrow the government. I said that
> fitnah is worse than murder. Now they [the government]
> are doing the same, exactly the same. They are claiming
> that those of us who signed the Petition of Fifty are plot-
> ting to assassinate the leaders and take over the govern-
> ment. So history is repeating itself. The PKI said that
> Yani and I and the others were preparing to take over
> from Sukarno. And that was never the case. And now
> it is the same. The government is saying that maybe we
> are planning to murder the president. And not even the
> PKI said that we intended to murder Sukarno. They [the
> government] are murdering us when they spread these
> slanders.[33]

---

us. If I want to arrest these [fifty] people tomorrow and send them
to Buru I can have a Hercules [from the Air Force] just like that."

33. Interview with General Nasution.

While the press briefing seemed an amazing case of overreaction, an attempt by senior officers to smooth the ruffled feathers of those on high, the government did show that it had at least learned some lessons from earlier experiences in the field. At the briefing, Yoga announced that there would be no arrests of the government's critics, because arrests would only give the petitioners the martyrdom they sought. However, the government would press ahead with its plans to strike back in other ways at those who had spoken out. They would, he said, be isolated; their expiring work permits and business licenses would not be renewed; their credit lines to state banks would be cut off; their requests for exit permits would not be approved; and they would not be permitted to participate in government tenders.

Such actions, which a former minister of mines, Slamet Bratanata, described as "an attempt to strangle people to death by economic means,"[34] were typical of the Suharto government and had a double aim. On the one hand they would punish those who had stepped out of line. On the other, they would serve as a warning to anyone else who might seek to challenge those in authority. Often these "punishments" were of a particularly spiteful nature, as in the case with General Hugeng, the former chief of police. A modest and unassuming officer with a reputation for probity and idealism, Hugeng had been forced to resign in 1971 after tracking down an import racket that led to Madame Suharto.[35] But Hugeng also had another string to his bow; an accomplished entertainer, he had been performing Hawaiian songs on Indonesia's state-owned television network for twelve years. Immediately after he added his name to the petition, Ali Murtopo, now minister for information, announced that Hugeng's popular TV show was to be axed on the grounds that Hawaiian music "does not reflect the national culture"--a ban which did not extend to such programs as Ellery Queen and The Flintstones. At the subsequent briefing for editors, Sudomo chimed in with some gratuitous remarks about the former police chief. "Don't look on Hugeng as an innocent guitar player or Hawaiian singer," he said. "We must not exclude the possibility that he will one day sing a revolutionary song and incite people to riot."[36]

The outcry over Suharto's remarks in March and April had become pervaded by a general sense of unreality, and at the briefing for Indonesian editors it began to lurch decisively towards total con-

---

34. Interview with Slamet Bratanata.

35. Details of the first lady's alleged involvement in the multimillion dollar smuggling racket were aired in court during the trial of Sawito Kartowibowo late in 1977. See David Jenkins, "Trial touches raw nerves," FEER, January 13, 1978. Hugeng was dismissed four days after he revealed details of the racket. See Crouch, Army and Politics in Indonesia, p. 292, n.

36. Confidential communication, June 5, 1980.

fusion and absurdity. Within Indonesia, the talk of plots and assassination bids, of illegal documents and illegal transfer of power, had been recognized for what it was--a rather hamfisted and theatrical way of putting the damper on further criticism. But then foreign news organizations heard of the briefing and began taking some of the more bizarre and ill-considered remarks at face value. Foreign bankers began making worried telephone calls. Western embassies started to fret about a downturn in foreign investment. This roller-coaster descent into absurdity--a consequence, it is true, of the overreaction, if not the grotesque ineptitude, of some high officials--only served to obscure the more important aspects of the debate stirred up by Suharto's speeches.

One interesting development was that, as the protest wave gathered momentum, the critics had become increasingly daring and outspoken, more inclined to thumb their noses at government leaders. At a seminar to commemorate the 20th anniversary of the Atma Jaya Catholic University in Jakarta several days before the security briefing to editors, Ali Sadikin had spoken out against the growing tightness of the political system--and heaped scorn on Ali Murtopo for dissembling about the ban on Hugeng's Hawaiian music. His remarks, delivered in an easy, off-the-cuff manner, had produced an extraordinary response, the hall ringing with applause and acclamation.

Having taken a swipe at the pettiness of the government's actions, Sadikin continued, in a more statesmanlike manner, with an outline of what he saw as the fundamental questions that were being asked in Indonesia. The struggle to establish democracy, he said, would be a long one; it was not just a matter of general elections in 1982 or 1987. And it was a struggle that would have to be waged by the younger generation. "Never mind the generation of 1945 [the independence fighters]," said Sadikin. "They are all *brengsek* [rotten], I know because I'm one of them." Later, turning to the dwifungsi of the military and the question of a gradual increase in civilian responsibility, the former Jakarta governor said: "We know who screwed up the political parties."[37] That tart observation was also met with resounding applause.

The mood of men like Jasin and Sadikin could be summed up in the word *nekad*--they were obstinate, even reckless in their new mood of defiance, ready in some cases to risk almost everything in their struggle against the government. Until now, the regime had tended to feel that there was little to fear from disaffected generals. It had generally been assumed in Jakarta that these people could be kept in line by calls for solidarity or, if that failed, by the withdrawal of the government patronage on which so many of them depended. "Most of these people," one member of the ruling group said, "are just as corrupt as anyone else. We have a laundry list. We can hit back if they want that."[38] That might have been true.

---

37. Ibid.

38. Confidential communication.

But if the wave of criticism persisted, many felt, laundry lists might not be enough, as the government seemed to admit. No one believed for a moment that a group of retired generals and ex-ministers were about to bring down the New Order government. But, in the long run, continuing criticism of this kind was likely further to erode Suharto's claim to legitimacy.

Shadows Behind the Screen

By mid-1980, the Petition of Fifty had become the central talking point of Indonesian politics. However, few people stopped to ask who was behind it. The answer, as with so many other protests at this time, was that it was in large measure the work of retired generals. The petition appears to have been inspired by Mokoginta's April 18 letter to Jusuf, in which the former Sumatra commander commented on the president's Pekanbaru speech. Although Mokoginta felt there was a need for a more comprehensive statement after Suharto had spoken again at Cijantung, he believed it would look foolish to write another letter so soon after the first. Accordingly, he suggested that Slamet Bratanata draft a document of concern and this, after three drafting sessions, the last chaired by Daan Jahja, became the petition.[39] Given the involvement of the "ex-Fosko" generals, it might appear surprising that none of the three members of the FKS "daily board" (Dharsono, Sukendro, and Sudirman) appended their names to the document. (Djatikusumo, a member of the original Fosko presidium, had by this time dropped out of the group.)[40] Why, it might be asked, had members of the FKS leadership remained aloof from a document that had been so much their own work when most ordinary members of their group had signed? The answer, according

---

39. Interview with Slamet Bratanata, March 4, 1982. In an interview (November 7, 1981) Maj. Gen. Sukendro said of the Petisi 50: "Memang buat disini" (at the FKS office). ("Indeed, it was prepared here.") General Nasution confirms that the initiative for the petition came from retired generals, particularly those in the FKS. (Interview, June 23, 1980.) No one has linked Nasution with the preparation of the petition and he has stressed that he remained aloof from the planning, leaving this to others.

40. Djatikusumo's withdrawal from the Fosko grouping coincided with his appointment as deputy chairman of the DPA (Supreme Advisory Council). According to General Jasin, the reason was that Djatikusumo had been provided with a generous salary and with various "facilities." (Interview with Lt. Gen. Jasin, May 23, 1980.) According to Jusuf Wanandi, Jasin taunted Djatikusumo and said, "You're too old to sign. You've lost your teeth." Djatikusumo is said to have answered, "No, that's not the way to do it." (Interview with Jusuf Wanandi, June 17, 1980.) According to Wanandi, Djatikusumo had changed a lot in two years and was now "very pro the old man [Suharto]."

to some in the government, was that this was an indication of the essential deviousness, if not cowardice, of these men.   Dharsono and Sukendro, it was alleged, were "too clever" to sign the petition. Having helped set the wheels in motion, it was suggested, Dharsono and Sukendro had withdrawn to safe ground to watch the ensuing melee, safe from any government reprisals.   This, it was true, provided a convenient explanation for the government side and one which had the advantage of impugning the character of two of its principal adversaries.   However, it would seem to ignore other considerations that were apparently in the minds of these three men.

One reason why Dharsono, Sukendro, and Sudirman did not sign the petition was that, as office bearers of the FKS, they wanted to keep their lines of communication open to General Poniman.   When Fosko had been obliged to change its name in 1979, its leaders, anxious to maintain the official link that Widodo had provided, had gone to considerable lengths to comply with his ruling that they keep their deliberations and suggestions private.   In a document issued early in 1980, the FKS stressed that the army chief of staff was the only person who received copies of their recommendations, although they said they hoped that he would "process and evaluate" the results of their labors and forward them to such people as the minister for defense and the president.[41]   The document went on to stress that FKS had been formed merely as a *dapur sosial* (social kitchen) and had no relations with any other organization.   In April 1980, shortly before the petition was drawn up, Widodo had been replaced as chief of staff by Poniman.   The "Fosko" group was keen to retain the lines of communication which Widodo had, at some cost to himself, established and maintained, particularly as Poniman seemed prepared to continue what Widodo had begun.[42]   In a meeting with Brig. Gen. Slamet, the Fosko liaison officer,[43] Poniman had said that he would "continue the policy of Mr. Widodo."[44]   Accordingly, the FKS leaders were at some pains to avoid taking any action which, like the participation of Fosko in the 1979 National Awakening Day celebrations, might jeopardize those links.   If the three FKS daily board members appended their names to the petition, it was feared, it would drag Fosko into a skirmish that might well threaten its last remaining links with the army leadership.

Another reason was that Sudirman and Dharsono had already sent their own protest letter to Poniman, using language that was considerably stronger than that in the petition.   "I didn't sign,"

---

41.   *Fosko Brosur 1980*.

42.   Fosko, according to Slamet Bratanata, was "lying low" at the time of the petition in order to preserve these links.   Interview, 1980.   Jasin, confirming this, said, "We [would] like to maintain the umbrella."   Interview, May 23, 1980.

43.   The former liaison officer, Maj. Gen. Sugih Arto, had dropped out of the group by this stage.

44.   Interview with Jasin, May 23, 1980.

Sukendro noted, "because the language in the letter to the Kasad was stronger: "We considered that we had sent a stronger letter already and that it was not necessary to sign. Besides, the petition is external while our letter is internal."[45]

---

45. Interview with Maj. Gen. Sukendro, November 7, 1981.

CHAPTER EIGHT

DISENCHANTMENT AND RETRIBUTION

Have you seen [Jasin's] book? It's crazy!

--Lt. Gen. Benny Murdani, 1979[1]

Lt. Gen. Mohammad Jasin, who was to prove the most prickly of all the retired generals, was a man who had come to judge contemporary Indonesia by the strict standards of his own upbringing and who, having found it wanting, was resolved to see it corrected at all costs. There was in his make-up a strong puritanical streak, and this, combined with a rather doctrinaire and inflexible nature, led him to take actions which he saw as correct and necessary and *berani* (brave, daring) and which others, particularly those of the contemporary elite, saw as reckless, un-Javanese and, in the final analysis, unforgivable. Jasin, in their view, had acted in a way which offended the Javanese sense of propriety.

Some of the initial motivation for the Jasin crusade may well have stemmed, as his critics suggested, from events of a more particular and personal nature. But in the end it was his sense of probity, the outrage he felt at things he saw as morally reprehensible, that drove him on.[2] He became in the end a man obsessed with the rightness of his cause. And if he lost the support of many along the way--describing the president as a hypocrite was hardly the stuff of everyday Javanese politics--then there were others, including a number of prominent figures in the army, who stood by him and gave their moral support to what he had done.

Jasin was born in Aceh on July 22, 1921, the eldest son of a harbor technician from East Java and his Jakarta-born wife.[3] He received his entire education in Taman Siswa schools, and his character appears to have been shaped to a quite extraordinary extent by the

_____

1. Interview with Lt. Gen. Benny Murdani, August 14, 1979.

2. "I think at that time [the early 1970s] you can say the motivation was personal," General Nasution said in an interview (July 7, 1980). "At the beginning it was personal motivation. But that is now a long time ago."

3. The material in this section is based on an interview with Lt. Gen. Jasin on May 23, 1980 and on interviews with his former colleagues.

values inculcated in these institutions. The Taman Siswa schools had been established by Ki Hadjar Dewantoro (Suwardi Surianingrat), an educational reformist who, concerned that Western education was undermining Indonesia's sense of its own identity, had fashioned a curriculum that was a blend of Montessori's ideas and traditional Javanese culture. Students were imbued with a strong sense of national and personal identity in surroundings that called for rigid self-discipline.

Jasin, after spending the first thirteen years of his life in Aceh, had attended a "middle school" in Medan in the early 1930s, before going on to junior high school in Yogyakarta. His life there was spartan in the extreme. After a brief period as a teacher, Jasin joined the Peta, the Japanese-sponsored self-defense forces, before going on, like so many others, to take part in the revolutionary struggle against the Dutch. In 1960, after a period as an instructor at SSKAD (Staff and Command School) in Bandung, he was sent to Aceh as military commander by Nasution with the task of negotiating an end to the rebellion there. He carried out the job successfully, thanks in part to the help of some former colleagues of Daud Beureueh, the so-called "strong man of Aceh," who headed the armed rebellion against the Indonesian government from 1953 to 1962. Jasin was given the job, because he knew Aceh and the Acehnese but was still a man of the center.[4] He was later posted to Moscow as military attaché.

In 1965, after Jasin had been in Moscow a year, Suharto called him back to Jakarta and said he would like him to remain in the Soviet Union for another year. In 1966, Suharto recalled Jasin for good, giving him a second star and one of the plum jobs in the Indonesian military hierarchy--command of Kodam VIII Brawijaya (East Java). East Java, with 25 million people, and Suharto's home province of Central Java, together accounted for more than 40 percent of Indonesia' population, and both were critical areas in the tense days following the 1965 coup attempt. After Jasin replaced Sumitro in East Java in early 1967, he distinguished himself by the very tough measures he took against Sukarnoist remnants in the Brawijaya itself, the KKO (Marines), the police, and the PNI.[5] When in that same year remnants of the outlawed PKI were said to be preparing a comeback at South Blitar, according to Lt. Gen. Sutopo Juwono, at that time head of Bakin, Jasin at first refused to believe there was any such danger:[6]

---

4. I am indebted to Prof. Ben Anderson and General Nasution for making this point.

5. See Crouch, *Indonesian Army in Politics*, pp. 498-500 and pp. 561-62.

6. Interview with Lt. Gen. Sutopo Juwono, July 21, 1981.

It is interesting that at the time we had the conclusion that [the PKI would resurface in East Java] and maybe in these particular places. We went to the Panglima Brawijaya, at that time General Jasin, and General Jasin told me that "I am the commander and there is nothing happening in East Java." It was very hard for us to convince him that some months from then it could happen like this and maybe in these places." He said to us, "But that is nonsense. I am the commander here and I see nothing here." Later he had to admit that I was right.[7]

Once he accepted that a danger did exist from an underground PKI, Jasin took all necessary steps to suppress it. Operation Trisula, launched against "Communist remnants" in mid-1968, was noted for its ferocity. Jasin was equally forceful in putting down anti-Chinese riots in Surabaya in 1968.

When, in 1980, Jasin forwarded his controversial letter to the DPR, he would claim that one of his objectives "was to change the system, change the system of democracy." As commander of the Brawijaya, however, Jasin gave little indication that he saw his job as upholding the sanctity of the democratic process. In the late 1960s, he clamped down on the PNI and NU and dragooned villagers into Golkar with the same sort of zeal he had shown in combatting Communists and rioters. He also worked actively to ensure that military authority was established at all levels in East Java. As General Sumitro was wont to observe: "In the late 1960s the Panglima were always happy if they knew that all the kepala desa [village heads] were military men. . . . People can lie at the moment. But I'm within the process and I know exactly that the Panglima in West Java, even Jasin [in East Java] at that time, they are both very happy if all the kepala desa there are ex-soldiers. And the camat too. They were all soldiers too."[8]

Like other retired generals whose recommendations were often at variance with their actions while in uniform, Jasin may well have seen things from a different perspective in his retirement. But his about-face on the value of free expression provided ammunition to

---

7. Ibid.

8. Interview with General Sumitro, December 12, 1981. Crouch has argued (personal communication) that Jasin's actions were mainly directed against the PNI, not so much the NU, and that dragooning people into Golkar only really took place after Jasin had left East Java. Sumitro and Nasution are among those who take a different view. Nasution says that prominent figures in both the PNI and the NU had told him at the time that they had been hit by the actions taken by Jasin. Written communication, March 4, 1983. Jasin moved to Jakarta in January 1970, eighteen months before the general elections on July 3, 1971.

those around Suharto who looked on Jasin with anger and contempt, and who saw him as being as munafik (hypocritical) as almost anyone else. In any event, it seems clear that concern about political repression was not in the forefront of his thinking in the late 1960s. Jasin's first serious doubts about Suharto stemmed, in fact, from three "watershed experiences" in the early 1970s.

Having succeeded in his assignment in East Java, Jasin was again rewarded by Suharto; in 1970 he was promoted to lieutenant general and made deputy chief of staff of the army. It was while serving in this position in Jakarta that Jasin began to entertain his first doubts about the Suharto government. During the 1971 election campaign, he says, the president called him in to his office and offered him five-ton trucks for use in connection with the campaign.[9] Jasin says he refused to accept vehicles of this size, objecting that rural roads were not adequate for five-ton trucks in many parts of the country. He asked instead for 2 1/2 ton trucks. Suharto, whose aides reportedly had made arrangements with a large Japanese motor company for delivery of the larger vehicles, is said to have responded, "If you don't like five-ton trucks you can forget about having any transportation."[10] In the event, Jasin was obliged to accept the larger vehicles. This incident, and others of a similar nature, offended Jasin's sense of propriety, and his opposition grew as he came to the conclusion that the government was unaware of, or indifferent to, the sort of moral values that had figured so prominently in his own life. This sense of disaffection was accelerated by two other developments, one of which Jasin saw as an affront to his family and another which struck at his own self-esteem.

The first incident involved Maj. Gen. Bustanil Arifin. Arifin, who was later to achieve considerable success as head of Bulog, the national logistics office, was in almost every respect the direct antithesis of Jasin. A freewheeling military entrepreneur who enjoyed particularly close relations with the first family, he stood for almost all the things that Jasin found distasteful. Jasin was a fighting general, Bustanil Arifin a palace general and fix-it man. Jasin was slightly built, wiry, and somewhat severe, an implacable moralist with a rather melancholy disposition. Arifin was rotund, jolly, and self-indulgent; a man who enjoyed the good things of life. If Jasin was known as a man of abstemious ways, then Bustanil Arifin was known for his high living. If Jasin was known for his probity and parsimony, Bustanil was seen as an indefatigably wheeler-dealer, a man, the local press implied, who had been associated with some questionable business dealings and had done very handsomely out of them. If Jasin had a reputation as a rather straight-laced figure, then Bustanil enjoyed a certain notoriety as a ladies' man. In 1973, Bustanil's inclinations in this direction were to bring the two generals into collision. At the airport to bid farewell to his 22-year-old

---

9. Interview with Jasin, May 23, 1980.

10. Ibid.

daughter as she set off, on her first trip abroad, to study English in London, Jasin noticed that Bustanil Arifin was taking the same flight. He asked him, as one officer to another, to keep an eye on the girl. When Jasin's daughter arrived in London, she wrote to her father that Arifin had been *kurang ajar* (literally, "less than educated") on the flight.[11]   Infuriated, Jasin asked Suharto to discipline Arifin. Nothing was done, however, apparently because Arifin enjoyed such close relations with the first family and was a particular favorite of Madame Tien Suharto.   (Arifin's wife was related to Madame Suharto.) When Jasin tried once more to raise the matter with Suharto, the president refused to receive him.[12]   Still smouldering over the affair, Jasin summoned Arifin to his home in Kebayoran Baru and, according to his account, struck him across the face and punched him.   Arifin, being only a one-star officer did not, it seems, seek to defend himself. (According to the account of one of the senior generals in the Suharto group, Jasin did not strike Arifin himself but ordered a younger officer to do it for him. In the view of this officer, Arifin may have had something of the sort coming to him.   But, it is argued, Jasin behaved improperly in not doing the job himself.   Jasin insists that he was the one who dealt the rebuke to Arifin.)[13]

Later that year, when General Umar Wirahadikusumah stood down as chief of staff, Jasin was confident that he, as deputy chief of staff, would move up to this highly prestigious position, thus becoming the first officer from the Brawijaya to hold that post.[14]   He was bitterly disappointed when he was passed over and Suharto appointed in his stead General Surono Reksodimedjo, a former com-

---

11.   Interview with senior military officer, July 3, 1980.   As this officer noted, *kurang ajar* could mean anything.   "He may have said something that wasn't right or tried to kiss her.   But you can't do much more with 100 people watching."   On the other hand, if Arifin had merely tried to kiss the girl, it is unlikely that Jasin would have wanted to complain to the palace in person.

12.   Interview with Jasin, May 23, 1980.

13.   Jasin, according to a senior officer, may have struck Bustanil once or twice but had had a junior officer punch him.   That, in this officer's opinion, "was not right."

14.   The officers who have filled the position of army chief of staff have all come from either the Siliwangi or the Diponegoro.   No one has been able to offer a particularly plausible explanation for this, although Jasin claims that it is because East Javanese are too strong-willed.   (Interview, May 13, 1980.)   In fact, it may simply have been an accident of history.   Given that Sumitro rose to become deputy commander of the armed forces and commander of Kopkamtib, it can hardly be argued that East Javanese have been excluded from the upper reaches of the army command system.   In view of the greatly circumscribed power of the army chief of staff, there may no longer be any significance in having a Kasad from the Brawijaya.

mander of Military Region VII (Diponegoro). Jasin was moved out of the army, becoming secretary general of the Department of Public Works, a position he held until he resigned and went into private business in 1974 following a post-Malari decree, more honored in the breach than in the observance, that the relatives of officials must not be involved in business. (Jasin's wife was so involved.) He was at this time an embittered man. He nursed a grudge against Suharto for ignoring his repeated complaints about Bustanil Arifin and he had been taken aback by the appointment of Surono. And in the Department of Public Works he had been presented with further evidence of the way in which Suharto did business.

Jasin's feelings of bitterness over the way he had been treated went hand in hand with a growing disillusionment about the extent of practices which, to his comparatively puritanical nature, were beyond the bounds of all propriety. This, in a man of such moral rectitude, was to prove an explosive mix. His sense of being slighted seems to have provided at least some of the motivation for what was to develop into a singular one-man campaign against corruption and delinquency in general and the person of Suharto in particular.

After his retirement, Jasin began to turn his attention, almost obsessively, to the question of "correcting" the system. And his conviction in the rightness of his cause and his determination to pursue it to its logical limits strengthened, as one senior official after another sought to persuade him that corruption was not all that serious in Indonesia and that the issue had been blown out of all proportion. To Jasin, it became increasingly obvious that the government was not sincere about corruption, and he saw each new profession of concern as evidence of a hypocrisy that extended through all layers of the government. He became an inveterate writer of letters and memos. He chided ministers when they suggested that corruption was not a problem and made the point that so-called "leakages" were depriving the state of vast amounts of money.

The development of Jasin's thinking and his growing disenchantment with Suharto were plainly visible in the letters he wrote to prominent officials in the years that followed his retirement. On June 28, 1974, he forwarded a strongly worded ten-page letter to Suharto offering his thoughts about the problem of implementing a 1974 decree dealing with "Restrictions on the Activity of Government Servants in Private Business."[15] The tone was respectful but direct. Jasin wrote that he was offering his conclusions and suggestions with sincerity and purity, based merely on a realistic attitude and without political motivation. His view at this time, he said in a subsequent interview,[16] was that the government was not at all serious in its

---

15. The text of this letter is to be found in M. Jasin, *Apakah Perlu Pemerintah Dikoreksi?: Persembahan Untuk Generasi Muda* (Jakarta: n.p., 1979), pp. 35-44.

16. Interview, May 23, 1980.

purported determination to prevent civil servants from taking outside jobs. The decree banning such activity, he felt, was merely "camouflage" for the government in the wake of the Malari Affair--an attempt to persuade the students that the government was clean. In Jasin's view, it was essential that the government take the decree seriously and implement it fully.

Several years later, the minister of home affairs, Lt. Gen. Amir Machmud, was reported to have said in Bandung that it was "rumored" that the government apparatus was very involved in corruption; this, the minister had replied was not true at all.[17] Jasin was appalled. He wrote immediately to Amir Machmud, saying that corruption was not merely something that was rumored but that the indications of it were plainly visible. It was present at every echelon, from the bottom to the top.[18]

On January 2, 1979, it was reported that the minister of health, Dr. Suwardjono Surjaningrat, had said that if small groups of people were claiming that the development program had been a failure, such statements were without foundation and untrue.[19] During Repelita I (the first five-year plan) expenditure in the state budget had been Rp 1 trillion. But in Repelita II it had been Rp 4 trillion and in Repelita III Rp. 6 trillion. Once again, Jasin felt compelled to respond. In a letter dated January 4, he reminded the minister that the former minister for research, Dr. Sumitro, and the chairman of the National Audit Board, General Umar Wirahadikusumah, had estimated that waste and corruption accounted for 30-40 percent of the state budget. If one took 35 percent of Rp 5 trillion (Pelita I and II) it came to Rp 1.75 trillion, or more than the total of Repelita I. This was money which had produced no development.[20]

Jasin published these and other letters in a "white book" entitled *Apakah Perlu Pemerintah Dikoreksi?: Persembahan Untuk Generasi Muda.*" ("Does the Government Need Correcting?: Dedicated to the Young Generation.") In the foreword, he explained how the letters had come to be written and the response, if any, they had evoked. He urged people to be berani in calling on the government to make corrections, and added an extra sting to some of the observations he had made in the original letters. Thus, Amir Machmud was now said to have been *sangat* munafik (extremely hypocritical) in

---

17. A report of Amir Machmud's comments, as published in *Sinar Harapan* on February 23, 1977, is included in *Apakah Perlu*, p. 28.

18. Jasin letter to Amir Machmud, February 24, 1977. *Apakah Perlu*, pp. 24-27.

19. The *Antara* report of these comments, which appeared on January 2, 1979, is included in *Apakah Perlu*, p. 13.

20. Jasin letter to Suwardjono Surjaningrat, January 4, 1979, published in *Apakah Perlu*, pp. 11-12.

saying that corruption was only something talked about by rumor-mongers.[21]

Meanwhile, Jasin continued with his letter-writing campaign. On September 7, 1979, he sent a letter to General Darjatmo, chairman of the MPR/DPR, taking issue with a comment he had made and requesting an appointment with him.[22] Darjatmo received Jasin at his office on September 10. Three days later, Jasin wrote thanking the MPR/DPR chairman and again calling for reform of the system.[23] By now, his criticisms were getting closer and closer to the president. In his letter of September 13 he recalled General Darjatmo's question: "How can a battalion commander take action against his subordinates if he himself is dishonest?" In the same letter, he employed the word kemunafikan (hypocrisy), typed in capital letters, to describe the nature of the national leadership.

In October, Jasin summarized his views in a "Contribution of Thoughts" submitted to the "Fosko Purna Yudha ABRI."[24] This document took more than a veiled swipe at the behavior of Suharto and his family.

In 1978, Jasin had been a founding member of Fosko TNI-AD and had been appointed to the presidium of that body. Now, starting with his visit to Darjatmo, he began calling on prominent army officers in the government to express personally his concern about the need for correction in the government. (Under the rules of Fosko TNI-AD, a member was permitted to take any individual action he deemed fitting so long as he reported on his actions to the Fosko board.) Jasin had little difficulty in setting up his initial meetings. As a former commander of the Brawijaya and deputy chief of staff, he had close personal links with many of those in the upper echelons of the government and, initially at least, his former colleagues were ready to give him the sort of respectful hearing that was due an old associate.

In October, Jasin called on the army chief of staff, General Widodo. The two men had never had much opportunity to become close friends—Jasin, who was five years older, had been commander of the Brawijaya at a time when Widodo was chief of staff of the Diponegoro, under Surono. But Widodo, who had already been criticized for his closeness to the Fosko generals, was ready to listen to what the former deputy chief of staff had to say. The attorney gen-

---

21. See Kata Pengantar, *Apakah Perlu*, p. 8.

22. Jasin letter to Gen. Darjatmo, September 7, 1979. Copy made available by General Jasin.

23. Jasin letter to Darjatmo, September 13, 1979. Copy made available by General Jasin.

24. See Jasin, "Sumbangan Pikiran Dalam Rangka Mengumpulkan Data² (kapita selecta) unt: Fosko Purna Yudha ABRI," October 29, 1979. Copy made available by General Jasin.

eral, Lt. Gen. Ali Said, was also prepared to listen. Ali Said had been Jasin's assistant V (territorial) in East Java, and when Jasin called on him in January 1980 he found it easy to "talk to him frankly."[25] During the meeting, Jasin says, he told Ali Said he no longer had any respect or trust in Suharto. As a loyal member of the Suharto group, the attorney general may have felt a little uncomfortable to hear his former commanding officer speak in this manner of the president. However, it would have been impolite and improper for him to rebuke his "bapak," and he seems to have settled on the course of saying as little as possible. "I have no reaction, Bapak Jasin," Ali Said supposedly replied at the end of Jasin's statement. "You were my commanding officer before. I know about your character."[26]

Jasin also considered himself to be close to Jusuf--while still a colonel, Jasin had been panglima Aceh when Colonel Jusuf was panglima South Sulawesi and both had been favorites of Sukarno--and on October 27, 1979, he had written to the defense minister requesting an appointment to see him. His letter, however, had contained a blistering attack on Suharto, and Jusuf, perhaps not surprisingly, had failed to respond. Now, on February 27, 1980, he wrote again to Jusuf, summarizing his views "in a short and clear fashion": "I no longer believe in or trust President Suharto because the national leadership at every level is munafik and I have proof of this hypocrisy both in the economic and in the political sectors."[27]

By now, Jasin was on a collision course with the president, carried along by his conviction that something was fundamentally wrong with the national leadership. It only remained for him to take one more step--sending his May 9 letter to the DPR--for his disaffection to become a national issue.

Afterwards, when the Jasin affair had become a cause celèbre, senior officers in Suharto's circle were to imply that the former deputy chief of staff had somehow gone "off the rails." (In not untypical fashion, the arguments of the ruling military group were to be given their most fulsome expression by civilians closely associated with those in power; often, they tended to adopt an angry and patronizing attitude towards Jasin that went beyond that of the general's military colleagues.) However, a number of prominent officers--including at least two retired four-star generals--were prepared to stand by Jasin. Nasution gave his moral support--and his endorsement--to the actions Jasin had taken: ". . . strategically, he is right, I think. You have to argue and he uses this argument. Tactically, he may be said to be too hasty. But I am not against this. I have explained to people that in an army you have commando

---

25. Interview with Lt. Gen. Jasin, May 23, 1980.

26. Ibid.

27. Jasin letter to General Jusuf, February 27, 1980. Copy made available by General Jasin.

units as well as the infantry. You cannot have only infantry, you need also commandos. But not everybody must be a commando."[28]

Sumitro, although he could not agree with Jasin's tactics, was also sympathetic. "I know his weaknesses," the former Kopkamtib commander noted nine months after the Jasin document had been presented to the DPR. But "I still admire him."[29]

Cutting the Lifelines

Suharto is very good to his friends but revengeful towards his enemies.

--Maj. Gen. Sukendro[30]

In his meeting with senior editors on June 3, 1980, General Yoga Sugama had given assurances that the government would strike back at those who had signed the petition. This it did without delay. As we have seen, the Suharto government derived much of its power from the skillful distribution of patronage, and this gave it considerable room to "remind" those who failed to play by its rules --particularly retired military men--that they could be squeezed out and left to suffer. It was, said Lt. Gen. Benny Murdani in mid-June, a denial of government privileges: "Normally when people retire [from the army] they come to us and see what they can get in the way of business. And normally people like this get first priority on government contracts and tenders. They can make US$1-2 million on commissions and that sort of thing and put it in the bank and sit back for life. So what we have done in this case is tell them to go to the bottom of the list."[31]

In fact, this was very much more than a mere denial of government privileges. In the months that followed, the Suharto government was to display a truly Nixonian facility for victimizing its political "enemies," hounding them with a meanness of spirit that brought little credit to either the president or those who enforced his will. As threatened, the government took steps to "isolate" those associated with the petition. Their expiring work permits and business licenses were permitted to lapse. Their credit lines to state banks were cut, and they were not permitted to participate in government tenders. This had the effect of driving many retired officers out of business. Ali Sadikin was obliged to relinquish his position with at least one major company. Dharsono found it necessary to give up his post of

---

28. Interview with General Nasution.

29. Interview with General Sumitro, March 3, 1981.

30. Interview with Maj. Gen. Sukendro, November 7, 1981.

31. Lt. Gen. Benny Murdani in a discussion with Warwick Beutler on June 14, 1980. Communication with Beutler, June 15, 1980.

chairman of P. T. Propelat, the Siliwangi holding company in West Java.[32] Sukendro, who had been president of the government-owned holding company which managed thirty-nine of Central Java's trading and industrial companies, was obliged to step down from this position on June 12, 1980.[33] (Although neither Dharsono nor Sukendro had signed the petition, they had been associated with its drafting.) Jasin was obliged to give up his post as chief supervisor of three companies he ran. And Slamet Bratanata, who ran a small business as a consultant to foreign oil firms, saw his clients threatened, and in a number of cases withdraw from their business dealings with him.

These measures, by their very nature, could only be used against those who were dependent to some degree on government largesse or permits. To penalize those who were not--and to underscore official displeasure with those who were--the ruling group introduced a comprehensive network of related "punishments."

One such punishment was a ruling that those associated with the Petition of Fifty were not to travel abroad,[34] a policy enforced with a certain self-interested "flexibility." For example, former prime minister Mohammad Natsir was banned from attending an International Commission of Jurists seminar in Kuwait on "Islam and Human Rights."[35] But Nasution was permitted to accompany his wife to Manila where Mrs. Nasution was to receive the Magsaysay Award for her services to charity.[36] The exception was made, apparently, to avoid official embarrassment over the denial of a visa to the former defense minister.

Under another ruling, the Foreign Ministry "recommended" that signatories to the petition should be taken off the official invitation lists of foreign embassies for the time being "to avoid any embarrassment."[37] A third ruling--and one that smacked of extreme pettiness--centered on official invitations to the National Day celebrations at the Merdeka Palace each August 17. It was a custom in Indonesia for former prime ministers, of whatever political coloration, to be given a place of honor at these celebrations. Suharto, however, was so angered by the actions of the petition's signatories that he ordered aides to see to it that no further August 17 invitations be issued to Natsir, Burhanuddin Harahap, or Sjafruddin Prawiranegara. It was, thought Natsir, the action of a man with limited education and a lim-

---

32. Interview with Lt. Gen. Dharsono.

33. Interview with Maj. Gen. Sukendro.

34. The travel ban was confirmed by the director general for immigration, Maj. Gen. Nichlany. See *Merdeka, Pelita* and *Harian AB,* July 3, 4, and 6, 1981.

35. Interview with Mohammad Natsir, November 9, 1981.

36. Interview with General Nasution.

37. See Reuters report in *Straits Times*, October 21, 1980.

ited world view. In 1933-34, Natsir had conducted a polemic with Sukarno about Islam. The exchanges had been sharp, but neither man had said anything that would have been "painful" to the other. There had been no personal animosity. This spirit had characterized all their differences. When, twenty-five years later, Sukarno had announced his *konsepsi* for Indonesia, Natsir had attacked it bitterly in a newspaper article. "But on January 1, 1958," said Natsir, "he invited me to the palace and said not a word about [my criticism]. Everyone was aghast. Suharto is not able to do that. After the Petisi 50 no one is invited to August 17 at the palace. . . . We don't exist any more."[38]

Meanwhile, steps were also taken against academics who had signed the petition. On June 9, 1980, the rector of the (Catholic) Atma Jaya University in Jakarta was summoned by the inspector general of the Department of Education and Culture and told to take action against Chris Siner Key Timu, the forty-year-old head of the student bureau at the university. The reason given was that Timu had signed the petition. On July 22, the department threatened that the status of the university and all the aid that had been given until then would be "reviewed" if Atma Jaya failed to take action against Timu. On July 28, Timu felt obliged to tender his resignation.[39] Timu had been a signatory of the petition, Education Minister Daud Jusuf said, and he had a job that dealt with students, who were a factor in the frequent occurrence of trouble on campus. "If he were a sweeper," the minister said, "there would be no problem."[40] At the end of August, Dr. Judilherry Justam, was discharged as an assistant at the University of Indonesia School of Medicine, owing to his "redundancy." Judil, who had nominated himself for president in the 1978 MPR session, said it was beyond doubt that his dismissal was due to the fact that he signed the petition. The same fate befell Professor Dr. Kasman Singodimedjo and Dr. Anwar Haryono, both of whom were lecturers at the Jakarta Sjarief Hidayat Institute of Islamic Studies (IAIN).[41]

Many believed that Hugeng's signature on the petition further estranged him from the president and Madame Suharto. Hugeng had agreed to give away his niece at her marriage (her father having died), and when he did not in fact do so, it was said this was because of objections from the first family, who were acquainted with the groom's family and were attending the wedding. The decision to cancel Hugeng's "Hawaiian Seniors" television program, many believed, had been taken at least partly at the behest of Madame Suharto. (The first lady, it was said, not only remembered Hugeng's anticorruption campaign with disfavor but had for some time taken of-

---

38. Mohammad Natsir interview, November 9, 1981.

39. For details, see *Tempo*, September 13, 1980. USE.

40. *Merdeka*, September 12, 1980.

41. Ibid.

fense at the sight of lightly clad "Hawaiian" girls appearing on her television screen.)

Now, there were signs that the first lady was taking an active interest in a campaign aimed at Nasution's wife. Mrs. Nasution was the founder and chairman of the Coordinating and Supervising Body for Social Welfare activities (Badan Pembina Koordinasi dan Pengawasan Kegiatan Sosial, BPKKS), a body that enjoyed a high reputation for its charitable work in Jakarta, and chairman of the Indonesian National Council on Social Welfare (Dewan Nasional Indonesia untuk Kesejahteraan Sosial, DNIKS), a national umbrella organization of charitable bodies. However, the BPKKS had long been a thorn in the side of Madame Suharto, who was founder and president of the Our Hope Foundation (Yayasan Harapan Kita). The first lady wanted to "acquire" the BPKKS, and Nasution's involvement with the petition was evidently seen as providing this opportunity. Under plans drawn up in Jakarta, the Department of Social Welfare began, early in 1981, to summon all BPKKS branch secretaries and instruct them to set up a new central organization, a move which was seen within the organization as a fairly heavy-handed attempt to depose Mrs. Nasution. Under this plan, the government would sever the links between the provincial branches and the foundation's headquarters in Jakarta and would install Mrs. Nelly Adam Malik, wife of the vice president, as chairman of a new foundation. To accomplish this task, the director of a state bank was instructed to "freeze" all BPKKS funds. These efforts did not allow for Mrs. Nasution's resourcefulness and the strength of the informal ties she was able to call on. Adam Malik was a relative of Nasution. On learning of the move to have Mrs. Malik installed in her place Mrs. Nasution went to see the vice president, emerging with an assurance that his wife would have nothing to do with the new institution. The coordinating minister for people's welfare, General Surono, had at one time been Nasution's ADC, and when Mrs. Nasution called on him to complain about the government's moves she found him sympathetic. (Surono was described by one military officer as "an army man, not a Golkar man.") At a wedding ceremony, Mrs. Nasution approached the director of the government bank which handled the BPKKS funds and said she was aware that he was "trying to cut" her money. The manager confirmed that he had instructions to do this but said that, while he had cut the money of "the others," the BPKKS money was not in Mrs. Nasution's name and could not be touched. Nasution himself was prevented from delivering a Lebaran sermon, an action which, he complained, was in breach of both Article 29 of the Constitution and in violation of injunctions in the Koran.[42]

Meanwhile, further action was being taken against Sukendro. Not only was he obliged to step down as president of the holding company of the Central Java government; he was also prevented from completing his part-time academic studies. (The former army intelli-

---

42. Interview with General Nasution.

gence chief, who turned 57 in 1980, was preparing a dissertation in business administration, looking at administrative reform within regional corporations.) In July 1980, four months before his work would have been finished, he received a letter saying that he would not be permitted to complete his academic work.[43]

Clearly, the Suharto government was prepared to go to quite extraordinary lengths to ensure that its "enemies" paid for their audacity in criticizing the presidential statement at Pekanbaru. The government banks and the immigration department took to keeping "black lists" to ensure that no one from the group of fifty was able to participate in a government tender, was granted a state bank loan, or was allowed to leave the country. The government also took steps to ensure that academic signatories were obliged to resign their teaching posts, that men like Nasution were not permitted to speak at mosques or write in the newspapers. It had also barred elderly nationalist leaders from attending national day celebrations at the palace. "The idea," said Sukendro, "is that all your lifelines should be cut."[44] Nothing quite like this had ever happened before, not in Dutch colonial times, not in Sukarno's time. It was, in short, an extraordinary display of presidential sensitivity to criticism, and inevitably, it produced an angry reaction. "We feel insulted at the way they have cut us off from everything," Ali Sadikin complained. "There were many in our group who fought for this country, before, during and after the revolution. And they are treated like this. But there are Chinese who did nothing, nothing, and they share in everything."[45]

---

43. Interview with Maj. Gen. Sukendro, November 7, 1981.

44. Ibid.

45. Interview with Lt. Gen. Ali Sadikin, June 19, 1980.

CHAPTER NINE

THE HANKAM PAPER

> We have agreed that the conclusion of this book should be that the dwifungsi should be continued in principle but that the implementation should be *disempurnakan* [perfected].
>
> Brig. Gen. Nugroho Notosusanto[1]

What had become abundantly clear by early 1980 was that criticism of the existing system was coming not only from retired (and therefore possible disgruntled) officers. Two of the most powerful men in the military command system--the minister of defense/commander of the armed forces and the army chief of staff--had made it plain that they shared in this concern over the implementation of ABRI's dwifungsi. Others in senior positions were likewise concerned. In the final analysis, however, this support amounted to very little. It was a measure of the president's extraordinary control over the system that he was able to silence these voices with his March 27 speech in Pekanbaru.

Not long after that speech, the difference of opinion between the "pragmatists" and those committed to a more "principled" approach was to give birth to a third--and very different--paper on the dwifungsi, one that was drawn up at the behest of the Hankam pragmatists, if not the president himself. The "Hankam paper"[2] would serve as both a rebuttal of the key dwifungsi sections of the "Widodo paper" and a justification for ABRI's extensive and continuing involvement in nonmilitary activities. However, those commissioned to prepare the Hankam paper, while paying due regard to the views of their sponsors, were to argue strongly that the dwifungsi should be implemented more correctly, and to suggest that the armed forces should be far more selective in placing military personnel in non-Hankam jobs.

---

1. Interview with Brig. Gen. Nugroho Notosusanto, November 21, 1981.

2. The full title of the "Hankam paper" was *Pejuang dan Prajurit: Konsepsi dan Implementasi Dwi Fungsi ABRI* [Fighters and Soldiers: The Concept and Implementation of ABRI's Dual Function]. The paper was published by Sinar Harapan in book form in 1984.

In the view of the authors of the Hankam paper, Widodo had virtually come out in favor of the "Turkish model"--the notion that the military should withdraw to the mountain top and only become involved in times of national crisis.[3] This was not entirely correct. Although Widodo did favor a reduction in ABRI's nonmilitary role, it was implicit in the Nasution-Abdulkadir Besar thinking which he and the army staff endorsed that ABRI, whatever else it might give up, would always be represented in the MPR. This would ensure that, at the very least, the armed forces had a say in the formulation of the Broad Outlines of State Policy (GBHN) and in the selection of the president. On the other hand, the officers committed to a more principled approach were advocating something akin to the Turkish model. The officers believed it was necessary to establish a "national consensus" among the various political groupings that, if a non-Golkar party were to win the elections, the successful party should be allowed --with one proviso--to take office. The proviso was that, should this party deviate from the Pancasila and seek, for example, to establish a Negara Islam, the ABRI would take steps to crush it.[4] This line of thinking, dangerously liberal in the view of the ruling group, seemed to run parallel to that of Jusuf. If Widodo had disturbed some key officers by his support to those who sought to undermine the existing orthodoxies, then Jusuf seemed to those officers to be even more unrealistic. Not only was he propagating the notion that ABRI should be above all groups; he also seemed inclined to do away with the military's kekaryaan function, at least in its existing form. And the appointment of ABRI officers as karyawan was the cornerstone of military control over the civilian sector.

In January 1980, Jusuf announced that he was calling back all Akabri (Military Academy) graduates serving as ADCs outside the Hankam structure. Not long afterwards, he seemed to some officers to be ready to call back *all* active officers serving in a kekaryaan role. This, in their view, would have severely weakened the army's control over the apparatus of government. There were in 1980 some 16,000 military men serving in a kekaryaan role, half of them still active and half retired.[5] Jusuf appeared to take the view that all ac-

---

3. Nugroho interview, November 21, 1981.

4. Interview with Brig. Gen. Abdulkadir Besar, March 22, 1982.

5. The figures for November 1980 were 8,156 active (of whom 1,957 were MPP (preretirement) and 8,674 retired, for a total of 16,830. See "Jumlah Anggota ABRI Yang Ditempatkan di Luar Bidang Hankam/ ABRI," included in *Pejuang dan Prajurit*, pp. 378-79.

The ABRI terminology, as many senior officers are ready to admit, is confusing. In theory, one might have thought, it does not make much sense to say that a retired military man is serving in a kekaryaan (nonmilitary) capacity. In fact, ABRI distinguishes between two kinds of kekaryaan. One category is the "organic kekaryaan," consisting of active military personnel, and the other the

tive officers should be recalled, and that kekaryaan duties should be left to retired officers. In the words of one officer, "General Jusuf seems to be inclined towards the Turkish model. If given his way he might withdraw all armed forces people from non-Hankam jobs and only if things got bad would the armed forces intervene." According to this officer, who played a key role in shaping the eventual "Hankam paper," that view "is not popular among everyone else."[6] In short, Jusuf's views caused considerable consternation within the upper echelons around Suharto. Darjatmo, who had served as chief of staff for functional affairs (Kaskar) for nine years (1969-78) and who had presided over the vast expansion of kekaryaan activities, openly opposed the minister's concept, if only because experience had shown that it was difficult for Hankam to exercise effective control over retired military men. As he observed in January 1980: "from one side it is a good idea because the strength of the armed forces

---

"nonorganic kekaryaan," made up of retired military men. Interview with General Darjatmo, January 21, 1980.

6. Interview with Brig. Gen. Nugroho Notosusanto, July 27, 1981. This may have been an accurate statement if by "everyone else" Nugroho was referring to the inner circle around Suharto. There was, however, a good deal of support for Jusuf's idea among other groups, particularly among the "military professionals" who had been eased out of key positions at the time of Malari. Thus General Sumitro, who had given much thought to this matter at the time of the restructuring of the armed forces in 1969, took the same view as Jusuf, this being one of the few points on which he saw eye to eye with the minister. (Sumitro interview, March 6, 1981.) The governor of Lemhannas, Lt. Gen. Sutopo Juwono, shared their opinion. Jusuf's proposal, he felt, was "very logical." It was true, as General Darjatmo had pointed out, that the withdrawal of active military men would create a problem from the army viewpoint and affect the dwifungsi. "But actually we hope we don't need that any more." (Sutopo Juwono interview, July 23, 1981.) The position of Lt. Gen. Charis Suhud, who had been appointed Kaskar in 1978, was not entirely clear. According to Sutopo Juwono, Charis Suhud shared the view that, in principle, active officers should be withdrawn from kekaryaan duties. However, as we shall see, it was Charis Suhud, apparently concerned over Jusuf's plans, who was to commission the "Hankam paper." That paper came out in favor of pruning unnecessary kekaryaan posts (which seemed to strike primarily at retired or soon-to-be-retired military men) while endorsing a continuing role for organic kekaryaan officers.

Brig. Gen. Abdulkadir Besar also believed that Jusuf was inclined towards the Turkish model. Jusuf, he felt, was not much interested in politics and wanted to concentrate on ABRI's role as a professional military force. Jusuf, he thought, accepted that ABRI had a social-political function but was not inclined to pay much attention to it. Interview with Abdulkadir Besar, March 22, 1982.

can be maintained. Also there is no waste of money because the salary is the salary of the armed forces and they [work] for the armed forces. But on the other hand, it is easier to handle people of the organic group because they are still disciplined, their promotions are dependent on the Manhankam/Pangab while retired people are just other citizens.[7]

For Darjatmo, there was not much to commend the view that "once an ABRI man, always an ABRI man." Once a man had been away from the armed forces for some time, he felt, the discipline was "not so tight."[8] Lt. Gen. Charis Suhud, Darjatmo's successor as Kaskar, was equally concerned. According to one officer with a close knowledge of these matters, Suhud believed that Jusuf was not only on the verge of recalling all active officers but was toying with the idea of abolishing the Kaskar job altogether.[9] (Such fears would seem to have been unfounded, if only because it is highly unlikely that Suharto would ever have countenanced such a move.) As a result of this concern, it is said, Charis Suhud decided to commission a paper of his own on the dwifungsi. Towards the middle of 1980, he asked Dr. Nugroho Notosusanto, director of the Center for Armed Forces' History and an honorary brigadier general in the TNI, and three other men--Brig. Gen. (retd.) A. S. S. Tambunan SH, Maj. Gen. (retd.) Subiyono SH, and Drs. Hidayat Mukmin--to set out their own views on the dwifungsi without being bound by any doctrine.[10] Inviting the four men to write as scholars, Suhud told them that, if they felt that the dwifungsi principle or the position of Kaskar should be abolished, then they should say so, setting out their reasons.[11] At first sight, it might appear that Suhud was opening up a Pan-

---

7. Interview with General Darjatmo, January 21, 1980. Sumitro takes issue with Darjatmo on this point. According to Sumitro, the "original idea" in the army headquarters in the late 1960s was that only nonactive officers would be assigned as karyawan. There were practical considerations for this. If, for example, an officer had served two five-year terms as a governor or bupati "how the hell are you going to absorb him back into the normal military system?" Interview with General Sumitro, March 6, 1981.

8. Darjatmo interview, January 21, 1980.

9. Confidential communication. If Charis Suhud had taken the same view as his former mentor, Sumitro, he would presumably have agreed with Jusuf's apparent intention of recalling all serving officers. Evidently, he felt compelled to take a different view from Sumitro on this point.

10. Ibid. Nugroho described the paper as a "semi-official" work. "We are official people but we are given the freedom not to espouse the party line."

11. Ibid. The team was made up of one historian (Nugroho), two lawyers (Tambunan and Subiyono) and one political scientist (Hidayat Mukmin).

dora's box. In fact, the careful selection of the four-man review team virtually ensured that the eventual paper would be sympathetic to the views of the "realists." Nugroho, who had written his doctoral dissertation on the Japanese-sponsored Indonesian auxiliary army (Peta) formed during the wartime occupation, was known to be sympathetically disposed towards the views of the ruling group.[12] And the other members of the team were no less sympathetic. A.S.S. Tambunan, a member of the fraksi ABRI (ABRI grouping) in Parliament, was known to be a "violent opponent" of both Abdulkadir Besar and the sort of thinking expressed in the Widodo paper.[13] Subiyono was also a fraksi ABRI member of Parliament. The one civilian in the group, Drs. Hidayat Mukmin, a political scientist from Gajah Mada University in Yogyakarta, had been a lecturer at Seskoad since 1959 and was a member of the staff of the coordinating minister of people's welfare, General Surono.[14]

Almost immediately after their appointment, the team began to gather material for the study. Tambunan and Subiyono held consultations with the political parties and Golkar. Hidayat Mukmin talked at length with civilian bureaucrats. By April 1981, the team had come up with a preliminary (green cover) draft, a copy of which was forwarded to the president by Charis Suhud. A more complete (red cover) version was issued in June; this ran to 326 pages (not counting appendixes) and was entitled *Pejuang dan Prajurit: Konsepsi dan Implementasi Dwifungsi ABRI*. The paper was divided into two parts,

---

12. Nugroho, for many years the director of the Institute of History of Hankam, had been the co-author (with Colonel Ismail Saleh) of a publication entitled *The Coup Attempt of the September 30 Movement in Indonesia* (Jakarta: Pembimbing Masa, 1968), the Indonesian army's version of the 1965 coup affair. Early in 1982 he was installed as the rector of the University of Indonesia. When Suharto unveiled his Fourth Development Cabinet the following year, Nugroho was named minister of education. In 1981, Ismail Saleh, by now a major general, was appointed attorney general. In May 1984, Lt. Gen. Ismail Saleh was named minister of justice.

13. Interview with Nugroho Notosusanto, July 27, 1981. Abdulkadir Besar acknowledges this, but says that Tambunan was an opponent "because he misunderstood my point of view." Abdulkadir says that his approach in both the Seskoad and Widodo papers had been "behavioral"; he had interpreted the dwifungsi in cultural terms. Tambunan had misunderstood his approach and concluded that he, Abdulkadir, was adopting a "quantitative" approach, suggesting that everything could be measured precisely and quantitatively. Abdulkadir says he has never held such a view "because social action cannot be measured exactly and mathematically." Interview, March 22, 1982.

14. Mentioned by Drs. Hidayat Mukmin in a meeting on November 19, 1981. Subiyono and Hidayat Mukmin had both taught part-time at the University of Indonesia.

the first historical, the second structural. The historical section, which dealt with the dwifungsi since 1945, was written in its entirety by Nugroho. The structural part was divided into three chapters --one by Tambunan on the concept of the dwifungsi, one by Subiyono on its implementation (past and present), and one by Hidayat Mukmin on the future of the dwifungsi, including its implementation. Nugroho, who oversaw the project, supplied a comparative introduction for the volume.

Although commissioned by the chief of staff for functional affairs--on the orders, according to one senior officer, of the president and his associates[15]--the paper was not something that the government was obliged to accept. Ostensibly the private views of a four-man group, it was, in the words of Nugroho, a staff study proposing ideas which could either be accepted or rejected by the leadership.[16] There was little likelihood, however, that such a rejection would be necessary. Quite early in their deliberations, the four-man editorial team reached the conclusion that ABRI's dwifungsi should, in principle, continue. This being so, the authors felt, it would be quite wrong to dismantle the Kaskar position; so long as the dwifungsi doctrine existed an agency would be needed to take care of these functions.

In many ways, the report provided not only a rebuttal of the sort of thinking found in the Widodo paper but a justification of ABRI's continuing involvement in the nonmilitary sector. If Widodo and Jusuf were in fact leaning towards the "Turkish model," their views found no support in the Hankam paper. "We don't adhere to the Turkish model," Nugroho remarked.[17]

> We think that according to our experience it's safer to have the ABRI get involved completely, although we know there are certain disadvantages--that ABRI, going down in the mud, will get spattered also by the mud. While if it remains on horseback it remains clean. So this is the disadvantage. During the Sukarno period we were actually shifting towards the Turkish model. And the result was Lubang Buaya [the "Crocodile Hole" where the bodies of the six murdered generals were thrown after the September 1965 coup attempt]. So at least the present generation is apprehensive to try this again. So the basic idea [of ABRI] is to get involved completely--realizing the consequences of being unable to maintain its cleanliness, as the last resort of the nation to clean up. This means that ABRI is fully responsible for what happens to the

---

15. Confidential communication.

16. Nugroho interview, July 27, 1981.

17. Ibid.

nation. So if the nation goes down the drain--to use an
extreme example--ABRI is responsible.[18]

In one critical area--ABRI's control of the high ground of the
Indonesian political and military system--the authors of the Hankam
paper come down firmly in favor of the status quo. The paper's
basic theme is that ABRI should implement its dwifungsi at the apex
of the government pyramid. Its hold over the legislative and representative branch should be secured by its continuing dominance of
the DPR and MPR. At the very least, the paper implies, ABRI will
continue to insist on seventy-five of the 460 seats in the DPR and on
one-third of the seats in the MPR; control over the MPR will ensure
that it is not possible for any hostile political group to exercise Article 37 and change the Constitution, an unlikely enough event in the
foreseeable future.[19] ABRI's hold over the executive branch is to be

---

18. Ibid. It is, in fact, very much open to question whether Indonesia was moving towards the "Turkish model" during the Sukarno
period. After the Presidential Decree of July 5, 1959, under which
Sukarno dissolved the Constituent Assembly and adopted the 1945
Constitution, there was a steady, even relentless, expansion of the
army's involvement in the social-political field.

19. The "fear" that certain groups were bent on changing the Constitution has been something of a preoccupation with Suharto, and at
various times he has offered suggestions about ways in which the
sanctity of this document can be preserved. As we have seen, in his
Pekanbaru speech in March 1980, the president suggested that, if
two-thirds of the MPR members wished to change the Constitution, it
would be ABRI's duty "to use weapons" to prevent them. Rather
than using weapons, he said, "we had better kidnap one out of the
two-thirds who wish to make the change." (See above, p. 157.) In
a speech in 1981 to Indonesians resident in Bangkok, Suharto raised
the possibility of a referendum being held before any change was
made in the Constitution. In his Independence Day speech in August
1981 Suharto devoted no less than four pages to the question of the
appointment of members of the MPR and DPR, and returned to the
theme of a referendum. The main consideration behind the appointment of one-third of the members of the MPR, he said, was to secure
a "constitutional safeguard" against the possibility of any alteration of
the Constitution or of any replacement of the Pancasila as the basis of
the state. In this context a "consensus" had been reached to have
one-third ABRI appointees. If the appointed armed forces members
failed to attend an MPR sitting, it was still possible for the non-ABRI
members to sit and put through a constitutional amendment "although
that possibility is extremely small." After some discussion of this and
related points, Suharto returned to the theme of blocking any potential change of the Constitution, however remote that might seem.
"Should the MPR indeed wish to alter the existing consensus and consider doing away with the institution for the appointment of one-third
of the members of the assembly it is necessary to determine another

maintained by its retention of the top executive positions, in particular the presidency and the ministries of Defense and Home Affairs. Because Home Affairs is still considered a sensitive ministry, one can conclude that it is likely to be the last nonmilitary department to witness the withdrawal of high-level kekaryaan ABRI personnel. A military minister of home affairs, surrounded, as at present, by a phalanx of senior military administrators, is likely to be a fact of life well into the future.

If Nugroho and his colleagues were not prepared to give ground on the need for a continuing ABRI involvement in society, they did at least take the view that the army should relinquish a large number of civilian posts. The Hankam paper argued that the army should be much more selective in placing ABRI people outside the Defense Ministry. There was, it is true, a good deal of room for pruning. In barely twenty years, the armed forces had moved in on the civilian sector in a big way.

The appointment of army officers to nonmilitary positions had begun modestly enough in 1957.[20] But it had soon gathered momentum, and by 1977 the number of ABRI personnel serving outside the Defense Ministry had risen to 21,118.[21] And though the number fell by more than 4,000 to 16,830 in 1980, this was not due to any conscious policy to reduce numbers but was more a result of natural attrition.[22] The bulk of the military men who left during this period were middle-echelon officials who had been serving in government departments; as they had reached retirement age their places had been taken by qualified civilians from a lower age bracket.[23] Into the

----

method of safeguarding." The method the president had "considered" was a decree from the MPR that, before that body make any such change through the exercise of Article 17, the people ought first to be asked about it through a referendum. (See Address of State by President Suharto before the DPR, August 15, 1983, State Secretariat, Jakarta, 1981.) In other words, the president appeared to be suggesting that what was necessary was not merely a two-thirds vote of the MPR, as the framers of the Constitution had decreed, but a referendum *as well*. It is difficult to escape the feeling that this preoccupation with the dangers posed by the free exercise of the constitutional processes reflected a deep and abiding distrust of the good judgment of the Indonesian people. It also implied that, in Suharto's eyes, there were major differences in perception between the government leaders and the people as a whole, the talk of ABRI-people unity notwithstanding.

20. Nasution, in an interview (November 10, 1981), dated ABRI's direct involvement in nonmilitary activities to this time.

21. See "Jumlah Anggota ABRI Yang Ditempatkan di Luar Bidang Hankam/ABRI" in *Pejuang dan Prajurit*.

22. Ibid.

23. Interview with Brig. Gen. Nugroho Notosusanto, July 27, 1981.

midst of this situation came the Hankam paper with its calls for a substantial reduction in the number of military men serving in a kekaryaan capacity.

At present, military men serving in this capacity--the most visible physical manifestation of ABRI's dual role in society--are divided into three separate categories--*penugaskaryaan*, *penyaluran*, and *perbantuan*. Penugaskaryaan, which in late 1980 accounted for 8,725 men, involves placing active military men in nominally civilian positions. These men, who can later return to Hankam, are the responsibility of the Kaskar, not the assistant for personnel. In theory; such placement must be based on the military man's usefulness to the people and the nation in such a position, on his moral qualities, on his expertise, his acceptability in the environment in which he is to be placed, and on his previous experience. In practice, the appointment of men to penugaskaryaan positions is sometimes done with an eye not on the urgency of an ABRI man holding a particular position but more on a desire to reward a friend or colleague with a comfortable post. The appointment of prominent military officers as ambassadors is one of the more obvious examples of this kind of practice.

The penyaluran category, which in November 1980 accounted for very nearly as many ABRI personnel as the penugaskaryaan, is somewhat different in composition. It is made up of officers and men who, although still on the active list at the time of their civilian appointment, are approaching retirement and not expected to return to Hankam. Thus, an ABRI man who will soon be retiring might, because of his distinguished record in the revolution, be put into a civilian slot that allows him "to spend the rest of his life peacefully."[24] Although expected to perform his job in a dutiful manner and set an example, he is not given any specific mission to accomplish or any particular target to meet. In November 1980, this subgroup accounted for 7,031 people or almost 42 percent of all kekaryaan positions. More often than not, appointments were simply "retirement presents" from headquarters.

The perbantuan category is different again. A military man so designated is merely attached to a certain position on a short-term basis to perform a particular task or solve a particular problem. He may serve, for example, as an adviser to a governor, as a member of a special committee or advisory council, or may be attached to a certain factory to solve a problem of labor unrest. In most regards, perbantuan simply means short-term penugaskaryaan. However, a military man serving in this capacity is not put under the kekaryaan administration. His career remains in the hands of the assistant for personnel, and is not taken over by the Kaskar. Many of the ADCs to ABRI functionaries were included under this heading. However, by 1982 almost all of these officers had been recalled by Jusuf.

---

24. Interview with Brig. Gen. Nugroho Notosusanto, November 21, 1981.

The primary concern of the authors of the Hankam paper was that penugaskaryaan positions should in future be filled with much greater selectivity than was currently the case. Before any ABRI man was put into a civilian position, they argued, it should first be clear that the appointment was essential. There were two reasons for this. First, the armed forces could not afford to squander their limited manpower. Second, many civilians had now been trained--in such places as the Institut Pemerintahan Dalam Negeri (Civil Service Institute of the Department of Home Affairs)--to serve as bupati and so on. These people, being professionals, were well qualified to assume responsibility, and an ABRI man should only be brought in over their heads if the position were still considered *rawan* (vulnerable), either physically or politically.

A secondary and closely related concern centered on the penyaluran category. The authors of the Hankam paper argued strongly that the Ministry of Defense should abandon the practice of putting military men out to grass in a penyaluran capacity. Many of these appointees, they said, were considered *brengsek* (rotten) by the community at large, and this was harming ABRI's image. If the military was looking for some way to cut the fat from its kekaryaan structure, the paper suggested, then abolition of penyaluran appointments was an obvious first step. That sort of reasoning seemed to find ready acceptance at the top. When President Suharto received senior officers at the palace after the Rapim ABRI (ABRI Commanders Call) in April 1981, his speech reflected not just the view that the dwifungsi should remain in place but also that the penyaluran should not be treated as a dumping ground for unwanted personnel. "Kekaryaan ABRI," the president said, "should not be just a matter of channeling individuals into comfortable positions." (*"Kekaryaan ABRI jangan sampai menjadi penyaluran."*)[25] The suggested abolition of penyaluran appointments also found favor with General Sumitro, who had been responsible for restructuring the armed forces in 1969. As he noted

> I do not agree with such appointments. If an officer reaches the time of MPP [preretirement] or retirement, give him his retirement. Don't try to find any other jobs for these people. It will create resentment and disappointment among the civilians. But on the other hand, it is a challenge for the civilians to make themselves better. . . . I accept that professionally all these officers are nothing if you compare them with a civilian with the professional educational background. He [the officer] is nothing! But he's got the guts to do something. The training to take decisions. And he's bold. Sometimes without this [his head]. Very bold![26]

25. See speech by President Suharto, April 1981.

26. Interview with General Sumitro, December 12, 1981.

Table V. *Total ABRI Members Serving Outside Hankam*

No.	Officers/Groupings	Total 1977 (May)		Total 1980 (Nov.)	
	Central Government				
1.	Ministers, Heads of High State Institutions	17	(42,5%)	19	(47,5%)
2.	Secretaries General	14	(73,6%)	14	(73,6%)
3.	Inspectors General	18	(29,5%)	18	(29,5%)
4.	Directors General	15	(78,9%)	15	(78,9%)
5.	Heads/Chiefs Nondepartmental Institutions	8	(44,4%)	8	(44,4%)
6.	Ministerial Secretaries, Assistant Ministers (one level)	21	(84%)	21	(84%)
	Total	76	(53,5%)	76	(53,5%)
	Regional Heads/Representatives Abroad				
7.	Governors	19	(70,3%)	19	(70,3%)
8.	Bupatis	136	(56,4%)	137	(56,6%)
9.	Mayors	19	(31,6%)	20	(33,3%)
10.	Ambassadors	24	(41%)	28	(44,4%)
11.	Chargés d'affaires	1	(50%)	1	(50%)
12.	Consuls General	4	(25%)	4	(25%)
13.	Indonesian Consuls	2	(9,5%)	2	(9,5%)
	Total	31	(31,9%)	35	(34,3%)
	Groupings				
14.	Penugaskaryaan	--		8725	
15.	Penyaluran	--		7031	
16.	Perbantuan	--		1071	
	Total	--		16830	
	Status				
17.	Active	8715		6199	
18.	MPP (Pre-retirement)	12405		1957	
19.	Pensioned	--		8674	
	Total	21118		16830	

Table V. (Continued)

No.	Officers/Groupings	Total	
		1977 (May)	1980 (Nov.)
20.	Legislative (MPR/DPR)	1806	1480
21.	Executive	19312	10203*
	Source		
22.	Army	17004	12873
23.	Navy	926	823
24.	Air Force	698	777
25.	Police	2490	2357
	Total	21,118	16,830

*Although these figures are obviously incomplete, there has been a clear and dramatic fall in the number of ABRI officers serving in the executive branch.

SOURCE: *Pejuang dan Prajurit: Konsepsi dan Implementasi Dwi Fungsi ABRI.*

In the view of the authors of the Hankam paper, Pepabri should take over the process of penyaluran from ABRI. Pepabri should know what vacancies exist in the civilian sector and should suggest the names of ex-ABRI men who could fill these positions. This, it was argued, would prevent a situation in which ABRI continued to influence such appointments. At the same time, the authors believed that the phasing out of the penyaluran category should be done carefully and gradually. If it were done abruptly, they feared, those currently in such positions might "join other political forces."[27]

From even a cursory glance, it is clear that the Hankam paper called for some fairly significant changes in the implementation of ABRI's dwifungsi. It said in effect that, when those currently in kekaryaan functions retired, they should not be replaced by other ABRI people unless strictly necessary. This would entail a dramatic and substantial--but "natural"--reduction in the number of military men serving in nonmilitary positions by the mid-1980s. By implication, there would be fewer military governors, fewer bupati, fewer camat, fewer ambassadors, fewer middle-level functionaries. Even in private, the authors of the paper were unable to say just what this proposal, if implemented, would mean in terms of numbers. However, Nugroho conceded that it could mean that the number of military governors and bupati would be halved.

In mid-1981, after completing the second draft, the authors of the paper sought some feedback on their views from within the system. Initially, mid-career officers at Seskogab, the Joint Services' Staff and Command School, were asked to read and comment on the paper. The response is said to have been very favorable. Later, the authors asked Lt. Gen. Sutopo Juwono if they could present their work to a selected team of people from Lemhannas. The outcome of this encounter proved to be somewhat unexpected. The authors say they had anticipated a fierce attack on their suggestions regarding the dwifungsi doctrine and were surprised to find that their basic proposals went unchallenged. When a copy of the paper was forwarded at about the same time to Lt. Gen. T. B. Simatupang, the former armed forces chief of staff found himself in almost complete agreement with the recommendations and used some of the thoughts contained in the document as the basis of a series of editorials he wrote in *Sinar Harapan*.[28]

The national leadership also seemed pleased with the paper. Suharto, as we have seen, drew on sections of it when he addressed senior officers following the Rapim ABRI in April 1981. When, six months later, he spoke at the October 5 Armed Forces Day celebrations at Cilegon, West Java, he seemed to put his imprimatur firmly on the paper's assessment of where ABRI stood in society. ABRI, he

---

27. Nugroho Notosusanto interview, November 21, 1981.

28. Ibid. Confirmed by Lt. Gen. Simatupang in an interview, March 19, 1982.

said, would not go in the direction of militarism, authoritarianism, or totalitarianism.[29] In December 1981, the Hankam paper was accepted by senior ABRI officers who assembled in Bandung for the Preliminary Commanders Call, and in 1984 it was published in book form.

Some, however, were not impressed. General Sumitro, who was in favor of a progressive--but not unlimited--transfer of power to civilians, found nothing new in the proposals. "It is not a new idea! It is not new! Nothing new! Even during my time [there was talk about this]! You can ask Darjatmo if he's honest enough! Darjatmo! Charis Suhud! Topo Juwono! Nothing new!"[30]

---

29. See "Kemanunggalan ABRI dan Rakyat," (Amanat Pada Upacara Peringatan Hari Ulang Tahun ABRI Ke XXXVI, Pada Tanggal 5 Oktober 1981, Di Cilegon, Jawa Barat), in *Mimbar Kekaryaan ABRI* (Jakarta: Hankam, Edisi: 130, Oktober 1981), pp. 3-7. In his speech, Suharto said that with the unity of ABRI and the people and with the implementation of the dwifungsi, the role and activities of ABRI as fighters and soldiers must always constitute a safeguard to the Pancasila for the realization of social justice for the entire Indonesian people. Within this framework, the role of ABRI as fighters and soldiers was not sliding towards militarism, authoritarianism, or totalitarianism (*tidak akan meluncur pada kekuasaan yang militeristis, otoriter atau totaliter*). See also "Peranan ABRI Tidak Meluncur ke Militeristis," *Merdeka*, October 6, 1981. The president repeated these assurances in March 1982 when he addressed nearly 2,000 senior officers who had participated in the Commanders Call in Bandung. (*Indonesian Times*, March 15, 1982.) Earlier, Jusuf had said that the military's dual function was aimed at spurring the growth of political and economic democracy. ABRI's involvement in nonmilitary affairs would not kill democracy or society's initiative in the political or economic sphere. (*Indonesian Observer*, March 15, 1982.)

It is interesting to note that General Surono, deputy commander of the armed forces and spokesman for the ABRI faction in the MPR, had made much the same point during the plenary session debate that preceded Suharto's reelection in 1978. ABRI's dual function, he said, was "an essential element of our political system," and was not a reflection of militarism or disguised militarism. *Kompas*, March 16, 1978.

30. Interview with General Sumitro, December 12, 1981. Sumitro believed that it was time to start handing positions back to the civilians. But he argued that there were three important steps that had to be followed. First, there had to be an overall concept and a clear policy that certain positions would continue to be "occupied" by ABRI people. (This was in line with the Nugroho group's proposals, although Sumitro was not familiar with their paper or, it seems, particularly in sympathy with Nugroho.) Second, it was necessary to make an evaluation of all ABRI bupati. Perhaps half of them or a third of them were good--"accepted by the civilians, by everyone." "They have their achievement, their performance is very good, excellent and

Senior members of the ex-FKS group felt the recommendations did not go far enough. Nasution doubted that the key proposals of the Hankam paper would ever be implemented. As he noted in November 1981: "The whole problem is what you are saying is not what you are doing. I think that when they are talking about this they are still upholding some idealism, and so they are speaking for the record. But they are still doing the same. . . . The number of kekaryaan appointments is still growing, still growing. They are going down, even the lurah and so on. So it's increasing, not decreasing."[31]

Jusuf had proposed that kekaryaan duties be reserved for retired officers, Nasution noted. But Darjatmo had opposed this because he had felt that the government would lose control. "What Darjatmo is saying is the policy of the government," said Nasution. "But they are not speaking openly."[32] Fosko had proposed that there were enough retired officers to serve as members of Parliament and so on. But the President had refused. "He likes to have active officers because you can order them, control them." Nasution felt that the outlook of active military officers was too "ABRI-centric." He did not feel such an approach would be enough or long lasting. This was a national problem and therefore it was necessary to have a national approach, one based on the 1945 Constitution.

In the view of a number of retired officers, the refusal of those in power to contemplate an easing of the military's grip on the most important institutions was totally unacceptable. As Nugroho himself admitted: "they say we should withdraw completely from politics and sit on the mountain and look down on the people in the valley caring for the country. And if anything should go wrong--but only then--should the people here go down. This is the Turkish model."[33]

Whatever the reservations of the retired generals, the Hankam paper was clearly of importance in the continuing debate over ABRI's role in Indonesian society. There are, however, two intriguing questions that remain unanswered. Who precisely was behind this paper?

---

so on. Why not use them? And the rest, you kick them out! Give them training, give them money or something and let them do something else." Finally, it was necessary to make an honest evaluation of potential civilian bupati and select those who were "ripe enough to be exposed." (Ibid.) If the Hankam paper was suggesting that ABRI, as a matter of principle, withdraw military bupati wherever possible, Sumitro did not agree; he took the view that the good ones could be left where they were. This may have amounted to much the same thing, as Nugroho and his group had allowed for the need for incumbents to be phased out gradually.

31. Interview with General Nasution, November 10, 1981.

32. Ibid.

33. Nugroho interview, November 21, 1984.

And why was such a document proposed at this particular time? On the face of it, the initiative came from Charis Suhud. He was the officer who "commissioned" Nugroho and the others to prepare such a document, and he was the one who ushered it through its prepublication phase, forwarding a preliminary draft to the president himself. Yet there are grounds for believing that Charis Suhud was no more than an instrument of others in this, an obedient servant who followed the instructions that were given to him. In the view of a number of senior officers, Charis Suhud had been a disappointment as Kaskar. "Many of us feel Charis Suhud has failed," a prominent two-star officer noted in 1981. "He is not strong."[34] In the years when Darjatmo had served as chief of staff for functional affairs, he had been an important and influential figure. A trusted associate of Suharto, whom he had known since 1950, he served as chief karya not only for the minister of defense but for the president as well. When Darjatmo was Kaskar, he had a decisive say on the selection and appointment of all key karyawan and played a central role in drawing up the GBHN. He had been deeply involved in all manner of political problems, and not simply those touching on army matters. He had made it a point to keep in regular contact with political leaders, particularly from the younger generation, and met them twice a month in his office. He had been very well informed. He had, in short, been the very model of a modern political commissar. And when he moved across to the DPR, he seemed to take many of those key functions with him, leaving Charis Suhud with little more than administrative responsibilities.

Charis Suhud was a thoughtful and reflective man. Like Sutopo Juwono, he was from that stream within army intelligence which believed certain moral precepts should guide government actions.[35] Like Sutopo Juwono, he was very much in agreement with those in the armed forces who believed in conciliation. In his view, it was important for the army leaders to maintain links with the dissident generals, not to cut them off and treat them as enemies. But, like so many others in senior positions in the army, he was caught between the demands of his superiors and the demands of his conscience, a handicap made all the more difficult by the fact that the more "principled" officers within the intelligence establishment had lost influence at the time of the Malari Affair and were still regarded with some reserve by their more "pragmatic" colleagues. Lacking a close personal

---

34. Confidential communication, November 11, 1981.

35. Intellectually, Charis Suhud had been a pupil of the late Maj. Gen. Suwarto, a man frequently described as "PSI" in outlook. Charis Suhud and Sutopo Juwono, who were instructors at Seskoad in the late 1950s, were two of Suwarto's closest assistants. They are unlikely, however, to have shared Suwarto's PSI outlook, and their tie with him was probably more through their Siliwangi and intelligence activities. (I am indebted to Prof. Ben Anderson for making the latter point.)

connection with Suharto, lacking perhaps the political skills and dynamism of his predecessor, and left with a job that had been stripped of some of its most important functions, Charis Suhud seemed to many to be little more than a military bureaucrat. Before long, he seemed to lose touch with the civilian political leaders --Darjatmo, at the DPR, was taking care of that--and senior officers who had once made a point of attending his twice-monthly briefing sessions began sending their excuses; Charis Suhud, they complained, was not his own man. The briefings, said one officer, were "a waste of time and energy." Charis Suhud could not even say, "Take it or leave it. I am just following orders." He gave no impression that he would fight, as Yoga, Sutopo Juwono, or Ali Murtopo would have done, for something he believed in.[36]

If not Charis Suhud, then who? The answer may have been someone below him--Nugroho Notosusanto is one obvious possibility --or someone above him. Nugroho had in the past written any number of papers on ABRI's role in society--his most recent effort in this direction had been the first part of Jusuf's blue book in 1979--and he may well have suggested such a project to Charis Suhud. Alternatively, the idea may have come from Suharto himself, or, at any rate, from someone close to him, perhaps Darjatmo. If this was, in fact, the case, it raises the equally intriguing question of whether Suharto had become convinced, amid the furor that had followed the Pekanbaru speech, that it was necessary to make a fundamental adjustment to ABRI's role. The senior leadership may have decided that the time had come to limit military involvement in the civilian sector, at least at the middle and lower levels. But on the evidence available, there is room for skepticism. The leadership may publicly endorse the recommendations contained in the Hankam paper. But it remains to be seen whether those proposals are implemented. In the meantime, Indonesians are confronted with the paradox that appeared at the time of Golkar's Second National Congress in 1978. As the talk of a pullback increased, the military's grip over the institutions of the state was growing still tighter.

---

36. Confidential communication.

CHAPTER TEN

THE VIEWS OF GENERAL NASUTION

When I was Commander of the Siliwangi (aged 28 years)
the Siliwangi was my pride. Siliwangi meant everything
to me.   Then when I became deputy Commander-in-Chief
(aged 30 years) and later army chief of staff, the TNI
was my pride. After becoming chairman of the MPRS, I
emphasized my dedication to the people. But now, the
older I become, it is God's will that is most important to
me.

--General Nasution, 1977[1]

Of all the retired generals who locked horns with the government in the late 1970s and early 1980s, none was more important than
Abdul Haris Nasution. Nasution had been a dominant figure in the
armed forces since the early days of the revolution and had earned a
reputation not only as a tactician and strategist of considerable re-
nown, but also as a shrewd--if sometimes hesitant--actor on the political stage.

Nasution was less than three years older than Suharto and most
of the other key members of his group. But his career had blossomed much earlier--he had been a major general when Suharto was
still a captain--and he seemed at times to be of an entirely different
generation. In a sense he was. An Outer Islander and a graduate
of the prewar Royal Military Academy in Bandung, Nasution did not
have a great deal in common with the Japanese-trained--and largely
Javanese--officers in Peta. His sense of values tended to be more in
line with those of the prewar civilian politicians (albeit with a more
authoritarian streak), and his commitment to Islam contrasted with the
more permissive attitude of the largely abangan Javanese. Moreover,
Nasution's age advantage, although slight, was to give him a very
different perspective from that of the Peta officers. The dominant
experience in the lives of these men had been the Indonesian revolu-
tion--the period of revolutionary ardor (semangat) and struggle that
had culminated in the overthrow of Dutch colonial rule. Nasution,
who had come to maturity during the Japanese occupation, tended to
take a more detached view of the years of physical revolution, and

1. General Nasution in an address to Siliwangi "seniors" in 1977.
Mentioned by Nasution in a written communication dated November 14,
1981.

was able to note the shortcomings as well as the advantages of the *pemuda* (youth) struggle.

Nasution's career had been rich in accomplishment. Elected the first commander of the Siliwangi (West Java) division in 1946, he had served as deputy Commander-in-Chief of the Armed Forces (1948) and later as the head of the Java Military Command. He had had two terms as chief of staff of the army (1950-52 and 1955-62), had served as chief of staff of the armed forces after 1962 and been minister of defense between 1959 and 1966. Instrumental in mapping out the strategy that was to stalemate the Dutch, he had gone on to play a central role in forging a modern, professional army out of the disparate group of pemuda struggle organizations that had carried the revolution to success. Later, he had been successful in crushing a series of regional rebellions and in suppressing Muslim militants bent on the creation of an Islamic state. Equally important, he ranked as a major military theoretician. His book *Fundamentals of Guerrilla Warfare* has been described as a classic on insurgency and ranked with the works of Mao Zedong and Vo Nguyen Giap. Nasution was the man who formulated many of the doctrines on which the TNI was based. In 1958, he set out his famous "Middle Way" formulation of the army's political role, in which he affirmed that the armed forces should neither seek to dominate the political processes nor exist merely as a "dead tool" in the hands of a civilian government. He elaborated this concept in his Armed Forces Day speech in 1963, foreshadowing later theories of the military's dwifungsi, a concept formally adopted at the first army seminar in Bandung in April 1965 and developed still further at the second army seminar the following year.

Nasution was pushed into a parliamentary backwater as the forces around Suharto gathered self-confidence in the postcoup period, and by 1968 the estrangement between him and the new president was complete; although after that date they would exchange ritual pleasantries if they met by chance at some social function, they had no further communication. As far as Nasution was concerned, the catalyst for this falling out was the president's decision to restructure the MPRS "to his own liking," and then "virtually ignore" both the body and its chairman. For the following four years, Nasution lived in a kind of limbo; although chairman of what was nominally the highest institution in the nation, he was increasingly ignored and isolated by the new powerholders.

Critics have suggested that there was some fatal flaw in Nasution's character, a flaw which hampered his effectiveness at critical times. Military men, particularly those around Suharto, sought to focus attention on his seeming immobility at several critical points in the nation's history, most particularly in the wake of the 1965 coup attempt. A number of explanations have been advanced for this, not least that Nasution had narrowly escaped an assassination attempt, in which his small daughter had been fatally wounded and his aide also killed, and he was in an obvious state of shock. There can be little doubt that this was the case. But nevertheless some prominent Indonesians contend, the defense minister failed to take command at a time when this was necessary and when it would have been possible. On the evening of October 1, Adam Malik, a relative of Nasution, went to the defense minister at the hospital where his daughter had been taken and urged him to rally the non-Communist forces. "Now there is only you," Malik said. "You are the senior general. Go to Kostrad. Take over. Everyone will support you."[2] Nasution is said to have replied, "How can I leave the hospital, my daughter?" To which Malik responded that he and his wife would look after Nasution's wife and daughter, and repeated his insistence that Nasution take over. Nasution answered, "We already decided this afternoon to support Suharto. So support Suharto." Malik, recounting this tale, concluded with the question, "How can you have a general like that at a critical time?"--a sentiment frequently echoed by members of Suharto's inner circle, who say that Suharto offered Nasution the command of the army on no less than four separate occasions. Nasution counters, that, in fact, the situation was never so straightforward. Sukarno, who had managed to shunt Nasution aside in 1962, succeeded not only in opposing any moves to restore him to a position of power in the postcoup period but in persuading the four key Java commanders also to oppose Nasution's return.

Prior to 1962, Nasution agrees, he had had the power to take over the country, had he so wished.[3] He had not done this, the repeated entreaties of certain officers and civilian politicians notwithstanding, he says, because he did not believe it was the army's role to assume power. After 1962, he notes, he was no longer in command and thus no longer had it within his capacity to take over, even if he had wanted to. Now, as events unfolded in the wake of the coup, he was outmanoeuvered not only by Sukarno but by the army commanders who remained loyal to the president and who had little desire to see Nasution return to a position of authority.

With Yani's death, Suharto had, under written standing procedures, automatically become acting commander of the army. Later, after Sukarno had been forced to dismiss his own interim candidate for this post, General Pranoto Reksosamudro, Suharto became full commander of the army. And it is not true, Nasution insists, that Suharto offered him the leadership four times. Suharto did ask Nasution's permission to propose his name as chief of the Koti staff, a position previously held by Yani. However, Sukarno is said to have refused, and Suharto did not persist. On another occasion, several regional councils suggested that Nasution be named vice president. This proposal was equally unacceptable to Sukarno, and Suharto, without consulting Nasution, reportedly issued a statement saying there was no need to fill this position. On yet another occasion, Suharto told Nasution he would propose him as vice minister of the defense department. But again Sukarno was supposedly unyielding,

2. Interview with Adam Malik, March 1, 1984.

3. Interview with General Nasution, March 11, 1982.

reportedly saying on one occasion, "The commanders have to choose between me and Nas." Finally, when the MPRS was being convened, Alamsjah went to Nasution's house on behalf of Suharto and asked him to become chairman of this body, a proposal which Nasution said he was willing to accept. But here too Sukarno made his displeasure known, Nasution says, particularly over a provision by which Nasution would have become acting president in his absence. The compromise eventually hammered out named Suharto, not Nasution, as acting president in Sukarno's absence. In these circumstances it is difficult to escape the conclusion that Suharto's four "offers" to Nasution were more a matter of form than substance. And given Suharto's increasingly strong position, Nasution seems to have had very few cards to play. On the other hand, it is equally difficult to escape the conclusion that Nasution's explanation turns on an almost excessively legalistic interpretation of the situation, an approach not necessarily appropriate in the circumstances. In this regard it might be pointed out that Suharto deliberately chose to ignore certain legal and constitutional niceties in the difficult days of 1965-66 in the interests of what he doubtless saw as the greater national good. In retrospect, there probably was only a brief moment on October 1 when Nasution could have made an attempt to take control. And his failure to seize this opportunity, for whatever reasons, give his subsequent eclipse an air of inevitability, his career falling victim this time not just to the manoeverings of Sukarno and certain senior officers but to his own inability to act as well.

Be that as it may, Nasution remained a major figure in Indonesia, exercising a moral authority over many who were still in uniform; he was respected for his idealism, his probity, his sense of justice. He was, as men like Murdani were prepared to admit in private, the critic who disturbed the government most. Late in May 1980, after the "Petition of Fifty" had been presented to the Parliament and the battle joined over the president's interpretation of Pancasila, senior officers from Hankam, including Murdani, began giving special briefings to middle-ranking officers from all over Indonesia to reinforce their basic indoctrination. This continued for about six weeks. On one occasion, all of the country's Kodim commanders (about 200 in all) were assembled in Bandung for a briefing by officers from army headquarters about the "errors" of those who sought to criticize the government. "We know many of these [officers] still have a lot of respect for people like Nasution," Murdani admitted afterwards, "but we need to show them that they must be loyal to the present ABRI leadership."[4] Jusuf Wanandi, a long-time associate of Murtopo and Murdani, made much the same point when answering suggestions that the government might take strong action against the former minister

---

4. Murdani made this comment in a discussion with Warwick Beutler, the Australian Broadcasting Commission (ABC) correspondent in Jakarta, on June 14, 1980. Communication with Beutler, June 15, 1980. The "loyalty briefings" were attended by all officers above the level of major.

of defense. "Nasution is the last person they would touch," he said. "They still recognize him as the senior. He is the only one who is clean."[5]

There were, running through Nasution's contemporary criticisms, three major, interrelated themes.[6] First, the man who in the late 1950s had pioneered the successful campaign for a return to the 1945 Constitution, was in the late 1970s and early 1980s calling on the government to implement that document in a "pure and consistent" manner. Second, the man who had introduced the doctrine of the dwifungsi was calling on those same leaders to purge it of its transitional and emergency excesses, to strip away the accretions that had built up since the coup, accretions which were, in his opinion, seriously distorting the original doctrine. Third, the man who had served as the right-hand man to the late General Sudirman, the 1945-50 Commander-in-Chief of the Indonesian armed forces, was calling on the army leaders to implement Sudirman's last message before his death: that ABRI must stand above all groups in society and not side with any particular faction. In doing this, Nasution was taking issue with those in power who had thrown the army's support behind Golkar (another, albeit radically altered, product of Nasution's thinking about functional representation) in order to help it romp home in successive general elections.[7] Finally, and more generally, Nasution argued that the government was concentrating "almost exclusively" on security and economic growth, and was postponing the solution of fundamental social problems.[8] At the same time, there was a continuing stress on the anticorruption theme, a cause he had pursued con-

---

5. Interview with Jusuf Wanandi, June 5, 1980.

6. Nasution did not adopt this categorization himself, or always distinguish clearly between the various arguments, many of which tended in any case to run into one another. However, this is, I believe, a useful way of examining the criticisms he makes of the present system.

7. The following analysis of Nasution's political thinking is based on interviews with the former defense minister over the period 1979-83 and on a study of other material, published and unpublished, in which he has outlined his views. I am particularly grateful to General Nasution for a sixteen-page typewritten response to questions submitted to him. In this document, which was dated June 7, 1980, he set forth his views in some detail. Other material was drawn from interviews held on May 10 and 11, 1979; June 23 and July 7, 1980; March 2, July 24, and November 10, 1981; March 11 and 23, 1982; and August 9, 1983.

8. See, for example, the report in *Antara*, September 17, 1977. Nasution elaborated on these matters in interviews with the correspondents of *Reuters* and the *Economist* in October 1981. Copies of these replies were made available by General Nasution.

sistently since the days of the Operasi Budhi campaign during the Guided Democracy period.

These points are worth looking at in some detail, even if--indeed, precisely because--Nasution's actions while in power sometimes fell well short of the constitutional propriety he now demanded from others, and even if he was vulnerable to the charge that in creating the dwifungsi doctrine, not to mention "baptizing" it with a name and identity of its own, he had, with what seemed to some a fairly cavalier disregard of the consequences, laid the foundations for the very excesses of military intervention he now so roundly condemned.

a) *The Call for a More Faithful Implementation of the Constitution*

> When the TKR [Tentara Keamanan Rakyat, People's Peace-keeping Army, the precursor of the TNI] was founded, it was implanted that the Constitution is the basis and policy of the army.

> --Gen. Nasution, 1979[9]

> October 17, 1952, was half a coup. It split the army into two camps. . . . Since then I have not believed in coups, I believe in loyalty to the Constitution.

> --Gen. Nasution, 1959[10]

From 1957-62, when Nasution exercised far-reaching powers under the SOB (State of War and Siege) regulations, he acted in a manner which was often every bit as authoritarian as that of the current ruling group and one which had next to nothing to do with the Constitution. He banned political activities, suppressed newspapers,

---

9. Nasution, in a letter to *Tempo*, June 9, 1979. The doctrine that the Constitution was the basis and policy of the army (*UUD adalah azas dan politik tentara*) was formulated by President Sukarno early in 1946 and issued as an *amanat* (message, or order of the day). It found immediate support at the top levels of the armed forces. Sudirman, according to Nasution, was "a good military man" and said, "Sukarno said that. We will stick to that." Although technically the doctrine dates from early 1946, Nasution always referred to it as the "45 message." Interview with General Nasution, November 10, 1981.

10. Quoted in Louis Fischer, *The Story of Indonesia* (New York: Harper, 1959), p. 289. Nasution says that this was "half a coup" in the sense that it was against Parliament but not against the president. (Interview, March 11, 1982.) Looked at in one way, it has been suggested, the logic here is that the only reason for holding to the Constitution is to prevent the army being split.

imprisoned opposition figures, and generally dealt harshly with all those who stood in the army's way. He also formulated a doctrine under which the military claimed for itself a permanent role in the social, political, and economic affairs of the state. In later years, Nasution sought to project himself as a strict constitutionalist--at least insofar as the 1945 Constitution was concerned--and in many ways he had indeed become one. But those who recalled his activities while in power regarded all this with a certain amount of skepticism, and there were, by Nasution's own admission, certain areas where the commitment to constitutionalism was less than total. Be that as it may, the constitutional thread that runs through his writings is unmistakable.

Nasution, who fought and won the battle to return to the 1945 Constitution, stresses that even in an emergency situation the Constitution should be the basis of government action. The main task facing the Indonesian leadership, he argues, is to implement the Constitution in a pure and consistent manner "in a programatic way in the not-too-distant future."

The New Order government has gone through the motions of adhering strictly to the Constitution, he maintains, holding general elections at periodic intervals, providing for the existence of the MPR/DPR and other institutions, allowing these bodies to debate the Broad Outlines of State Policy, the budget, and so on. But in truth, the spirit of the Constitution has not been observed. The army has moved onto center stage, and its role has become "far greater than we had planned."[11] The major props supporting New Order rule are, in his opinion, patently unconstitutional. The army leadership, he says, is underpinned by the emergency powers conferred by both the decree establishing Kopkamtib and by the so-called Supersemar decision of March 11, 1966, under which President Sukarno transferred executive authority to General Suharto. What is more, Suharto, as the holder of the authority vested in him by the Supersemar decree, has made excessive use of the transition powers (kekuasaan-kekuasaan peralihan) granted to him; these powers enabled him to nominate members of the MPRS and put military men into nonmilitary positions at all levels and echelons of society "from village head to president, from chairman of the DPRD [Regional Legislative Assembly] to the chairman of the MPR."[12] With the authority vested in him by the Kopkamtib and Supersemar decrees, executive power has centered on Suharto, and he has made full use of the army in order to achieve his objectives. Gradually, Nasution argues, Suharto assumed a central position in the political and legislative processes. For example, in 1966, the DPR leadership authorized Suharto, as mandataris (mandatory) of the MPRS, to increase the membership of the lower house by 50 percent through nominations. Expanded by the addition of governmental nominees, the DPR had then forwarded a

---

11. Interview with General Nasution.

12. Ibid.

resolution that Suharto should change and add to the membership of the MPRS. Subsequently, the DPR had approved the General Election Law and the law relating to the system for installing people's representatives and party delegates in the MPR/DPR, which Suharto then implemented. Early in 1968, Suharto changed the house membership on a large scale, thus producing the dominant Golkar fraksi (grouping). The purpose of these steps, Nasution argues, was not only to ensure that no attempt could be made to change the Pancasila or the 1945 Constitution but also, as a matter of practical politics, to guarantee Suharto's continuation in office.[13]

Nasution's thinking on this subject in the late 1970s is best reflected in a letter he sent to the MPR, and in particular to the ABRI faction, during the 1978 MPR session. The theme of this letter was that ABRI, with its decisive position within the MPR, should make up a program to implement the basics of the Constitution gradually. Nasution referred to three specific areas. To begin with, he called for the implementation of Article I of the Constitution. Sovereignty was in the hands of the people, he pointed out, and this meant that the people's representatives should be candidates from, and chosen by, the people. In reality, he noted, only 39 percent of the MPR members were elected. In making this point, the former army commander drew attention to the fact that his proposal in the 1950s to return to the 1945 Constitution had been accompanied by a call for general elections to be held on a district, not a proportional basis, with one member being returned by each district. Under such a scheme, it would be possible for nonactive or retired ABRI members to stand as candidates.[14]

Secondly, he called for the implementation of Articles 27-34 of the Constitution, dealing with the basic rights and duties of citizens. These included freedom of expression, of meeting, and of forming associations. In 1966-68, he noted, the MPRS had, in fact, drawn up a bill dealing with this topic, but this work had not been continued by the MPR of 1973 or 1978. The MPRS of 1968 had been unable to finish its work on the *hak-hak azasi* (basic rights), Nasution says, because the fraksi Golkar refused to participate. (This is not entirely correct. Muslim opposition to provisions concerning the freedom to change religion was an important factor in the bill being shelved.)

Thirdly, he called for the abolition of the extraconstitutional powers vested in the president and the commander of Kopkamtib; if there were a need for emergency rule, he said, it could be provided for under Article 12 of the Constitution, which gives the president

---

13. Interview with General Nasution, June 17, 1980.

14. The 1969 Election Law, Nasution pointed out on a later occasion, had been drawn up at the behest of MPRS Decree No. XI; this stipulated that the MPR and the DPR must be produced by elections held in accordance with the sovereignty of the people. General Nasution made this point in a written communication dated November 14, 1981.

the right to proclaim martial law. All state regulations should be derived from the Constitution; however, there were still laws and regulations that were improper and deviated from it. Moreover, there were also Penpres (presidential decisions) which did not accord with the Constitution, one of these being the Subversion Law dating from the Old Order. Not directly referred to in the note to the MPR, but of continuing concern to Nasution, was the program, dating from the time of the Hatta Cabinet of 1948, for the existing professional army system to be gradually transformed into a people's army system, where ABRI would serve as the kernel, as specified under Article 30 of the Constitution.[15]

If these proposals were implemented, Nasution argued, ABRI members could still be chosen as members of Parliament and sit in the MPR as representatives of the armed forces, as provided under Article 2 of the Constitution. And with the implementation of Article 1 and Articles 27-34 dealing with civil rights, Nasution reasoned, democracy would be established and parties would develop. The TNI's role would be to defend the state and to take care of deviations from the Constitution. This, he noted, had been the standpoint since 1945--that the Constitution was the foundation and policy of the army. Nasution felt it would be unrealistic to expect the government to introduce all the proposed reforms at once. But, he argued, a start should be made. Accordingly, his 1978 note to the MPR asked for a program in stages to implement the fundamental principles of the Constitution. He also argued that the MPR should once again be given the formal power to decide the aims and objectives of state policy.

This blend of idealism and realism was characteristic of Nasution's approach. Although he wished to see the nation return to the constitutional path, he had no illusions about the obstacles that stood in the way of this goal. In the final analysis, he recognized, everything depended on the political will of the president, and he saw little to justify optimism that change was imminent. Nasution is fond of pointing out that the third army seminar of 1972 concluded that it was necessary for the '45 Generation, and in particular those holding positions of authority, to purify and correct themselves in order to guarantee the continuation of the "'45 struggle." (Nasution was among those who put purification as a *sine qua non*, because, in his opinion, there had been considerable "ideological erosion" within the ranks of the '45 Generation, with the result that the new generation, military as well as civilian, was not being given the sort of example they needed.)

> However, the implementation of purification, which means the establishment of a clean government, the pure and consistent implementation of the Constitution, the establishment of the rule of law, the implementation of the

---

15. Interview with General Nasution, 1979.

people's army system, and so on all depend on the political will of the president. And since 1972 I have not seen any consistent effort to execute the objectives of the third army seminar, which in reality is nothing but the outlining of the follow-up of the second army seminar of 1966 in which the army formulated the guidelines for implementing the New Order as a "total correction" based on mental attitude and covering social, political, economic, and cultural fields.[16]

The constitutional thread that ran through all of Nasution's utterances found periodic expression in the Indonesian press. In a letter to *Tempo* in June 1979, the former defense minister congratulated General Sumitro for his initiative in publicly and responsibly discussing matters which had been regarded as taboo, "like the matter of 'succession', which should have been an ordinary matter in constitutional life and which, in fact, is the right and duty of every citizen to discuss."[17] He conceded, however, that it was not just the present leadership that had made this a sensitive subject. "In the Old Order, for example, you would be subject to the Presidential Directive on Subversion when you talked about the matter." In the letter, Nasution also referred to the failure of the MPRS in 1968 to approve a draft of "constitutional rules of the game," owing to the lack of cooperation from the ABRI and functional faction. "I believe that on the basis of experience with past upheavals, without constitutional rules of the game, it will be like a game of soccer where only the side that plays roughly will score goals."[18]

In an article in *Prisma* in 1981, Nasution stressed yet again the need for the pure and consistent implementation of the Constitution, warning of the dangers that were inherent in the existing system.

In the future, all extra-constitutional authority and institutionalization should be ended, particularly where they are expressly defined by the Constitution. If this is not implemented it may lead to disharmony between the military, other social groups, and the people. This in turn could negate ABRI's unity with the people and bear negatively upon national defense and security. If the definition and implementation of civil participation were to be deprived of elements of transition and emergency, as my

---

16. Ibid. At the second army seminar it was stated that the "New Order is a mental attitude, its aim is to create a social, political, economic, and cultural life that is [spirited by] Pancasila morals, particularly a belief in God Almighty."

17. *Tempo*, June 9, 1979. USE.

18. Ibid.

lecture [at] Seskoad proposed, the [scale] of this negative threat would be reduced.[19]

If Nasution is a firm believer in the Constitution and the need
for free and fair elections, then it is with one important caveat--he
would not permit the Communist party to participate in elections. If
the PKI had won a majority of votes in an election in the early 1960s
it would have been necessary, in Nasution's view, for the army to
block any takeover of state power. In Nasution's opinion, such a
takeover had been a distinct possibility. "If Aidit had not staged the
coup," he says, "the PKI would have become the majority party with
the majority in Parliament and then become the government. Sukarno
was helping them."[20] The Muslims might have opposed such a development, he concedes, but they had been very much handicapped by
the participation of many of them in the PRRI rebellion of 1958-61,
and the PKI leaders had Sukarno on their side. In Nasution's view,
opposition to a Communist takeover, albeit a constitutional takeover,
would have been justified "because it's another Indonesia [they would
build]. It's no longer the Indonesia of 1945."[21] The nation had lost
so many lives in securing its independence, and the Communist ideology was contrary to its struggles. "I am convinced that we would
[have] become a satellite of Peking or Moscow." Moreover, "as a religious man, I cannot tolerate communism." On the other hand,
Nasution says that an individual Communist or ex-Communist should
always be permitted to vote, unless he or she has been stripped of
that right by a court decision. (It is not sufficient, he believes, for
Kopkamtib to strip a person of a right guaranteed under the Constitution.)

There is, clearly, an area of potential conflict here between
possibly incompatible demands of the Pancasila and the 1945 Constitution. The army is sworn to uphold the Constitution, and thus, in
theory, the principle of free elections and majority rule. But it is
also bound to defend the five principles of the Pancasila, including
the sila which emphasizes a "belief in God." If the army was convinced that a certain political party stood in violation of this principle
(the PKI always insisted that belief was a matter for the individual),
was it justified in preventing that group from coming to power if the
group in question had the popular support necessary to do so
through elections? If one were to argue that the army was bound to
accept the will of the majority of the population, then Nasution's
constitutionalism, which excluded a Communist party, would in principle be no less flawed than Suharto's, which excluded "extremists" of
both the right and the left. Nasution's answer--and indeed the answer of the officer corps as a whole--was that communism was in conflict with the principles of the Pancasila, and in particular with those

---

19. *Prisma*, March 1981, p. 42.

20. Interview with General Nasution, July 7, 1980.

21. Ibid.

silas dealing with belief in God and nationalism. Because of this, he argued, it was neither appropriate nor possible to recognize the PKI as a party. As Lev has noted, for many who were quite committed otherwise to concepts of legality, "the Communists, revolutionary threat that they were, stood outside the circle of acceptability."[22]

Finally, it should be noted that Nasution admits that he must accept much of the blame for failing to make Sukarno adhere to the Constitution prior to 1965. "We all failed, especially me," he says. "I was at the top. I was his assistant. It was precisely because of this failure, that the second army seminar formulated a doctrine which said, inter alia, that there had been a deviation from the Constitution during the Old Order period and a departure from the principle of people's sovereignty:

> Since the [seminar] I have always said we have to stick to this. And they [members of the ruling group] are always going back before this. Maybe I was always against the parties before that. But maybe the position of the army was not yet clear; it became clear after Gestapu [the coup attempt]--adherence to the Constitution. So all my criticism is about this. But they are always replying [by talking about my actions] in the past.[23]

b) *Nasution and the Changing Interpretation of Dwifungsi*

> What is very much needed in the 1970s is the purification of the meaning and the implementation of the dwifungsi concept.
>
> --Nasution in his last lecture at
> Seskoad, 1969[24]

The failure to apply the Constitution in a pure and consistent manner is closely related, in Nasution's view, to what he sees as the misuse by the Suharto group of the dwifungsi doctrine. When in 1957 a standing committee of the Dewan Nasional (National Council) had formulated the concept of going back to the 1945 Constitution, he argues, it was understood that it was not just the armed forces which had a dual function but also all other groups in society, including workers, peasants, youth, religious teachers, and so on. A member of any one of these owed his first duty to the state as a citizen and his second to his group or profession. In the New Order period, this concept was dropped, with the result that only the armed forces

---

22. Daniel S. Lev, "Judicial Authority and the Struggle for an Indonesian Rechtsstaat," *Law and Society* (Fall 1978), p. 52 (footnote).

23. Interview, March 11, 1982.

24. The lecture was delivered in September 1969.

was said to have a dual function. This dual function, Nasution argues, was materially enhanced by General Sumitro's restructuring of
the armed forces in 1969; under the new system, he says, ABRI's
kekaryaan function was elevated to a new plane.

> In the past, the territorial doctrine [*pembinaan wilayah*]
> was the tree, and from this tree you had various branch-
> es, including civic mission and kekaryaan. With the re-
> structuring introduced by General Sumitro in 1969,
> kekaryaan became the tree while the tree, territorial, be-
> came no more than a branch. Because of this change of
> structure, the territorial apparatus has become a tool of
> kekaryaan.[25]

Under Suharto, Nasution argues, the territorial system has
been politicized and bent to the needs of the ruling group. According to its doctrine, the army is above all groupings. However, since
1969 territorial officers have come under the control of the chief of
staff for functional affairs (Kaskar Hankam) and become a tool of
kekaryaan. Kekaryaan has, in turn, become a tool of Golkar. If the
territorial apparatus had remained the trunk of the tree, then ABRI
would indeed be at one with the people. But with kekaryaan as the
tree, territorial officers are obliged to ensure that Golkar wins each
election. A military bupati might, in theory, be answerable to the
provincial governor and the Department of Home Affairs. In practice,
he has to follow the dictates of the local Korem commander. Likewise,
a military governor is obliged to follow the guidelines laid down by
the local military commander, the latter being the chairman of the
Dewan Kekaryaan. The territorial branch should be at one with the
people, Nasution argues, but under Suharto it is being used in the
most partisan fashion; it is working not for the people but for the
ruling group. There are dangers too in the nonpolitical field, he
feels. When farmers are unable to repay their loans under the Bimas
rice intensification project, territorial officers are sent to recover the
debt. This practice, so reminiscent of the operations of the colonial-
ist army, is, in Nasution's view, opposed to the whole concept of territorial defense and ABRI-people unity.

At the same time, Nasution argues that the emergency powers
conferred on the army leadership as a result of the birth of
Kopkamtib on October 2, 1965, not only considerably enhance the
power of the army leaders but extend downwards and outwards to the
laksus-laksus (pelaksana khusus, or special executors of Kopkamtib)
in the provinces. Amongst other things, he notes, Kopkamtib and its
provincial agencies have had responsibility for screening candidates
for the general elections, administering the post-1977 antigraft operation (Opstib), checking on the prices of essential commodities, and
providing permits for religious meetings. This army power has been
further enhanced, he suggests, by the formation of a Muspida in each

---

25. General Nasution in written communication, November 14, 1981.

province.   The Muspida, which consists of the panglima (military commander), the governor, the police chief, and the local representative
of the Attorney General's Office, amongst others, is chaired by the
panglima in his capacity as Laksusda (regional representative of
Kopkamtib).   In theory, the Muspida is only a *wadah musyawarah*
(consultative body).   However, Nasution says that, because it brings
together all local powerholders, it is in practice the most powerful institution in the province.[26]

Under the Supersemar decree of March 11, 1966, Nasution argues, the dwifungsi of the army was even further extended.   As we
have seen, acting pursuant to the powers conveyed in that instruction, Suharto was twice able to change the composition of the DPR
(GR) and the MPRS en masse in the years 1966 and 1968.   As a result of the exercise of this emergency power, Nasution argues, the
government has been able to stifle many fundamental rights of the Indonesian people.   For example, Article 28 of the Constitution guarantees the freedom to unite and assemble, to express one's opinions
both verbally and in writing.   But no attempt has been made to produce even a bill on this subject.   Constitutional regulations are very
necessary in building the life of the state and ensuring equality of
law and justice.   Yet up till now, only the commander of Kopkamtib
can regulate these matters, meaning that they fall within ABRI's
jurisdiction.   At the same time, there are regulations from the period
of the Old Order which, although formally treated as laws, are not in
accordance with the 1945 Constitution.   This was the case with the
law (No. 11/PNPS/1963) regarding subversion, until the introduction
of a new law on this matter in 1982.

In practice, any decision regarding the exercise of the
said political rights is in the hands of the Pangkopkamtib
or the police and so it is felt that the authority of regu-
lating politics is in the hands of ABRI officials.   This situation is not in accordance with the 1945 Constitution
and, although these sorts of things are supposed to be
dual functional, in reality that is not the case.   That is
why in my last lecture at Seskoad in 1969 I said that
what was very much needed for the seventies was the

---

26.   Ibid.   The panglima was always chairman of the Muspida, even if
he was a two-star officer and the governor a three-star.   The rationale was that the governor, being in a kekaryaan role, was not on the
active list.   Thus, when Maj. Gen. Witarmin was panglima Kodam VIII
Brawijaya (East Java), he chaired the Muspida, even though the governor, Lt. Gen. Sunandar Prijosudarmo, was more senior in rank.
The same situation existed in Jakarta at the time when Maj. Gen. G.
H. Mantik was panglima Kodam V Jaya and Lt. Gen. Ali Sadikin was
governor, although in that case Sadikin was, of course, a Marine
Corps officer.

purification of the meaning of the dwifungsi concept and
its implementation.[27]

In the period since he held office as chairman of the MPRS,
Nasution has been proposing that the People's Congress establish the
limits of ABRI's involvement in society under the dual function doctrine: "I have proposed that every five years the MPR should determine the guidelines of ABRI's involvement in civilian functions so that
in effect the people remain truly sovereign."[28] This, of course, was
hardly the sort of suggestion that was likely to commend itself to the
Suharto government.

Because of the way the system has been structured, Nasution
sees no real prospects for political change via the electoral process so
long as Suharto is president. The general elections in 1982 and the
presidential elections in 1983, would, he correctly predicted, simply
repeat the pattern that was established in 1971-72 and 1977-78. The
general election system, plus the large percentage of appointees in
the MPR/DPR, lead him to the conclusion that Article 1 of the Constitution has not been applied consistently. Because there is no true
social control, he feels, opportunities exist for those in authority to
manipulate their powers. To illustrate this point, Nasution cites the
process relating to the nomination of the president. This, he maintains, is virtually in the hands of the leadership of the five fraksi
within the MPR, including the ABRI, Golkar, and provincial delegates'
groupings "where the leadership is with the president himself."
Moreover, as it has become the practice for the political party leaders
to state during the campaign that they all support the same candidate
for president, the results of the presidential elections are known even
before the general elections are held. When, in the 1978 MPR session, the PPP fraksi decided that more than one presidential candidate
should be nominated (in order for voting to take place), the move
was thwarted by the party presidency, namely Idham Chalid and his
colleagues.

---

27. Nasution interview, June 17, 1980. As we have seen, another
prominent retired general (and former Kopkamtib commander),
Sumitro, shared the view that Kopkamtib should be disbanded.
Sumitro says he first urged Suharto to dissolve the body in 1971.
The continuing existence of Kopkamtib a decade and a half after the
emergency situation that led to its birth has been a matter of peren-
nial complaint with student groups. As suggested elsewhere in this
monograph, Suharto may have retained the body not only because of
its convenience but also--and perhaps more importantly--because it
was an integral part of the artfully balanced command structure he
had erected over the years; the disappearance of Kopkamtib would
have upset the harmonious balance he sought between subordinate officers.

28. *Prisma*, March 1981, p. 43.

As a matter of practical politics, Nasution concludes, it is not possible to choose a candidate other than the ruling president. The presidential appointment of a large number of DPR members is similar, he argues, to the system in South Korea under President Park Chung Hee and the system in Spain under General Franco: "In colonial times we also found it in several places outside Java where village heads were chosen by giving more than 20 percent more votes to the son of the person to be replaced for the sake of stability and continuity."[29]

By and large, Nasution maintains, the formation and working pattern of representative institutions and political groupings in Indonesia is oriented to the political system as it existed in 1966. However, the situation at that time was one of emergency and one that had a transitional character. This "authority system" has ensured its own stability through both the electoral arrangements and the appointment of a very large percentage of the DPR and MPR members. Because of this, Suharto's position has become entrenched. This state of affairs not only allows for a situation of executive domination but creates a "political dependency" on the part of DPR and MPR members. As a result, Nasution maintains, the nation is faced with a lower house which has merely a "responsive character," and is unable to take much initiative. The ruling group is not only in a position to screen candidates, he argues, but is able, because of its links with amenable party leaders, to have troublesome representatives recalled at any time. A revision is needed to bring back the equilibrium envisaged by the Constitution. The electoral process makes possible, in theory at any rate, a dynamic and self-renewing system. However, because the political rights of the candidates are circumscribed and the majority of the MPR members are mere appointees, the "representative" bodies are in fact no more than subsystems of an entity dominated by the executive in general and the president in particular.

Nasution, as we have seen, has been at pains to emphasize that the official doctrine of the armed forces is that the Constitution is the basis and policy of the armed forces. (Suharto stressed precisely the same point and indicated that he was prepared, if necessary, to "use weapons" to defend the Constitution. The difference between the two men was that, while Nasution was saying he was now prepared to trust the people, Suharto, more "pragmatic" and aware of the implications of such a move, was content with constitutional form rather than substance.) Nasution does not expect Suharto to change his mind on this issue, but he does see some grounds for optimism in the future. Because since its birth ABRI has been indoctrinated to defend the 1945 Constitution, "I feel certain that it can't be involved in continuously ignoring important sections of the Constitution, like the sections dealing with people's sovereignty, citizen's rights and so on, as we have experienced during the former regime."[30]

---

29. Interview with General Nasution, June 17, 1980.

30. Ibid.

While Nasution makes a cogent and closely argued analysis of the constitutional shortcomings of New Order rule, there is a certain irony in the fact that it has fallen on him to detail these excesses. Nasution argued throughout the 1950s for a strong and vigorous presidential system and urged that the army be given a generous say in the decision-making process. Now he is in opposition to what has become, in effect, a self-perpetuating presidency, a presidency, moreover, that is dominated by a retired army officer making full use of the doctrines bequeathed to him by Nasution. In short, as he now readily enough concedes, Nasution failed to spell out the acceptable limits to military involvement in society. But, whether, had he done so, this would have altered the subsequent course of events greatly is very much open to question.

c) *Above All Groups: The Army in the Electoral Process*

The government may change every day; the army remains the same.

--General Sudirman, 1947[31]

. . . the only national property that is still whole and unchanging notwithstanding all sorts of challenges and changes is the Indonesian National Army.

--General Sudirman, 1949[32]

It would have been difficult to find two Indonesian nationalist leaders as different in training and temperament as the 1945-50 Commander-in-Chief, General Sudirman, and his 1948-49 deputy, Colonel Nasution, and relations between them were not always smooth. However, while the two men frequently clashed on military matters, Nasution tended to defer to Sudirman when it came to politics, conceding that the commander was "more mature" in this field.[33] Later,

31. According to Nasution, Sudirman had stressed this line "since the early days of the TNI." (Written communication, November 14, 1981.) In an interview, Nasution said the phrase *"ganti setiap hari"* was first used by Sudirman in about 1947.

32. Quoted in Nasution, *Sekitar Perang Kemerdekaan Indonesia*, 2: 349.

33. Interview with General Nasution, November 10, 1981. In many ways the direct antithesis of Sudirman, Nasution was a Dutch-educated military professional, an Outer Islander committed, above all, to the rationalization of the command system. Sudirman, a product of Japanese military training, was Javanese, with a deep mystical streak. As McKemmish has observed,

after Sudirman's death in 1950, Nasution took over many of Sudirman's concepts about the army's role in society and, as his own political thinking developed, fashioned them into the "Middle Way" doctrine of 1958.

Nasution, as we have seen, had been the one who publicized Sudirman's *hak milik nasional* letter to Sukarno in his book *TNI*, published in 1953. (See above Ch. 3, n. 1.) In later years, it became customary for senior army officers to refer to this statement when ad-

---

> Sudirman's precepts and sense of morality stemmed from the traditions of the *wayang*, the *satria*-warrior and Javanese mysticism; Nasution's from the harsher, less tolerant, more legalistic tradition of Islam as practiced in North Sumatra, reinforced by his training under the Dutch, and quite alien to the Javanese experience. (McKemmish, "Political Biography of Nasution," p. 26.)

When, on November 12, 1945, an all-Java meeting of TKR commanders had met to elect a leader, Nasution favored the election of Urip Sumohardjo, a former KNIL major. He was deeply disappointed when Urip lost out to Sudirman.

Nasution admits that at various times there was "some friction" in his relationship with Sudirman. On one occasion, Nasution, as commander of the Siliwangi, had felt it necessary to take action against some of the troops under his command; the troops had then complained to Sudirman. On another occasion, Nasution had criticized Sudirman's headquarters because it did not have an overall strategy, leaving each front to take its own initiative; when Nasution personally submitted a concept for an overall strategy, there was no response from Sudirman. In 1948, when the Hatta cabinet was pushing through its plans to rationalize and restructure the TNI, there were further differences of opinion between the two men. This was due in large part to the fact that Sudirman remained neutral when the PKI, which was opposed to the Hatta cabinet, launched a stinging attack on both the Siliwangi and its commander. Despite these frictions, Nasution says he was never admonished by Sudirman and the two men were able to maintain good relations; Sudirman's ADC, Major (later Lt. General) Suprapto, and his former ADC, Colonel (later Brig. Gen.) Abimanju, were also personal friends of Nasution and took care that the relationship between the two men was not destroyed.

These differences of opinion ended after the Madiun affair. Sudirman, who had succumbed to illness, turned the leadership of the headquarters over to Nasution. With free rein to act, Nasution was able to push through the reorganization that he had always wanted. In the guerrilla period that followed the Second Dutch "Police Action" of December 1948, Nasution was able to carry out his duties as commander of the Java Command without intervention from Sudirman. (General Nasution, written communication, November 14, 1981.)

dressing the question of ABRI's place in society. Nasution looked with equal favor on Sudirman's dictum about the army remaining constant as governments came and went. Whenever there were political problems in Yogyakarta during the revolution, Nasution says, Sudirman had always emphasized that the government could change every day because that was the political system. "But" Sudirman had added, "the army cannot change."[34]

This was, as Nasution is prepared to concede, a fairly embryonic formulation of the army's role in society. And it was one that did not necessarily make allowance for the sort of political role that Nasution would later seek to establish and legitimize. Nevertheless, for him it captures the essentials of his preferred relationship between army and government. Sudirman had said that the army always remained the same, and in his speeches in the 1950s Nasution sometimes added a line of his own at the end of Sudirman's formulation--"dan rakyat adalah tetap rakyat" ("and the people remain the people").[35] For Nasution, the army and the people were constant and unchanging, a lesson that had been driven home in December 1948 when, as he saw it, the government had "surrendered," and the army and the people had gone on fighting.[36] In Nasution's view, the most important components were the tentara (army) and the rakyat, not the pemerintah (government). In later years, however, this had changed. "Since Yani, it is pemerintah and tentara. Together! It is like the Shah of Iran. Not strong!"[37] The Shah had built his government on the power of the army but, as events were to show, that "power" was illusory.

Sudirman, of course, had not had to address the question of the TNI's role during an election campaign. But he did have to deal with a situation in which political groups were trying to influence the army, or at least some parts of it. His attitude was that the TNI should not allow itself to be the tool of any one group in society; the TNI was an instrument of the nation. In Nasution's view, it was logical that the army should, in any election, adhere to the Sudirman doctrine that the army remain independent of contending political factions.

During his time as chief of staff, Nasution had gone to some lengths to keep the army from backing one or another of the political

---

34. Interview with General Nasution.

35. Nasution, written communication, November 14, 1981.

36. He wrote: "In Indonesia, the people and the armed forces together were able to maintain effective security following the disbandment of the government by the enemy on December 19, 1948. Yugoslavia fared similarly well during the Second World War." See A. H. Nasution, "The Dual Function of ABRI: Origins and Current Situation," Prisma (March 1981), pp. 38-39.

37. Interview with General Nasution, July 24, 1981.

parties (indeed, he had spent a good deal of his time criticizing the practices of the various parties), and although he had played a key role in the formation of Golkar in 1964, he had no time for the view that the army, being so closely identified with Golkar, should lend the organization its support during an election.[38] The army seminars in 1966 and 1972, he liked to point out, had reaffirmed that ABRI must be above all political groupings. However, due to a lack of consistency in implementing the formulations of those seminars, "a sort of cold war" had come into existence. During the 1977 general election campaign, Nasution issued a press statement reminding ABRI to stand above all groups and not to side with any contestant, because that would involve a deviation from Sudirman's last message. In this, his thinking appeared to be very much in line with that reflected in the public statements of active officers like Jusuf.

d) *The Obsession with Security and National Development*

Beyond his anxieties regarding the Constitution, the dwifungsi and the need for ABRI to remain above all groups, Nasution is also concerned that the Suharto government is concentrating "almost entirely" on the issues of security and economic growth. Because of this "onesidedness," it is, he believes, postponing the solution of fundamental social problems. As he sees it, attention should be focused on education ("the main investment for development"), on the building of a social and political system based on the Constitution, and on economic growth—in that order. Under the current government, he argues, the gap is widening between rich and poor, between town and country, between the center and the regions and between the elites and the masses—a line of argument almost identical to those of Alamsjah in his 1977 Menado speech. There has been an erosion of national and social discipline, a misuse of power among officialdom, and a very great increase in corruption. The government's excessive concern with security, he feels, is manifested in the apparent "Islam-phobia" of the ruling group, its predisposition to find evidence of an "anti-Pancasila" attitude in even the most moderate expression of dissent. There is not one Islamic organization that is not committed to upholding the Constitution, he contends, but still the government

---

38. The Joint Secretariat of Golkar had not been created directly by ABRI but by Nasution in his capacity as vice chairman of the National Front. The front was headed by Sukarno; Nasution, as vice chairman, represented the armed forces and unaffiliated organizations. There had been an attempt, at the initiative of the Supreme Advisory Council, to eliminate organizations that were not affiliated to any party. Nasution says that to "save" these fairly strongly anti-Communist organizations, among them HMI (Islamic Student Association), Muhammadiyah, and PGRI (Association of Indonesian Teachers), he formed the Golkar Joint Secretariat. Written communication, November 14, 1981.

treats Islamic groups with suspicion. The complaint in Islamic circles, he says, is not that the Constitution or the Pancasila should be
changed, but that there should be greater religious freedom; at
present, it is necessary to have a license to carry out many religious
activities, particularly *dakwah* (missionary work). If one listens to
the *khutbah* (sermons) in the mosques, one can hear complaints of too
much supervision of religious activity by the government security
services.

Here, as earlier, it is possible to see Nasution's preoccupation
with the need to purify and correct the social and political ills he
finds around him. Although he is not unaware of the obstacles that
stand in the way of such an undertaking, he believes it is essential
for him, as both a Muslim and a nationalist, to make his views known.
There is, in his concern about corruption and moral laxity, a strong
"Calvinist" revulsion at the ways of the new elite, at the steady erosion of the "old" values. There is, too, the concern of a pious Muslim at the obstacles placed in the path of the Muslim community and a
concern that the government's policies are once again creating a
Java-centric Indonesia. Many of these sentiments, in the view of the
ruling elite, are admirable but "unrealistic."

How Far Has Nasution Himself Been Consistent?

> If I followed the dictates of my heart I'd suppress all
> political parties.
>
> --Nasution, 1958[39]

> I think you better not listen to Pak Nas. He's more au-
> thoritarian than anyone else. Really! He is more totali-
> tarian. When he was still in office he could not stand
> opposition or other ideas. Really, I tell you, he cannot
> talk too much. I know him very well. People like me.
> Although I respect him, because he's got his merits dur-
> ing the guerrilla war. But after that he's not an example
> anymore.
>
> --General Sumitro, 1981[40]

---

39. Quoted in Fischer, *Story of Indonesia*, p. 294. Nasution says
he *never* (his emphasis) openly demanded the dissolution of the political parties. Asked about this quotation, he said, "Maybe Fischer was
not thorough in writing my quotes on the parties." (Written communication, November 14, 1981.)

40. Interview with General Sumitro, December 12, 1981. Sumitro's
view of Nasution may have been colored in part by personal animosity. Sumitro, it is said, felt that Nasution had not given him an

As a 22-year-old cadet at the prewar Royal Military Academy in Bandung, Nasution is said to have been much influenced by structures stressing power. According to Simatupang, who admittedly has little time for Nasution, blaming him in particular for the fashioning of a doctrine that gave the army a permanent place in the political process, Nasution was an admirer of Baldur von Schirach, the leader of the Hitler Youth, and sought a state in which youth was organized and militarized. During the Japanese occupation, he was enrolled in the Japanese-run Seinendan youth organization, which was more or less a militarized Boy Scout movement. Like the framers of the 1945 Constitution, who started not with individual rights but with the organic entity of the state, he seemed basically hostile to notions of "liberalism." On the other hand, it would be wrong to make too much of this. (D. N. Aidit, who in 1951 became the chairman of the PKI, had, according to Nasution, belonged to his youth organization in 1943-44 and been an admirer of Joseph Goebbels.) During the Japanese occupation--and indeed for a number of years thereafter-- Nasution was not politically mature. Like many members of his generation he had been attracted and influenced by Germany's post-1918

---

opportunity to have a career in the Brawijaya. Nasution's answer was that this had been Sukarno's decision, not his, a statement which may not give the full picture. According to Nasution, there were, in the late 1950s, two "crown princes" in the Brawijaya--Sumitro and Surachman. Surachman, he says, was a Sukarno man and Sumitro was not. "At that time," said Nasution, "you could not make a decision about the Brawijaya panglima without Sukarno. Brawijaya meant something special for Sukarno. I was not free. About the Siliwangi I could make the decision myself." (Interview, March 2, 1981.) Anderson has argued that Surachman, "an extreme right-winger, *anti*-Sukarno, indeed strongly suspected of masterminding subversive Gerakan Anti-Sukarno, Anti-PKI etc.," may in fact have been an ideal Nasution man for that period, like the panglima of the "Three Souths" (South Sulawesi, South Kalimantan, and South Sumatra), who all banned the local PKI on Nasution's prodding. Surachman, he argues, was already a lieutenant colonel in 1955 and chief of staff of the Brawijaya and way above Sumitro, who was merely a chief of staff of one of Kodam VIII's three brigades. In other words, he concludes that there never were "two crown princes." (Written communication, February 9, 1984.) If this is so, Nasution would seem to have had several good and compelling reasons for appointing Surachman. Sumitro, in discussing his relationship with Nasution, makes no mention of this matter. In his view, the former army chief of staff looked on him with disfavor because of his refusal to back the abortive October 17 movement in 1952. This seems fanciful. Nasution was a colonel in 1952 and Sumitro only a captain and the views of the latter could hardly have counted for much. Nor is it entirely true that Nasution had a free hand in Siliwangi appointments; as we have seen, in 1959 Sukarno had been able to appoint Ibrahim Adjie chief of staff of the Siliwangi, Nasution's reservations notwithstanding.

rise from the ashes of defeat. But he knew little about political systems in general and still less, it seems, about fascism. By his own
account, he saw history in terms of personalities and patriotism, of
heroic leaders and eventful deeds. He may not have taken issue with
the views of von Schirach, he says, but he did not look to him for
guidance. Rather, his heroes were men like Hindenburg, de Gaulle,
and Mustapha Kemal.

In later years, a number of writers were to draw attention to
what they saw as an authoritarian streak in Nasution's political thinking.[41] A number of fellow officers, Simatupang included, thought
they detected a "Bonapartist" element in his make-up. And officers
associated with the Suharto group have suggested that there is not
only a trace of sour grapes in Nasution's criticisms but more than a
trace of hypocrisy as well. Nasution, it is said, is a man who con-
demns practices that he himself took part in while in power, when he
never hesitated to take steps which severely curtailed many of the
democratic rights he now advocates. He is the man who pioneered
the return to the 1945 Constitution, a document that greatly
strengthened the executive branch. And if the Suharto government
is in error, military leaders assert with some exasperation, then they
are doing no more than "Pak Nas" bade them to do. If valid, these
criticisms would undermine some of Nasution's moral authority in making his current statements, and on this ground alone they deserve
serious study.

Nasution, perhaps more than any other postwar leader, was
very much influenced by the lack of cohesion during the revolutionary period, a point which has been well made by Jean Taylor: "Where
others have drawn edifying examples of self-sacrifice and patriotism,
Nasution has drawn conclusions of a different nature. He has seen in
the physical revolution a terrible object-lesson on the necessity for a
competent and integrated leadership and for a well thought-out national programme."[42] Where others saw a nation fired by an over-
powering sense of revolutionary spirit, Nasution saw a plethora of
pemuda struggle groups, many of them at odds with one another.
Nasution wanted to establish control over this situation, to bring cohesion and coordination out of the chaos.

---

41. See, for example, McKemmish, "Political Biography of Nasution,"
p. 8.

42. J. S. Taylor, "Some Indonesian Perceptions of the Revolution, A
Study in Indonesian Historiography" (MA thesis, University of Melbourne, 1968), p. 109.

Anderson has pointed out that the main reason for Nasution
feeling this way was the thrashing his troops took in July 1947 from
the Dutch in their first "Police Action." This led to the abandonment
of West Java under the terms of the Renville Agreement, a big humiliation for him, which he blamed on poor organization. (Written communication, February 9, 1984.)

But although Nasution emphasized the relative importance of *teknik* versus semangat (fighting spirit) and placed stress on discipline, training, and strong and purposeful leadership--"Western" values held in contempt by many pemuda leaders--he was not in any sense apolitical. He distrusted those like Simatupang who sought to build an essentially Western professional army, one that was detached from the conduct of nonmilitary activities. In part, this may have been a reflection of Nasution's own view that the army had a continuing contribution to make in the postrevolutionary period, in part a recognition that the army as a whole subscribed to this view and that it would be all but impossible to restrain it from playing such a role.

In many cases, it would be pointless to sluice through the tracings of contemporary history, looking for signs of ideological consistency in the words and deeds of one or other of the main political actors. All too often, the central actors in a political drama may only have been responding to developments in their immediate surroundings. Nasution was himself frequently merely reacting to events, with his most important objective doubtlessly to enhance his own power or position and exclude from decision making those he considered rivals. However, it is also possible to detect a good deal of consistency in Nasution's positions over the past thirty years, to find a thread of continuity between what he advocated in the early 1950s and what he is advocating in the early 1980s.

Nasution and the Political Parties

During the revolution, Nasution was persistently at odds with civilian party politicians, and he clashed with them often, largely because the troops affiliated with particular political organizations were often unwilling to obey commands from the central army leadership. The parties had reciprocated by attacking Nasution through political channels. This dissension continued even during the period of Nasution's close cooperation with the Hatta Cabinet of 1948-49 over its plans to reorganize and rationalize the armed forces. While serving as army chief of staff from 1950 to 1952, Nasution continued to skirmish with political party leaders, who, in his opinion, wanted to go too far in interfering with the TNI and its security operations. He was, in any case, rather ill-disposed (*sentimen*) towards many of the political party representatives in Parliament, arguing in the period before the 1955 elections that two-thirds of them were representatives of the puppet states created by the Dutch and led by people whom the Republicans viewed as "traitors" and "collaborators."[43] Nasution wanted to rid the parties of those elements who had collaborated with the Dutch against the Republic.

For Nasution, one of the most important lessons of the revolutionary years had been the overwhelming need for strong and pur-

---

43. Written communication, November 14, 1981.

poseful leadership, not just in the army but in the nation as a whole. Another lesson--and one that had been driven home by the civilian government's surrender to the Dutch in December 1948--was that the armed forces had a right and a duty to play a role in nonmilitary matters. The lesson Nasution had learned from the abortive October 17 Affair of 1952 was that, while the army was entitled to play an important role in the decision-making process, its efforts to secure such a role should not be advanced through nonconstitutional means.

In the period 1950-52, Nasution was, by his own admission, "politically naive."[44] However, during the three years of enforced retirement that followed there was a significant development of his views. The main shoots of Nasution's political thought--a belief in strong government, constitutionalism, and army participation in decision making--had been evident at the time of his dismissal as chief of staff in 1952. By the time of his reappointment in 1955, these shoots were developing into a cogent and coherently argued philosophy, one that was built around a return to the 1945 Constitution and the need for a close and continuing military involvement in nonmilitary affairs. In formulating these doctrines, which would find expression in such statements as the "Middle Way" speech of 1958, Nasution owed much to the late Professor Djokosutono, Dean of the Faculty of Law at the University of Indonesia and professor of constitutional law at that institution. Nasution had first become acquainted with Djokosutono in 1951 when, as army chief of staff, he had established the Military Law Academy. In subsequent years, Nasution frequently exchanged views with the professor, a man regarded as one of the foremost Indonesian authorities on government.[45] Djokosutono was very preoccupied with the idea of ordering the political dynamics, in ordering both the people and the army. In this regard, he provided much of the theoretical framework for Guided Democracy.

After 1952, according to Susan McKemmish, the army chief of staff, began openly to reject a parliamentary and liberal democratic system in which the army had no stake. "His ideas after 1952 appear to have changed dramatically."[46] In this period, she notes, Nasution

> was developing a comprehensive critique of the existing system of government in Indonesia. Foremost among his targets were the political parties. Since 1950, he claimed, no thorough and consistent defense and military policy had ever been formulated, with serious consequences for the armed forces. With such an unstable system of government and the changes in direction brought about by the frequent cabinet changes, it was impossible to pursue any consistent policy.[47]

---

44. Quoted in McKemmish, "Political Biography of Nasution," p. 85.

45. Written communication, November 14, 1981.

46. McKemmish, "Political Biography of Nasution," p. 86.

47. Ibid., p. 90.

Indeed, in his view, stable government was not possible under the existing parliamentary system. "Because of this," he wrote in 1956, "personally I feel it would be better if we returned to the original Constitution of the 1945 Proclamation."[48] The role of the army was to protect and support the national struggle, based on the ideals of the 1945 Constitution and Pancasila.

As Nasution saw it, the Republic had abandoned the 1945 Constitution due to "the politics of compromise" with the Dutch,[49] and it was necessary, on this ground alone, to return to this original Constitution. There were, however, two additional reasons for such a return. First, the 1945 Constitution guaranteed secure and stable government for a period of five years. Second, Article 2 of the 1945 Constitution could be interpreted as providing for representation of functional groups, thus giving the army a permanent place in policy making as distinct from the temporary authority vested in it under the martial law decrees. (As Lev has pointed out, this was a somewhat specious argument. For neither in 1945, when a kind of functional group concept was first introduced, nor in 1957, when Sukarno revived the concept, were the armed forces considered a functional group.)[50] Later, after the outbreak of the PRRI-Permesta rebellion, Nasution found another reason to justify a "return to 1945." With the original Constitution, he argued, the government would be able to call on members of the PRRI to return to the lap of the Republic, to reunite with all '45 fighters. In 1962, after the conclusion of operations against the PRRI and the Darul Islam, Nasution, by now minister of defense, made the point that there would not have been such an extensive revolt if from the beginning the government had upheld constitutional life; because the Constitution had not been upheld, provinces and groups had felt it necessary to resort to the use of force.[51]

During his three years in retirement, Nasution's formulation of the army's role in society acquired a depth and maturity it had previously lacked. By 1955 he was calling not only for a return to the 1945 Constitution but forcefully advocating the view that the military had a role to play, not just in implementing state policy but in shaping it as well. In an article in *Pedoman* in June 1955, four months

---

48. A. H. Nasution, "Bahan-Bahan Guna Menjelaraskan Pribadi TNI Kepada Pribadi 1945 (1956), quoted in Ibid., p. 91. Nasution had first suggested the idea of a return to the 1945 Constitution in his writings in 1952-55 and had become a firm exponent of the idea by the time of the 1955 elections.

49. Nasution, written communication, November 14, 1981.

50. See Daniel S. Lev, *The Transition to Guided Democracy: Indonesian Politics, 1957-1959* (Ithaca: Cornell Modern Indonesia Project, 1966), pp. 224-25.

51. Nasution, written communication, November 14, 1981.

before his reappointment as army chief of staff, Nasution wrote that the army was not simply a dead instrument of the state but "an instrument of state which lives as a national army, whose members are citizens, whose ideology is the State Constitution." The army was not a "political" body but one which implemented government policy. However it should share in deciding that policy.[52] Nasution expanded on these themes when, several months later, Sukarno asked him to write his Order of the Day speech for Armed Forces Day, October 5. In this speech, Nasution stressed that "the ideology of the Armed Forces is the State Constitution" reiterating that "the Armed Forces are not dead instruments of state."[53]

In 1958, three years after he had been reappointed army chief of staff, Nasution delivered his most important speech on the TNI's role in society, arguing that the position of the TNI was not like that of an army in a Western country, in which the military was solely an "instrument of the government" (*alat pemerintah*), neither was it like that of various Latin American armies which monopolized political power. Rather, the TNI was one of the forces of the people's struggle which was at the same level and which fought shoulder to shoulder with other forces, such as parties.[54]

Nasution's concerns had always transcended that which was purely military. Now, he emerged as a military theoretician who was to have a decisive influence on the political contours of post-independence Indonesia. His enthusiastic support for the return to the 1945 Constitution (together with the fear in certain circles that the army might be preparing to seize power) paved the way for the sort of strong government he favored. His concept of the dwifungsi and the related notion that the military should pursue a "Middle Way" provided both a framework for and a legitimization of a substantial military role in society.

Nasution does not dispute that as *Penguasa Perang* (martial law authority holder) he often took actions against the press and political parties. However, he makes three points about such actions. First, he stresses that they occurred during periods of revolt or at the beginning of such periods. Second, he argues that all his actions were taken under the emergency law provisions in the Constitution. Finally, he makes the point that it would be wrong to see all of his actions at this time as stemming from his own initiative; in many cases, he says, actions were taken at the behest of the government of the day, whether it was the prime minister when the 1950 Constitution

---

52. A. H. Nasution, "Tentera dan Politik," *Pedoman*, June 29, 1955, quoted in McKemmish, "Political Biography of Nasution," p. 92.

53. *Antara*, October 5, 1955, Sukarno's Perintah Harian (Order of the Day), quoted in McKemmish, "Political Biography of Nasution," p. 106.

54. As we have seen, it was Prof. Djokosutono, not Nasution, who dubbed this "the army's middle way." (*Jalan tengah tentara*.)

was in force or the president after 1959, under the 1945 Constitution.[55]

These arguments are not particularly convincing. For one thing, it was not only during periods of incipient revolt that Nasution acted in this way: the harshest repression was against the PKI, which was a strong supporter of the government. For another, there are no emergency provisions in the Constitution, except for Article 12, which provides for the proclamation of martial law, which is why the actions of 1957 were taken under the State of War and Siege (SOB) provisions, a nonconstitutional carry-over from colonial days.

If Nasution is prepared to admit that he frequently criticized the political parties and took actions against them, then he steadfastly rejects the notion that he wanted to eliminate them altogether. That distinction, he suggests, belongs to President Sukarno. "Bung Karno was the one who openly demanded the disbandment of the parties in 1956." (In fact, Sukarno only "dreamed" at that time that they would dissolve themselves. And whatever he may have said in the mid-1950s, he strongly supported them in 1960 against those who wanted to absorb them into the National Front.) It is true, Nasution says, that he often criticized party practices. But he says he never questioned their right to exist. What he had emphasized was "putting in order," not disbandment.[56]

It may be true, as critics sometimes suggest, that Nasution displayed "Bonapartist" tendencies during his formative years at the Military Academy in Bandung. It is certainly true that he emerged from the revolution with a firm belief in the need for strong government and for the exercise of military influence in the nonmilitary sector. It is also clear that, as chief of staff of the army in the late 1950s, he did much to advance both these objectives. The return to the 1945 Constitution conferred enormous powers on the president and the Middle Way doctrine legitimized a continuing army involvement in society, an involvement that was expanding rapidly as a result of three factors--Nasution's takeover of Dutch enterprises in 1957-58 under the SOB provisions, takeovers which provided the lifeblood for the army in 1959-65; the PRRI-Permesta rebellion; and the declaration of Martial Law.

It is impossible to know what sort of political format Nasution might have chosen had he, rather than Suharto, come to power, and in fact the chances of that happening were always fairly remote, Nasution having been outmanoeuvered by Sukarno in 1962 and stripped at that time of much of his strength. From 1955 to 1962, it is true, Nasution presided over an army that was growing more powerful by the day and this has made his critics (not least those around Suharto) cynical about his calls for political restraint by the armed forces. That expansion was legitimate for a number of reasons,

---

55. Written communication, November 14, 1981.

56. Ibid.

Nasution argues, not least because it was taken to offset the growing power of the PKI.   But, he says, there was no justification for the still greater expansion of the army's role that took place after 1965.

Nasution's stated desire for the pure and consistent application of the 1945 Constitution appears to be quite genuine, the only exception he would make to a rule about free expression being that there should be no "anti-Pancasila" parties.

Meanwhile, the former defense minister's desire to see a more rule-based system is reinforced by several other factors.   For one thing, Nasution has become a member of an out-group and out-groups traditionally, and quite naturally, stress the rights that are their due under the formal rules.   Second, he is an Outer Islander, and those from outside Java have traditionally emphasized the need for strict adherence to rules that allow them to maintain their position vis-a-vis Java.   Finally, Nasution has moved closer of late to student and middle-class groups in Jakarta and Bandung, and concern with the observation of laws and procedures is something very dear to the hearts of people in these groups.[57]

------

57.   I am indebted to Professor Daniel Lev for making this point. For an exposition of this argument see Lev, "Judicial Authority and the Struggle for an Indonesian Rechtsstaat."

CHAPTER ELEVEN

CRITICS AND CRITICISM ANALYZED

Now we have stability. Even if you say we have no democracy, it's all right [because] we have stability. And
the most important thing is that development can take
place.

Admiral Sudomo, 1983[1]

The Retired "Seniors": A Profile

What is most striking about the officers who were so critical of
Suharto is their age. This was, almost by definition, a movement of
middle-aged or old men. In 1980, the retired senior officers associated with Fosko and the LKB (see Table VI) ranged in age from Air
Vice Marshall Suyitno Sukirno (who was 50) to Rear Admiral Nazir
(who was 70). Fifteen of the twenty whose ages we have identified
were between 55 and 64. There were two reasons for this. First, it
was important, given the deference shown to age and authority in Indonesia, that Suharto's challengers should be of his own age and
rank. The officers who joined bodies like Fosko and the LKB had all
participated in the independence struggle and had had long and in
many cases distinguished careers. They felt they had not just a
right but a duty to draw attention to what they saw as the shortcomings of a military-backed government, the more so in that those in
power were in many cases their former subordinates. Second, it
would have been impractical, given Suharto's tight control over the
system, for younger and/or active officers to have participated in
such a movement; any such involvement would have proved suicidal in
career terms.

A second feature of this group is that, while much of the initial
reforming drive had come from retired army officers, the inclusion of
retired officers from the navy, the marines, the air force, and the
police lent an appropriate multiservice coloring to the criticisms that
were being made.[2] There were two officers of flag rank from the

---

1. Interview with Admiral Sudomo, August 6, 1983.

2. The army had always been politically more active than the other
services, the "Seventeenth of October Affair" being but one manifestation of its determination to play a political role. It was the army
chief of staff (Nasution) who had introduced the dwifungsi concept

navy (Rear Admiral Nazir and Rear Admiral Kamal), two from the
marine corps (Lt. Gen. Ali Sadikin and Brig. Gen. J. J. Sahulata),
one from the air force (Air Vice Marshall Suyitno Sukirno), and one
from the police (General Hugeng). These six nonarmy officers are of
some interest. For one thing, none of them had ever been particularly close to Suharto. Nazir, one of the founders of the navy, had
stood down as navy chief of staff in 1949 when Suharto was still a
lieutenant colonel. Kamal had been very close to Nasution and had
served in a senior staff position when Nasution was chief of staff of
ABRI after 1962. Air Vice Marshall Suyitno Sukirno, a former deputy
to the air force chief of staff, had been eased out very soon after
Suharto came to power. Hugeng, although appointed chief of the national police in 1968, had been pensioned off in October 1971 after
becoming too much of a thorn in the side of the ruling group. Ali
Sadikin, a Sukarno appointee whose term as governor of Jakarta had
been extended by Suharto in 1971, had been dropped, with an almost
audible sigh of relief, in 1977. In this sense, the nonarmy officers
were carry-overs from the pre-New Order period. For another thing,
they included in their ranks two men (Ali Sadikin and Hugeng) who
were prominent and well-liked and whose opinions still commanded
considerable respect.

A third feature was the fairly exalted rank and/or status of
those who participated in the movement. With the exception of
Kawilarang and one or two others who had been "frozen" at the rank
of colonel in the late 1950s, all these men were of general officer
rank. There were two four-star generals (Nasution and Hugeng),
eight lieutenant generals (not to mention a number of nonarmy officers of equivalent rank), eight major generals, and six brigadier
generals. The roll-call of the government's critics in the mid- to late
seventies included some of the most prominent names in recent Indonesian military history: Nasution, Simatupang, Djatikusumo,
Kawilarang, Mokoginta, Dharsono, Jasin, Sukendro, Kemal Idris,
Hugeng, Ali Sadikin, Nazir, and Azis Saleh. It was this fusion of
high rank and "big names" which gave the criticism of the retired officers its astringency. Civilian critics could, if they dared, loudly
criticize the government and yet have little effect. The retired "seniors" were different. These were men whose names still counted for
something and who had the capacity to influence to some extent the
course of events. Besides, civilians could be arrested easily, while
one had to think twice about touching a general, even a retired one.

Another characteristic, particularly of Fosko, was the prepon-
derance of officers from the Siliwangi (West Java) and Brawijaya (East
Java) military regions. The original Fosko "daily board" (consisting
of the three-man presidium plus the secretary general) reflected a
strong Siliwangi-Brawijaya configuration. Although Djatikusumo was
from neither of these divisions, Sudirman was Brawijaya, Sukendro

---

which sought to define and legitimize the role of the armed forces in
society.

Table VI. *Retired Senior Officers Critical of Suharto Government 1975–80*

Name	Rank	Year of Birth	Pre-military Education	Ethnic Background	Divisional/ Service Affil.	Religion
1. FOSKO						
Djatikusumo	LG	1917	Technical High School	C. Javanese	--	Muslim
Sudirman	LG	1913	Teachers High School	E. Javanese	BRA	Muslim
Sukendro*	MG	1923	Senior High School	C. Javanese	SIL	Muslim
Dharsono	LG	1925	Instit. of Technology	C. Javanese	SIL	Muslim
Mokoginta**	LG	1921	Senior High School	Gorontaloan	SIL	Muslim
Daan Jahja	BG	N.A.	Medical student	Minangkabau	SIL	Muslim
Jasin	LG	1921	High School	E. Javanese	BRA	Muslim
Agus Prasmono	BG	N.A.	N.A.	E. Javanese	BRA	Muslim
Munadi	MG	1923	Junior High School	C. Javanese	DIP	Muslim
Iskandar Ranuwihardjo	MG	N.A.	N.A.	C. Javanese	DIP	Muslim
Brotosewoyo	MG	N.A.	N.A.	C. Javanese	DIP	Muslim
Broto Hamidjojo	BG	N.A.	N.A.	C. Javanese	DIP	Muslim
Sugih Arto	LG	1923	N.A.	C. Javanese	SIL	Muslim
Muamil Effendy***	MG	N.A.	N.A.	C. Javanese	DIP	Muslim
Kawilarang	Col	1920	Senior High School	Menadonese	SIL	Christian
Chandra Hasan	Col	N.A.	N.A.	Madurese	BRA	Muslim
Harun Sohar	MG	N.A.	N.A.	S. Sumatran	SRI	Muslim
Sukanda Bratamenggala	Col	1917	Teachers' College	Sundanese	SIL	Muslim
Ishak Djuarsa	MG	1925	High School	W. Javanese	SIL	Muslim

* Sukendro died in 1984.

** Mokoginta was a member of both Fosko and the LKB. He died in 1984.

*** Muamil Effendy died in February 1982.

Note: Although not mentioned in Fosko membership lists, Lt. Gen. Ibnu Sutowo took an active part in the early Fosko deliberations on economic matters.

Table VI (continued)

Name	Rank	Year of Birth	Pre-military Education	Ethnic Background	Divisional/ Service Affil.	Religion
2. LKB						
Nasution	Gen	1918	Senior High School	Tapanuli Batak	SIL	Muslim
Azis Saleh	MG	1914	Jkt Medical Faculty	Sundanese	SIL/DIP	Muslim
Hugeng	Gen	1921	N.A.	C. Javanese	Police	Muslim
Ali Sadikin	LG	1927	N.A.	Sundanese	Marines	Muslim
Nazir*	Rear Adm.	1910	N.A.	Minangkabau	Navy	Muslim
Suyitno Sukirno	Air V. Marshal	1930	Senior High School	C. Javanese	Air Force	Muslim
Isa Edris	BG	N.A.	N.A.	E. Javanese	BRA	Muslim
Hidayat Martaatmaja	LG	1916	N.A.	Sundanese	SIL	Muslim
H. M. Kamal	Rear Adm.	N.A.	N.A.	Minangkabau	Navy	Muslim
Surakhmad	Col.	N.A.	N.A.	E. Javanese	BRA	Muslim
Sahulata	BG	1920	Technical High School	Seramese	Marines	Christian
H. Sadikin	BG	1916	Mamba'ul Ulum, Solo	Sundanese	SIL	Muslim

* Rear Admiral Nazir died in August 1982, aged 72.

Note: Maj. Gen. Azis Saleh had been a member of both the Siliwangi and Diponegoro divisions. During the first guerrilla period he was in the Siliwangi; during the second he was in the Diponegoro, serving as a commander of the Republican forces in Semarang. Although very much a product of the Siliwangi, Lt. Gen. Mokoginta likewise spanned both divisions, having served at one stage as chief of staff of the Diponegoro. Brig. Gen. Abimanju, who participated in the discussions that led to the formation of Fosko, had served in each of the three big Java divisions and had commanded the Siliwangi.

and Dharsono from the Siliwangi. In all, no fewer than eight of the eighteen members of Fosko were from the Siliwangi. Moreover, there was also a strong Siliwangi "presence" in the LKB. The founder and most senior military member of this body, General Nasution, was the "father of the Siliwangi" and three of its other senior military partici-pants were from the same division. Lt. Gen. Kemal Idris, although associated with neither Fosko nor the LKB, was also from the Siliwangi, as was Brig. Gen. Abimanju, who, though he declined an invitation to join Fosko, had taken part in the Brasildi meetings of 1977. All told, included in Fosko and the LKB were five of the first nine Siliwangi commanders--Nasution (Panglima ke I), Daan Jahja (II), H. Sadikin (IV), Kawilarang (V), and Dharsono (IX) and there would have been six had Abimanju (Panglima III) joined them. Of the twen-ty-five army officers identified in Table VI, almost half were from the Siliwangi. Another six were from the Brawijaya. The Diponegoro (Central Java) military region was somewhat underrepresented, at least at the leadership level. Five Diponegoro officers belonged to Fosko, but only two were of any consequence--Maj. Gen. Munadi, a onetime assistant V (territorial) Diponegoro who had gone on to serve as governor of Central Java between 1966-74, and Maj. Gen. Muamil Effendy. Neither played a central role in the Fosko leadership. On the other hand, Maj. Gen. Azis Saleh, who had spent at least part of his career in the Diponegoro, was chairman of the LKB.

In the view of such officers as Dharsono, the disproportionate number of Siliwangi officers was both a result of, and a protest against, a "de-Siliwangi-ization" process instigated by Suharto.[3] Suharto, it was argued, had tended to surround himself with trusted colleagues from the Diponegoro, and while some retired generals, Sukendro included, were prepared to admit that this was understand-able, others, like Dharsono, felt strongly that this had gone hand-in-hand with a deliberate attempt to curb the influence of the Siliwangi.[4] (Some in Fosko believed the ruling group had pursued a parallel, although less drastic, policy of "de-Brawijaya-ization").[5]

Whatever the truth of these assertions, the lopsided influence of the Siliwangi group was important. As has often been noted,

---

3. Interview with Lt. Gen. Dharsono, November 7, 1981.

4. Sukendro believed that this was "logical and understandable." Interview, July 11, 1981.

5. According to Sukendro, the "phase of de-Siliwangi-ization" started in 1969 or 1970. Once the "de-Siliwangi-ization" had been achieved, he said, "you feel they are trying to cut the Brawijaya." However, the steps taken against the Brawijaya had not been as drastic as those against the Siliwangi. In the same interview, Su-kendro qualified this by saying that what had occurred was not so much the "de-Siliwangi-ization" or "de-Brawijaya-ization" as the emer-gence of the "ruling officers' class" around Suharto. The members of this "class" had been associated with Suharto "since the days of the Mandala Command" (that is, 1962). Interview, July 11, 1981.

Siliwangi officers were generally better educated and more cosmopolitan in outlook than officers of other divisions. This was due to historical circumstances. "The higher proportion of socially and educationally advantaged officers in the Siliwangi Division," wrote McVey, "derived in good part from the fact that Bandung and Batavia were principal centers of residence and education for the Western educated Indonesian elite in the colonial period."[6] Most of the institutes of higher learning in colonial Indonesia, including the Bandung Technical Institute, were in West Java, as was the Dutch Military Academy.

Within the mainstream of army life, the importance of divisional affiliations has been declining. The next generation, it has been pointed out, is much more identified with various specialized services and schools than with the localized combat experience and comradeship of the revolution.[7] However, the three Java "divisions" still figure prominently in the thinking of the retired officers in whose lives they played so central a role, even if old rivalries have been put aside for the sake of a unified campaign against the present "in" group. Given the disproportionate number of Siliwangi officers in the "opposition" movement and the disproportionate number of Diponegoro officers in the inner circles around Suharto, the statements and criticisms of a number of prominent members of the so-called Barisan Sakit Hati ("Sick at Heart Brigade") may be seen, at least in part, as a final working out of divisional rivalries that date back to the fifties.

A fifth feature of the above list is that three of the most prominent army officers (Nasution, Mokoginta, and Kawilarang) were graduates of the prewar Royal Military Academy in Bandung. (Lt. Gen. T. B. Simatupang, an equally prominent retired officer and a man whose concern about "a drift into militarism" had led to his involvement in the Sawito Affair in 1976, was likewise a graduate of the RMA.) The professional military training these officers received set them apart from the much larger (and slightly younger) group of officers who were to receive their first military instruction at the hands of the Japanese.

At the Military Academy, cadets underwent a rigorous two-year course, with due emphasis being given to staff work. Those Indonesian youths who graduated as platoon commanders (*shodancho*) and company commanders (*chudancho*) in the Japanese-sponsored Peta were also given intensive and effective military training and subjected to strict military discipline. (Battalion commanders (*daidancho*) were usually political figures, much older and not seriously trained.)[8] But Peta graduates received only two to six months' instruction, and none

6. See McVey, "Post-Revolutionary Transformation of the Indonesian Army," p. 133.

7. See "Current Data on the Indonesian Military Elite," *Indonesia* 29 (April 1980): 157.

8. See Benedict R. O.'G. Anderson, *Java in a Time of Revolution* (Ithaca: Cornell University Press, 1972), p. 21.

were trained to command anything larger than a battalion. At the same time, the academy's graduates, coming in many cases from second-generation Dutch-speaking homes, tended to be better educated than the Peta officers. As a result of all this, they not only had a clear professional edge over their Japanese-trained colleagues but also in some cases a sense of hubris that tended to color their relationships with those from Peta, something that tended to become more pronounced after Peta officers replaced them in senior command positions. The prewar military cadets had belonged to a select group chosen to study at the Military Academy. Most of the Peta officers had less imposing credentials; Suharto, for example, had only reached junior high school, Amir Machmud had attended a technical vocational school. What is more, the better-trained academy graduates had moved, at a very early age, into senior staff and command positions. Simatupang was appointed chief of staff of the armed forces in 1950 at the age of twenty-nine. Nasution, one year his senior, became army chief of staff at the same time. (One of the retired generals, when invited to the unveiling of the statue of General Sudirman in Magelang, is said to have sniffed that he would not attend any gathering at which "that sergeant" [Suharto] was officiating.)[9]

On the other hand, the RMA graduates were to be recruited into the KNIL, a colonial army whose prime task was not external defense but internal repression. In other words, men like Nasution, Simatupang, Mokoginta, and Kawilarang were tainted initially by the fact that they had enrolled for what amounted to mercenary and antinationalist operations, and they had to work off the collaborator image. Peta was at least a patriotic army, even if it had been sponsored by the Japanese and even if some of its members (Suharto among them) had themselves served, albeit at a low level, in the KNIL.

Finally, it might be pointed out that the comparatively exalted military education in the RMA tended to buttress divisional affiliations; all three Military Academy graduates were later to enter the Siliwangi.

If the distinction between Javanese and Outer Islanders remains of some importance in the Indonesian army, it is difficult to draw too many conclusions from the above listing, which represents a fairly even mix between the two. It has been argued that the central army leadership is today made up of a disproportionate number of Javanese, a statement that is hardly open to dispute. According to recent surveys by the editors of the Cornell University bi-annual journal *Indonesia*, almost 80 percent of the high command officeholders whose ethnic identity can be determined have been Javanese.[10] Moreover, as we have seen, the members of the "inner core group" around Suharto--Yoga Sugama, Ali Murtopo, Sudomo, and Benny

---

9. Confidential communication.

10. *Indonesia* 29 (April 1980): 157.

Murdani--were all Javanese, as were other key officers like Sudharmono and Darjatmo. At the same time, it should not be forgotten that there was a fairly strong non-Javanese presence at or close to the top of the military pyramid. (The two men who served as minister of defense between 1968-83 were Outer Islanders, although able Javanese officers, including Surono, Sumitro, and Widodo, were available.) Several reasons account for this. One is that it was still necessary to maintain a harmonious ethnic and regional balance in the army, just as in the cabinet. Thus Panggabean had been for many years the senior Batak in the army and Jusuf the senior officer from South Sulawesi. Likewise, Amir Machmud had been the senior Sundanese in the government. A second reason had to do with power considerations; an Outer Islander was hardly likely to pose the sort of threat to the incumbent president that a powerful and popular Javanese officer might. In this sense, Javanese officers, although accounting for a disproportionate number of senior positions, have been kept at some distance from key military leadership posts.

Within the military, where the prevailing outlook was decidedly abangan and Christian, there was, as we have seen, a deep-seated suspicion concerning Muslim aims and objectives. And insofar as men such as Nasution and Lt. Gen. R. Sudirman appeared to some in the military to be unduly close to Islamic groups, it might be supposed that they could be depicted as sympathizing with the so-called "ultra-Rightist Pancasila" group. However, it would be difficult to support such an assertion. Nasution and many other devout Muslims had played a central role in the suppression of the Islamic fundamentalists in the Darul Islam/Tentara Islam Indonesia and frequently made the point that there was no need to juxtapose religion and Pancasila. If one looks at the religion of those in the above list, it becomes obvious that all but a very few (such as Simatupang and Kawilarang) were Muslim. Some of the retired officers were known to take their religion very seriously; others were by way of being nominal Muslims.

Politically, the retired senior officers were a mixed grouping. Initially there were some suggestions that Fosko was too "Sukarnoist" in outlook, Sukendro, being characterized in certain quarters, as a "100 percent Sukarnoist." Agus Prasmono, Djatikusumo, Jasin, and Chandra Hasan were also allegedly, in varying degrees, "Sukarnoist" in outlook. So too was Mokoginta. "I didn't join Fosko," one prominent retired brigadier general said in 1982, "because I am anti-Sukarno and there were too many officers there who were pro-Sukarno."[11] This argument is not especially persuasive. Sukendro may well have had a certain residual regard for Sukarno--this, after all, was common enough in the armed forces--but he had also clashed with, and been banished by, Sukarno. (In the early 1980s, Sukendro liked to portray himself as "more PSI" in outlook.)[12] Moreover, it might have been thought that the Sukarnoist sympathies of

---

11. Confidential communication, March 7, 1982.

12. Interview with Maj. Gen. Sukendro, March 15, 1982.

some would have been canceled out by the anti-Sukarnoist attitudes of others in and around Fosko. Dharsono and Kemal Idris had led the anti-Sukarno campaign in 1966-67 and yet Dharsono was able to work closely with Sukendro on the Fosko daily board. The various differences, while they existed to some extent, were not really very influential. This was not a movement which took its bearings from the ideological disputes of the 1950s and early 1960s, but one which looked more towards the rather generalized ideals of 1945. Within the Brasildi, and later the Fosko and the LKB, there was a fairly conscious effort to leave behind the idea of *kekelompokan* (compartmentalization). The starting point was 1945. At that time, the retired officers suggested, everyone had been represented in a broad movement and no one had fought for the *kelompok*. This, of course, presented a rather idealized version of the situation in 1945. If individuals had not fought singlemindedly for the interests of their own particular group or cluster in 1945, it was due in large part to the efforts of leaders like Sukarno who, recognizing the dangers of a divided and disputatious nationalist movement, stressed broad goals that were acceptable to all. In the late 1970s and early 1980s, the various dissident groups in Indonesia, did much the same thing.

While, as we have seen, there were differences in the way various officers had entered the armed forces, there were equally important distinctions in the timing and manner of their retirement.

The Sakit Hati Brigade

There has never really been a period in postindependence Indonesia in which there were not at least some disaffected military officers sitting out their time on the sidelines. The intense political infighting of the early 1950s, the October 17 Affair in particular, and the regional rebellions of the late 1950s, created situations in which a number of prominent military officers were forced into premature retirement, either of a temporary or permanent nature. The most notable figure affected in this way was Nasution, who was forced to step down as army chief of staff following the failed "half coup" of 1952; he was to remain on the sidelines until recalled as chief of staff in 1955. However, many others faced similar and, in most cases, more permanent exclusion. Simatupang, who had served as chief of staff of the armed forces in the early 1950s, was forced into retirement--at the age of 35--when his job was abolished in 1955. Colonels Husein, Lubis, and Simbolon had been dishonorably discharged from the army at the beginning of the PRRI rebellion in February 1958, for an alleged attempt to assassinate Sukarno and "attempting to change the state and government by violence."[13] Col. Alex Kawilarang was dis-

---

13. See Sundhaussen, *Road to Power*, p. 107. Husein and Simbolon were amongst the rebels in Padang who proclaimed a Revolutionary Government (PRRI) on February 15, 1958.

charged from the army--but never prosecuted--after he and a large number of Permesta rebels surrendered in April 1961.

These eruptions had seen the departure of a fairly steady stream of officers, but the collapse of the Old Order and the "purification" of the command structure created a situation in which much greater numbers of officers found their services no longer required. When Suharto was appointed defense minister in 1966, the Indonesian military establishment was not only top-heavy with generals and air marshalls but was staffed with many pro-Sukarno and left-leaning officers, particularly in the air force and the navy. Suharto's very success in establishing his hold over the military establishment and his ouster of so many Old Order figures, greatly augmented the pool of retired officers, some of whom felt no compunction in criticizing those who were now at the top.

In the late 1960s, a falling-out amongst New Order officers produced the first post-Sukarno crop of "sakit hati" officers. The first wave to find themselves pushed to one side were Siliwangi figures whom Crouch has described as New Order "militants." In 1968, as we have seen, Nasution was manoeuvered into a parliamentary backwater. In 1969, following a heavy-handed attempt to bring the various parties in West Java together into "two groups," Dharsono, the Siliwangi commander, and his colleague Kemal Idris, the Kostrad commander, were replaced. These officers, like others who had seen the abrupt termination of once promising careers, were later to turn up in the Barisan Sakit Hati.

If the New Order "militants" tended to be at odds with the Suharto leadership over matters of policy, there were stirrings, many of which went unnoticed at the time, among another group of officers who took exception to the corruption already becoming apparent under the New Order. This second wave of New Order dissidents included Hugeng, Jasin, and Ishak Djuarsa. Although the motives of these men, Hugeng excepted, may not have always been as straightforward as they might have liked to suggest, resentment over orders from above to abandon corruption investigations figured prominently in the disenchantment of at least two of them.

Hugeng, as we have seen, had been something of a carry-over from the Sukarno era. Although on good terms with Suharto at the time of his appointment as chief of the national police in mid-1968, he soon found that Suharto "did not have the same open attitude towards me as President Sukarno had shown."[14] One point of dissension concerned the role of the national police force. Under the restructuring plans drawn up by Sumitro in 1969, the four armed services were to be unified under one command. Hugeng, who had quite good relations with Sumitro, accepted this, but argued that the national police should be simply a civilian law enforcement agency, not a separate

---

14. See "Former police chief speaks out on regime," *Tapol*, Bulletin 13 (December 1975), p. 4.

military force and not in any way a plaything of the armed forces. This apparently conflicted with the intentions of the ruling army officers, and Hugeng, whose character allowed no room for compromise on points of principle, came increasingly to be seen as a troublesome and obstinate man. When, in 1971, Hugeng ordered his subordinates to ensure that no intimidation occurred during the general election campaign, the exasperation of the army generals grew still more pronounced.[15] In the meantime, Hugeng's unswerving stand on law and order matters had brought him into personal conflict with the minister of defense/Kopkamtib commander, General Panggabean, and with President Suharto. At a cabinet meeting in 1970 Hugeng learned from Foreign Minister Adam Malik that Yap Thiam Hien, a prominent lawyer and government critic, had been arrested several days earlier by the Jakarta police chief, Maj. Gen. Subroto. When Hugeng contacted his deputy he found not only that the report was true but that Subroto had followed Panggabean's orders in arresting Yap without even knowing the reasons for it. Infuriated at what he saw as thoroughly unprofessional behavior, Hugeng ordered Yap's immediate release, bracing himself for an angry rejoinder from Panggabean. In the event, Panggabean did nothing. However, he is said to have borne a grudge towards Hugeng from that day.[16]

In 1971, Hugeng was summoned to the president's home on a Sunday morning and asked to drop the case against a smuggler and set the man free; his refusal to do so greatly annoyed the president. The same year, police captured an Indonesian Chinese confidence man who went under the alias Haji Drs. Djokosuwarno SH and who was wanted in connection with business frauds in Jakarta, Palembang, Padang, Medan, and Kota Raja in Aceh. When the CID searched the man's house they found photographs of him with Madame Suharto and several of her younger brothers. They also found documents bearing the first lady's signature. Hugeng, genuinely concerned about the good name of the president, handed the material to Suharto the following day in the presence of the attorney general, Maj. Gen. Sugih Arto, and the state secretary, Maj. Gen. Sudharmono, and suggested it would be wise if measures were taken to prevent any recurrence of such an event. Suharto, who said he had already advised his wife not to get involved in such matters, appeared taken aback and embarrassed by the disclosures.

For the New Order leaders, the last straw came in September 1971 when Hugeng zeroed in on a huge smuggling racket at Tanjung Priok, the port of Jakarta. Hundreds of expensive cars had been imported duty-free by a smuggling ring headed by Robby Tjahjadi, a young Indonesian Chinese who was said to be in league with a Hankam staff officer who acted on behalf of certain members of the first family. Hugeng, who had already broken one such ring, planned to raid the port on September 19, 1971. However, instead of

---

15. Interview with General Sumitro.

16. Confidential communication.

being rewarded for his enterprise, he was dismissed from his post. On September 2, he was summoned by Panggabean and told, in the presence of Sumitro, that the president had decided that his term as chief of the national police was "considered finished." He was offered the post of ambassador to the Netherlands, which he declined.[17] In 1976, according to evidence given at the trial of Sawito Kartowibowo, Hugeng told the head of the Roman Catholic Church in Indonesia, Cardinal Justinius Darmojuwono, that he had reported to both the attorney general, Sugih Arto, and to Suharto himself that Madame Tien Suharto was involved in the smuggling racket. However, Hugeng had said, the smuggling had gone on regardless. According to the court witness, the smuggling involved billions of rupiahs. "Mrs. Suharto should have been tried before the courts," the witness said, "because she had been involved in smuggling."[18] The previous year, Hugeng had given a Dutch television interviewer his opinions about the moral dissolution of the times. "It seems," he said, "as if some people take a pride in becoming rich overnight."[19]

If the chief of police was disturbed by the illegality he saw around him, so too was General Jasin, the former deputy army chief of staff. As we have seen, Jasin was to trace his disenchantment with the Suharto regime to the instruction he was given to use unsuitable trucks in the 1971 election campaign.

Ishak Djuarsa, who had shared many of the sentiments of the early New Order militants like Dharsono and Kemal Idris, had also been reined in when he had sought to crack down on smuggling while serving as military commander in Aceh in 1965-67. According to evidence given at the Sawito trial in November 1977, Ishak Djuarsa had been abruptly ordered to halt these efforts "on orders from higher up." In the words of one of his colleagues in Fosko, Ishak Djuarsa had in 1966 been "shocked into disbelief" by the illegal activities of members of the Suharto family in both Aceh and Palembang.[20] In 1976, as the Sawito trial was to make clear, a disillusioned Ishak Djuarsa, by then ambassador to Yugoslavia, was to play a central role in the plot to force Suharto step down.[21] (Ishak Djuarsa's own activities in Aceh had caused even greater shock in certain quarters. As panglima between 1965-67 he presided over an anti-Communist campaign of exceptional brutality.)[22]

---

17. Ibid.

18. See David Jenkins, "Trial Touches Raw Nerves," *FEER*, January 13, 1978.

19. *Tapol*, Bulletin 13.

20. Confidential communication, March 25, 1982.

21. *FEER*, January 13, 1978.

22. Although well known for his zeal in combatting illegality, Ishak Djuarsa was a man who had a reputation for extreme brutality. Apart from his activities in Aceh, while he was serving as panglima in South

In the years after 1970, a number of key officers around Suharto either fell from favor or chose to distance themselves from the government they had once served so willingly. In 1974, four men--Sumitro, Sutopo Juwono, Sajidiman, and Charis Suhud--resigned or were reassigned as a result of the Malari Affair. The following year, Ibnu Sutowo was "honorably discharged" as the president director of Pertamina. In 1980, Widodo was dropped as army chief of staff. However, these men had for many years been members of the ruling elite and, whatever reservations they might have had about Suharto, they tended to keep their criticisms to themselves or to express their concern in the most oblique way. The longer an officer had been close to Suharto, it seemed, the more muted his criticism of the government. This was also true to some extent of those from the Suharto group who, like Sugih Arto, were to join Fosko. Sugih Arto, who had served as ambassador to India after his four-year (1966-70) term as attorney general, was a founding member of Fosko in 1978. But few people were aware of this, and in time he found it prudent to step back from the group. Munadi, the former governor of Central Java, was likewise muted in any statements he made.

From the above observations, certain conclusions can be drawn about Suharto's military critics in the late 1970s and early 1980s. These officers tended to be as old as, or older than, the members of the ruling group and had in a number of cases been the commanding officers of those whose actions they now found unacceptable. Initially at least, they were disproportionately drawn from the army and disproportionately also from the Siliwangi. They tended to be more idealistic than members of the government, more inclined to advocate "radical" solutions to problems which were often of great complexity.

The "Sakit Hati" Officers: What They Sought

An analysis of the criticisms, both private and public, expressed by the "Sakit Hati" officers shows that, beneath a generalized disenchantment with "the situation" in Indonesia, there existed three overlapping areas of concern. First and foremost, these offi-

---

Sumatra (1967-70) a number of PKI detainees are said to have been executed in their cells, with the chief of the military police in Palembang reportedly taking the strongest exception to these actions. Confidential communication, March 21, 1982. Between 1971 and 1975 Ishak Djuarsa was the senior officer at Kopkamtib in charge of ASEAN/Indochinese affairs. He served briefly as ambassador to Cambodia in 1975 and was named ambassador to Yugoslavia in 1976. Detained at the time of the Sawito Affair in 1976, he was later quietly released and went into business with General Sumitro. Interview with Ishak Djuarsa, February 28, 1981. See also Arief, *Indonesian Military Leaders*, pp. 89-90. (This book mistakenly lists Ishak Djuarsa's birth date as 1926, instead of 1925.)

cers shared a feeling that under Suharto the political, social, and economic role of the armed forces had expanded beyond acceptable limits. ABRI's political role, they argued, was built on extra-constitutional pillars and on "emergency" decrees which had long since served their purpose. And, these officers felt, the ruling group's preoccupation with public order was stifling legitimate political expression. As Horowitz has observed: "Many analysts have noted that the common military conception of public order consists essentially of an 'absence of social conflict', disturbance, or unpredictable action, 'an apolitical calm', 'the stability of a vacuum, a state undisturbed by the erratic movements of partisan bodies."[23]

The opposition generals, although they may once have supported the notion of depoliticizing a volatile and intensely politicized nation, had come to believe that this process had been carried too far, and that its continuation might provoke a serious backlash. None of these officers, with the exception of Mokoginta, were in favor of a "return to the barracks." They were committed to the notion that ABRI had an important role to play in society and saw the dwifungsi doctrine as providing a legitimation of such a role. But they wished to rid the existing system of its "excesses." On the whole, they were inclined to take a more mature and generous view of civilian society, to recognize its potential strengths rather than being preoccupied by its apparent weaknesses. ABRI's continuing involvement in an extensive range of business and economic activities was likewise condemned. In the view of many retired officers it was time to "regularize" a situation in which the line between *penguasa* (power holder) and *pengusaha* (entrepreneur) had become dangerously blurred.

A second area of concern was that there had been an enormous increase in--and apparent indifference to--corruption under Suharto. A number of retired officers, schooled in a stricter discipline than those who assumed power in the mid-1960s, found the level of corruption morally reprehensible. (A number of others, it is true, found it prudent to refrain from comment on this topic, having themselves grown enormously wealthy through the systematic plunder of the public purse.) They felt that the system should operate not on the basis of what Feith has described as the "judicious distribution of patronage," but through a system that was essentially legal and predictable. In this, they were at one with the student critics of the regime. Corruption was a matter of real concern to men like Nasution, Sudirman, Kawilarang, and Hugeng, officers of a "Calvinist" bent who regretted the passing of the old values. Indeed, in Kawilarang's case, an abhorrence of the corrupt practices of the "Yogya-Solo" officers seemed to have been one of the main factors--if not the main factor--in the decision to join Fosko.

---

23. See Donald L. Horowitz, *Coup Theories and Officers' Motives: Sri Lanka in Comparative Perspective* (Princeton: Princeton University Press, 1980), p. 169.

Finally, many of these officers felt that the Javanese *abangan* and Christian generals around Suharto were taking an unduly narrow and repressive view of Islam in general and political Islam in particular. This concern tended to take two forms. Some retired officers, Nasution for example, sympathized with the Islamic cause. Others were wary of Islam but feared that heavy-handedness might make the situation worse.

There was no unanimity on the relative importance of the various items in this catalog of grievances. Some retired officers, Nasution and Sudirman for example, focused on all three areas, even if they tended to put primary emphasis on the need for constitutional purification. Some, like Jasin, Kawilarang, and Hugeng, stressed the spread of corruption under the New Order. Many voiced a concern about the government's negative view of Islam. (Others, like Simatupang, a prominent member of the Christian community, tended to accept the notion that certain former Masyumi leaders, Natsir in particular, were bent on the eventual creation of an Islamic state.)[24]

In the late 1970s, these streams came together in one major current of dissent. Moreover, these retired officers' views had much in common with the sort of criticism being expressed both within the army and from outside civilian groups. By 1980, there was a broad and somewhat unique alliance between a number of retired senior officers and "retired politicians," with linkages to the student movement. Their views found expression in both Fosko and the LKB and in such things as the Petition of Fifty.

Although the critics were linked more by a sense of what they opposed than what they sought to build, and although they in no way posed a substantive threat to the government, they did succeed in chipping away at the moral authority and legitimacy of the ruling group. To the government, the criticism of the retired officers proved particularly irritating. These retired "seniors" enjoyed an immunity--initially at least--that did not extend to their civilian counterparts, and their prominent "names" gave their criticism additional weight and respectability. The government, not taking kindly to this, evinced its displeasure in a number of ways.

The Official View of the Criticism

The government attitude, as articulated by such officers as Sudomo, Benny Murdani, and Yoga Sugama, was not one of forbearance or understanding. These officers tended to take a cynical view of the motives of the government's critics. They allowed little room for the possibility that the criticism derived from anything other than self-serving motivations and were loath to concede, in public at any

---

24. This was a recurrent theme in Simatupang's thinking and one which found expression in interviews on June 10, 1980, July 31, 1981, and March 19, 1982.

rate, that there might have been a genuine undercurrent of concern in these expressions of discontent.

Essentially, those in power took the view that the retired generals were members of an "out" group and that most, if not all, would fall into line if the price was right. According to Jasin, Suharto's reaction, when Adam Malik showed him the Jasin letter, was: "Jasin is just sakit hati because he didn't get facilities. It is a [small] matter."[25] Harmony, the ruling group seemed to believe, could be maintained through the distribution of patronage. And there was, of course, some justification for this sort of cynicism. When, in 1980 and 1981, attractive inducements were offered to a number of dissident generals on the condition that they abandon their antigovernment stance, a number quietly accepted, if only out of a concern for the welfare of their families. However, this fairly deep-seated cynicism about the motivation of former comrades was clothed, in public at least, with quasi-sociological explanations about why these troublesome old men acted as they did. In Sudomo's opinion, these officers were unhappy victims of the "post-power syndrome." They were men, he suggested, who had once been powerful figures in society, whose opinions had helped determine national policy, and who, in their time, had commanded respect and obedience. They had been provided with large houses and chauffeur-driven limousines. Their children had attended the best schools. Now they were nothing. They had been pensioned off and left, or so it seemed to them, to fend for themselves. (In fact, as other serving officers were quick to point out, most had been well set up for their retirement, with access to generous bank credit and other facilities. It could not be said that the New Order did not look after its own.) Cut off from the institution that had been a dominant influence in their lives--sometimes while still in their forties--these men had grown embittered and disillusioned. They had become sour and ungrateful, nurturing a grievance against those who were still in office.

There was, it must be said at once, some truth in this characterization. Several officers had never really come to terms with their exclusion from the decision-making process. This, combined in some cases with a sense of hubris, an awareness that they had been displaced by men they still tended to look on as subordinates, did influence the criticisms of some retired officers.

Another charge from those in power was that the retired officers had never shown much aversion to a strong military-backed government when they were in office. Murdani, for example, was wont to make the point that Nasution was the man who had paved the way for strong presidential rule, who had formulated the dwifungsi doctrine which legitimized the military's social role, who had come up with the notion of ABRI as the "dynamizer and stabilizer" of society, and who had presided over the birth of Sekber Golkar. In the 1950s, as members of the ruling group would note, "Pak Nas" had

---

25. Interview with Lt. Gen Jasin, May 23, 1980.

been the one who wanted to take firm measures against the political parties, and for him to present himself as a born-again democrat was hypocritical.[26] Sumitro, whose attitudes remained very much in tune with those of the ruling elite, took a similar view.

> If Pak Nas were president he would do the same things. Believe me, he would do the same things. The best navigator, the best captain, is on shore. . . . Oh, Nas! He's worst. He is authoritarian! Really! That's why in 1971 or 1972 I was warning him: "Once you do it, I'll detain you. Using that Mimbar Bebas [Free Forum, a seminar at the University of Indonesia prior to the 1971 elections]. . . . I told him, "You belong to the past. You had your chance actually but you didn't have the courage to grasp it."[27]

Much the same sort of criticism, some of it justified, was directed at men like Dharsono, Jasin, and Ishak Djuarsa, all of whom had exhibited authoritarian tendencies while in office and none of whom had been particularly noted for a commitment to the free expression of the popular will. In the view of the ruling group, these officers had left their criticism too late. Murdani, who seemed deeply offended that men like Ali Sadikin, Nasution, and Hugeng could act as they did, said in 1980: "My answer is: 'Why didn't you say these things when you had stars on your shoulders?'"[28] (The answer, members of Fosko and the LKB were quick to reply, was that men like Nasution, Dharsono, and Hugeng had done just that and had paid the price for it.) Having retired, it was argued, these officers should have had the grace to sit back and let their successors get on with the job. There was something improper, it was suggested, in the fact that these old generals kept carping about the performance of a new group of leaders--particularly as they brought all of ABRI's dirty linen out into public view. In Yoga's view, if everyone was able to adjust himself to the thought that "there's a time to come, there's a time to go" then no one would be frustrated.

> Take my case, for instance. I will be happy if I can leave my active duty. . . . Somebody will replace me. And I will adjust myself because mentally I'm already prepared for this. I don't expect any special treatment from

---

26. Nasution's answer, as we have seen, was that the dwifungsi doctrine was meant to be implemented with restraint, that ABRI was supposed to work as a partner of the civilian groups, not seek to dominate the landscape. In 1981, Nasution argued that military men should not serve as the heads of large government-owned corporations or as heads of economic institutions. Interview, March 2, 1981.

27. Interview with General Sumitro, July 18, 1981.

28. Interview with Lt. Gen. Benny Murdani, July 3, 1980.

the state when I am retired. I will be happy to become a normal, ordinary citizen. And I will easily adjust myself and forget what I have been before. I have considered myself as being a player in a certain story, a *wayang* story. When the dalang thinks he needs you, you could be put into the play. When the dalang is finished then you can be put into the box. If you are content with that kind of philosophy, I don't think there is anything in this world that could make you frustrated. When the dalang is finished with you it will be time for you to go into the box. . . . I'm just somebody who plays a certain act in a certain story. The story happens to be the Revolution Indonesia, the Republic of Indonesia. I played my part, so I can retire. You cannot always be playing your part. There is always some beginning and some end. . . . These chaps, they have had their chance. . . . Why come now, after the government doesn't need them anymore? . . . When I am finished I will be nothing anymore. I should not come and say, "The government should do this, should do that!" I have had my time to say my piece. I had my chance to do that if I wanted. Why now? They are retired. That's wrong.[29]

Sumitro, who was not unlike Yoga in a number of ways, took pre-cisely the same view. Most officers, he felt, shared the view that it was necessary to reduce ABRI's involvement. But it should not be done by making speeches, by criticizing the government.

The retired officers still want to have their say. But they should accept that they *are* retired. Take me, for instance. I was in army for thirty-two years. But I don't have any expectations because I believe that who-ever succeeds me will be better than me. Without me the Republic will go on. Don't consider yourself very impor-tant. No! If you want to share your opinion, give ad-vice but do it in a mature way. Because by fighting you gain nothing, you gain nothing.[30]

To men like Nasution, an ABRI man was an ABRI man until the day he died; he had a responsibility to fight for what he believed was right. To Yoga and his fellow officers in the ruling circle, an ABRI man fought for his beliefs while still in uniform and then went gracefully "into the box," a philosophy which of course had its obvi-ous attractions to an "in" group. The retired officers not only re-jected this philosophy on principle but, being in their view all too fa-miliar with the ways of the dalang, had no inclination to allow the "excesses" to go by unremarked. It was possible also to detect some-

---

29. Interview with General Yoga Sugama, July 15, 1981.

30. General Sumitro interview, July 18, 1981.

thing self-serving in the argument of the ruling generals that, after retirement, they would be heard from no more. Being of the ruling group and largely in agreement with its policies (which, of course, they had helped shape) they would have no need to criticize, except in the unlikely event that a radically different group were to come to power.

A fourth criticism was that, with the exception of Nasution, Hugeng, and perhaps one or two others, the retired generals were just as corrupt as those they sought to criticize. "Most of these people," one of the Ali Murtopo's colleagues said in 1980, "are just as corrupt as anyone else. We have a laundry list. We can hit back if they want that."[31] There was some truth in this assertion, many officers having helped themselves to the spoils that had been available to those in authority for the past twenty years. But these remarks would seem to overstate the extent of corruption among the retired officers. Certainly there were more than a few officers who were prepared to maintain their criticisms of the government, threats of this nature notwithstanding.

The Official Response

In coping with the dissident generals, Suharto relied on both carrots and sticks, both of which were in ample supply. The initial approach, as so often in the past, was to seek to coopt the critics by offering them all manner of perquisites and privileges in exchange for a cessation of their criticism; given the government view that the critics tended to be dissatisfied because of a denial of "facilities," there was a certain logic in this. In pursuing the campaign to disarm his opponents, Suharto relied to a considerable extent on Sumitro, who was seen more and more around town in the early 1980s and who seemed to be increasingly back in favor. Sumitro shared some of the concerns of the dissident group. He felt, for example, that Kopkamtib should be dismantled and was disturbed that patrimonialism was still "shadowing" the Indonesian political process.[32] However, Sumitro seemed to be talking more about fine tuning the existing system; he was not talking about the sort of fundamental changes that the critics had in mind. Moreover, he seemed anxious to persuade Suharto that he had harbored no ambitions in 1974, giving every indication that he sought to win back a place on the Suharto team, however difficult that might seem. By early 1981, Sumitro was making periodic visits to Suharto's office and benefitting from his willingness to play by the established rules of the game. He owned PT Rigunas which had a forest concession of 300,000 hectares in Irian Jaya and managed PT Tjakra Sudarma which operated in the field of ABRI equipment purchases. He was also the chief supervisor of PT

---

31.   Interview with Jusuf Wanandi, 1980.

32.   Interview with General Sumitro.

Riasima Abadi, a pharmaceuticals company in Citeureup, West Java.[33] The former Kopkamtib commander had also been entrusted with several special government assignments. One of these involved working with the minister of research, Dr. J. B. Habibie, on long-term defense planning. Another centered on a government attempt to develop Irian Jaya. In the eyes of some of the critics, Sumitro had been bought off by those in power. His philosophy, said one retired general, was "typically Javanese--if you can't beat them, join them."[34] Sumitro, in fact, saw things from a very different perspective; he was not "joining" the Suharto group, he had never really left it. Sumitro seemed to nurture the hope that he might make some sort of a "comeback," perhaps in a ministerial capacity, a forlorn expectation as it turned out. And though it was purely coincidental that this partial reemergence of Sumitro came at a time when other retired generals were becoming increasingly critical of the government, Suharto was quick to seize on the opportunity it presented. Well versed in the frailties of human nature, the president was always ready to give those around him a chance to prove both their usefulness and loyalty. Early in 1978, for example, Dr. Mochtar Kusumaatmadja, acting foreign minister and eager to land the Foreign Ministry post in the upcoming Suharto Cabinet, had been given the somewhat distasteful job of going around the ASEAN capitals and gaining postfacto support for Suharto's decision to remove Dharsono as secretary general of ASEAN. Successful, he had been rewarded with the position he sought. Now, early in 1981, Sumitro sought to prove his loyalty to Suharto by prevailing upon certain dissident generals to abandon their confrontationist position.[35]

Sumitro had already gone into business with Ishak Djuarsa,[36] and he is said to have had authority to offer certain guarantees to dissident generals who might be persuaded to call off their criticism. If these generals agreed to cooperate, Sumitro is alleged to have said, they would be awarded "big projects."[37] The former Kopkamtib commander is said to have told one retired general: "Don't criticize and you can say where you would like to sit; here, here, or here." Those who cooperated, it was alleged, could have their own company to run. Several generals who, like Sumitro, had one or more families to support, were in difficult financial straits and felt compelled to bow out of the protest movement.[38] Their withdrawal was one of the more recent examples of the government's dependence on, and successful employment of, patronage distribution. As we have seen, for

---

33. *Tempo*, November 22, 1980.

34. Confidential communication.

35. Confidential communication, March 1981.

36. *Tempo*, November 22, 1980.

37. Confidential communication.

38. Ibid.

those who refused to play ball the government had other methods, some of which were exceptional in their pettiness and meanness of spirit.

These various efforts by the ruling group took their toll. Men like Djatikusumo dropped out of the "ex-Fosko" grouping, partly because they came to adopt the opinion that more could be gained from working within the system, partly too for other reasons. Ishak Djuarsa, Harun Sohar, and Daan Jahja also dropped out. By March 1981, even Jasin was out of the picture, having formally apologized to Suharto, largely, it appears, because of the intense pressure brought to bear on his family. But many retired senior officers associated with the "ex-Fosko" group and with the LKB doggedly soldiered on, as did many prominent civilians associated with these bodies. By 1983, five major civilian and military "protest" organizations had converged in a loose Forum Komunikasi Nasional, which brought together representatives from the Petition of Fifty, the "ex-Fosko" group, the LKB, the Lembaga Sukarno-Hatta, and the Silaturrahmi 45. (The Lembaga Sukarno-Hatta was a reform-minded body set up by Sukendro and Mokoginta. The Silaturrahmi 45 was a body made up of representatives from the nine political parties which had contested the 1971 elections.) Many of the Forum Nasional's "council of elders," which included Nasution, Mohammad Natsir, Sanusi Hardjadinata, Ali Sadikin, Dharsono, and Sudirman, now took the view that it was necessary to build bridges to those in the government.

Men like Sukendro, Dharsono, Hugeng, Sudirman, and others of the "ex-Fosko" grouping continued to meet each Friday morning in a shabby conference room at the Graha Purna Yudha (Veterans) Building, joined as often as not by civilians like Slamet Bratanata. A strong sense of shared purpose and camaraderie marked these sessions. Men who had in their time held high office in the armed forces and the government shuffled into the room in tennis shirts and slacks, and the air was rich with the aroma of tobacco smoke, the talk of new petitions and protest papers. The deliberations were characterized by a lot of good-natured bantering and by a wry, though sometimes angry, acceptance of the increasing pressures to which all were being subjected. The meetings, however, seemed increasingly irrelevant and time began to take its own toll on the participants. In 1982 the group was saddened by the news that Maj. Gen. Muamil Effendy had died, in 1983 by the news of the death of Maj. Gen. Iskandar Ranuwihardjo. In the same year Sukendro suffered a crippling brain haemorrhage and Mokoginta was hospitalized with serious spinal trouble; by 1984 both men were dead and the ex-Fosko grouping robbed of two of its more dynamic members.

CONCLUSION

By 1980, it was possible to discern two distinct schools of thought within ABRI over the question of the army's appropriate role in society. First, there was the "leadership group," a tightly knit and extraordinarily powerful body of men, centered on the president and including the key members of his inner circle. This group was broadly committed to a system, largely of its own creation, in which the armed forces occupied all manner of positions in Indonesian society and enjoyed immense influence over everyday affairs. This pattern of influence and control seemed likely to remain operative, with only slight modifications, for as long as Suharto remained in power. There were several reasons for this. For one thing, the position of the president was so secure and his powers of patronage so extensive that few dared openly to challenge his authority. For another, the army was disproportionately abangan Javanese in composition, inclined by orientation and indoctrination to go along with the basic tenets of the ruling group, even if there were occasional doubts in some quarters about the wisdom of certain of its policies. Third, the rigid hierarchy of the "modern" army command system reinforced a preexisting and "traditional" cultural disposition to accord extraordinary respect and deference to those in authority. Acutely status-conscious, aware of the penalties of stepping out of line, and willing in any case to bide their time until they were themselves in senior command positions, middle-ranking officers left decisions on such topics to their superiors, men who could claim the aura of revolutionary legitimacy and who were more experienced in social-political affairs.

A second--and much more heterogeneous--group of officers felt that it was necessary for ABRI to take a more enlightened and indulgent view of Indonesian society and yield up a good deal of its control. Among these were active army officers from the operational side of the armed forces, including such men as Jusuf, Widodo, Sajidiman, and Abdulkadir Besar, one of the army's leading theoreticians. Widjojo Sujono was thought to share these views to some extent. Also in agreement with this type of thinking were two prominent but displaced intelligence officers--Sutopo Juwono, the former head of Bakin and an advocate of a more principled approach to intelligence matters, and Charis Suhud. A significant number of prominent retired officers were also associated in one way or another with these views, among them Nasution, Simatupang, Djatikusumo, Sudirman, Sukendro, Dharsono, Mokoginta, Jasin, Kawilarang, Sugih Arto, Kemal Idris, and Ishak Djuarsa. As we have seen, two characteristics of the retired military critics were that they included a disproportionate number of former Siliwangi officers, and that Nasution exercised a continuing influence over them. Nasution's political thinking found expression in both the Seskoad and Widodo papers and his organizational skill manifested itself in the activities of the LKB. At the same time, he maintained close ties with retired army officers in Fosko, most notably with Sudirman and Mokoginta.

The various criticisms were in no sense a threat to the stability or the security of the Suharto government, there being insufficient support in the community for any concerted opposition the president's rule and more than a little cynicism about the motives and sincerity of former military leaders who were now so ready to condemn institutions in which they once served so diligently. Even so, their criticisms gave the leadership pause for thought. It is one of the minor conceits of senior officers that ABRI men, whether sergeants or generals, are uniquely qualified to lead, and the history of the Republic, they feel, has amply borne out this contention. The fact that so many "big name" retired officers were expressing criticism was, in the government's eyes, something that needed to be handled with care.

Initially, it sought to stem the unrest by summoning and rebuking critics like Kemal Idris and Dharsono. But as the movement gathered momentum, greater efforts were made to buy off the opposition with offers of money and "facilities," often apparently quite generous. This tactic, as we have seen, had some success. However, when it became apparent that most critics were immune to, or contemptuous of, such blandishments, the government adopted a tougher line. In the wake of the Petition of Fifty, it undertook a serious campaign aimed at "cutting the lifelines" of its critics.

In the introduction to this paper it was suggested that two central issues were being debated within the Indonesian armed forces during the period 1975-82. One was the question of ABRI's stance vis-a-vis the various political groupings in the country. The other was the question of the "purification" of the dwifungsi and the possible reduction in the number of military men serving outside the defense structure as such. By 1982 it seemed clear that, despite intimations of change during the late 1970s, the ruling group envisaged no meaningful realignment of ABRI's relations with the political forces. Fearful that there were elements bent on changing the 1945 Constitution and the Pancasila and disinclined to see the army yield up its very extensive power over the system, the president was insisting that ABRI "choose friends" who truly supported the accepted doctrines and, by extension, the status quo. Suharto, it is true, had begun assuring senior officers in 1981 that ABRI would in future play a less prominent role in the affairs of Golkar and would not openly support it in the 1982 general elections. But this was misleading. ABRI could afford to be less visible during the campaign precisely because Golkar was, at the national level, totally under the control of the ruling group. Suharto's decision in 1978 to become chairman of Golkar's central supervisory board had signalled the likelihood that this would not change while he remained president. The vigor of his remarks at Pekanbaru in March 1980 had underscored the depths and dimensions of his feelings regarding ABRI-Golkar relations. There was, clearly, an unbridgeable chasm between the basic philosophy that ABRI was "above all groups" and President Suharto's strictures that the armed forces should "choose friends," a chasm that no amount of sophistry could disguise.

As we have seen, there had been some valiant obscurantism on this issue at the annual Golkar leadership meeting in 1979. At that time it was suggested that ABRI in its capacity as a stabilizer was indeed above all groups, but that ABRI in its capacity as a social-political force was still a functional group and a component of Golkar. From this line of reasoning there developed the notion that ABRI was the New Order's "champion" and thus entitled to guide and direct it via Golkar. ABRI as a social-political force, it was suggested, was far from neutral; it had not only brought forth Golkar but was entitled to give it its full backing. This rather disingenuous attempt to have things both ways did not attract widespread support either in Golkar or in the armed forces. To many of Golkar's members it was all simply a matter of semantics, a debate which had about as much relevance as discourses in mediaeval Europe about how many angels could dance on the head of a single pin. As a member of Ali Murtopo's circle observed with customary frankness, ABRI and Golkar were the same thing and where was the point in arguing about it? The "rationalization" suggested in 1979 was hardly more popular within the armed forces. When it was debated at the ABRI Commanders Call in Bandung in March 1982 the argument was not found to be particularly persuasive, and the meeting broke up without succeeding in formulating a doctrine which bridged the two points of view.[1] In the final analysis, a fundamental contradiction remained between the "pure" doctrine, requiring the armed forces to be above all groups, and the injunctions of those in command to weigh in behind Golkar. Given the structure of the system, it was practically impossible for serving officers to reject or resist the policy that came from the line of command. On the other hand, the "pure" doctrine still commanded widespread support within the armed forces (and within the army in particular) and it was by no means certain that its eclipse would be so pronounced under another leader.

If the debate over ABRI's relations with the political groupings had led back to square one, the same did not happen with the parallel discussion over the dwifungsi doctrine and the future of the kekaryaan ABRI. At the Commanders Call in 1982, the leaders of the armed forces endorsed the notion that, while the dwifungsi as a philosophy was everlasting, its *implementation* was dependent on the situation at any given time. The mission of the dwifungsi, it was said, was to stimulate Pancasila democracy in all fields. This included the preparation and encouragement of civilian cadres to take over many of

---

1. Interview with Brig. Gen. (Hon.) Nugroho Notosusanto, March 12, 1982.

the functions still being handled by military men. (In a parallel decision, the meeting decided that only those military men who were actually needed by a particular department would go into kekaryaan
duties.)[2] On the surface, this sounded very much like a string of
earlier and equally pious declarations that implied an imminent scaling
back on ABRI's involvement in society. This time, however, there
were reasons for believing that the armed forces' leaders were indeed
contemplating a reduction in military involvement in the civilian sector, at least at the middle and lower levels. These had to do with
the quantity and quality of military personnel available to handle
these functions. As we have seen, the appointment of military men to
kekaryaan positions in the mid-1960s not only allowed the army to enhance its grip on society at a time of dislocation and upheaval. It
also made it possible for the armed forces to "demobilize" effectively
many officers and men of the revolutionary generation, shunting them
into comfortable positions while at the same time pruning the military
establishment back to a more manageable size. By 1980, there was,
for the first time, a shortage of officers available for kekaryaan
duties. The armed forces had been pared back to 300,000 men (not
counting the 100,000-man national police force) and was finding it increasingly difficult to maintain 17,000 men (or nearly 6 percent of its
force) in kekaryaan positions. (If those serving in a territorial capacity were added to those fulfilling a kekaryaan role, roughly one-
third of the 300,000-man defense force was occupied in noncombat
duties.) As karyawan of the 1945 generation retired, the problem
became more acute.[3]

At the same time, there was a widespread feeling at the upper
levels of the armed forces that insufficient younger officers had the
necessary skills and qualifications to serve as karyawan. To some
extent, this view stemmed from one of the more understandable conceits of the Generation of '45, or at least of some of its members. In
their own self-image, these men had been members of a unique movement of youthful activists who, fired by nationalism and a burning
revolutionary ardor, had helped wrest independence from the Dutch.
Tempered by war and tested by the political, economic, and military
challenges of the postindependence period, they saw themselves as
uniquely placed to "stabilize and dynamize" the nation, and tended at
times to look somewhat askance at the capabilities of others who might
aspire to such office--including the men they had selected as their
eventual successors. There appeared, however, to be some justification for those doubts. By 1980 it had become clear that the Military
Academy (Akabri) at Magelang was not attracting the cream of the
nation's youth, the obvious possibilities for self-advancement in the

---

2. Interview with Lt. Gen. Sutopo Juwono, March 22, 1982.

3. In 1982 ABRI was having difficulty not just in finding enough
personnel for its combat units but for its territorial organization as
well. In one of its decisions, the 1982 Commanders Call stressed that
efforts must be made to strengthen the territorial structure.

military sphere notwithstanding. The best and the brightest students were seeking admission to prestigious centers of learning, like the University of Indonesia or the Bandung Institute of Technology (ITB). There were a number of reasons for this. First, most Indonesian families had no strong tradition of military service, even if, as is the case, more than half of the Akabri cadets are the children of ABRI members.[4] Indeed, there is a certain disdain for those in the armed forces. Second, opportunities were growing rapidly in the civilian sector. Finally, as in many other countries, the peacetime army seemed to hold little attraction for many young people. Given all this, there was a feeling, even amongst senior military officers, that Akabri was in some ways a "second-class" institution. The Military Academy offered cadets a four-year course, with the time being divided almost equally between "pure" military and more general social-political subjects. And while this compared favorably with the stronger "military" emphasis in academies in most neighboring countries, there was a feeling in some quarters that insufficient attention was being given to nonmilitary subjects. This, it was feared, would make it difficult in later years for military officers to hold their own with their better-educated civilian equivalents.

By 1982, President Suharto and his key military advisers seem to have accepted the need for a progressive reduction in the number of military men serving in a kekaryaan capacity, as recommended by the authors of the Hankam paper. Such a reduction would owe much to the difficulties noted above of locating sufficient younger officers with the necessary qualifications to serve as karyawan. But it would also reflect a fairly widespread feeling in society that it was becoming increasingly difficult to justify the large number of ABRI personnel in key civilian positions. At the same time, it was frankly conceded in ruling circles that ABRI intended to go on controlling the upper levels of the legislative, executive, and judicial branches of government. This being so, the changes should be seen as only a very qualified reduction in the scale of kekaryaan activity. The number of karyawan might decrease but no one could say by what amount. More important still, the cutback would be carried out from the bottom up, leaving military control over the commanding heights essentially intact.

All of this is taking place at a time when the members of the so-called "Magelang Generation"--officers admitted to the Military Academy in the years since 1957--are moving into senior staff and command positions, replacing members of the Generation of 1945 and the (scarcely younger) members of the "bridging generation." Given that the members of the younger generation will also "inherit" the military's dominant role in society, the central question that arises concerns the likely orientation and outlook of the members of this

---

4. See Donald E. Weatherbee, "Indonesia's Armed Forces: Rejuvenation and Regeneration," *Southeast Asian Affairs 1982* (Singapore: Institute of Southeast Asian Studies, 1982), p. 27.

"generation." Will they be inclined to play a greater role in society, or are they likely to preside over a gradual "recivilianization" of the government?

First, it must be said that surprisingly little is known about the social and political outlook of the younger officers. Few outsiders have been vouchsafed entry into their circle and even when communication is established the results tend to be disappointing; wary of incurring their superiors' displeasure, the officers in question are reluctant to offer opinions about anything of much substance. On the other hand, access is possible at one remove--via those older officers who have served as the instructors and mentors of the Magelang generation. Here, opinions tend to be very much at opposite poles. Some senior officers hold out high hopes for the new generation; others harbor the most serious misgivings about them and what they might do. (Interestingly, and perhaps not surprisingly, those senior officers who tend to take a generally benign view of society and who call for decreasing military involvement tend on the whole to be optimistic. In this sense, those we have described as being of a more "principled" cast of mind are optimists when it comes to the new generation. The more "pragmatic" officers associated with the present ruling group tend on the whole to be surprisingly pessimistic about their successors--despite the very considerable opportunity they have had to mould their character and select and promote those who most conform to their own image.)

There can be little gainsaying that the intellectual horizons of the younger officers are not especially wide. As Weatherbee has noted, the curriculum at Akabri is "narrow and intellectually constrained, stressing traditional military virtues of discipline, conformity and duty."[5] Moreover, the "ideological quotient" is high, great stress being put on the inculcation and acceptance of ABRI doctrine (as currently interpreted) and world view, particularly regarding the link between security, stability, and development. (Much the same criticism can be levelled at the curriculum at the Army Staff and Command School [Seskoad] in Bandung, the disclaimers of senior officers notwithstanding.)[6] At the same time, the younger military officers would certainly seem to have greater professional and military skills than the current generation of military leaders. This, however, is precisely where the problems arise.

Militarism or Military Professionalism?

"Professionalism" is a possible departure point for two very different types of development. One such development could arise from what might be described as "professionalism narrowly defined." The

---

5. Ibid., p. 26.

6. For details of the Seskoad course, see Charles Donald McFetridge, "Seskoad--Training the Elite," *Indonesia* 36 (October 1983): 87-98.

younger generation, it is pointed out by some senior officers, have not had the experiences of the Generation of '45 and thus have a very different perception of the dwifungsi. By and large, it is claimed, they take pride in their military professionalism and pay insufficient attention to their social-political role. As we have seen, the best of the younger officers will have served as Kodim commanders before attending Seskoad. Similarly, the best of the Seskoad graduates will have been sent abroad as military attachés or been given a Korem command. Despite this heavy official stress on the social-political function, it is suggested, the younger officers do not particularly favor such responsibilities, even if they accept their necessity in order to "get on" in the system. More concerned with ABRI's function as a defense force, some senior officers fear they may be in danger at times of "giving up" their social-political role and abandoning the field to civilians. In this sense, they are thought to be in danger of moving towards the "Western" model, in which the army is merely an instrument of the state. Put another way, the younger officers are becoming less "red" and more "expert." At Seskoad, where the die is cast for senior career appointments, lecturers have noted that with each new crop of mid-career officers the perception of the dwifungsi grows thinner.

If members of this group fear that the younger generation is becoming more military-minded in the sense that its officers have little interest in the social-political function, there is another, diametrically opposed, school of thought. Members of this school believe that the younger officers are in danger of becoming more authoritarian and impatient, more inclined to use the army's power to effect political and social change. This argument carries a good deal of weight.

The "younger" officers--and some, it should be remembered, are not far off 50--are certainly better trained and more professional than members of the revolutionary generation, or indeed most members of the small but influential *generasi jembatan* (bridging generation), officers trained in the years 1950-57. But this hardly means that they will eschew a political role. Indeed, their whole training has been based on the notion that ABRI has a central and everlasting role to play in the social-political field, and they appear to accept this notion without question. What is more, their progression up through the ranks exposes them, as we have seen, to both military and social-political functions. This means that by the time a 45-year-old becomes a Kodam commander he will have had extensive experience in social-political matters. Already there is a good deal of evidence to suggest that the lieutenant colonels who emerge from Seskoad are inclined to be more, not less, active in these areas than an earlier generation of military men, pushing the local bupati (regent) to do more, to achieve more, to meet the planning targets. In ABRI, where promotion is on the basis of merit, it never hurts to have a 150 percent success rate.

In these circumstances it would be rash to see the Magelang man as some sort of Jeffersonian democrat with a tolerant disposition and a belief in the perfectability of human nature. The curriculum at

Akabri is narrow in the extreme, the horizons of its graduates decidedly limited. The new generation is made up of men who carry
their historical knowledge lightly, who seek their intellectual nutri-
ment in the pages of *Harian AB*, the drab and unimpressive armed
forces daily, not in the works of the great political or social philoso-
phers. The Magelang graduates may not be carbon copies of the men
produced in the South Korean military institutions, but they have
some of the same impatience, the same intolerance, the same mild contempt for what they see as the ineptitude of civilians and the "failure" of civilian institutions. They tend to lack, some fear, the political skill and sophistication of the present leaders and are likely to be
less tolerant of the roles of other social and political actors. According to one officer,

> It is possible that the new generation through impatience
> and lack of sophistication will produce a new New Order
> in which even the outward forms of *musyawarah* and
> *mufakat* (consultation and consensus) give way to com-
> mand. The new generation is inheriting a political system
> they did not build. They may not be able to manipulate
> it so skillfully.

> Rather than attempt to mediate social and political ten-
> sions the next generation might be tempted to greater co-
> ercion, replacing the oligarchic style with a more thor-
> oughgoing praetorianism.[7]

This is a fear which is echoed in both military and civilian circles in Indonesia. The new breed of officer, it is feared, will be
more impatient and more intolerant, less inclined to "waste" resources
on what he sees as socially disruptive activities. The "overbearing"
attitude of many of the military men who served in the provincial
Golkar establishment prior to 1977 is seen by this group as a harbin-
ger of things to come. According to one officer associated with the
ruling group

> our main worry is that the younger generation will move
> in the direction of totalitarianism. They are impatient,
> they want to get on with the job. They want to grasp
> the power. We are worried about that. I think we are
> moving towards the type of officers you see in South
> Korea. The spirit of the South Korean officers is dif-
> ferent from ours but perhaps our younger generation will
> move in that direction--highly professional but with a
> strong desire to succeed.[8]

---

7. See Weatherbee, "Indonesia's Armed Forces," pp. 32-33.

8. Confidential communication.

There was evidence of this attitude, this officer felt, at the time of the student unrest in both 1974 and 1978. Younger officers, surveying the antigovernment and anti-ABRI tone of the criticism, had reacted with almost knee-jerk praetorianism. "We will deal much more firmly with this sort of thing," a captain had said at the time. "We will sweep it all away. These young people are irresponsible. They can afford to study quietly at their parents' cost and yet they curse us, they curse those who are serving the country and say we are brengsek [rotten]."[9]

It is too early yet to predict with any certainty the sort of political format that might commend itself to a new generation of military officers; indeed, the current generation's reluctance until recently to transfer power to younger officers virtually ensures that there will be little serious debate on this question until perhaps the late 1980s or the early 1990s. However, it seems unlikely that a new generation of officers, whatever forms their "military professionalism" may take, will voluntarily relinquish the sort of role that ABRI now plays in Indonesian society. The officers who have graduated from Akabri in the years since 1960 have had extensive exposure to social and political problems while serving in territorial posts. Their experience as Kodam commanders in areas outside Java will have sharpened their skills in dealing not only with purely military matters but with all manner of "sospol" matters as well. Indeed, given the nature of the system, the stress placed on the sospol role, and the conscious rejection of those officers who fail to perform adequately in this field, there is a process of "natural selection" in which only those with proven political capacity are brought forward. The Magelang officers who come to power during the 1980s and 1990s will be men in their late forties and early fifties with up to three decades of active involvement in nonmilitary matters. Moreover, strenuous efforts have been made to ensure that they are in the correct ideological mould. The new generation officers accept (or go through the motions of accepting) the basic tenets of New Order rule and seem committed to the notion that ABRI has a unique and important role to play in guiding and developing Indonesia. In view of this, it seems unlikely that the new generation will lightly contemplate a major reduction in the army's role or feel in any sense inadequate to the task of providing the nation with the necessary leadership. From the evidence available, their commitment to Pancasila (as presently defined) and the 1945 Constitution would appear very much in tune with the thinking of the Suharto group. This is particularly so with those officers who have already been given Kodam commands. Others who may be less committed to the status quo are said to be content to bide their time, knowing that the present leaders are already old and cannot go on indefinitely, their penchant for frequently redefining and extending the retirement age notwithstanding. In short, ABRI is dug in on the commanding heights of the political, economic, and social landscape, and there is little evidence to suggest that the new generation of of-

---

9. Ibid.

ficers has any intention of lightly yielding up the vast powers they are about to inherit.

This is not to say that the younger officers will have an easy ride when they eventually reach the top. They will not be able to claim--as the present leaders can--that they possess revolutionary credentials that give them a special right to govern Indonesia, although they may well seek to award themselves some such legitimacy by claiming to be the defenders and upholders of the sacred principles of those who fought the revolution. Furthermore, as we have already seen, the decidedly narrow syllabus at institutions like Akabri and Seskoad has meant that officers of the new generation have a very narrow world view. Finally, it does not necessarily follow that officers, simply because they have been exposed to social and political problems on the way up, will have the sophistication to cope with the broader question of ABRI's role in a changing society. The only model with which they are familiar is the essentially static one found in contemporary Indonesia. Given their limited reading and narrow horizons, they may tend to accept the current system as the norm and apply it rigidly in all circumstances--with disastrous consequences.

It is precisely because the new generation of military leaders will become increasingly important in the years ahead, that those concerned about ABRI's role in the social-political field have been aiming their comments as much at them as at the current military leadership, a group which is seen, with some justification, as very set in its ways. For the same reasons, the ruling group has sought to insulate its protégés from the various heresies that are being propounded. At this stage, it is not possible to say how far they have been successful in this.

In conclusion, it might be worth making the point that, Suharto's current strength notwithstanding, the present system should not be seen as something fixed and immutable. ABRI's role has become increasingly institutionalized under Suharto, and the military have come to dominate much of society. But postcolonial Indonesia is still in a state of flux, and the pendulum, post-Suharto, may swing back somewhat in the other direction. For one thing, it is by no means certain that Indonesia will throw up another military leader with as much power as Suharto. Indonesia's second Head of State came to the presidency through an exceptional set of circumstances, seizing the initiative at a time when others wavered, and then securing his control over the levers of power. This gave him an opportunity to impose his own somewhat rigid views in such areas as civil-military relations and to brush aside any officers who took a different view. It is impossible to predict the way power may devolve to a new president. And though it would seem reasonable to expect that Suharto's successor would also be from the army, circumstances may dictate that the new man is more a *primus inter pares*, at least initially. That, and continuing doubts within the army leadership about the wisdom of the present course, could produce important modifications to the way in which ABRI uses its influence in society.

With hindsight, it seems clear that the views of the New Order "radicals" (many of them from the Siliwangi) were altogether too "progressive," and thereby unacceptable to the predominantly Javanese officer corps, with the result that the curbing of their power has come to appear increasingly inevitable. At the same time, it may be argued that the pendulum, under Suharto, has swung too far in the other direction, and that views which today compel support may be significantly modified after Suharto's departure.

This would be unlikely to involve much more than limited adjustments to the system of army dominance, all officers, active and retired, being committed to the notion of ABRI's continuing role in the social-political field. But from the army's point of view it might be seen to have very real advantages. If ABRI is "down in the mud" running society, there is always the danger, as Nugroho Notosusanto has noted, that the mud will spatter it. This has already happened.

The forces at work in one Southeast Asian nation may differ from those at work in another. Nevertheless, the events in Thailand in 1973 provide a warning of what can happen when a military regime spends too much of its time seeking to perpetuate its own rule and to contain change in society. When change eventually came in Thailand, the results were traumatic, not least for the army, which lost not only power and credibility, at least for the time being, but also its own sense of self-confidence and legitimacy. There is surely, a lesson here for Indonesia.

In 1982, ABRI's dilemma was much the same as it had been for the previous fifteen years. The army leaders knew that the political movement they had fashioned would not command a majority of the votes in a free election, and yet believed, often in all good conscience, that it was necessary for the army to rule Indonesia. This fundamental contradiction was the Achilles' heel of the regime and the dissembling and double talk about "constitutionalism" and following the "rules of the game" was necessary to paper over the gap between image and reality.

During the revolution, many officers had subscribed to the view that the army *was* the Republic. In 1982, after thirty-seven years of independence, the military leadership often acted as if the national interests of Indonesia, the corporate interests of the army, and the individual interests of the officer corps were identical and in no danger of conflict. What was good for ABRI was good for the Republic. This was not necessarily so. In these circumstances, it seems possible to suggest that one of the main legacies of the Generation of '45 to a new generation of officers is the problem of finding a more acceptable accommodation between military and civilian interests.

GLOSSARY

Abangan -- Nominally Muslim in orientation, influenced by pre-Islamic beliefs

ABRI -- Angkatan Bersenjata Republik Indonesia (Armed Forces of the Republic of Indonesia)

Akabri -- Akademi Angkatan Bersenjata Republik Indonesia (Indonesian Armed Forces Academy)

Asintelhankam -- Assistant for Intelligence at Hankam

Asintelkopkamtib -- Assistant for Intelligence at Kopkamtib

Aspri -- Asisten Pribadi (Personal Assistant)

BKR -- Badan Keamanan Rakyat (People's peace keeping body)

BPKI -- Badan penyelidik usaha-usaha Persiapan Kemerdekaan Indonesia (Body to investigate measures for the preparation of Indonesian independence)

BPKKS -- Badan Pembina Koordinasi dan Pengawasan Kegiatan Sosial (Coordinating and Supervising Body for Social Welfare Activities)

Babinsa -- Bintara Pembina Desa (NCO appointed to serve, with a small detachment of men, in a territorial capacity at the village level)

Bakin -- Badan Koordinasi Intelijen Negara (State Intelligence Coordinating Body)

BAKN -- Badan Administrasi Kepegawaian Negara (State Personnel Administration Board)

Bapilu -- Badan Pengendalian Pemilihan Umum (Body to Manage the General Elections)

Barisan Sakit Hati -- Sick at Heart Brigade

Bulog -- Badan Urusan Logistik Nasional (National Logistics Board)

Bupati -- Regent, sub-province chief

Camat -- Sub-district chief

Cukong -- Pejorative term for wealthy financiers, often Chinese

Dakwah -- Missionary work

Dalang -- Puppeteer

Dandim -- Komandan Kodim (Kodim commander)

Danrem -- Komandan Korem (Korem commander)

266

Darul Islam -- House of Islam, separatist movement in West Java in the 1950's and early 1960's

Desa -- Village

Departemen Juang -- Struggle Department

Dewan Hankamnas -- Dewan Pertahanan Keamanan Nasional (National Defense and Security Council)

Dewan Kekaryaan Daerah -- Regional Functional Affairs Board

Dewan Pimpinan Pusat -- Central Executive Board

Dewan Pimpinan Daerak Tk I -- Provincial Executive Board

Dewan Pimpinan Daerak Tk II -- Regency Executive Board

Dewan Pembina -- Control Board

Dewan Pembina Daerah -- Regional Control Board

Dewan Penasehat Daerah -- Regency Advisory Board

Dewan Pertimbangan Daerah -- Regional Assessment Board

DNIKS -- Dewan Nasional Indonesia untuk Kesejahteraan Sosial (Indonesian National Council on Social Welfare)

DPA -- Dewan Pertimbangan Agung (Supreme Advisory Council)

DPR -- Dewan Perwakilan Rakyat (People's Representative Council, Parliament)

DPR-GR -- Dewan Perwakilan Rakyat Gotong Royong (Mutual Assistance People's Representative Council)

Dwifungsi -- Dual function. Doctrine which states that the Armed Forces has both a defense and social-political role

Fosko TNI-AD -- Forum Studi dan Komunikasi TNI-AD (Army Forum for Study and Communication)

F.K.S. Purna Yudha -- Forum Komunikasi dan Studi Purna Yudha (Purna Yudha Forum for Communication and Study)

Gestapu -- Gerakan September Tigapuluh (Thirtieth of September Movement)

Golkar -- Golongan Karya (Functional Groups)

Golongan istana -- Palace group

GBHN -- Garis-garis Besar Haluan Negara (Broad Outlines of State Policy)

Hankam -- Departemen Pertahanan-Keamanan (Department of Defense and Security)

Hankamrata -- Total People's Defense Concept

HMI -- Himpunan Mahasiswa Islam (Islamic Student Association)

IAIN -- Institut Agama Islam Negeri(Institute of Islamic Studies)

IPDN -- Institut Pemerintahan Dalam Negeri (Civil Service Institute of the Department of Home Affairs)

IPKI -- Ikatan Pendukung Kemerdekaan Indonesia (League of Upholders of Indonesian Independence)

Kabupaten -- Regency

Kapusintelstrat -- Head of the Strategic Intelligence Center

Karyawan -- Military man serving in nonmilitary capacity

Kaskar -- Chief of Staff for Functional Affairs

Kaspri Pangad -- Chief of Staff of the Personal Secretariat of the Army Commander

Kebatinan -- Javanese mystic beliefs

Kecamatan -- District

Kekaryaan -- Nonmilitary, or functional

Kerakyatan -- Popular sovereignty

Khutbah -- Sermons

Kodam -- Komando Daerah Militer (Regional Military Command)

Kodim -- Komando Distrik Militer (District Military Command)

Komando Jihad -- Holy War Command

Kopassandha -- Army para-commando unit, formerly known as the RPKAD

Kopkamtib -- Komando Operasi Pemulihan Keamanan dan Ketertiban (Operational Command for the Restoration of Security and Order)

Koramil -- Komando Rayon Militer (Military Precinct Command). A force of 10-15 men at local level

Korem -- Komando Resort Militer (subprovince Military Resort Command)

Korpri -- Korps Karyawan Pegawai Republik Indonesia (Civil Servants' Corps of the Republic of Indonesia)

Kosgoro -- Koperasi Serba Usaha Gotong Royong (All-Purpose Mutual Help Cooperatives)

Kostrad -- Komando Cadangan Strategis Angkatan Darat (Army Strategic Reserve Command)

Kotoe -- Komando Tertinggi Operasi Ekonomi (Supreme Command for Economic Operations)

Kowilhan -- Komando Wilayah Pertahanan (Regional Defense Command)

KNIL -- Koninklijk Nederlands Indisch Leger (Royal Netherlands Indies Army)

Kraton -- Palace, court

Laksusda -- Pelaksana Khusus Daerah (Special Executor of Kopkamtib in the Regions)

Liga Demokrasi -- Democratic League

LKB -- Lembaga Kesadaran Berkonstitusi (Institute of Constitutional Awareness)

Leppenas -- Lembaga Penunjang Pembangunan Nasional (Institute of the Supporters of National Development)

Lurah -- Village headman

Malari -- Malapetaka Januari (January Disaster)

Manipol -- Manifesto Politik (Political Manifesto)

Masyumi -- Majelis Syuro Muslimin Indonesia (Council of Indonesian Muslim Associations)

Menhankam -- Minister of Defense

MKGR -- Musyawarah Kekeluargaan Gotong Royong (Family Mutual Help Association)

MPR -- Majelis Permusyawaratan Rakyat (People's Consultative Assembly)

MPRS -- Majelis Permusyawaratan Rakyat Sementara (Provisional People's Consultative Assembly)

MUI -- Majelis Ulama Indonesia (Indonesian Ulamas Council)

Muspida -- Musyawarah Pimpinan Daerah (Regional Leadership Council)

Nasakom -- nasionalis, agama, komunis (nationalist, religious, Communist)

Nefos -- New Emerging Forces

Negara Islam Indonesia -- Islamic State of Indonesia.   Proclaimed by the Darul Islam leader S. M. Kartosuwirjo in August 1949

Nekolim -- neokolonialisme, kolonialisme, imperialisme (neocolonialism, colonialism, imperialism)

NU -- Nahdatul Ulama (Muslim Scholars Party)

Oldefos -- Old Established Forces

Opsus -- Operasi Khusus (Special Operations)

Opsgalangan -- Operasi galangan (Guidance operations)

Pancasila -- Five principles.   State philosophy formulated by Sukarno in 1945

Pangab -- Commander of the Armed Forces

Pangad -- Army commander

Pangdam -- Panglima Kodam (Military commander)

Pangkopkamtib -- Commander of Kopkamtib

Panglima -- Military commander

Pembina Utama -- Chief Controller. Pembina and Pembinaan are peculiar army terms from the early 1960s. "Pembina" is sometimes translated as "supervisor" but the meaning is more "shaper," "moulder," "controller" (in the intelligence sense)

Penguasa Perang -- Martial Law Authority Holder

Penugaskaryaan -- The placing of an active military man in a nominally civilian position, often as a sinecure

Penyaluran -- The process of moving a military man into a civilian position prior to retirement

Pepabri -- Persatuan Purnawirawan Angkatan Bersenjata Republik Indonesia (Association of Retired Members of the Indonesian Armed Forces)

Pepelrada -- Penguasa Pelaksanaan Dwikora Daerah (Regional Authority to Implement Dwikora)

Peperti -- Penguasa Perang Tertinggi (Supreme War Authority)

Perbantuan -- The process of attaching a military man to a civilian position on a short term basis to perform a particular task

Peta -- Pembela Tanah Air (Defenders of the Fatherland)

Perusahaan daerah -- Regional enterprises

PDI -- Partai Demokrasi Indonesia (Indonesian Democratic Party)

PKI -- Partai Komunis Indonesia (Indonesian Communist Party)

PN -- Perusahaan Negara (state corporation)

PNI -- Partai Nasional Indonesia (Indonesian National Party)

PPP -- Partai Persatuan Pembangunan (United Development Party)

PPP-AD -- Pusat Pendidikan Perwiraan-Angkatan Darat (Army Officers Training Centre)

PRRI -- Pemerintah Revolusioner Republik Indonesia (Revolutionary Government of the Republic of Indonesia)

PSI -- Partai Sosialis Indonesia (Indonesian Socialist Party)

PSII -- Partai Sarekat Islam Indonesia (Indonesian Islamic Union Party)

PT -- Perusahaan Terbatas (limited company)

Rapim ABRI -- Rapat Pemimpin (ABRI Commanders Call)

Rapat Gubernur -- Governor's Meeting

RPKAD -- Resimen Para Komando Angkatan Darat (Army Para-Commando Regiment)

Santri -- Devout Muslim

Sapta Marga -- Seven Pledges

Satgasintel -- Satuan Tugas Intelijen (Intelligence Task Unit)

Sekber-Golkar -- Sekretariat Bersama Golongan Karya (Joint Secretariat of Functional Groups)

Sekwilda -- Sekretariat Wilayah Daerah (Regency secretary)

Semangat -- Revolutionary ardor, fighting spirit

Seskoad -- Sekolah Staf Komando Angkatan Darat (Army Staff and Command School)

Seskogab -- Sekolah Staf dan Komando Gabungan (Joint Services' Staff and Command School)

SOKSI -- Sentral Organisasi Karyawan Sosialis Indonesia (Central Organization of Indonesian Socialist Workers)

Sospol -- Social-political affairs

Spri -- Staf Pribadi (Personal Staff)

Syariah -- Islamic law

Team Poleksos -- Political, Economic and Social Team

TKR -- Tentara Keamanan Rakyat (People's Peacekeeping Army), October 5, 1945-January 7, 1946

TNI -- Tentara Nasional Indonesia (Indonesian National Army), since June 3, 1947

USDEK -- Undang-undang Dasar 45, Sosialisme a la Indonesia, Demokrasi Terpimpin, Ekonomi Terpimpin Kepribadian Indonesia (1945 Constitution, Indonesian Socialism, Guided Democracy, Guided Economy, Indonesian Personality)

Wanbinda -- Dewan Pengurus Daerah (Regional Executive Board)

Wanbintu -- Dewan Pembina Daerah -- Tingkat 1 (Regional Supervisory Board)

Wanbinpus -- Dewan Pembina Pusat (Central Supervisory Board)

Yayasan Harapan Kita -- Our Hope Foundation

YLKB -- Yayasan Lembaga Kesadaran Berkonstitusi (Foundation for the Institute of Constitutional Awareness)

NAME INDEX

Abdulkadir Besar: 61-62, 94, 113-14, 116, 119-20, 124 n.34, 189, 190 n.6, 192, 255

Abimanju: 67-68, 86, 91, 222 n, 237 n, 238

Abu Darda: 57

"Abu Firman" (pen name): 80, 81 n.57

Achir: 124 n.33

Achmadi: 97

Adjie, Ibrahim: 3, 142, 226 n

Agus Prasmono: 67, 86, 109, 236, 241

Aidit, D. N.: 215, 226

Alamsjah Ratu Perwiranegara: 22-23, 35, 77-79, 80 n.54, 98, 127-28, 208, 224

Ali Murtopo: 13, 16, 20-25, 29-32, 36, 41-42, 44 n.27, 49-52, 54 n.7, 56n, 57-59, 62n, 70-73, 79, 98, 113, 122, 127-28, 130 n.52, 136, 151, 159-60, 169-70, 204, 208, 240, 252, 257

Ali Sadikin: x, 75, 102, 105-08, 143-44, 147, 149-50, 162, 170, 183, 187, 218 n, 235, 237, 250, 254

Ali Said: 21, 182

Ali Wardhana (Dr.): 17

Amin Iskandar: 106, 163

Amir Machmud: 20-21, 24, 25 n.24, 47, 49, 85, 122, 127-28, 136, 180, 240-41

Amir Murtono: 38 n.12, 48-49, 130 n.52, 149, 151

Anwar Haryono (Dr.): 102, 185

Arif Rachman: 102 n

Ateng Jailani: 57

Awaluddin Djamin: 124 n.33

Awan Karmawan Burhan: 153

Azis Saleh: 102, 104-05, 108, 110, 235, 237-38

Batubara, A.: 69 n.33

Batubara, Cosmas: 49

272

SOUTHEAST ASIA PROGRAM DATA PAPERS

120 Uris Hall
Cornell University
Ithaca, New York 14853

In Print

Number 18 CONCEPTIONS OF STATE AND KINGSHIP IN SOUTHEAST ASIA, by Robert Heine-Geldern. 1956. (Fourth Printing 1972) 14 pages. $3.50.

Number 46 AN EXPERIMENT IN WARTIME INTERCULTURAL RELATIONS: PHILIPPINE STUDENTS IN JAPAN, 1943-1945, by Grant K. Goodman. 1962. 34 pages. $2.00.

Number 49 THE TEXTILE INDUSTRY--A CASE STUDY OF INDUSTRIAL DEVELOPMENT IN THE PHILIPPINES, by Laurence David Stifel. 1963. 199 pages. $3.00.

Number 54 CATALOGUE OF THAI LANGUAGE HOLDINGS IN THE CORNELL UNIVERSITY LIBRARIES THROUGH 1964, compiled by Francis A. Bernath, Thai Cataloguer. 1964. 236 pages. $3.00.

Number 55 STRATEGIC HAMLETS IN SOUTH VIET-NAM, A SURVEY AND A COMPARISON, by Milton E. Osborne. 1965. (Second Printing 1968) 66 pages. $2.50.

Number 57 THE SHAN STATES AND THE BRITISH ANNEXATION, by Sao Saimong Mangrai. 1965. (Second Printing 1969) 204 pages. $4.00.

Number 61 RAJAH'S SERVANT, by A. B. Ward. 1966. (Second Printing 1969) 204 pages. $2.50.

Number 71 AMERICAN DOCTORAL DISSERTATIONS ON ASIA, 1933-JUNE 1966, INCLUDING APPENDIX OF MASTERS' THESES AT CORNELL UNIVERSITY 1933-JUNE 1968, by Curtis W. Stucki. 1968. (Second Printing 1970) 304 pages. $4.00.

Number 72 EXCAVATIONS OF THE PREHISTORIC IRON INDUSTRY IN WEST BORNEO, Vol. I, RAW MATERIALS AND INDUSTRIAL WASTE, Vol. II, ASSOCIATED ARTIFACTS AND IDEAS, by Tom Harrisson and Stanley J. O'Connor. 1969. 417 pages. $5.00 each set.

Number 73 THE SEPARATION OF SINGAPORE FROM MALAYSIA, by Nancy McHenry Fletcher. 1969. (Second Printing 1971) 98 pages. $2.50.

Number 75 WHITE HMONG-ENGLISH DICTIONARY, compiled by Ernest E. Heimbach. Linguistics Series IV. 1969. (Second Printing 1979) 497 pages. $6.50.

Number 82 MAGINDANAO, 1860-1888: THE CAREER OF DATO UTO BUAYAN, by Reynaldo C. Ileto. 1971. 80 pages. $3.50.

Number 83 A BIBLIOGRAPHY OF PHILIPPINE LINGUISTICS AND MINOR LANGUAGES, with Annotations and Indices Based on Works in the Library of Cornell University, by Jack H. Ward. Linguistic Series V. 1971. 549 pages. $6.50.

Number 84   A CHECKLIST OF THE VIETNAMESE HOLDINGS OF THE WASON COLLECTION, CORNELL UNIVERSITY LIBRARIES, AS OF JUNE 1971, compiled by Giok Po Oey, Southeast Asia Librarian. 1971. 377 pages. $6.50.

Number 85   SOUTHEAST ASIA FIELD TRIP FOR THE LIBRARY OF CONGRESS, 1970-71, by Cecil Hobbs. 1971. 94 pages. $3.50.

Number 87   A DICTIONARY OF CEBUANO VISAYA, Vols. I and II, by John U. Wolff. 1972. Linguistics Series VI. 1,200 pages. $8.00.

Number 88   MIAO AND YAO LINGUISTIC STUDIES, Selected Articles in Chinese, Translated by Chang Yu-hung and Chu Kwo-ray. Edited by Herbert C. Purnell, Jr. Linguistics Series VII. 1972. 282 pages. $4.00.

Number 89   A CHECKLIST OF INDONESIAN SERIALS IN THE CORNELL UNIVERSITY LIBRARY (1945-1970), compiled by Yvonne Thung and John M. Echols. 1973. 226 pages. $7.00.

Number 90   BIBLIOGRAPHY OF VIETNAMESE LITERATURE IN THE WASON COLLECTION AT CORNELL UNIVERSITY, by Marion W. Ross. 1973. 178 pages. $4.50.

Number 91   SELECTED SHORT STORIES OF THEIN PE MYINT, Translated, with Introduction and Commentary, by Patricia M. Milne. 1973. 105 pages. $4.00.

Number 92   FEASTING AND SOCIAL OSCILLATION: A Working Paper on Religion and Society in Upland Southeast Asia, by A. Thomas Kirsch. 1973. 67 pages. $5.00.

Number 98   THE CRYSTAL SANDS: THE CHRONICLES OF NAGARA SRI DHARRMARAJA, translated, edited and with an introduction by David K. Wyatt. 1975. 264 pages. $6.50.

Number 101   AN ANNOTATED GUIDE TO PHILIPPINE SERIALS, by Frank H. Golay and Marianne H. Hauswedell. 1976. 131 pages. $5.00.

Number 102   NO OTHER ROAD TO TAKE, Memoir of Mrs. Nguyen Thi Dinh, translated by Mai Elliott. 1976. 77 pages. $6.00.

Number 103   DIRECTORY OF THE CORNELL SOUTHEAST ASIA PROGRAM 1951-1976, compiled by Frank H. Golay and Peggy Lush. 1976. 88 pages. $3.00.

Number 106   COMMUNIST PARTY POWER IN KAMPUCHEA (CAMBODIA): DOCUMENTS AND DISCUSSION, compiled and edited with the introduction by Timothy Michael Carney. 1977. 86 pages. $4.50.

Number 109   THE STATUS OF SOCIAL SCIENCE RESEARCH IN BORNEO, edited by G. N. Appell and Leigh R. Wright. 1978. 117 pages. $5.75.

Number 111   CAMBODIA'S ECONOMY AND INDUSTRIAL DEVELOPMENT, by Khieu Samphan, translated and with an introduction by Laura Summers. 1979. 122 pages. $5.75.

Number 113 MEMOIRS OF THE FOUR-FOOT COLONEL, by General Smith Dun. 1980. 147 pages. $6.00.

Number 114 LAWYER IN THE WILDERNESS, by K. H. Digby. With a preface and notes by R. H. W. Reece. 1980. 123 pages. $5.75.

Number 115 THE MANIYADANABON OF SHIN SANDALINKA, translated by L. E. Bagshawe. 1981. 132 pages. $7.00.

Number 116 COMMUNICATIVE CODES IN CENTRAL JAVA, by John U. Wolff and Soepomo Poedjosoedarmo. 1982. 188 pages. $7.50.

INDONESIA, a semiannual journal, devoted to Indonesia's culture, history, and social and political problems.

    *No. 1, April 1966, *No. 2, Oct. 1966, *No. 3, April 1967
    *No. 4, Oct. 1967, *No. 5, April 1968, *No. 6, Oct. 1968
    *No. 7, April 1969, *No. 8, Oct. 1969, *No. 9, April 1970
    *No. 10, Oct. 1970, *No. 11, April 1971, *No. 12, Oct. 1971
     No. 13, April 1972, No. 14, Oct. 1972, $4.50 each, $8.00 both
     No. 15, April 1973, No. 16, Oct. 1973, $4.50 each, $8.00 both
     No. 17, April 1974, No. 18, Oct. 1974, $4.50 each, $8.00 both
    *No. 19, April 1975, No. 20, Oct. 1975, $4.50 each
     No. 21, April 1976, No. 22, Oct. 1976, $5.00 each, $10.00 both
     No. 23, April 1977, $5.00 each, *No. 24, Oct. 1977
    *No. 25, April 1978, No. 26, Oct. 1978, $6.00 each
     No. 27, April 1979, No. 28, Oct. 1979, $6.00 each, $12.00 both
     No. 29, April 1980, No. 30, Oct. 1980, $6.00 each, $12.00 both
     No. 31, April 1981, No. 32, Oct. 1981, $6.50 each, $12.00 both
     No. 33, April 1982, No. 34, Oct. 1982, $6.50 each, $12.00 both
     No. 35, April 1983, No. 36, Oct. 1983, $7.50 each, $14.00 both
     No. 37, April 1984, No. 38, Oct. 1984, $7.50 each, $14.00 both

STUDY AND TEACHING MATERIALS

Obtainable from Southeast Asia Program
120 Uris Hall, Cornell University, Ithaca, New York 14853

THAI CULTURAL READER, Book I, by Robert B. Jones, Ruchira C. Mendiones and Craig J. Reynolds. 1970. (Second revised edition 1976) 517 pages. $7.50.

THAI CULTURAL READER, Book II, by Robert B. Jones and Ruchira C. Mendiones. 1969. 791 pages. $8.25.

INTRODUCTION TO THAI LITERATURE, by Robert B. Jones and Ruchira C. Mendiones. 1970. 563 pages. $7.00.

A.U.A. LANGUAGE CENTER THAI COURSE, by J. Marvin Brown, Books 1, 2, 3. $4.50 each. Tape Supplements for Books 1, 2, 3, $2.00 each. SMALL TALK (Dialogue Book A), $5.00. GETTING HELP (Dialogue Book B), $5.00. BOOK R (Reading and Writing Text), $5.00. BOOK W (Reading and Writing Workbook), $5.00.

BEGINNING INDONESIAN, by John U. Wolff. 1,124 pages. Part One, revised 1977, $12.50. Part Two, reprinted 1974, $12.50. INDONESIAN READINGS, 1978, $12.50. INDONESIAN CONVERSATIONS, 1978, $12.50. FORMAL INDONESIAN, 1980, $12.50. Tapes available at extra cost.

BEGINNING INDONESIAN THROUGH SELF INSTRUCTION, by John U. Wolff, Dede Oetomo, and Daniel Fietkiewicz. 1984. 900 pages. $25.00. Tapes available at extra cost.

INTERMEDIATE SPOKEN VIETNAMESE, by Franklin Huffman and Tran Trong Hai. 1980. $10.00.

Maps

Central Thailand. 7 x 10 inches; scale: 34 km to 1 inch. Price $.25 each; $1.00 set of five.

A. 1. Jangwat Outline Map. 1955.
    2. By Amphoe. 1947.
    3. Population Density by Amphoe. 1947.
    4. Proportion of Chinese by Amphoe. 1947.
    5. Concentration of Chinese by Amphoe. 1947.

Thailand. 13 x 22 inches; scale: 50 miles to 1 inch, except B-10 as noted. Price $.25 each; $1.00 set of six.

B. 6. By Amphoe. 1927.
    7. Population Density by Amphoe. 1947.
    8. Fertility Ratios by Amphoe. 1947.
    9. Concentration of Chinese by Amphoe. 1947.
   10. Untitled (Amphoe Outline Map). 16 x 44 inches, in two parts, each 16 x 22 inches; scale: 27 miles to 1 inch.

Maps and Gazetteer for 1964, 1969, 1974. Maps of Ethnic Settlements of Chiengrai Province, North of the Mae Kok River, Thailand. Prepared by L. M. Hanks. 1975. 35 pages. $8.00.

CORNELL MODERN INDONESIA PROJECT PUBLICATIONS

102 West Avenue
Ithaca, New York 14850

In Print

Number 6   THE INDONESIAN ELECTIONS OF 1955, by Herbert Feith. 1957. (Second Printing 1971) 91 pages. $3.50. (Interim Report)

Number 7   THE SOVIET VIEW OF THE INDONESIAN REVOLUTION, by Ruth T. McVey. 1957. (Third Printing 1969) 90 pages. $2.50. (Interim Report)

Number 16   THE DYNAMICS OF THE WESTERN NEW GUINEA (IRIAN BARAT) PROBLEM, by Robert C. Bone, Jr. 1958. (Second Printing 1962) 182 pages. $3.00. (Interim Report)

Number 25   THE COMMUNIST UPRISINGS OF 1926-1927 IN INDONESIA: KEY DOCUMENTS, edited and with an introduction by Harry J. Benda and Ruth T. McVey. 1960. (Second Printing 1969) 177 pages. $5.50. (Translation)

Number 32   PRELIMINARY CHECKLIST OF INDONESIAN IMPRINTS DURING THE JAPANESE PERIOD (March 1942-August 1945), by John M. Echols. 1963. 62 pages. $1.50. (Bibliography)

Number 37   MYTHOLOGY AND THE TOLERANCE OF THE JAVANESE, by Benedict R. Anderson. 1965. (Third Printing 1979) 77 pages. $5.00. (Monograph)

Number 39   PRELIMINARY CHECKLIST OF INDONESIAN IMPRINTS (1945-1949): WITH CORNELL UNIVERSITY HOLDINGS, by John M. Echols. 1965. 186 pages. $3.50. (Bibliography)

Number 43   STATE AND STATECRAFT IN OLD JAVA: A STUDY OF THE LATER MATARAM PERIOD, 16TH TO 19TH CENTURY, by Soemarsaid Moertono. 1968. (Revised edition 1981) 180 pages. $6.50. (Monograph)

Number 44   OUR STRUGGLE, by Sutan Sjahrir. Translated with an introduction by Benedict R. Anderson. 1968. 37 pages. $2.00. (Translation)

Number 45   INDONESIA ABANDONS CONFRONTATION, by Franklin B. Weinstein. 1969. 94 pages. $3.00. (Interim Report)

Number 46   THE ORIGINS OF THE MODERN CHINESE MOVEMENT IN INDONESIA, by Kwee Tek Hoay. Translated and edited by Lea E. Williams. 1969. 64 pages. $3.00. (Translation)

Number 47   PERSATUAN ISLAM: ISLAMIC REFORM IN TWENTIETH CENTURY INDONESIA, by Howard M. Federspiel, 1970. 250 pages. $7.50. (Monograph)

Number 48   NATIONALISM, ISLAM AND MARXISM, by Soekarno. With an introduction by Ruth T. McVey. 1970. (Second Printing 1984) 62 pages. $4.00. (Translation)

Number 49   THE FOUNDATION OF THE PARTAI MUSLIMIN INDONESIA, by K. E. Ward. 1970. 75 pages. $3.00. (Interim Report)

Number 50   SCHOOLS AND POLITICS: THE KAUM MUDA MOVEMENT IN WEST SUMATRA (1927-1933), by Taufik Abdullah. 1971. 257 pages. $6.00. (Monograph)

Number 51   THE PUTERA REPORTS: PROBLEMS IN INDONESIAN-JAPANESE WAR-TIME COOPERATION, by Mohammad Hatta. Translated with an introduction by William H. Frederick. 1971. 114 pages. $4.00. (Translation)

Number 52   A PRELIMINARY ANALYSIS OF THE OCTOBER 1, 1965, COUP IN INDONESIA (Prepared in January 1966), by Benedict R. Anderson, Ruth T. McVey (with the assistance of Frederick P. Bunnell). 1971. 162 pages. $6.00. (Interim Report)

Number 55   REPORT FROM BANARAN: THE STORY OF THE EXPERIENCES OF A SOLDIER DURING THE WAR OF INDEPENDENCE, by Major General T. B. Simatupang. 1972. 186 pages. $6.50. (Translation)

Number 56   GOLKAR AND THE INDONESIAN ELECTIONS OF 1971, by Masashi Nishihara. 1972. 56 pages. $3.50. (Monograph)

Number 57   PERMESTA: HALF A REBELLION, by Barbara S. Harvey. 1977. 174 pages. $5.00. (Monograph)

Number 58   ADMINISTRATION OF ISLAM IN INDONESIA, by Deliar Noer. 1978. 82 pages. $4.50. (Monograph)

Number 59   BREAKING THE CHAINS OF OPPRESSION OF THE INDONESIAN PEOPLE: DEFENSE STATEMENT AT HIS TRIAL ON CHARGES OF INSULTING THE HEAD OF STATE, Bandung, June 7-10, 1979, by Heri Akhmadi. 1981. 201 pages. $8.75. (Translation)

Number 60   THE MINANGKABAU RESPONSE TO DUTCH COLONIAL RULE IN THE NINETEENTH CENTURY, by Elizabeth E. Graves. 1981. 157 pages. $7.50. (Monograph)

Number 61   SICKLE AND CRESCENT: THE COMMUNIST REVOLT OF 1926 IN BANTEN, by Michael C. Williams. 1982. 81 pages. $6.00. (Monograph)

Number 62   INTERPRETING INDONESIAN POLITICS: THIRTEEN CONTRIBUTIONS TO THE DEBATE, 1964-1981. Edited by Benedict Anderson and Audrey Kahin, with an Introduction by Daniel S. Lev. 1982. 172 pages. $9.00. (Interim Report)

Number 63   DYNAMICS OF DISSENT IN INDONESIA: SAWITO AND THE PHANTOM COUP, by David Bourchier. 1984. 128 pages. $9.00. (Interim Report)